Governance of Arctic Offshore Oil and Gas

Global energy problems will remain a challenge in the coming decades. The impact of climate change and the melting of polar sea ice opening up access to offshore hydrocarbon resources in the Arctic Ocean raises questions for both civil society and the scientific community over drilling opportunities in Arctic marine areas.

Disparities in approach to the governance of oil and gas extraction in the Arctic arise from fundamental differences in histories, cultures, domestic constraints and substantive values and attitudes in the Arctic coastal states and sub-states. Differing political systems, legal traditions and societal beliefs with regard to energy security and economic development, environmental protection, legitimacy of decision making and the ownership and respect of the rights of indigenous people all affect how governance systems of oil and gas extraction are designed.

Using a multidisciplinary approach and case studies from the United States, Norway, Russia, Canada, Greenland/Denmark and the EU, this book both examines the current governance of extraction and its effects and considers ways to enhance the efficiency of environmental management and public participation in this system.

Professor Cécile Pelaudeix, Aarhus University

Professor Ellen Margrethe Basse, Aarhus University

Global Governance

Series Editor: John J. Kirton
University of Toronto, Canada

Global governance is growing rapidly to meet the compounding challenges of a globalised 21st-century world. Many issues once dealt with largely at the local, national or regional level are now going global, in the economic, social and political-security domains. In response, new and renewed intergovernmental institutions are arising and adapting, multilevel governance is expanding, and sub-national actors are playing a greater role and creating complex combinations and private-partnerships to this end.

This series focuses on the new dynamics of global governance in the 21st century by:

- Addressing the changes in the structure, operation and impact of individual intergovernmental institutions, above all their innovative responses to the growing global challenges they confront.
- Exploring how they affect, are affected by and relate to non-state actors of global relevance and reach.
- Examining the processes of cooperation, competition and convergence among international institutions and the many global governance gaps where global challenges such as terrorism, transnational crime and energy do not confront powerful international institutions devoted to their control.
- Dealing with how global institutions govern the links among key issues such as climate change and health.

In all cases, it focuses on the central questions of how global governance institutions and processes generate the effective, legitimate, accountable results required to govern today's interconnected, complex, uncertain and crisis-ridden world.

Local Politics, Global Impacts
Steps to a Multi-Disciplinary Analysis of Scales
Olivier Charnoz, Virginie Diaz Pedregal

The G8-G20 Relationship in Global Governance
Edited by Marina Larionova and John J. Kirton

China's G20 Leadership
John J. Kirton

The New Economic Diplomacy
Decision-Making and Negotiation in International Economic Relations
Edited by Nicholas Bayne and Stephen Woolcock

Membership in the World Trade Organisation
Russia, China and Ukraine
Anastasia Loginova and Irina Mikheeva

Governance of Arctic Offshore Oil and Gas

Edited by
Cécile Pelaudeix and Ellen Margrethe Basse

Routledge
Taylor & Francis Group
LONDON AND NEW YORK

First published 2018
by Routledge
2 Park Square, Milton Park, Abingdon, Oxon OX14 4RN

and by Routledge
605 Third Avenue, New York, NY 10017

First issued in paperback 2021

Routledge is an imprint of the Taylor & Francis Group, an informa business

Publisher's Note
The publisher has gone to great lengths to ensure the quality of this reprint but points out that some imperfections in the original copies may be apparent.

British Library Cataloguing-in-Publication Data
A catalogue record for this book is available from the British Library

Library of Congress Cataloging-in-Publication Data
A catalog record for this book has been requested

ISBN 13: 978-1-03-209675-9 (pbk)
ISBN 13: 978-1-4724-7150-5 (hbk)

Typeset in Times New Roman
by codeMantra

Contents

Figures and tables

Figures

Table

Contributors

Ellen Margrethe Basse is Professor of Environmental Law at the Department of Law, Aarhus University. She is a doctor habitation of environmental law and was awarded the jur.dr. (H.C.) at Uppsala University for her research education activities in this area. She is a former Professor of Procedural Law and Associate Professor of Administrative Law. She was the Director of the Interdisciplinary Social Science Research Centre (1992–2001) and the Chairman and Secretary of Aarhus University's Climate Panel (2008–2010). She has been a member of several research bodies, evaluation panels and think tanks in Denmark and other Nordic countries. She is the author of many books and articles on international, EU and national environmental, energy and climate law, public law and legal theory.

David Boertmann is Senior Researcher and Biologist at Aarhus University and an advisor to the Government of Greenland in environmental issues related to oil exploration. His areas of research concern ecology and taxonomy, with a focus on the distribution and occurrence of birds and marine mammals in Greenland and on mycology. He has recently mapped the distribution of breeding seabirds in the whole of Southeast Greenland.

Edward T. Canuel is a U.S. Foreign Service Officer with extensive international law experience. His career and scholarship have focused on energy, the Arctic, environmental sustainability and trade/investment issues, with overseas postings in Canada, Norway and Denmark. He has also served as the State Department's Visiting Professor at West Point and holds professorships at Aarhus University and American University. Dr. Canuel was named the US government's candidate to lead the Arctic Council Secretariat in 2012. His most recent legal publications at Duke University, West Point and the University of Texas deal with Arctic energy issues.

Vladimir Pacheco Cueva is Associate Professor at the School of Culture and Society, Aarhus University. His research interests include the socio-economic impacts and governance of non-renewable resource extraction in the Arctic and the Global South. Previous to this position, Cueva held senior roles in Australia with the Foundation for Development Cooperation, the Centre for Social Responsibility in Mining and the consulting firm WorleyParsons. His latest publication is a book chapter entitled 'From transnational trends to local practices: monitoring social impacts in a Papua New Guinea mining community' (Routledge, 2015).

Kim Gustavson is Senior Scientist at the Department of Bioscience/Danish Centre for Environment and Energy, Aarhus University. Presently, he is the work package leader in the EU project entitled 'Integrated oil spill response actions and environmental effects – GRACE'. He has key expertise with regard to the fate and effect of metals, oil and persistent organic pollutants in Arctic ecosystems. Since 2011, he has performed advisory work for the authorities in Greenland and Denmark within the field of mining and oil exploration in the Arctic. His publications include more than 40 scientific papers in international scientific journals.

Christoph Humrich is Assistant Professor of International Relations and Security Studies at the Department for International Relations and International Organizations, and Associated Researcher at the Arctic Centre at the Faculty of Arts, University of Groningen. His research focuses on Arctic security, Arctic international relations and Arctic governance.

Rachael Lorna Johnstone is Professor of law at the University of Akureyri, Iceland and at the University of Greenland. Professor Johnstone specialises in Polar law: the governance of the Arctic and the Antarctic under international and domestic law. She is the author of *Offshore Oil and Gas Development in the Arctic under International Law: Risk and Responsibility* (Brill 2015) and has published widely on the rights of indigenous peoples, international human rights law, international environmental law, due diligence, state responsibility and Arctic strategies.

Timo Koivurova is Research Professor and Director of the Arctic Centre at the University of Lapland. He is editor-in-chief of the *Yearbook of Polar Law* and the *Yearbook of International Environmental Law*, and he has led many international research projects including the project with Wuhan University on 'Arctic Law and Governance: The Role of China and Finland'. He is a specialist in Arctic law and governance.

Bent Ole Gram Mortensen is Professor at the University of Southern Denmark where he holds a chair in environmental and energy law, and is Section Head of Public Law and Head of the Research Unit Commercial Administrative Law. For the past 20 years, he has been engaged in the legal aspects of the energy industry and of exploitation of minerals (including oil and natural gas) in Greenland. He has contributed to a large number of articles and books in English, Danish and German. He is a member of the Danish Energy Board of Appeal and Chairman of the Valuation Authorities in Southern Denmark in compliance with the Danish Renewable Energy Act.

Anders Mosbech is Head of Research and Advisory Tasks at the Arctic Environment Group, Bioscience, Aarhus University. He has worked with biodiversity and environmental issues in Greenland for more than 25 years. Research interests include marine ecology, oil spill sensitivity analysis, and the delineation and identification of key marine habitats. He leads the joint Baffin Bay Environmental Study Program (Aarhus University and Greenland Institute of Natural Resources). He is Co-PI for the Arctic Council project *Adaptation Actions for a Changing Arctic (Baffin Bay-Davis Strait Region)* and Co-PI for the *THE NOW PROJECT: Living Resources and Human Societies around the North Water in the Thule Area, NW Greenland.*

Cécile Pelaudeix is Associate Professor at the School of Culture and Society of Aarhus University and research associate at PACTE, Sciences Po Grenoble. She has been a member of the Scientific Committee of the 'Chantier Arctique', CNRS (National Center for Scientific Research), Paris. Her research focuses on Arctic governance, the EU Arctic policy, Greenland politics and China's foreign policy in the Arctic. She is the work package leader in a research project on the Arctic for the European Defence Agency.

Pelle Tejsner is Assistant Professor at the Department of Anthropology, Aarhus University. His current research examines local receptions of plans for onshore and offshore resource exploration from 2015 by considering the rights of indigenous peoples (Inuit) rights, traditional notions of tenure, and custodianship vis-à-vis the interests of the state and multinational resource exploration companies. Tejsner is also a committee member of the International Arctic Research Council (IASC), Social and Human Working Group (SHWG) and a moderator for the *Greenlandic Society.*

Øyvind Ravna is Professor of law at UiT the Arctic University of Norway and Adjunct Professor, at the University of Lapland, Rovaniemi, Finland. His fields of research are indigenous people's law, human rights law, property law, land consolidation and legal history. He is the editor-in-chief, of the Arctic Review on Law and Politics. Ravna has published several monographs and many articles in the field of indigenous people's law, land rights and natural resources including the Finnmark Act of Norway.

Thierry Rodon is Associate Professor at the Political Science Department at Université Laval and holds a Research Chair in Northern Sustainable Development. He is also the director of the Interuniversity Centre for Aboriginal Studies and Research (CIERA) and of the journal *Études*

Inuit Studies. He specialises in northern policies and community development and has extensive experience working with Indigenous communities and northern institutions. He leads MinErAL an international research project on extractive industries and indigenous livelihood.

Roman Sidortsov, J.D. LL.M, is Assistant Professor of Energy Policy at Michigan Technological University and a non-resident Senior Global Energy Fellow at Vermont Law School's Institute for Energy and the Environment. His research focuses on legal and policy issues related to the development of sustainable energy systems, energy security and justice, comparative and international energy law and policy, energy geopolitics, risk governance, and Arctic oil and gas with a special emphasis on the Russian Federation, Norway and the United States. Dr. Sidortsov also serves as an editorial board member for *Energy Research and Social Science* for which he recently edited a special issue regarding energy development in the Arctic.

Kristoffer Svendsen holds an LL.B and LL.M from Bond University, an LL.M in Russian oil and gas law from Moscow State Institute of International Relations (MGIMO-University), and a PhD from the Arctic University of Norway. He previously worked for a Russian investment bank in Moscow and an NGO in Brussels on EU foreign policy towards Russia. Svendsen regularly guest lectures in Russia and the US, and publishes academic articles globally. He also maintains an 'of counsel' position at a Moscow law firm. He has been admitted as a lawyer in New South Wales, and is an Attorney-at-law in New York State. He is also a member of the NORDEM roster (the Norwegian Resource Bank for Democracy and Human Rights).

Acknowledgements

This collective volume is the outcome of two years of research activities on the governance of Arctic offshore oil and gas, carried out at Aarhus University and involving the Faculty of Arts, the Department of Law and the Arctic Research Centre (ARC). The research activities behind this volume have been part of the activities of the ARC and the Research Group on International and Transnational Tendencies in Law (INTRALaw) at the Department of Law.

The editors wish to express their gratitude to all the institutions that have supported the research activities and the editing of this volume, in particular INTRALaw for its support for the linguistic reviews of this volume.

We are grateful to the authors for their contribution to the volume.

We thank Mia Korsbæk for her essential support in the preparation of the manuscript and of the index.

We also extend our thanks to the people who have provided linguistic reviews: Nicholas Wrigley, Lucy Seton-Watson and Tinna Meyer.

List of abbreviations

AAC	Arctic Athabaskan Council
AANDC	Aboriginal Affairs and Northern Development Canada
Aarhus Convention	UNECE Convention on Access to Information, Public Participation in Decision-Making and Access to Justice in Environmental Matters
AC	Arctic Council
ACAP	Arctic Contaminants Action Program
ACHR	American Convention of Human Rights
ADRDM	American Declaration of the Rights and Duties of Man
ADRIP	American Declaration on the Rights of Indigenous Peoples
AEPS	Arctic Environmental Protection Strategy
AIA	Aleut International Association
AMAP	Arctic Monitoring and Assessment Program Working Group under the Arctic Council
ANILCA	Alaska National Interest Lands Conservation Act
ANSCA	Alaska Native Claims Act
ANWR	Alaska National Wildlife Reserve
AO	Arctic Ocean
AOGS	Arctic Oil and Gas Services
AOOGG	Arctic Offshore Oil and Gas Guidelines
AP95	Common conditions for the provision of works and supplies within building and engineering in Greenland
Basel Convention	UNEP Convention on the Control of Transboundary Movements of Hazardous Wastes and their Disposal
BAT	Best Available Technique
BEP	Best Environmental Practice
BIP	Business Incentive Policy (Canada)
BLM	Bureau of Land Management (U.S.)

BMP	Bureau of Minerals and Petroleum (a former Greenlandic authority now replaced by the MLSA)
BOEM	Bureau of Ocean Energy Management (U.S.)
BOEMRE	Bureau of Ocean Energy Management, Regulation, and Enforcement (U.S.)
BSEE	Bureau of Safety and Environmental Enforcement (U.S.)
CAFF	Conservation of Arctic Flora and Fauna Working Group under the Arctic Council
Cairn	Cairn Energy and its Greenlandic subsidiary Capricorn Greenlandic Exploration
CBA	Community Benefit Agreement
CEO	Chief Executive Officer
CERD	Convention on the Elimination of Racial Discrimination
CFC	Coastal Fishing Committee (Norwegian)
CJEU	Court of Justice of the European Union
CLC	International Convention on Civil Liability for Oil Pollution Damage
CLCS	Commission on the Limits of the Continental Shelf established under Anne II of the UNCLOS with the mandate set out in Article 76(8) on the limits of the continental shelf beyond 200 nm
COGOA	Canada Oil and Gas Operations Act
Commission	European Commission
COP	Conference of the Parties
Council	European Council
CSC	Convention on the Continental Shelf
CSR	Cooperate Social Responsibility
DCE	Danish Centre for Environment and Energy, Aarhus University
DOI	Department of Interior (U.S.)
EA	Environmental assessment
EBA	Economic Benefit Agreement
EBS	Environmental baseline studies
ECJ	European Court of Justice (before the Lisbon Treaty)
ECHR	European Convention of Human Rights
EDS	Electric Data Systems
EEA	European Economic Area
EEA Agreement	Agreement on the European Area, which was concluded in 1992 and entered into force in 1994
EEZ	Economic Exclusive Zone
EFTA	European Free Trade Association
EI	Extractive Industries
EIA	Environmental Impact Assessment

EIA Directive	Environmental Impact Assessment (2011/92/EU as amended by 2014/52/EU)
EIS	environmental impact statement
EISC	Environmental Impact Screening Committee
EITI	Extractive Industries Transparency Initiative
EL	Exploration Licence
EMSA	European Marine Safety Agency
EPA	Environmental Protection Agency (U.S.)
EPCM	Engineering, Procurement and Construction Management
EPPR	Emergency, Prevention, Preparedness and Response Working Group under the Arctic Council
ESA	EFTA Surveillance Authority (EEA/EFTA)
ESA	Endangered Species Act (U.S.)
Espoo Convention	UNECE Convention on Environmental Impact Assessment in a Trans-boundary Context
EU	European Union
EUOAG	EU Offshore Oil and Gas Authorities Group
EUR	Euro
FDI	foreign direct investment
FMSP	Framework Directive for Maritime Spatial Planning (2014/89/EU)
FOC	Flag of Convenience
FOC registration	Registration of ships in a state that the ships have no real connection with
FPIC	Free, Prior and Informed Consent
GCI	Gwich'in Council International
GINR	Greenland Institute of Natural Resources
GMES	Global Monitoring for Environment and Security
GNWT	Government of the Northwest Territories (Canada)
GIS	Geographic Information System
HELCOM	Baltic Marine Environment Protection Commission - Helsinki Commission
HSE	Health, Safety and Environmental standards
IBA	Impact Benefit Agreement
ICC	Inuit Circumpolar Council
ICCPR	International Covenant on Civil and Political Rights
ICES	International Council for the Exploration of the Sea
ICESCR	International Covenant on Economic, Social and Cultural Rights
IFA	Inuvialuit Final Agreement
IFC	International Finance Corporation
ILO	International Labour Organization

ILO Convention No. 107	ILO's Indigenous and Tribal Peoples Convention (from 1957)
ILO Convention No. 169	ILO's Indigenous and Tribal Peoples Convention (from 1989)
IPIECA	International Petroleum Industry Environmental Conservation Association
IMO	International Maritime Organization
INAC	Indian and Northern Affairs Canada
IOGP	Industrial Association of Oil and Gas Producers
IOPC Fund Convention	International Convention on the Establishment of an International Fund
IPGs	Institutions of public governance
IPIECA	International Petroleum Industry Environmental Conservation Association
IRC	Inuvialuit Regional Corporation
IRF	International Regulators Forum
IRP	Integrated Resource Planning
ISPS Code	International Ship and Port Facility Security Code
IUCN	International Union for the Conservation of Nature
IWC	International Whaling Commission
JCNB	Joint Commission on Narwhal and Beluga
JI	Joint Implementation
JNCC guidelines	British standards for seismic surveying
LLMC 76	IMO's International Convention on Limitation of Liability for Maritime Claims of 19 November 1976
LNG	liquid natural gas
London Convention	Convention on the Prevention of Marine Pollution by Dumping of Wastes and Other Matters
M&As	Mergers and acquisitions
MARPOL 1973/78	IMO's Convention for the Prevention of Pollution from Ships from 1973 as modified in 1978
MEPC	Marine Environmental Protection Committee of the IMO
MET	Mineral extraction tax (Russia)
MLG	Multilevel governance
MLSA	Mineral Licence and Safety Authority (Greenland)
mmBtu	million British thermal units

MMS	Mineral Management Service (U.S.)
MPAs	Marine Protected Areas
MSC	Marine Stewardship Council
MSFD	Marine Strategic Framework Directive (2008/56/EC)
NAFO	Northwest Atlantic Fisheries Organisation
NAMMCO	North Atlantic Marine Mammal Commission
NASDAQ	National Association of Securities Dealers Automated Quotation
NEB	National Energy Board (Canada)
NEBA	Response Strategy Development Using Net Environmental Benefit Analysis
NEPA	National Environmental Act (U.S.)
NGO	Non-Governmental Organization
NIRB	Nunavut Impact Review Board
NLCA	Nunavut Land Claims Agreement
nm	nautical miles
NORSOK	Norwegian standards for adequate safety in the petroleum industry
NOU	Norwegian Official Report
NPC	Nunavut Planning Commission
NPDES	the National Pollutant Discharge Elimination System
NRt	Norwegian Legal Journal – it is a court archive journal publishing the Supreme Court verdicts since 1833.
NTI	Nunavut Tunngavik Incorporation
NUNAGIS	Self-Government of Greenland's GIS portal
NWB	Nunavut Water Board
NWNB	Nunavut Wildlife Management Board
NWT	Northwest Territories (Canada)
NYMEX	New York Mercantile Exchange
O & G	oil and gas
OAS	Organisation of American States
OCS	U.S. Arctic Outer Continental Shelf
OCSLA	U.S. Arctic Outer Continental Shelf Lands Act (U.S.)
OCTs	Overseas Countries and Territories (of the EU)
OG21 and Energi 21	Norway's two strategies on Oil and Gas in the Twenty-first Century
OJ	Official Journal of the European Union
ONRR	Office of National Resources Revenue (U.S.)
OPA	Oil Pollution Act (U.S.)
OPRC	IMO Convention on Oil Pollution Preparedness, Response and Cooperation

OPRC-HNS Protocol	The Protocol under OPPRC on Preparedness, Response and Cooperation to Pollution Incidents by Hazardous and Noxious Substances
OSPAR	Convention for the Protection of the Marine Environment of the North-East Atlantic
OVOS	Russian acronym for the preparation of an EIA
PAME	Protection of the Arctic Marine Environment Working Group under the Arctic Council
PCB	Polychlorinated biphenyl
PIP	Preparatory Information Package
ppm	parts per million
PSA	Production-Sharing Agreement (Russian)
QIA	Qikiqtani Inuit Association
RAIPON	Russian umbrella organization, which organizes thirty-five regional and ethnic organizations of indigenous peoples in the regions where they live.
RF Government	Government of the Russian Federation
Rosnedra	Federal Agency for Mineral Resources (Russia)
Rosprirodnadzor	Federal Service for Oversight of National Resources (Russia)
Rostekhnadzor	Federal Service for Environmental, Technological and Nuclear Oversight (Russia)
SCJ	Standing Committee of Justice (Norwegian)
SEA	Strategic Environmental Assessment
SEA Directive	Strategic Environmental Assessment Directive (2001/42/EC)
SEA Protocol	Strategic Environmental Assessment Directive under the UNECE's Espoo Convention
SEIA	Strategic Environmental Impact Assessment (also called SEA)
SER	State Environmental Review
SDAP	Sustainable Development Action Plan
SDWG	Sustainable Development Working Group under the Arctic Council
SIA	Social Impact Assessment
SLA	Submerged Lands Act (U.S.)
SSA	Social Sustainability Assessment
SSRW	Same Season Relief Well
TAPS	Trans-Alaska Pipeline System
TEU	Treaty on European Union
TFEU	Treaty on the Functioning of the European Union
TNG	True North Gems Greenland A/S
Treaty	Treaty of Lisbon

UK	United Kingdom
UKNBP	United Kingdom National Balancing Point
UN	United Nations
UNCED	United Nations Conference on Environment and Development
UNCLOS	United Nations Convention on the Law of the Sea (also titled LOS Convention)
UNCTAD	United Nations Conference on Trade and Development
UNECE	United Nations Economic Commission for Europe
UNEP	United Nations' Environmental Programme
UNESCO	United Nations Educational, Scientific and Cultural Organization
UNFCCC	United Nations Framework Convention on Climate Change
UNDRIP	United Nations Declaration on the Rights of Indigenous Peoples
US	United States
USGS	United Nations States Geological Survey
WB	World Bank
WCED	World Commission on Environment and Development
WCIP	World Conference on Indigenous Peoples
WTI	West Texas Intermediate

1 Governance of offshore oil and gas in the Arctic

Between diversity and coexistence

Cécile Pelaudeix and Ellen Margrethe Basse

Widely covered with sea ice, the Arctic Ocean has been shielded from developments arising from globalisation until recently, when global warming started impacting the region at an unexpectedly fast pace. Shipping, tourism, fishing and offshore oil and gas activities have already increased in the Arctic Ocean due to the receding of sea ice. As a consequence of energy globalisation,[1] which has resulted in energy resources being transported over long distances, the Arctic Ocean is also now being targeted. One of the most significant features in the use of this sea area is the development of offshore oil and gas activities with potentially far-reaching consequences for the political, economic, social and environmental situation in the Arctic which raises questions about governance of environmental issues and public participation.

Exploration for and exploitation of hydrocarbons in the Artic are not new. Fossil-fuel activities began in the 1970s in very different areas of Russia, Norway, Canada and Denmark/Greenland. In the Greenlandic area, they ceased in the 1980s and resumed in 2000.[2] Offshore oil and gas exploitation started around the world more than a century ago, but as reserves are depleted in shallow waters, greater depths are being targeted. In the space of just a few years, the petroleum industry has embarked on the conquest of the deep offshore (over 500 ft or 152 m), and the deep offshore has emerged as a key source of new reserves for the future.

A conjunction of factors explains why the Arctic coastal states are looking with renewed interest for offshore potential in the north, including in the deep offshore of the Arctic Ocean. First, high oil and gas prices in the period from 2004 to 2008 were an incentive to invest in offshore exploitation. As oil prices have declined, some exploitation projects in the Arctic have slowed down, but the relative lull is accompanied by the opening of new areas. For instance, 33 companies showed an interest in the 23rd licensing round in Norway for blocks located farther east and farther north than ever before. In 2016, the 24th licensing round extended petroleum activities on the Norwegian coastal shelf even farther, and oil and gas activities continue in the Russian Arctic as well. Second, in the aftermath of the 2006 gas crisis between Russia and Ukraine, after which gas supplies to European countries were cut off, energy security rose high on the political agenda and directed attention to the Arctic region. One result of this development was that the

European Union (EU) developed an Arctic policy. Third, reserves are currently being depleted in conventional fields such as the onshore Prudhoe Bay Oil Field in Alaska and in the North Atlantic, whereas the Arctic is thought to hold immense reserves of gas and oil. In this context, the 2008 US Geological Survey (USGS) estimates on the amount of Arctic oil and gas resources made an even bigger impact. According to this survey, the Arctic holds 13 percent of the world's undiscovered resources of oil and 30 percent of undiscovered gas resources.[3] Even so, these numbers, although they are widely used and much cited, represent only potential reserves and are based only on geological probability rather than on drilling results. Finally, world energy demand is experiencing a sharp increase, mainly due to rising demand from emerging countries such as China and India. It is expected to rise by more than one-third from 2011 to 2035.[4] Remote fossil-fuel fields are being targeted as a result.

The Arctic Ocean presents huge challenges for the exploration and exploitation of offshore oil and gas owing to the low resilience of the region's ecosystems, its extreme natural-climate conditions (low temperatures, icing, icebergs, ice floes, high winds, rapidly changing conditions, darkness during the winter season), and its remoteness from basic infrastructure. The Arctic is a highly diverse region constituting a composite of very specific areas in terms of geography, and parameters such as depth of sea, icebergs and sea ice vary greatly. Consequently, every Arctic region faces challenges when it comes to the offshore exploitation of hydrocarbon resources. Due to the Gulf Stream, the southern parts of the Norwegian Barents Sea are free of ice, but Norway has ambitions further north. As already stated, Norway has opened new areas of exploration in the Barents Sea, which are approaching the marginal ice zone. In Russia, the exploitation of the Pechora Sea Shelf is taking place in a water depth of only 20 meters, but these are also ice-infested waters. Ice floes constitute a threat in the Beaufort Sea in Canada and off the Greenlandic west coast, where glaciers calve and produce many icebergs, and yet exploration activities have taken place at a depth reaching 1,000 meters (Figure 1.1).

Accidental oil spills at sea can actually occur in at least four ways. Oil tankers can run aground due to human error, mechanical failure or bad weather. This is what happened with the *Exxon Valdez* (which ran aground on a reef off the Alaskan coast in 1989), the *Torrey Canyon* (which was wrecked off the British coast in 1967), the *Erika* (which sank off the French coast in 1999) and the *Prestige* (which broke in two off north-west Spain in 2002). These accidents had severe consequences, despite occurring in waters more benign than waters north of the Arctic Circle. Accidents can also damage long-range cargo ships, which carry substantial amounts of fuel oil. Oil can escape during the drilling or extraction process, as with the blow-out of the Deepwater Horizon rig in the Gulf of Mexico in 2010, making this question prominent in the public debate, with a focus on the special risks in the Arctic. Finally, oil spills can occur during the exploration phase: in

Figure 1.1 Map of the circumpolar Arctic
Source: © Arctic Portal

2012, the Kulluk rig drifted ashore during its transport from Alaska to the United States, but, luckily, the accident did not result in an oil spill. The Arctic Ocean is characterised by particularly vulnerable ecosystems that are already under pressure of climate change.

Just as the lack of infrastructure (Arctic-class drilling vessels, ice breakers, support and oil spill response vessels and deep water ports, for instance) hinders the capacity to prevent and respond to the risks of an oil spill, so does the lack of knowledge. Knowledge is still needed with regard to the adequate modelling of offshore drilling activity, local weather forecasting, observing and monitoring sea ice and iceberg mobility, oil-spill detection in ice-infested waters and oil fate in sea ice.[5] At the same time, the risks connected with the offshore activities for the local societies are huge: indigenous coastal communities rely on marine species as a means of subsistence, and fisheries account for a large part of the economy of Arctic coastal areas in Norway, Russia and Greenland. The consequences of oil spills in the Arctic can therefore dramatically affect both marine ecosystems and local economies.

In addition to the threat of oil spill and its environmental consequences for fish, marine mammals and ecosystems, fossil-fuel activities contribute to the Arctic paradox: the burning of fossil fuels contributes to climate change, which causes the receding of sea ice, which in turn facilitates access to fossil fuels – while the extraction and use of these resources contribute to climate warming. In the Arctic, average temperatures have risen almost twice as fast as in the rest of the world.[6]

A further complexity in the Arctic situation lies in the fact that many Northerners are calling for local development in order to build prosperous regions whose economies lack diversification. Until recently, the Arctic has been used as a vast reservoir of natural resources to serve the world market, and economic benefits have been very unequally distributed throughout the region: per capita economic output varies significantly depending on available resources and population density, but also depending on land claims and impact benefit agreements (IBAs) concluded by developers with the local governments, indigenous peoples and other local residents.[7] However, the social, economic and environmental impacts of the extractive industries are mixed. Offshore extraction in the form of large-scale industries can generate sizeable negative impacts.[8]

The challenges connected to the development of offshore oil and gas activities in the Arctic are defined not only by the environmental and social risks of these activities but also by the costs of minimising these risks in relation to the economic benefits expected from the activities. So who makes the decisions about offshore hydrocarbon activities in the Arctic marine areas, and how are those decisions made? Who is impacted by them and by the unfolding activities in the region, and how? This volume explores issues connected with the governance of offshore hydrocarbon extraction in the Arctic marine area, including the seas of the coastal states (Norway, Russia, the United States, Canada and Denmark/Greenland),[9] with the aim of clarifying the legal and political dimensions of the governance process in the Arctic area.

The governance approach

The concept of governance may be a relevant analytical tool to understand the management of the environment and of public participation in connection with activities taking place in the marine Arctic area. Based on the Westphalian model of international relations with its principles of sovereignty and reciprocity, the states retain jurisdiction over their energy activities in the offshore areas inside their exclusive economic zones (EEZ) and extended continental shelf. Both inside and beyond the states' territorial jurisdiction, many different actors play a part in the governance of offshore hydrocarbon extraction in the Arctic: international and regional state-based institutions, governmental agencies, territorial self-governments, advisory bodies, corporations, organisations representing indigenous peoples and non-governmental associations (NGOs). This complex situation, characterised by a multilevel governance system, has the potential to lead to a situation of *legal pluralism*, in which legal systems overlap.[10]

Offshore activities in the Arctic have mainly been studied with regard to international law[11] and the issue of fragmentation of law.[12] In this volume, the impact of globalisation, devolution and pluralism on the governance of the Arctic marine areas is the main focus. It is the first volume to analyse, on an interdisciplinary basis and with a circumpolar approach, the governance systems and processes that have been designed to address issues related to energy policies, environment protection and public participation.[13] 'Governance' in this volume is understood in reference to the definition of the Commission on Global Governance, which characterises governance as:[14]

> the sum of many ways individuals and institutions, public and private, manage their common affairs. It is a continuing process through which conflicting or diverse interests may be accommodated and cooperative action taken. It includes formal institutions and regimes empowered to enforce compliance, as well as informal arrangements that people and institutions either have agreed to or perceive to be in their interest.

The concept of governance, which first emerged in the field of public policy, entered the field of international relations in the late 1980s to properly analyse increasing regulatory activities on the international level in addition to domestic decision-making processes, and, additionally, to highlight the role of non-state actors in the mechanism of political regulation. As a concept underlying the fact that the nation states' governments no longer possess the monopoly of legitimate authority, how should the governance of offshore hydrocarbon activities be analysed when states usually retain jurisdiction over these activities? The question is of particular relevance in the Arctic, as this region is impacted at once by both globalisation and devolution processes. Globalisation can be defined as the process of intensification and acceleration of communications and international exchanges, the development of transnational relations – for instance, in the Arctic, the role of the Inuit Circumpolar Council (ICC) – and new roles for states. It encompasses globalisation of issues such as sources of energy, whose production has become entangled in faraway locations and events.[15] Globalisation also encompasses mechanisms including the spreading of ideas and the expansion of international law, leading to obligations being imposed on state parties and normative pressure being exercised on non-state parties. Devolution refers to processes of transfer of powers to regional/territorial governments and to administrations. Devolution processes started in the Arctic region in the 1970s with the need to exploit natural resources and address the remoteness of decision-making centres, as well as increasing recognition of the rights of indigenous peoples. The conceptual framework of this volume thus also relies on the concept of multilevel governance as an analytical approach to tackling the overlapping competences between levels of governments and the interaction of various actors across those levels. This volume provides a picture of Arctic governance that goes beyond the single issue of fragmentation at the international and supranational levels, so as to encompass national and regional levels and analyse how the interactions between those levels structure the policy process and impact the efficiency of environmental management and public participation, including the participation of indigenous peoples.

Volume outline

This volume addresses governance issues related to the need for environmental protection in a national and transboundary context and to the need to connect national energy and climate-related policies, in the wake of the Paris Agreement (COP21) under the UNFCCC, which strengthened the ability of states and other actors to deal with the challenges connected to climate change – national energy and climate-related policies. This volume is also addressing issues related to the need for democratic legitimisation of the offshore hydrocarbon activities in the Arctic – a demand that involves a widespread consent in the local communities in the implementation of and compliance with safety rules.[16] As a consequence of this comprehensive approach, and of the diversity of challenges posed by offshore oil and gas activities in the Arctic, the contributions in this volume offer analytical perspectives from various academic disciplines: political science, law, anthropology and biology. Approaches might differ, as legal studies tend to focus on normativity, whereas the approaches of political science focus more on the analysis of a process of decision-making.[17] And some contributions engage less than others in the governance and multilevel governance approach and propose a more technical angle. The result of the multidisciplinary approach adopted in this volume is a complementarity of analysis, and some contributions show a high degree of interconnectedness between policy and law.

This volume consists of four parts, which reflect the various levels of governance at stake and their interactions (international and supranational; national; national and subnational; and the local level of implementation and enforcement that focuses more on regulatory instruments).

Part I outlines the effects of globalisation, supranationalism and internationalisation in the Arctic, all phenomena that increasingly influence states in their approach to energy production in the offshore sector in particular. Globalisation in this part includes the spreading of ideas (such as the discussed idea of a "scramble for resources between states" or the campaigns of NGOs against oil drilling in the Arctic) and the expansion in the use of concepts (such as the concept of sustainable development) and their potential impacts on the unfolding of oil and gas activities in the Arctic offshore. Supranationalism refers to the specific institutional setting of the EU and the normative impact of the EU, not only on the legislation of EU member states but also on the legislation of EEA countries, as well as on the operations of EU companies outside the EU. Internationalisation implies the codification of norms, like the rights of indigenous peoples, in international conventions and declarations, which states can decide to ignore, or to fully or partially endorse. Part II analyses the five states and sub-state perspectives (the US, Russia, Norway, Canada and Greenland) on the offshore regulation and points not only to differences owing to political heterogeneity, energy policies and distinct legal traditions but also to similarities arising from common challenges and cooperation mechanisms. Part III examines the state-based approach in its specific relation with indigenous sub-state entities to assess the extent to which indigenous peoples are associated with the decision-making processes in the domestic and international regimes. This part of the book looks into cases from Canada, Norway and Greenland. Finally, part IV focuses on the regulatory instruments and the issue of enforcement as the final level of implementation. It addresses the provisions and mechanisms relating to the environment and society.

Some issues are cross-cutting and are taken up in all parts of the volume. This is the case regarding the dependence of communities on the environment and indigenous peoples' rights, which are dealt with as part of an internationalisation process when considering international law development (part I). The importance of the relation between the environment and society is also highlighted as a factor potentially constraining national policies, such as energy policies (part II). The issue is part of the analyses of the domestic and territorial policies when looking into devolution processes (part III), and of the analyses of the agreements known as IBAs (part IV). Another example of cross-cutting issues is the special case of Denmark's competences and responsibilities with regard to the offshore hydrocarbon activities of Greenland, which is described in part I, part II and part IV.[18]

The role of industry in the governance of offshore oil and gas is another cross-cutting issue in this volume. The chapters do not include a direct corporate view on governance, but the specific role of corporations in the governance process is addressed through different contributions. In their respective chapters (part II), Sidortsov and Pelaudeix touch upon the contexts in which regulatory frameworks provide incentives for corporate investments. Cueva and Mortensen's chapters (part III) look into the enforcement level and the flexibility that corporations enjoy in the way they implement IBAs.

Part I analyses the impacts of globalisation, supranationalism and internationalisation on the development and regulatory aspects of offshore oil and gas activities. The first two chapters discuss framings and concepts such as sustainable development related to the issue of oil and gas exploitation in the Arctic. The two following chapters address transnational governance aspects and the role of law in the setting of norms, as exemplified by the EU's role in the development of marine environmental law and the rights of indigenous peoples under international law. In the first chapter of part I – 'Framing the Problem in Arctic Offshore Hydrocarbon Exploitation' – Timo Koivurova analyses four framings of the 'problem' and discusses their validity in the analysis of governance options. He first deconstructs the wrong perception of a scramble for resources between Arctic states, before arguing against the idea that Arctic fossil fuels can drive national politics and political economy. Koivurova then highlights the need for a stronger climate change regime, and finally acknowledges that even if there are many regulatory tools for the extraction, there is no doubt that there will be risks associated with drilling for oil in some parts of the Arctic marine areas. He concludes that in defining what is problematic in Arctic hydrocarbon exploitation, we are bound to rely on our nation states and on the current regulatory systems that are in place, but that academic experts and the institutions of civil society must also play their role as responsible actors in assessing the risks connected with offshore hydrocarbon activities.

In the next chapter – 'Sustainable Development in Arctic International Environmental Cooperation and the Governance of Hydrocarbon-related Activities' – Christoph Humrich outlines how the sustainable development concept, based on the shared values, morals and ethics of an increasingly interconnected and interdependent world, became ingrained as a policy concept in Arctic international environmental cooperation. Humrich analyses the shift in the discursive context of the concept, which he links to the acknowledgement of the relevance of Arctic economic development, the broadening of the notion of development, the redefinition of the character of Arctic nature and environment, and finally the externalisation of threats to the Arctic environment. He concludes that in the present context of Arctic international environmental cooperation, the concept of sustainable development can no longer serve as a suitable policy-guiding frame for identifying what is problematic about Arctic oil and gas activities, because it is unlikely to result in any notable constraining effect on further oil and gas activities.

Ellen Margrethe Basse's chapter – 'The EU's Role as Facilitator in the Development of Environmental Law in the Arctic with Focus on Offshore Hydrocarbon Activities' – explains the ecosystem-based approach in the EU's marine and maritime directives and highlights how the Offshore Safety Directive has extended the scope of the Environmental Liability Directive, which now, based on her analysis of the European Court of Justice (EUCJ) and the EFTA Court, also includes all the marine areas of EEA/EFTA member states. The main theme of her chapter is how far the EU can rely on the territorial jurisdictions of the Kingdom of Denmark and the Kingdom of Norway in the Arctic as its basis for taking a more active role in the governance of Arctic offshore hydrocarbon activities. Basse describes how the judgments of the EUCJ are driving forces in the vertical harmonisation of international/regional obligations through the EU's secondary legislation as well as the extraterritorial effects of the EU's environmental standards and principles. The EU's membership of OSPAR and other regional and international regimes addressing the protection of the marine area is highlighted as another important issue in the chapter.

In 'Indigenous Rights in the Marine Arctic', Rachael Johnstone demonstrates that hydrocarbon development in the marine Arctic can be undertaken in a manner compatible with the internationally recognised indigenous rights. She shows that the key consideration is the right of indigenous peoples to self-determination and that land rights (including rights to traditionally used coastal and marine areas), resource governance and rights to property, culture, food and health are the main substantive rights at stake. These rights are complemented by procedural rights to information, consultation and participation (as a minimum), or to free, prior and informed consent, and to economic rights to compensation, and benefit-sharing. Johnstone explains, however, that in the event of significant interference owing to offshore activities, which affect living marine resources and/or have significant repercussions for human rights and indigenous rights, restitution is likely to be impossible, and compensation will be the alternative outcome. The author is of the opinion that the central principle of free, prior and informed consent, which is not (yet) a hard law requirement in every case, can be applied both by developers and by the states governing such procedural rights, reducing the potential risk of states being liable for economic loss.

Part II of the volume focuses on states and sub-state perspectives on offshore regulations and looks into the political, economic and cultural specificities of the national contexts (and sub-national context in the case of Greenland) in which oil and gas exploration and exploitation activities unfold. In 'Alaska and Offshore Hydrocarbon Extraction: A Legal and Socio-Economic Review', Canuel analyses the complex US regulatory framework and the various legal mechanisms influencing Arctic US hydrocarbon development. Canuel describes how these mechanisms provide a roadmap of issues, which are useful for diverse Arctic constituencies. Related issues include the implementation of the Alaska National Interest Lands Conservation Act (ANILCA), affecting and shaping Alaskan land-use law. Additionally, the impact and importance of Native Alaskan rights is discussed through a brief survey of US state and federal tribal law. In addition to surveying key issues affecting multiple stakeholders, the author suggests that increasing Arctic interest has created enhanced opportunities for cooperation. The author also illustrates that the Native Alaskan legal challenges to hydrocarbon development have challenged certain links within the complex regulatory scheme and have built upon a growing US case recognising the effects of climate change.

In her chapter, 'Governance of Offshore Hydrocarbon Activities in the Arctic and Energy Policies: a Comparative Approach in Norway, Canada and Greenland/Denmark', Cécile Pelaudeix analyses three regulatory systems, two of which were designed by states and one by a sub-state, with a focus on three criteria: economic incentive, environment protection and public – in particular indigenous – participation. She shows not only that the regulation of offshore oil and gas activities reflects technical rationality, but also that there is a correlation between the energy strategies of Canada, Norway and Greenland and their regulatory framework with regard to the hydrocarbon offshore sector. Norway, Canada and Greenland/Denmark conceptualise energy differently: energy is considered mainly as a commercial commodity in Canada, as a public commodity in Norway, and as a strategic commodity in Greenland. Pelaudeix explains how these conceptions have various impacts on the regulatory framework.

The principal thesis of Roman Sidortsov's chapter – 'The Russian Offshore Oil and Gas Regime: When Tight Control Means Less Order' – is that despite its seemingly tight control over offshore oil and gas development in the Arctic, the Russian regulatory framework lacks balance between financial incentive and appropriate environmental and socioeconomic checks. Sidortsov reviews the applicable policy, legal and regulatory framework with an emphasis on access to offshore hydrocarbon resources and the conditions governing the development. He explains that the strengthening of the vertical power policy by President Putin has left the region without authority over many matters, including offshore oil and gas development. Sidortsov shows that the two-step process of access to oil and gas resources relies on unclear criteria and that environmental protection is now only in the preliminary stages of commissioning research on ecosystem protection and sustainable development. Sidortsov concludes that for a nation that plans to maintain its current economic status by prioritising Arctic offshore development, Russia needs to have more aspects of its policy, legal and regulatory system in working order.

Betsy Baker's chapter, 'The Arctic Offshore Hydrocarbon Hiatus of 2015, Climate Change, and Integrated Management: An opportunity to revisit regulation around the Pole', offers an overview of trends in offshore regulation around the Arctic by stepping back to consider more broadly the detailed discussions of national regulatory systems in the three previous chapters of part II – the chapters written by Canuel, Pelaudeix and Sidortsov. Baker then proposes ways to revisit Arctic offshore regulatory regimes under three general headings: the Drilling Downturn, Climate Change, and Integrated Management. She explains how climate change and integrated management based on a dialogue between regulators, industry and stakeholders actually have the potential to reshape how offshore oil and gas could be regulated in the Arctic in a more sustainable manner.

Part III of the volume analyses the state-based approach to the question of regulatory frameworks, and the relation of this approach to devolution processes and indigenous sub-state entities. As mentioned earlier, the devolution processes vary greatly in the Arctic states. This part of the volume offers the opportunity to compare the challenges of devolution with regard to indigenous peoples' rights in the offshore context in Canada, Greenland and Norway. Thierry Rodon, in 'Offshore Development and Inuit Rights in Inuit Nunangat', describes the Canadian approach, which recognises only those rights that are established by the Supreme Court and protected by section 35.1 of the constitution. And yet – as he describes – the Supreme Court has insisted that indigenous peoples have no right to "veto" the developments. The land claims agreements that have been signed to date in Canada offer the Inuit little control over offshore development. Inuit organisations and communities can participate in decision-making through the co-management boards and the various formal and informal consultation processes, but final decisions are made by a territorial or federal minister or by a federal regulatory agency. Rodon explains that this is a situation very far from the acceptance of the 'free, prior and informed consent' principle of UNDRIP. He then explains the differing approaches taken in Nunavut and in the Inuvialuit settlement regions in terms of their differing historical contexts.

The next chapter, 'Securing the Coastal Sámi Culture and Livelihood' by Øyvind Ravna and Kristoffer Svendsen, deals with the legal protection of the coastal Sámi's substantive culture and livelihood – assessed in the light of the potential threat represented by offshore industry. In relation to the risk that affects the coastal Sámi, there is particular reason to focus on oil tankers sailing along the Norwegian coast. Ravna and Svendsen also survey the rights of the indigenous Sámi in general and the special rights of the coastal Sámi to coastal fishing as explored by, among others, the Sámi Rights Committee and the Coastal Fishing Committee (CFC). They analyse the legal protection of the coastal Sámi with respect to the impact of the oil industry, particularly in connection with oil spills, and conclude that their historical rights have little protection at present. Ravna and Svendsen conclude that it is urgent to raise the question of whether Norway is complying with its international legal obligations in respect to the protection of the coastal Sámi culture.

Pelle Tejsner's chapter – 'Indigenous modes of ownership: (re)opening the case for communal rights in Greenland' – briefly reviews the rights of indigenous peoples as they relate to resource extraction, and assesses historical and contemporary indigenous notions of ownership and territorial rights in Greenland. Tejsner reminds us that traditional conceptions of territory and related usage practices in Greenland vary not only according to the form of extraction involved (i.e. hunting, fishing or farming) but also according to the nature and modes of social integration and traditional community structures. Tejsner argues that recognition of community understandings may offer a way to reconnect historically fractured jurisdictional domains while addressing aspects of social exclusion, sustainable development and governance in Greenlandic coastal areas. He concludes that integrated strategies for long-term land, sea and resource management in Greenland's offshore areas have to be achieved through due recognition of indigenous customary ownership in the coastal zone.

Part IV of the volume focuses on the regulatory instruments and scientific basis for decision-making. As key tools provided to ensure that local sustainable development is promoted in the context of the development of offshore oil and gas activities, IBAs are discussed in two chapters. Cueva's chapter focuses more on the industry's perspective on the instrument, while Mortensen looks into Naalakkersuisut's (the Greenlandic Government) perspective and the design of the act regulating the IBAs. The final chapter by Mosbech et al. introduces a new actor in the governance of offshore oil and gas, which is the scientific community and its involvement as a source of expertise in regulatory and monitoring activities in environmental matters.

In his chapter, 'Impact Benefit Agreements and Economic and Environmental Risk Management in the Arctic', Vladimir Pacheco Cueva explores, by examining industry cases from Canada and Greenland, the various means by which improved governance of IBAs could result in more effective mechanisms for local sustainable development and environmental management. He concludes that, as they stand, IBAs rarely include local sustainability and environmental risk management criteria as part of their objectives for governing offshore projects. This form of negotiated regulation falls within the realm of what, in legal pluralism, is called 'negotiated justice': a regime that provides legitimation and regulation without direct prescription from the government of the relevant state. Cueva explains that even though increasing local content and participation in offshore oil and gas projects is possible – via a combination of company corporate social responsibility commitments and state regulation – the resulting outcome leaves much to be desired.

Bent Ole Gram Mortensen analyses 'Impact Benefit Agreements in Greenland' as a tool provided by the Greenlandic Raw Materials Act.[19] First, an attempt is made to define the legal nature of an IBA. Second, the issues regarding regulation of the use of IBAs are discussed. No formal definition of an IBA exists in the relevant Act, as it only refers to 'agreement on social sustainability and other socio-economic issues'. The wording of the Act stipulates that Naalakkersuisut[20] must decide on a discretionary basis whether to oblige the licensee to enter into an IBA as a condition for receiving a licence. Analysing parts of both the "draft model IBA agreement" that was designed as a prototype and the IBAs signed to date, Mortensen concludes that the IBAs used in Greenland so far contain very unclear obligations. These agreements are consequently not easy to enforce. He states that the definition of 'Greenlandic workers' in the agreements represents a particular problem. This is an unclear term intended to cover the people in the local societies, who are expected to benefit from the conditions stated in the agreements.

The last chapter of part IV of the volume is 'The Interplay Between Environmental Research and Environmental Regulation of Offshore Oil Activities in Greenland', by Anders Mosbech, David Boertmann, Susse Wegeberg and Kim Gustavson. The authors briefly introduce the challenges related to adequate management of the marine ecosystem and the regulatory framework used for oil exploration and exploitation activities in Greenland. They describe how research and monitoring are an integrated and important part of maritime spatial planning, the mitigation of pollution and the regulatory process of oil-exploration activities. They illustrate how the Greenlandic authorities in some cases have to deal with considerable uncertainty due to a lack of basic knowledge. It is their conclusion that the authorities manage to do so in an adaptive manner.

In this volume, all the authors point to complex situations in the governance of offshore oil and gas operations in the Arctic Ocean. The complexities arise from a great diversity in the region at the political, legal, geographical and cultural levels, as well as from the lack of capacity-building and knowledge. Drawing on the findings of the contributions, the conclusion highlights limits in the multilevel governance system, which remains very much state centred and is characterised by an insufficient commitment to the development of legally binding international standards on the protection of the Arctic marine area and public participation. Finally, the conclusion proposes paths of reflection to enhance the efficiency of environmental management and public participation, including the participation of indigenous peoples.

Notes

1 Overland 2016.
2 For a review of oil and gas activities in the Canadian North, see Nuttall 2010, 31–45.
3 Bird et al. 2008.
4 International Energy Agency 2012.
5 Barber et al. 2014a; Barber et al. 2014b.
6 CAFF 2013.
7 Duhaime and Caron 2006.
8 Rodon and Lévesque 2015.
9 The relevant Arctic marine areas covered by this volume are: the marine areas of Canada above 60° N; the marine Danish areas above the southern limit of the Greenland exclusive economic zone (EEZ); the Norwegian marine areas above the Arctic Circle; the United States' marine area along the mainland of Alaska to the Aleutian Islands above 24 nautical miles south of these islands, and in the Bering Sea; and the marine Russian areas above the coastlines of the White Sea, the Barents Sea, the Kara Sea, the Laptev Sea, the East Siberian Sea and the Chukchi Sea, and the mouths of the rivers flowing into these seas seaward.
10 Berman 2007, Zumbansen 2010, and Callies and Renner 2009.
11 Johnstone 2015.
12 See the definition of fragmentation of law in the section on international and supranational levels of this introduction. Koivurova and Hossain 2008. For an analysis of international cooperation, see also Humrich 2013.

13 For an analysis of oil and gas in the Arctic areas of North America, see Nuttall 2010. See also Mikkelsen and Langhelle 2008.
14 Commission on Global Governance 1995, 4.
15 Overland 2016.
16 Habermas 1981.
17 Pelaudeix 2014.
18 See the chapters by Basse in Part I, Pelaudeix in Part II, and Mortensen in Part IV.
19 Inatsisartut Act of 7 December 2009 on Mineral Resource and Mineral Resources Activities, with amendments.
20 The Government of Greenland is known as Naalakkersuisut.

References

Barber, D.G. et al. 2014a. 'Research Gaps in Scientific Understanding of Oil in Sea Ice.' Paper submitted to the Tanker Safety Expert Panel. Phase II: Ottawa: Transport Canada, Government of Canada.

Barber, D.G. et al. 2014b. 'Climate-Change and Ice Hazards in the Beaufort Sea.' *Elementa: Science of the Anthropocene* 2 (1). doi:10.12952/journal.elementa.000025 elementascience.org.

Berman, P.S. 2007. 'Global Legal Pluralism.' *Southern California Law Review* 80: 1157–1237. Available at: http://scholarship.law.gwu.edu/cgi/viewcontent.cgi?article=1097&context=faculty_publications.

Bird, K.J. et al. 2008. *Circum-Arctic Resource Appraisal: Estimates of Undiscovered Oil and Gas North of the Arctic Circle.* Fact Sheet 2008–3049. Reston, Virginia: US Geological Survey. Available at: www.usgs.gov.

CAFF (Conservation of Arctic Flora and Fauna). 2013. *Arctic Biodiversity Assessment: Status and Trends in Arctic Biodiversity.* Akureyri: Conservation of Arctic Flora and Fauna.

Callies, G.P. and M. Renner. 2009. 'Between Law and Social Norms: The Evolution of Global Governance.' *Ratio Juris* 22 (2): 260–280.

Commission on Global Governance. 1995. *Our Global Neighborhood.* Oxford: Oxford University Press for Commission on Global Governance.

Duhaime, G. and A. Caron. 2006. 'Economic and Social Conditions of Arctic Regions.' In *The Economy of the North*, edited by S. Glomsrød and I. Aslaksen, 11–23. Oslo: Statistics Norway.

Habermas, J. 1981. *Theorie des Kommunikativen Handelns. Bind I: Handlungsrationalität und Gesellschafdicke Rationalisierung.* Berlin: Suhrkamp.

Humrich, C. 2013. 'Fragmented International Governance of Arctic Offshore Oil: Governance Challenges and Institutional Improvement.' *Global Environmental Politics* 13 (3): 79–99.

International Energy Agency. 2012. *World Energy Outlook 2012.* Paris: International Energy Agency.

Johnstone, R. 2015. *Offshore Oil and Gas Development in the Arctic under International Law.* Leiden: Brill.

Koivurova, T. and K. Hossain. 2008. *Offshore Hydrocarbon: Current Policy Context in the Marine Arctic.* Background Paper. Rovaniemi: Arctic Centre/Arctic Transform. Available at: www.ecologic.eu/sites/files/publication/2015/offshore_hydrocarbon_background_paper.pdf.

Mikkelsen, A. and O. Langhelle. 2008. *Arctic Oil and Gas: Sustainability at Risk?* London: Routledge.

Nuttall, M. 2010. *Pipeline and the Arctic Energy Frontier*. Doc. No. 126. Copenhagen: International Work Group for Indigenous Affairs. Available at: www.iwgia.org/publications/search-pubs?publication_id=451.

Overland, I. 2016. 'Energy: The missing link in globalization.' *Energy Research & Social Science* 14: 122–130.

Pelaudeix, C. 2014. 'What is "Arctic governance"? A critical assessment of the diverse meanings of "Arctic governance".' *The Yearbook of Polar Law* 6: 398–426.

Rodon, T. and F. Lévesque. 2015. 'Understanding the Social and Economic Impacts of Mining Development in Inuit Communities: Experiences with Past and Present Mines in Inuit Nunangat.' *The Northern Review* 41: 13–39.

Zumbansen, P. 2010. 'Transnational Legal Pluralism.' *Transnational Legal Theory* 1: 141–189.

Part I

Globalization and supra-nationalism in the Arctic

2 Framing the problem in Arctic offshore hydrocarbon exploitation

Timo Koivurova

Introduction

There has been a lot of discussion related to Arctic hydrocarbons. The reasons for this are obvious. Climate change in the region is proceeding at twice the rate seen in the rest of the world. Melting sea ice and other changes present us with challenges as well as opportunities, one of the most recent of which is extending offshore oil and gas activities further out to sea.

The Arctic is very frequently regarded as the next province for oil and gas. According to the US Geological Survey, the Arctic Ocean contains approximately 13 per cent of the world's undiscovered oil reserves and 30 per cent of its undiscovered natural gas resources.[1] These reserves also have a geopolitical significance. Even if currently the boom in interest in oil and gas exploitation has subsided, it will likely rise again in the near future. The world is still fossil-fuel dependent, especially for transport, and the world's population is on a steep increase, especially in Asia.

In this chapter, I will present four framings of what can be seen as problematic in offshore oil and gas exploitation in the Arctic. It is these framings of the problem as regards Arctic offshore hydrocarbons that define what is seen as problematic. By the same token, it is these framings that define what type of legislative frameworks can be said to be applicable in addressing the problems perceived. Yet, elements of each of these framings contain arguments that reveal what is genuinely problematic in the current political and legal reality of the Arctic, and it is on those real problems that we should focus our efforts. The conclusion of the chapter will provide some ideas as to the type of issues on which law and policy related to Arctic offshore hydrocarbons should focus at this present moment.

The four framings: what is problematic in Arctic offshore hydrocarbon exploitation

'Framing' is understood in this chapter to mean an intentional choice that is intended to present reality in a particular manner. Framing is built on constructivism: the innate complexity of phenomena around us is such that as social beings we simplify the reality around us in order to grasp it. We rely on frames in our social world, as well, without intending to influence them. Yet wherever there is activity that involves perceived human losses and benefits – and offshore hydrocarbon exploitation is such an activity – many actors are bound to behave strategically in order to build different frames that will serve their interests or validate their values.[2] As argued by Annika Nilsson in her study of the framings of knowledge and policy-making in the field of climate policy, in particular that of the Arctic Climate Impact Assessment:

> Frames depict the basic cognitive structures that guide how the world around us becomes visible to us [footnote omitted]. In scientific assessments, framing influences what features of an issue are included or excluded within a specific context. Framing is important because it molds the rhetoric of policy debates.[3]

What follows is an exploration of these four framings and the narratives they produce of what is perceived as problematic in the extraction of Arctic offshore oil and gas. Each particular problem-framing steers us to seek specific types of policy and legal solutions, and these will also be examined. Policy/legal solutions are not sought for the first framing, however, simply because this is considered to be a clear misunderstanding of the situation.

Scramble for resources between states

The idea of a scramble for resources taking place originated from two events that occurred almost simultaneously. First, in August 2007, the Russians planted their flag on the seabed below the North Pole; almost immediately came the news in September 2007 that Arctic Ocean sea ice was reducing with dramatic speed. The media and some international relations scholars came to the conclusion that since the Arctic Ocean contains vast amounts of hydrocarbons that are now being revealed by climate change, the coastal states of the Arctic Ocean are now trying to occupy as much as possible of the sea floor for their companies.[4]

Much publicity was collected around an article ('Arctic Meltdown: The Economic and Security Implications of Global Warming') published in 2008 in *Foreign Affairs* by Scott G. Borgerson, international affairs fellow at the Council on Foreign Relations and a former lieutenant commander in the US Coastguard. He argued that climate change is opening the Arctic to a resource game, in an area where rules and institutions are scarce:

> ... the Arctic countries are likely to unilaterally grab as much territory as possible and exert sovereign control over opening sea-lanes wherever they can. In this legal no man's land, Arctic states are pursuing their narrowly defined national interests by laying down sonar nets and

> arming icebreakers to guard their claims. Russia has led the charge with its flag-planting antics this past summer…[5]

His ideal solution to this unfortunate state of affairs is this:

> The ideal way to manage the Arctic would be to develop an overarching treaty that guarantees an orderly and collective approach to extracting the region's wealth. As part of the ongoing International Polar Year (a large scientific program focused on the Arctic and the Antarctic that is set to run until March 2009), the United States should convene a conference to draft a new accord based on the framework of the Arctic Council. The agreement should incorporate relevant provisions of UNCLOS and take into account all of the key emerging Arctic issues. With a strong push from Washington, the Arctic states could settle their differences around a negotiating table, agree on how to carve up the region's vast resource pie, and possibly even submit a joint proposal to the UN for its blessing.[6]

At approximately the same time, the EU High Representative and Commission issued a joint paper on climate change and international security, in which the Arctic was identified geo-economically as a new frontier.[7] Other than this, there have been no further serious proposals to advance Borgerson's ideas, as he himself nowadays concedes. In a later article published in 2013, Borgerson reversed his claim, and now admits that:

> Just a half decade ago, the scramble for the Arctic looked as if it would play out quite differently. In 2007, Russia planted its flag on the North Pole's sea floor, and in the years that followed, other states also jockeyed for position, ramping up their naval patrols and staking out ambitious sovereignty claims. Many observers – including me – predicted that without some sort of comprehensive set of regulations, the race for resources would inevitably end in conflict. 'The Arctic powers are fast approaching diplomatic gridlock,' I wrote in these pages in 2008, 'and that could eventually lead to… armed brinkmanship.' But a funny thing happened on the way to Arctic anarchy. Rather than harden positions, the possibility of increased tensions has spurred the countries concerned to work out their differences peacefully. A shared interest in profit has trumped the instinct to compete over territory. Proving the pessimists wrong, the Arctic countries have given up on saber rattling and engaged in various impressive feats of cooperation… None of this cooperation required a single new overarching legal framework. Instead, states have created a patchwork of bilateral and multilateral agreements, emanating from the Arctic Council and anchored firmly in UNCLOS. By reaching an enduring modus vivendi, the Arctic powers have set the stage for a long-lasting regional boom.[8]

What many analysts thought was a scramble for resources was, in fact, the states mapping and collecting scientific information for the purposes of making submissions to the Commission on the Limits of Continental Shelf on the basis of the UN Law of the Sea Convention.[9]

Arctic fossil fuels driving national politics and political economy

But even if there is no competition between states over the Arctic offshore hydrocarbons, the potential deposits are within the national jurisdiction of the Arctic Ocean coastal states, so there may still be problems within the nation-states. After all, as some scholars have pointed out, rather than a blessing, abundance in natural resources sometimes appears to be something of a curse.[10] According to the resource-curse hypothesis, several factors may lead a country with plentiful natural resources to a condition in which it actually suffers from those resources, e.g. volatility in global market prices, or simply that all domestic actors want to receive their share from those resources. There was indeed a noticeable increase in offshore oil and gas exploration in the Arctic from 2007 onwards,[11] with oil companies entering the new Arctic hydrocarbon province. Even with the current downturn, it seems likely that this increase in activities will gradually resume if the world continues to rely on fossil fuels.

If the problem is increasing competition between oil companies, especially in the near-shore areas of the Arctic where some other sectors of industry are also active, such as fishing and transportation of goods, the governance solution could be to accommodate the various uses of these marine areas via various management tools such as a strategic environmental assessment or, perhaps more viably, maritime spatial planning. Yet if we take a larger view of what the opening of a new hydrocarbon province in the near-offshore areas of a particular coastal state might mean, it is apparent that it might involve not only accommodating various uses of the sea but also much more difficult issues such as wealth distribution or, in some areas of the Arctic, the impact of these activities on indigenous peoples and their evolving rights.

The largest view of a resource-curse stemming from Arctic offshore hydrocarbon development affecting any particular self-governing entity (such as Greenland) is that it could set that nation on a long-term development path whereby it would become heavily dependent on one particular non-renewable. This would mean not only that the national economy would be focusing too heavily on extracting natural resources – which obviously presents future dangers, since the economy would thus be relying too much on, e.g., offshore hydrocarbons and not sufficiently diversifying its base – but also ultimately that people's values might be affected by one dominating industry that could influence the electorate's values and ultimately even law-making as well. Rather than calling for immediate governance solutions, this largest view of the resource-curse challenges us to be critical about the kind of governance processes we have for making decisions about our natural resources in general and offshore oil and gas in particular.

Arctic fossil fuels as a final push towards global climate catastrophe

Greenpeace among NGOs has been particularly active with its Save the Arctic campaign[12] to try to stop the opening of the last oil province. This was shown most dramatically by Greenpeace activists scaling the Prirazlomnaya platform located in the Pechora Sea.[13] As Greenpeace argues, 'Arctic oil drilling is a really bad idea' because:

> Our climate can't afford it. As the impacts of climate change become more visible and the danger becomes greater, drilling for and burning more fossil fuels is pretty much the last thing we should be doing, especially in somewhere as fragile and untouched as the Arctic.[14]

Greenpeace is referring here to the so-called Arctic climate paradox. Even if we should be discontinuing the use of oil in particular in order to avoid exceeding the two degrees warming threshold, we are opening a new oil province in the area that is most heavily impacted by climate change.

Implicit in this message is that we should leave the Arctic offshore oil resources where they are. This is because the world community has already legally committed itself to prevent dangerous interference in the climate system in the UN Framework Convention on Climate Change (UNFCCC). 'Dangerous interference' is defined in the climate regime to be two degrees warming from the preindustrial era.

Why then is the Arctic so important in the climate-change combat? Recent research results published in *Nature* confirm that many fossil-fuel sources in the world should be left unexploited, especially in the Arctic, if we want not to exceed this tipping-point.[15] The Arctic is seen by many as of vast importance because it is a new frontier whose development, once opened, would likely become path-dependent even if its oil resources were at some point in the future no longer economically viable.[16]

This perception also received some policy attention. In the legislative consultation process that was issued in the EU parliament's Offshore Safety Directive, the parliament's Committee on the Environment, Public Health and Food Safety issued an opinion on 21 June 2011 that the Directive should 'Call for a moratorium on any offshore hydrocarbon exploration and extraction operations in the Arctic due to the vulnerability of its unique environment.'[17] This call for a moratorium was not endorsed when the Directive was adopted.[18] Member states that were also members of the Arctic Council were urged to give special attention to the Arctic offshore oil and gas standards,[19] and the Commission was also obliged to 'promote high safety standards for offshore oil and gas operations at international level in relevant global and regional forums, including those relating to Arctic waters.'[20]

There are some authors who claim that international law in its totality – international environmental law, human rights law, and so on – already now prohibits touching the Arctic offshore hydrocarbons.[21] This is a difficult argument to make in view of the failure of even the special and highly sophisticated climate-change regime to give a price signal that will significantly reduce fossil-fuel use because the parties to the regime have not been willing to commit themselves to stronger legal reductions in greenhouse-gas emissions. From the political perspective, however, the Greenpeace campaign has used the Arctic offshore fossil fuels very effectively. By demonstrating that states are not curtailed by the climate-change regime from embarking on offshore oil drilling even in an area where climate change occurs twice as fast as anywhere else on the planet, Greenpeace has shown how weak the climate regime currently is. Yet, with the adoption of the Paris agreement, we still have hopes of curtailing the advancement of climate change.

Offshore oil spill may cause a major Arctic environmental catastrophe

Greenpeace's campaign, like that of the World Wide Fund for Nature,[22] also targets an additional problem related to offshore oil drilling, namely that it may cause large-scale devastation to the region's vulnerable ecosystems. For Greenpeace, from this perspective, oil drilling is a bad idea for several reasons. Relief wells are harder to drill in the Arctic because winter ice cuts the drilling season short; oil recovery is near impossible in ice; there is not nearly enough oil-spill response capacity, especially because the Arctic is so remote; and here, nature is even less capable of absorbing oil than in lower latitudes, since winter and cold weather mean that oil takes more time to break down and/or will stay locked under the sea ice. Ultimately, in this framing of the likely impact of offshore oil drilling, the only governance solution is to prohibit it altogether.

It seems clear that Greenpeace's framing simplifies things, as, indeed, all frames do. Oil drilling in general has been going on in the Arctic for quite some time (Greenpeace's campaign is targeted mostly at offshore oil exploitation but also at all other oil drilling in the region). In some regions, offshore oil and gas operations have commenced and are very likely to continue, e.g. in the Barents Sea, because operational conditions here are fully different than in the ice-infested regions on the other side of the Arctic.

Offshore oil and gas exploitation, including in the Arctic and its waters, is fully regulated – mostly by national legal systems, but also by a fair amount of applicable international law[23] together with the efforts of the predominantly intergovernmental Arctic forum – the Arctic Council – to prevent oil spills from happening. The Council's Arctic Offshore Oil and Gas Guidelines,[24] a soft-law instrument, can still be considered a living instrument, as the Guidelines have already been revised twice.

The Guidelines recognise a uniform understanding of the minimum actions needed to protect the Arctic marine environment from unwanted environmental effects caused by offshore oil and gas activities. They also present a set of recommended practices for the regulation of offshore oil and gas exploration and extraction, including the transportation and onshore activities that are an integrated part of offshore operations in the Arctic. They emphasise the requirement of having an environmental impact assessment procedure, as well as plans for emergencies and responses. Since each oil spill is unique as to the local environmental conditions and the specific types of oil spilled,[25] the Guidelines provide prior risk assessments to identify accidental events that may occur. Overall, the Offshore Oil and Gas Guidelines is a comprehensive document that specifically addresses the concerns of the offshore Arctic. Even if it is not a legally binding instrument, the Guidelines encourages Arctic Council members to incorporate the recommendation into their national legislations.

In the most recent ministerial meeting of the Arctic Council, the Arctic states adopted the Agreement on Cooperation on Marine Oil Pollution, Preparedness and Response in the Arctic, a legally binding agreement that was negotiated under the auspices of the Arctic Council and targeted to respond to oil-spill emergencies, allocating responsibility areas and coming up with joint measures to tackle such emergencies in the region.[26] The Agreement applies not only in Arctic Ocean waters but also in the Baltic Sea (the northern part of the Gulf of Bothnia); there are, in addition, non-legally binding appendices. All Arctic countries are supposed to create a national system for responding promptly to oil emergencies, to provide notification to other states, and if need be, to provide assistance to counter the oil-pollution incident. The Agreement is firmly anchored in broader agreements that are applicable to the Arctic states, such as the 1990 International Convention on Oil Pollution Preparedness, Response and Cooperation.[27] Currently, the Arctic Council is working with an instrument that has as its aim the prevention of offshore oil and gas spills.[28] This work has led to the creation of a new co-operative forum between the eight Arctic states, namely the Arctic Offshore Regulators Forum (AORF). This is a forum including the safety agencies of the eight Arctic states, and having as its purpose e.g. to converse and evaluate safety-related threats and opportunities and encourage a high level of safety in petroleum activities in the Arctic. Corporate social responsibility standards have also been promoted under the Council's auspices.[29] Even if some of the arguments posed by Greenpeace are exaggerated, and even if there is plenty of law available, there is no doubt that there will be risks associated with drilling oil in some parts of the Arctic marine areas.[30]

Conclusion

Like all framings, the four framings studied in this chapter as to what is problematic in Arctic offshore oil and gas exploitation have shown how differently we can perceive the offshore oil and gas resources that lie in the Arctic shelf. They can be seen as triggering geopolitical games between the Arctic coastal states, or resource-curse dynamics within individual Arctic states. The offshore hydrocarbons of the region are seen by many as too dangerous to be touched, simply because otherwise we are dangerously interfering in our climate system and breaching the main goal of the global climate regime. Finally, offshore oil drilling in the Arctic is seen as entailing vast risks that, in the event of leaks on a large scale, would pose a tremendous threat to the environment of the whole Arctic Ocean.

The way in which the problem is framed very much dictates what type of governance tools are seen as most suitable for dealing with the problem. For instance, depending on the scale of the resource-curse cycle studied, the solution could, e.g., be introducing a maritime spatial planning system, or a deeper benefit-sharing arrangement (maritime spatial planning is part of EU law and therefore also an issue that could be relevant to the EU Arctic member states). It seems also likely that the more the global climate change regime is able to decrease the use of fossil fuels, the less the Arctic offshore exploitation will be seen as politically possible and desirable, and also economically viable. The recent Paris Agreement shows that there is currently a lot of political potential in taking worldwide measures in reducing greenhouse gas emissions.

In defining what is problematic in Arctic hydrocarbon exploitation, we are bound to rely first and foremost on our nation-states and on the current regulatory systems in place. Even international processes such as the Arctic Council guidelines or Arctic Offshore Regulators Forum primarily are to enhance national decision making rather than create international regulatory framework. The framing of Arctic offshore hydrocarbon extraction primarily as a spill risk issue supports state-centred approach to regulating offshore activities. Hence, it is primarily the Arctic states that have defined in an authoritative manner what is problematic in offshore hydrocarbon development in the Arctic. From their perspective, what is problematic in Arctic offshore oil and gas exploitation is not the geopolitical, resource-curse or climate impacts of these resources, but the very mundane human safety and environmental security risks posed by particular offshore oil or gas activities in very specific areas of the Arctic. All the Arctic maritime states have opened their maritime areas for oil and gas drilling (including the self-rule government of Greenland), even if these activities have in most regions not progressed beyond exploration.

This state-centred approach may be challenged in the future as other frames come to the fore. Many actors – for instance, NGOs like Greenpeace – already aim at internationalizing the question of offshore extraction. Moreover, the other framings taken up in this article influence on the way nation-states need to make decisions on what is problematic or not in Arctic offshore hydrocarbon exploitation. The future of Arctic offshore hydrocarbon regulation is directly connected to the workings of the global climate regime and if this regime induces stronger commitment from nation-states all over the world, it is clear that this process will have an impact on how nation-state decision-makers evaluate the prospects and benefits of Arctic offshore oil and gas. Even if they do engage in Arctic offshore oil exploitation, there is an increasing amount of work done in the Arctic Council and elsewhere in making sure that risky oil exploitation is done in an extremely cautious manner.

It is our nation states (apart from Greenland, which is a self-governing entity but still part of the Kingdom of Denmark) that have defined whether the level of risk posed by these activities is acceptable. Since there are no real alternative actors to make this judgment, we have to accept that this is the real-world problem diagnosis and that these are the measures in place. The assessment of whether risks and judgments are acceptable and minimised requires close and ongoing scrutiny of state actions by both academics and civil-society actors.

Notes

1 Bird et al. 2008, 4.
2 See two classic works on framing, which take up the intentional aspects of framing: Lakoff 2002, Fraser 2010.
3 Nilsson 2007, 6.
4 See Koivurova 2013, 21.
5 Borgerson 2008, 15.
6 Ibid.
7 'Climate Change and International Security', 2008.
8 Borgerson 2013. The present author is not convinced that there was real danger of international tensions at the time, an implicit message in Borgerson's article.
9 Koivurova 2011, 16.
10 Humphreys, Sachs and Stiglitz 2007. See also a critical view: Brunnschweiler and Bulteb 2008, 14.
11 Łuszczuk 2014.
12 Greenpeace 2015.
13 Pettersen 2012.
14 Greenpeace 2015.
15 McGlade and Ekins 2015, 3.
16 Sidortsov 2012, 3–12.
17 European Parliament 2011, at Para 35.
18 European Parliament and Council 2013.
19 Ibid, Para. 52.
20 Ibid, Article 33.3.
21 Sjafjell and Halvorssen 2014.
22 World Wide Fund for Nature 2015.
23 Koivurova and Hossain 2012.
24 Arctic Council 2009.
25 Arctic Council 1998.
26 Arctic Council 2013a.
27 International Maritime Organisation 1990.
28 See the work of the Task Force on Arctic Marine Oil Pollution Prevention, 2015.
29 Corporate social responsibility is a very important segment of any natural resource exploitation in the Arctic region, which for the most part is a remote area in which it is difficult for the government to oversee and enforce statutes and

other regulations. During the period of Swedish chairmanship, 2011–2013, the CSR standards were explored in the Arctic Council's Sustainable Development Working Group. Four workshops were convened, and the current multiple CSR standards were studied and shown to apply also in the Arctic: see Sustainable Development Working Group 2015, and especially UN Global Compact 2015. See also Extractive Industries Transparency Initiative 2015 (which applies to any company involved in the extraction of raw materials from the earth), and OECD 2015. In the Kiruna ministerial declaration, the CSR was endorsed not as a separate instrument, but as an encouragement for companies operating in the Arctic to respect the existing multiple CSR standards, also in natural resources exploitation. The Kiruna declaration states that the ministers representing the eight Arctic states, joined by the representatives of the six permanent participant organisations of the Arctic Council, 'welcome the Arctic Council's work on corporate social responsibility and sustainable business, and encourage enterprises operating in the Arctic to respect international guidelines and principles' (Arctic Council 2013b). The Council also established a task-force which created an independent Arctic Economic Council, which is supposed to advance these principles in the Arctic: Arctic Economic Council 2015.

30 Hossain and Koivurova 2012.

References

Arctic Council. 1998. 'Field Guide for the Oil Spill Response in Arctic.' Accessed 20 May 2015. www.arctic-council.org/eppr/completed-work/oil-and-gas-products/field-guide-for-oil-spill-response/.

Arctic Council. 2009. Protection of the Arctic Marine Environment Working Group. 'Arctic Offshore Oil and Gas Guidelines.' Accessed 20 May 2015. www.govmin.gl/images/stories/petroleum/Arctic_Offshore_Oil_and_Gas_Guidelines_2009.pdf.

Arctic Council. 2013a. 'Agreement on Cooperation on Marine Oil Pollution, Preparedness and Response in the Arctic.' Kiruna, 15 May 2013. Accessed 24 February 2017. http://arctic-council.org/eppr/agreement-on-cooperation-on-marine-oil-pollution-preparedness-and-response-in-the-arctic/.

Arctic Council. 2013b. 'Kiruna Declaration, 15 May 2013.' Accessed 21 May 2015. http://eu-arctic-forum.org/wp-content/uploads/2013/06/Final_Kiruna_declaration_w_signature.pdf.

Arctic Economic Council. 2015. Accessed 21 May 2015. http://arcticeconomiccouncil.com/.

Bird, K.J. et al. 2008. 'Circum-Arctic Resource Appraisal: Estimates of Undiscovered Oil and Gas North of the Arctic Circle.' *United States Geological Survey Fact Sheet 2008–3049*. Accessed 21 May 2015. http://pubs.usgs.gov/fs/2008/3049/fs2008-3049.pdf.

Borgerson, S.G. 2008. 'Arctic Meltdown: The Economic and Security Implications of Global Warming.' *Foreign Affairs* 87, 2: 63–77.

Borgerson, S.G. 2013. 'The Coming Arctic Boom: As the Ice Melts, the Region Heats Up.' *Foreign Affairs* 92, 4: 76–89.

Brunnschweiler, C.N. and E.H. Bulteb. 2008. 'The Resource-Curse Revisited and Revised: A Tale of Paradoxes and Red Herrings.' *Journal of Environmental Economics and Management* 55, 3: 248–264.

'Climate Change and International Security.' 2008. Paper from the High Representative and the European Commission to the European Council. Accessed 24

February 2017. www.consilium.europa.eu/uedocs/cms_data/docs/pressdata/en/reports/99387.pdf.

European Parliament. 2011. Committee on the Environment, Public Health and Food Safety. 2011.

European Parliament and Council. 2013. 'Directive on Safety of Offshore Oil and Gas Operations and Amending Directive 2004/35/EC Text with EEA Relevance.' 12 June. 2013/30/EU. Accessed 24 February 2017. http://eur-lex.europa.eu/legal-content/EN/ALL/?uri=CELEX:32013L0030.

Extractive Industries Transparency Initiative. 2015. Website. Accessed 21 May 2015. https://eiti.org/.

Fraser, N. 2010. *Scales of Justice: Reimagining Political Space in a Globalizing World.* New York: Columbia University Press.

Greenpeace. 2015. 'Saving the Arctic: The Expedition.' Accessed 20 May 2015. www.greenpeace.org/usa/arctic/.

Hossain, K. and T. Koivurova. 2012. 'Hydrocarbon Development in the Offshore Arctic: Can it be Done Sustainably?' *Oil, Gas and Energy Law Intelligence* 10, 2: 1–29.

Humphreys, M., J.D. Sachs and J.E. Stiglitz, eds. 2007. *Escaping the Resource-Curse.* New York: Columbia University Press.

International Maritime Organisation. 1990 'International Convention on Oil Pollution, Preparedness, Response and Cooperation, London: 30 October 1990.' 30 ILM 733.

Koivurova, T. 2011. 'The Actions of the Arctic States Respecting the Continental Shelf: A Reflective Essay.' *Ocean Development & International Law* 42, 3: 211–226. doi:10.1080/00908320.2011.592470.

Koivurova, T. 2013. 'The Dialectic of Understanding Progress in Arctic Governance.' *Michigan State International Law Review* 22: 1–21.

Koivurova, T. and K. Hossain. 2012. 'Hydrocarbon Development in the Offshore Arctic: Can it be Done Sustainably?' *Oil, Gas and Energy Law Intelligence* 10, 2: 1–29.

Lakoff, G. 2002. *Moral Politics: How Liberals and Conservatives Think.* Chicago: University of Chicago Press.

Łuszczuk, M. 2014. 'Developing Oil and Gas Resources in Arctic Waters.' In *The Strategic Assessment of Development of the Arctic: An Assessment Conducted for the European Union,* edited by A. Stępien, T. Koivurova and P. Kankaanpaa, 71–85. Rovaniemi: University of Lapland. Accessible at www.arcticinfo.eu/images/pdf/SADA_report.pdf.

McGlade, C. and P. Ekins, 2015. 'The Geographical Distribution of Fossil Fuels Unused When Limiting Global Warming to 2 degrees.' *Nature* 517: 187–190. doi:10.1038/Nature14016.

Nilsson, A.E. 2007. 'A Changing Arctic Climate: Science and Policy in the Arctic Climate Impact Assessment.' PhD dissertation, University of Linköping.

OECD. 2015. 'Guidelines for Multinational Enterprises.' Accessed 21 May 2015. www.oecd.org/corporate/mne/.

Pettersen, T. 2012. 'Greenpeace Occupying Prirazlomnaya.' *Barents Observer.* Accessed 20 May 2015. http://barentsobserver.com/en/arctic/greenpeace-occupying-prirazlomnaya-platform-24-08.

Sidortsov, R. 2012. 'Creating Arctic Carbon Lock-In: Case Study of New Oil Development in the South Kara Sea.' *Carbon and Climate Law Review* 1: 3–12.

Sjafjell, B. and A. Halvorssen. 2014. 'The Legal Status of Oil and Gas Exploitation in the Arctic: The Case of Norway.' Draft paper based on presentation in the Energy Law Conference: the Legal Issues Associated with the Development and Use of Arctic Energy Resources, Tromsø, 25–26 September 2014.

Sustainable Development Working Group. 2015. 'The Arctic Council's Work on Corporate Social Responsibility.' Accessed 21 May 2015. www.sdwg.org/the-arctic-councils-work-on-corporate-social-responsibility/.

Task Force on Arctic Marine Oil Pollution Prevention. 2015.

UN Global Compact. 2015. 'Transforming Business, Changing the World.' Accessed 21 May 2015. www.unglobalcompact.org/.

World Wide Fund for Nature. 2015. 'Arctic Oil and Gas.' Accessed 21 May 2015. http://wwf.panda.org/what_we_do/where_we_work/arctic/what_we_do/oil_gas/.

3 Sustainable development in Arctic international environmental cooperation and the governance of hydrocarbon-related activities

Christoph Humrich

Introduction

In the previous chapter of this volume, Timo Koivurova lists and discusses various different framings 'of what can be seen as problematic in offshore oil and gas exploitation in the Arctic'.[1] The framing provided by the concept of sustainable development, however, is missing from Koivurova's list. At first sight, this seems odd. The concept has undoubtedly served as a frame for policy-making in the field of international environmental cooperation in the Arctic since that cooperation began with the adoption of the Arctic Environmental Protection Strategy (AEPS) in 1991. In the AEPS the eight Arctic states recognised that resource-use plays an important role in the Arctic and stated that their strategy 'should allow for sustainable economic development in the North so that such development does not have unacceptable ecological or cultural impacts.'[2] The Arctic states saw both the strategy itself and cooperation under the AEPS as 'designed to guide development in a way that will safeguard the Arctic environment for future generations and in a manner that is compatible with nature.'[3] These formulations provide a frame for pondering at least three potentially problematic aspects of Arctic offshore oil and gas production: their immediate ecological as well as cultural impacts, and the long-term consequences for future generations. In the 25 years since the signing of the AEPS, the concept of sustainable development has become ever more deeply engrained in the international environmental cooperation between the eight Arctic states. Moreover, that cooperation has resulted in quite a number of recommendations and guidelines that refer implicitly or, indeed, explicitly to what can be seen as problematic in Arctic offshore oil and gas activities in respect to ecological and cultural impacts. Why, then, is sustainable development absent from Koivurova's list?

Taking a second look at sustainable development as a framing, an interesting internal tension in the concept comes into view. In a seminal volume edited by Aslaug Mikkelsen and Oluf Langhelle,[4] the question of what implications can be 'drawn from sustainable development for oil and gas in the Arctic' is explored.[5] One of the volume's chapters provides a thorough conceptual analysis of sustainable development as a framing for Arctic oil and gas.[6] With reference to the World Commission on Environment and Development (WCED) report, which brought the concept of sustainable development to international environmental politics, the authors point out that sustainable development means 'to meet the needs of the present without compromising the ability of future generations to meet their needs.'[7] What matters is thus not the preservation of a specific status quo, but the safeguarding of a certain level of needs-satisfaction for present and future generations. In this sense, oil and gas 'can be exploited in a meaningful sense' within a sustainable development framing.[8] Oil and gas activities are not problematic per se – and Koivurova would, accordingly, be right to exclude the sustainable development framing from his list.

Yet, the conceptual analysis of sustainable development might also yield the opposite conclusion. There is a 'sustainable development minimum,' namely, that economic development 'must not endanger the natural systems that support life on Earth.'[9] It is this minimum that points to what is, in fact, deeply problematic about increasing Arctic oil and gas production from a sustainable development perspective: that Arctic oil and gas extraction blatantly conflicts with the large-scale decrease in global carbon dioxide emissions necessary to prevent climate change. Once conceptualised as a global perspective, therefore, the sustainable development frame 'may become more and more constraining on further oil and gas activities in the Arctic.'[10]

However, what ultimately matters is less the conceptual implications of sustainable development as a frame than its leverage in a concrete political setting. In what follows, I will argue that sustainable development as a frame of Arctic international environmental cooperation will most likely not result in constraining effects of any significance on future increases in oil and gas extraction. The functional and discursive context in which the concept of sustainable development is embedded in Arctic international environmental cooperation in fact rather served to open up the Arctic for increased oil and gas activities, and it now shields these activities from being identified as an avoidable cause of global warming. The next section looks at sustainable development as a policy concept. It points out the functions it served for Arctic international environmental cooperation. The subsequent section then takes a closer look at the discursive context both of the concept and of the changes it underwent. These changes suggest that in the existing Arctic international environmental cooperation, the concept of sustainable development can no longer serve as a suitable policy-guiding frame for identifying what is problematic about Arctic oil and gas activities. Its normative substance, however, must be retained. This defines the challenge for the new vision of regional development in the Arctic that is so urgently needed.

The function of sustainable development in Arctic international environmental cooperation

By now, the story of Arctic international environmental cooperation has been told many times, and it is not the purpose of this section to tell it once more. Rather, the aim here is to point out the functional role sustainable development played in the emergence of that cooperation, and how it created a cooperation context, which does not prevent the opening up of the Arctic for increased oil and gas extraction but rather serves it.[11]

Research on international cooperation identifies three particular roles for concepts such as sustainable development. First, they can enable international cooperation in the first place, because they might provide a rationale for bringing together diverging interests or creating space within which positions can meet;[12] in other words, they can suggest and make possible issue linkages that enlarge the zone of agreement. Once institutionalised and thus transformed into principles and norms of a cooperative arrangement, such concepts can, second, help to sustain and develop cooperation by defining the legitimate range of bargains and norm interpretation within that arrangement.[13] Third and finally, concepts can not only serve to enable, sustain and develop a cooperative arrangement between states, but they can also direct the policies within the arrangement in tackling the problem for which it was necessary to set up the arrangement in the first place. The concept's function then changes from being generative to becoming operative or implementing.[14]

On the level of global environmental politics, sustainable development performed all three functions.[15] The WCED explicitly framed sustainable development as a concept that could create a zone of agreement between North and South that had not been there at the first big United Nations conference on environmental politics in Stockholm in 1972. On that occasion, developing countries still suspected that the North's interest in environmental protection was yet another ploy to keep the South from becoming a competitor in the global economy. The WCED's elaboration of the concept, however, emphasised the intimate connection between environment and development. At the United Nations Conference on Environment and Development in Rio 1992 (UNCED), broad global agreement around a set of principles and norms for sustainable development became possible. With these principles and norms, UNCED not only provided a frame within which many future bargains for international environmental cooperation were struck, but with Agenda 21, the conference outcome also arguably took a great step towards making the concept operational.

The inclusion of the sustainable development concept in Arctic international environmental cooperation followed in the wake of the WCED and later of UNCED.[16] The overall political context, however, was somewhat different, and for this reason, the concept functioned in slightly different ways. I argue that the concept first enabled cooperation on environmental protection in the Arctic in a rather paradoxical way. It transformed the narrow focus of the AEPS on environmental protection into a possible zone of agreement. However, once introduced, the concept of sustainable development provided a frame within which states could pursue their agenda for developing international environmental cooperation in the Arctic further. More concretely, the concept served as a vehicle for Canada to promote a broader agenda and the formalisation of cooperation in a regional body, the Arctic Council. Once the founding of the Arctic Council had put cooperation on a more formal basis, sustainable development became the frame for implementing the broader agenda, both within the newly created Arctic Council's sustainable development programme and within the Sustainable Development Working Group (SDWG).

Usually, the story of Arctic international environmental cooperation starts with Mikhail Gorbachev's Murmansk speech in 1987.[17] In this speech, Gorbachev sketched an extensive cooperation programme for confidence-building and rapprochement between the Soviet Union and the Western Arctic states.[18] Following up on the speech the next day, the Finnish government opened diplomatic communications with the other Arctic governments on the prospects for international environmental cooperation in the Arctic.[19] In 1989, the so-called Rovaniemi process was officially launched. Several rounds of diplomatic meetings of all eight Arctic states then led to the signing of the Rovaniemi Declaration on the Protection of the Arctic Environment, together with the AEPS, in 1991.[20]

Comparing the broad scope of Gorbachev's initial proposal for cooperation at Murmansk with the narrow environmental focus of the AEPS, as well as taking into consideration the process leading to the AEPS, diplomatic difficulties involved in achieving the cooperative arrangement come into focus.[21] Initially, it was not hard to agree that confidence-building efforts between the West and the Soviet Union were desirable. However, while the Soviet leadership badly needed some sort of foreign policy success as well as an international context that was more conducive to tackling their internal, mostly economic problems, the Western states were still too suspicious about being used for ulterior political purposes. Consequently, they were rather reluctant to embrace a broad cooperative agenda. The Finnish initiative thus tried to take the helm by focusing on the least contentious issue of the initial Murmansk programme – environmental protection. The Finns adapted the issue from the Murmansk programme to their particular interests and reframed it in conceptual terms. Their interests were mostly related to the very acute issue of cross-border pollution coming from the Soviet Union, and the desire to gain some influence over this in order to help prevent events such as another Chernobyl. The conceptual terms involved a switch from the concept of environmental security – which the Soviet leader had adopted and developed in some Soviet policy statements – to the less conspicuous concept of sustainable development. This had just been launched by the Nordic-led WCED and thus was not tarnished by being linked to the East–West confrontation.

However, it turned out that the Western states, particularly the United States, were uncertain about this new concept and the political consequences and repercussions it might have. Moreover, the United States overcame its reluctance to join an Arctic international environmental cooperation primarily because of public reaction to the *Exxon Valdez* oil-spill disaster.[22]

Committing to sustainable development in the Arctic rather than environmental protection plain and simple was not compatible with this background. While it thus might seem that, rather than enabling cooperation, sustainable development has served as a barrier to it, on closer inspection this is not the case. Sustainable development as it was finally incorporated into the AEPS enlarged the zone of agreement, because it could be read in two ways. On the one hand, it was used to acknowledge economic activities in the Arctic and to commit to making them more environmentally friendly. This served the Nordic concerns over transboundary pollution and the American government's need to satisfy environmentalist demands. On the other hand, the concept of sustainable development still had a significant overlap with and potential for taking up the broader agenda of Gorbachev's Murmansk speech. The commitment to sustainable development avoided the impression of a preservationist effort, which would have unduly constrained the economic development so urgently needed by the Soviet Union. Rather to the contrary, it could even provide a roadmap for modernising the vastly inefficient production from the Soviet Union's planned economy.

Even though sustainable development figured less prominently in the AEPS than originally envisioned in the Finnish initiative, the AEPS made a clear link to the WCED and thus also to the UNCED preparatory process, which was well under way when the AEPS was signed at Rovaniemi. Thus, sustainable development became part of the normative infrastructure of Arctic international environmental cooperation and its function subsequently shifted. Henceforth, it defined a range of legitimate bargains and provided an interpretive background for further development of the cooperative arrangements.

At least two challenges to the Rovaniemi agreement pressured for further development right from its inception. First, Canada had already brought up the idea of a more institutionalised regional intergovernmental forum with a broader focus in 1989, but had met resistance from the other Arctic states, particularly the United States.[23] But now that a first step was taken in circumpolar cooperation, the Canadians propagated their idea of a regional forum as next step. Sustainable development served as a justification to change the nature of the cooperative arrangement. In the Canadian view, the broader focus of sustainable development required a more formalised mechanism of cooperation than the AEPS entailed. Second, the Canadian idea was very much influenced by domestic processes, in which indigenous peoples had been successful in claiming and asserting their right to participation in the governance of their Arctic homeland.[24] In the other Arctic states, too, the Rovaniemi process had provided a focus for indigenous activities. The AEPS had emphasised and recognised the special relationships of indigenous peoples with the Arctic, but had not found adequate conceptual means to relate their concerns to the strategy. Thus, the AEPS's cooperation arrangement was challenged to better include indigenous peoples' concerns. The UNCED process and the Rio outcomes, particularly Chapter 26 of Agenda 21, supplied the needed conceptual means to meet this challenge.

Both these challenges formed a part of the political background to the second ministerial meeting of the AEPS, which took place in 1993 in Nuuk, Greenland,[25] a meeting which was visibly inspired by UNCED the year before.[26] Having agreed on the UNCED outcomes, no Arctic state could reasonably reject their application to the Arctic, a logic used by the Canadian and Danish governments in particular, both of which were influenced by and responsive to their country's indigenous populations. The Nuuk Declaration on Environment and Development in the Arctic explicitly affirms and reproduces several paragraphs from the UNCED final declaration. Moreover, the Arctic states 'recognise the importance' of applying UNCED's outcomes also to the Arctic region. A Task Force on Sustainable Development and Utilisation was created to explore the implications of this recognition.[27]

Yet again, at first sight sustainable development seems to have slowed down rather than smoothened the bargaining process. The United States was extremely reluctant to embrace the Rio process. Many in the United States saw sustainable development as an attack on the American way of life. The US government also had problems strengthening the recognition of indigenous peoples because it feared repercussions in its relations with US Native Americans. Finally, the AEPS cooperation had provided an opportunity to satisfy the demands of both environmentalists and preservationists in Washington. Because the question of sustainable development was linked to the politically hot and contentious topics in the area of natural resource use in the Arctic – read 'sealing,' 'whaling' and 'oil' – Washington stood to gain nothing by opening up opportunities to undermine its mostly preservationist stance in these matters. In a sense, therefore, for the United States in particular, sustainable development diminished the zone of agreement.

However, in the end, sustainable development continued to matter for the evolution of cooperation because the Canadians prevailed through relentless and persistent diplomatic efforts. The United States became convinced that it could best regain control over the process and agenda of Arctic international environmental cooperation if it joined the club and put a high price-tag on its willingness to join. The United States insisted on tight political supervision in the Arctic Council of any sustainable development activities. They demanded the direct involvement of the senior Arctic officials (the AEPS's and the Arctic Council's intermediate political level) in the work of the Sustainable Development Working Group. They also pushed for limiting the SDWG activities to individual projects proposed by the states themselves. Thus, the cooperation that followed in sustainable development differed markedly from the expert work that had taken place in the other AEPS and Arctic Council working groups. Until it came to the setting-up of the SDWG and the beginning of its work, however, the US insistence made the process of negotiating the steps towards making sustainable development operational in Arctic international environmental protection both arduous and slow.

The Ottawa Declaration on the Establishment of the Arctic Council institutionalised the council as a high-level forum 'for promoting cooperation, coordination and interaction [...] on common Arctic issues, in particular issues of sustainable development and environmental protection.'[28] The accompanying Joint Communiqué of the Governments of the Arctic Countries provided for the transition of the AEPS to the Arctic Council, and tasked the states with agreeing on the terms of reference for the sustainable development programme as its second pillar (in addition to environmental protection).[29] Thus, the four working groups that had been established under the AEPS were transferred by the last official AEPS meeting in Alta in 1997,[30] and the terms of reference for the sustainable development programme were adopted at the first Arctic Council ministerial meeting in 1998 in Iqaluit (where the SDWG was created).[31] At the second Arctic Council ministerial meeting in Barrow 2000, a sustainable development framework document was agreed upon,[32] and 2 years later the SDWG had developed and adopted operating guidelines for its projects.[33] Meanwhile the framework document evolved, and was elaborated as a Sustainable Development Action (SDAP) plan, tabled at the fourth Arctic Council ministerial meeting 2004 in Reykjavik and intended to inform subsequent work plans for the SDWG.[34] Since then, these work plans have been adopted at every consecutive ministerial meeting.

The Icelandic chairmanship of the Arctic Council 2002 to 2004 had made an Arctic Human Development Report one of its priorities, and this report was presented to the ministerial meeting in Reykjavik.[35] The report placed its emphasis on the human dimension of the changes occurring in the region; it was thus a manifestation of the particular function that sustainable development had assumed as operative concept. As has been said earlier, the AEPS had not provided the means to adequately incorporate the concerns of indigenous peoples in Arctic international environmental cooperation. With the Sustainable Development Working Group, a venue for these concerns was finally created, and the social dimension of sustainable development provided the rationale for initiating the various projects.

However, once the Arctic Human Development Report was published, the way in which sustainable development functioned as operative concept shifted from the social to the economic dimension of sustainability. When Russia took the rotating chairmanship of the Arctic Council in 2004 it had already conducted workshops on the Sustainable Development Action Plan and thus had shaped its agenda to some degree. The SDAP regrouped the six objectives of sustainable development that had been agreed upon in the sustainable development framework document into three clusters, referring to the economic, social and environmental dimensions of sustainable development. While the SDAP called for the identification of gaps in regard to these three dimensions, the regrouping already exposed the gap: it made clear that until 2004 the social dimension of the sustainable development agenda had dominated within the SDWG, while the remaining AEPS groups together had provided for the environmental dimension. What was missing was the promotion of economic development. At the 2006 Arctic Council ministerial meeting in Salekhard, Russia took that issue up, and the refocusing on the economic dimension materialised, for instance, in the form of projects on energy cooperation and natural resource development.[36]

Yet Russia was not the only Arctic nation pushing for an increased significance of economic cooperation in the region in the first decade of the new millennium. The increasing impact of climate change with record low levels of sea ice, together with new data about Arctic resources, created a certain opportunity structure that suggested a functional shift to promoting economic development. Moreover, incentives to take up the opportunity were provided by the record high oil price and the reaching of peak oil in more southerly wells in combination with the world economic crisis – and thus the other Arctic states followed suit.

The upshot of this brief review of the shifting functions of sustainable development as a concept in Arctic international environmental cooperation is that its introduction carried a liability from the beginning: sustainable development was incorporated into Arctic international environmental cooperation in addition to environmental protection, not as an overarching term of which environmental protection was an integral part. In the concrete context of the AEPS's inception, only as an addition to environmental protection could the Western side see economic development as constrained by the demand of sustainability, while the Soviet side could interpret the addition at the same time as enabling economic modernisation and being directed against a preservationist agenda. Once established, sustainable development could be used to legitimize the further intensification and extension of cooperation. The Canadian success in their push for the Arctic Council was heavily dependent on making environmental protection appear as too narrow an agenda and contrasting it with the much broader focus of sustainable development. But by now the terms for the relation of environmental protection and sustainable development had been set: an Arctic Council agreement could only be struck by explicitly adding sustainable development to environmental protection as the Arctic Council's primary topics for cooperation. The US rejection of any greater ambitions for sustainable development led to a paradoxical situation in which the four initial working groups for the AEPS's narrow environmental protection focus were retained, while just one new working group was established for the broad sustainable development agenda. While the Sustainable Development Working Group served the inclusion of the social dimension of sustainable development rather well, the setting also lent itself rather easily to the juxtaposition of environmental protection and sustainable development. Environmental protection was identified as being privileged and as subordinating the other concerns, among which the economic dimension was the most neglected. The Arctic states then agreed that this state of affairs required corrective action. The shift can be seen nicely when contrasting the AEPS's Nuuk Declaration,[37] which had introduced sustainable development to the Arctic in a quite comprehensive way, with the Kiruna Vision for the Arctic 20 years later.[38] The Nuuk Declaration had affirmed 'the Arctic states' commitment to the protection of the Arctic Environment as a priority,' while in Kiruna, the Arctic states declared that 'economic cooperation will be on the top of our agenda.'

Discursive shifts in the use of sustainable development

Putting economic development at the top of the agenda did not necessarily mean that the sustainable development concept could no longer work to constrain Arctic oil and gas activities. In order to make good on the claim that a restriction of an increase of these activities is not to be expected, the discursive context of sustainable development in Arctic international environmental cooperation needs to be examined. By tracing shifts of expressed meaning in the AEPS and Arctic Council declarations, I would like to show that this context evolved in four crucial respects. Together, these shifts undermine the foundation for claims that, as a policy concept, sustainable development will be interpreted to require the restriction of Arctic oil and gas extraction. These four are the relevance of Arctic economic development, the broadening of the notion of development, the redefinition of the character of Arctic nature and the Arctic environment and, finally, the externalisation of threats to the Arctic environment.

The *relevance of Arctic economic development* is implied in two discursive contexts: acknowledgement of the role and rights of Arctic indigenous peoples, and the importance of Arctic resources and industries for the Arctic states. In regard to the former, the AEPS had acknowledged indigenous peoples' concerns about threats to their Arctic homeland and their 'sound stewardship of nature and its resources' in 1991.[39] It had explicitly stated that Arctic resources should be used 'to the benefit and enjoyment of present and future generations, including indigenous peoples'[40] and that any development activities should include the 'health, social, economic and cultural needs and values of indigenous peoples'.[41] Overall, however, the wording of the AEPS did not treat the indigenous peoples as active subjects of the governance process. Rather, they appear as a part of the Arctic environment that requires protection. The Nuuk Declaration paved the way for a discursive shift in this regard. Referring to the UNCED outcomes, the Nuuk Declaration confirmed the important role of indigenous peoples in sustainable development and called for 'promoting of their effective participation in the achievement of sustainable development'.[42] Two years later, the Inuvik Declaration recognised and affirmed the 'right of all Arctic indigenous peoples to be represented in the AEPS'.[43] It set the tone for the unique arrangement of the Arctic Council, which accords to certain indigenous peoples' organisations the status of 'permanent participants', with the same participation rights as states, except for decision-taking.[44] Thus, the indigenous peoples had become full active members of the governance process.

The AEPS had merely stated that development should not conflict with the sustainable utilisation of resources by and for indigenous peoples. The latter's benefit from resource utilisation was explicitly included, but no need for development was stipulated. This changed with the acknowledgement of the indigenous peoples as active participants in the cooperation. The Inuvik Declaration emphasises 'the need for sustainable development in the Arctic for the benefit of indigenous peoples'.[45] The Ottawa Declaration then explicitly links sustainable development to the goal of improving living conditions for the indigenous peoples. This meant that sustainable development could not be interpreted anymore as being solely related to making existing industrial activities in the Arctic environmentally sustainable. Rather, from then on, human development was attached to sustainable development as an objective and remained a topic in the declarations of the Arctic Council.[46]

As the definition of relevance of Arctic economic development shifted, a *broadening of the notion of development* took place. The AEPS had acknowledged resource-related activities, but had considered these mainly on the level of small indigenous economies. One of the most protracted issues in the negotiations over the terms of the AEPS's sustainable development activities, and later of the Arctic Council's sustainable development programme, was the scale of economic activities to be promoted. An agreement was reached on a proposal by the Norwegian chair of the AEPS Task Force for Sustainable Development. He distinguished between local-level and industrial development on the one hand, and between the promotion of development and its assessment and regulation on the other. While local economic development was to be promoted by the sustainable development part of the Arctic states' cooperation, industrial development was to be assessed and regulated. However, this agreement which was still in line with the original functional role of sustainable development in the AEPS context, gradually gave way to the promotion of any economic development, at least from the Inari Declaration of 2002. Here, the Arctic's potential for the development of oil and gas (among other things) was already recognised,[47] breaking with the 'promotion of local activities only' principle. The next big step was taken with the Tromsø Declaration of 2009, where the Arctic Council took up the question of resource exploitation. The topic of energy – introduced in the SDWG workplan from 2006 as a field for cooperation – now received its own subsection,[48] of which the principal part was related to Arctic oil and gas activities. Central was the recognition 'that environmentally sound oil and gas activities may contribute to sustainable development in the Arctic region'.[49] Subsequent Arctic Council activities, both in policy and in regulatory output, then very much focused on guidelines and on the legally binding agreements to cope with potential challenges from increased hydrocarbon activities. Four years later, the Kiruna Declaration talked about wholesale economic development, without any qualifier. The Kiruna wording even went so far as to separate development from the notion of sustainability by mentioning 'sustainable resource use, economic development and environmental protection' as important elements of cooperation.[50] This discursive privileging of economic development at the expense of a context in which sustainability of the economy still carries environmental connotations continued during the second Canadian chairmanship of the Arctic Council from 2013 and 2015 and is epitomized in the setting-up of the Arctic Economic Council (AEC). The respective task force to facilitate the creation of the AEC defined the latter's task as '[f]ostering sustainable economic growth and development.' While the tasks of the AEC also included 'efforts to safeguard the environment', again the discursive separation from development clearly seems to suggest that 'sustainable economic growth' is best understood as *stable and continuing* and not in the first line environmental friendly growth.[51] Such suspicions are confirmed when consulting the AEC's web-presence: Here, the notion of sustainable development that is undeniably still linked to environmental protection has given way to the new concepts of responsible economic development.[52]

This refocusing, however, could not have taken place without a *redefinition of the character of Arctic nature and the regional environment*. In the AEPS and still in the 1993 Nuuk Declaration,[53] Arctic nature and environment are described not only as unique, but as fragile due to scarcity of light and life. The vulnerability of the Arctic is presented as requiring special protective measures. Economic and human activities appear as the exception rather than the rule. This latter aspect changed with the acknowledgement of indigenous peoples' needs and rights in the subsequent declarations. While the Inari Declaration recognises the potential for oil and gas development,[54] an explicit redefinition of the character of the region took place in the Reykjavik and Salekhard declarations. Both recognise 'the Arctic's rich natural environment.'[55] The Salekhard Declaration still emphasises that the 'environment is particularly vulnerable to human activities', but it does not mention the need for special protective measures as the AEPS did. The Nuuk Declaration of 2011 then also set the record straight in regard to the abundance of human and economic activities: 'the Arctic is first and foremost an inhabited region with diverse economies and societies.'[56] This was repeated in subsequent ministerial declarations. While in the Kiruna Declaration the vulnerability of the Arctic environment was mentioned again, this was only in relation to external threats.[57] This brings me to the last discursive shift.

This last shift placed a *stronger emphasis on the external challenges* to the region, thus effectively minimising any challenges that might be tackled from within. This externalisation had two sides. On the one hand, impacts on the Arctic environment generated outside the Arctic gained in importance in declarations; on the other hand, developments within the Arctic were externalised in the sense that they were presented not as outcomes of actions taken by the Arctic actors involved, but rather as events just happening. The AEPS, of course, had already recognised the harming effect of pollution generated beyond the Arctic. However, it also stated that damage to the Arctic environment could only be prevented 'through careful stewardship *by Arctic countries*.'"[58] But once the focus on economic development in the Arctic started to emerge, climate change framed as an outside threat entered the ministerial declarations as an important topic. The Inari Declaration put climate change in focus alongside sustainable resource use and human development.[59] Here, however, the Arctic mostly appeared as an indicator for global environmental change. When the Arctic Climate Impact Assessment was presented 2 years later at the Reykjavik meeting in 2004, its findings were noted with concern, but climate change was not yet externalised.[60] This happened partly in the Tromsø Declaration. Here, *global* climate change was identified 'as one of the greatest challenges facing the Arctic'.[61] Although regional countermeasures were pondered, too, the emphasis was on necessary global emission cuts. At the same time, the declaration recognised oil and gas exploitation as contributing positively to sustainable development. Necessary global emission cuts were then mentioned in all subsequent declarations. Nowhere, however, was the link between the promotion of Arctic economic development and the call for emission reductions explored. On the contrary, portraying Arctic economic development as something that simply happens to the Arctic meant that the link could be avoided. The wording suggests that influencing oil and gas activities lies beyond the capacity of the Arctic states. Already the SDAP had ominously stipulated that there will be 'growing pressure' to utilise Arctic resources,[62] insinuating that this is just something to which the Arctic states have to yield. The Salekhard Declaration then acknowledged 'rapid changes' and 'increased human activities' with significant impact on the Arctic environment, without explaining, however, where these came from.[63] The same was emphasised in the Tromsø Declaration, which recognised 'new opportunities for and challenges of economic development'.[64] Again, these were just recognised as a kind of *fait accompli,* appearing as given and thus, obviously, as mere facts to be accepted. The Nuuk Declaration 2 years later spoke of 'changing circumstances' and challenges faced in the Arctic.[65] This language, which does not identify the causes of the trends, at the same time decouples the promotion of economic development from its consequences for the Arctic. It thus helps to avoid the seeming cognitive dissonance of promoting and preparing for increased Arctic oil and gas extraction, while at the same time recognising that the Arctic is under severe threat as a result of climate change.

Conclusion

In the preceding sections I argued that sustainable development underwent a functional and discursive change in the course of international environmental cooperation between the eight Arctic states. I believe that the analysis presented must lead to the conclusion that there is little prospect that the concept of sustainable development will exercise constraining effects on an increase of Arctic oil and gas extraction. The evolution of the functional role of the concept has led to the opening up of the Arctic for economic development rather than to the latter's limitation. The discursive change sustainable development underwent as a policy concept in Arctic international environmental cooperation transformed the promotion of development into an obligation to meet the rights and needs of Arctic indigenous peoples. At the same time, the scope of the promoted development enlarged from local economies to wholesale industrial development. This was made possible by a redefinition of Arctic nature and environment. Formerly seen as fragile wilderness in need of protection, the Arctic came to be seen as an inhabited region with rich resources awaiting development. The apparent cognitive dissonance between acknowledging the challenges to the Arctic and, at the same time, contributing to their causes is avoided by an externalisation which places the causes of the challenges outside the region and beyond reach.

The greatest weakness of sustainable development was that the concept failed to resolve the conundrum of reconciling environment and development. Elsewhere, as in the Arctic, the concept has evolved 'more or less in conformity with the changing demands of a largely neoliberal global political economy'[66] and thus has ultimately privileged the economic dimension over the other two. The normative strength of the concept of sustainable development, however, lies in its consideration of and focus on human needs. The concept helped to anchor the increasing recognition of the rights of indigenous peoples in Arctic international environmental cooperation. This is certainly something to be appreciated. The challenge, then, is to find a frame which retains this normative substance without giving in to the hegemony of neoliberal economy. The two frames of climate change or oil spill from Koivurova's list will likely not be suited to this task.[67] They might too easily cash in the satisfaction of the needs of Arctic people for the avoidance of the stipulated pending disaster. Thus, the search for a better frame in which to grasp what can be seen as problematic with Arctic oil and gas extraction must still continue.

Notes

1 Koivurova 2017 (Chapter 2 in this volume).
2 AEPS 1991b, 6.
3 AEPS 1991b, 7.
4 Mikkelsen and Langhelle 2008a.
5 Mikkelsen and Langhelle 2008b, 4.
6 Langhelle, Blindheim and Oygarden 2008.
7 WCED quoted in Langhelle, Blindheim and Oygarden 2008, 19.
8 Langhelle, Blindheim and Oygarden 2008, 20.
9 Langhelle and Hansen 2008, 345.
10 Langhelle and Hansen 2008, 344f.
11 The insights presented here are based on 13 expert interviews conducted for and used in my unpublished graduate thesis. The interviews took place from

winter 1998 to spring 1999 with policy-makers involved in the Arctic Council and SDWG negotiation processes from Norway, Denmark, the ICC and WWF.

12 E.g. Haas 1980.
13 E.g. Keohane 1984; Goldstein and Keohane 1993.
14 E.g. Young 1996.
15 Cf. Bernstein 2000 and 2012.
16 Langhelle, Blindheim and Oygarden 2008.
17 E.g. Young 1998; Axworthy and Dean 2013.
18 Åtland 2008.
19 Axworthy and Dean 2013.
20 AEPS 1991a; b.
21 Scrivener 1996.
22 Young 1998.
23 Axworthy and Dean 2013.
24 Scrivener 1996.
25 AEPS 1993.
26 Langhelle, Blindheim and Oygarden 2008.
27 AEPS 1993.
28 Arctic Council 1996a.
29 Arctic Council 1996b.
30 AEPS 1997.
31 Arctic Council 1998.
32 Arctic Council 2000.
33 Arctic Council 2002.
34 Arctic Council 2004b.
35 Einarsson et al. 2004.
36 Arctic Council 2006.
37 AEPS 1993.
38 Arctic Council 2013b.
39 AEPS 1991b, 6.
40 AEPS 1991b, 7.
41 AEPS 1991b, 8.
42 AEPS 1993, 1.
43 AEPS 1995, 1.
44 Arctic Council 1996a.
45 AEPS 1995.
46 Arctic Council 1996a.
47 Arctic Council 2002.
48 Arctic Council 2009.
49 Arctic Council 2009.
50 Arctic Council 2013a.
51 Arctic Council-TFCBF 2013, 1.
52 www.arcticeconomiccouncil.com/about-us/. Accessed 09.12.2016.
53 AEPS 1991b; 1993.
54 Arctic Council 2002.
55 Arctic Council 2004a; 2006.
56 Arctic Council 2011.
57 Arctic Council 2013a.
58 AEPS 1991b, 7. My emphasis.
59 Arctic Council 2002.
60 Arctic Council 2004a.
61 Arctic Council 2009.
62 Arctic Council 2004b.
63 Arctic Council 2006.

64 Arctic Council 2009.
65 Arctic Council 2011.
66 Bernstein 2012, 379.
67 Koivurova 2017.

References

AEPS (Arctic Environmental Protection Strategy). 1991a. *Rovaniemi Declaration on the Protection of the Arctic Environment.* Rovaniemi.

AEPS. 1991b. *Arctic Environmental Protection Strategy.* Rovaniemi.

AEPS. 1993. *Nuuk Declaration on Environment and Development in the Arctic.* Nuuk.

AEPS. 1995. *Inuvik Declaration on Environmental Protection and Sustainable Development in the Arctic.* Inuvik.

AEPS. 1997. *Alta Declaration on the Arctic Environmental Protection Strategy.* Alta.

Arctic Council. 1996a. *Declaration on the Establishment of the Arctic Council.* Ottawa.

Arctic Council. 1996b. *Joint Communiqué of the Governments of the Arctic States on the Establishment of the Arctic Council.* Ottawa.

Arctic Council. 1998. *Iqualuit Declaration on the Occasion of the First Ministerial Meeting.* Iqualuit.

Arctic Council. 2000. *Barrow Declaration on the Occasion of the Second Ministerial Meeting.* Barrow.

Arctic Council. 2002. *Inari Declaration on the Occasion of the Third Ministerial Meeting.* Inari.

Arctic Council. 2004a. *Reykjavik Declaration on the Occasion of the Fourth Ministerial Meeting.* Reykjavik.

Arctic Council. 2004b. *Sustainable Development Action Plan.* Reykjavik.

Arctic Council. 2006. *Salekhard Declaration on the Occasion of the Fifth Ministerial Meeting.* Salekhard.

Arctic Council. 2009. *Tromsø Declaration on the Occasion of the Sixth Ministerial Meeting.* Tromsø.

Arctic Council. 2011. *Nuuk Declaration on the Occasion of the Seventh Ministerial Meeting.* Nuuk.

Arctic Council. 2013a. *Kiruna Declaration on the Occasion of the Eighth Ministerial Meeting* Kiruna.

Arctic Council. 2013b. *The Kiruna Vision for the Arctic.* Kiruna.

Arctic Council-TFCBF. 2013. *Report to the Senior Arctic Officials December 2013.*

Åtland, K. 2008. 'Mikhail Gorbachev, the Murmansk Initiative, and the Desecuritization of Interstate Relations in the Arctic.' *Cooperation and Conflict* 43, 3: 289–311.

Axworthy, T.S. and R. Dean. 2013. 'Changing the Arctic Paradigm from Cold War to Cooperation: How Canada's Indigenous Leaders Shaped the Arctic Council.' *The Yearbook of Polar Law* 5, 1: 7–43.

Bernstein, S. 2000. 'Ideas, Social Structure and the Compromise of Liberal Environmentalism.' *European Journal of International Relations* 6, 4: 464–512.

Bernstein, S. 2012. 'Grand Compromises in Global Governance.' *Government and Opposition* 47, 3: 368–394.

Einarsson, N., J.N. Larsen, A. Nilsson and O.R. Young. 2004. *Arctic Human Development Report.* Akureyri/ISL: Stefansson Arctic Institute/Icelandic Arctic Council.

Goldstein, J. and R.O. Keohane. 1993. 'Ideas and Foreign Policy: An Analytical Framework.' In *Ideas and Foreign Policy: Beliefs, Institutions and Political Change,* edited by J. Goldstein and R.O. Keohane, 3–30. Ithaca, NY: Cornell University Press.
Haas, E.B. 1980. 'Why collaborate? Issue-Linkage and International Regimes.' *World Politics* 32, 3: 357–405.
Keohane, R.O. 1984. *After Hegemony: Cooperation and Discord in the World Political Economy.* Princeton, NJ: Princeton University Press.
Koivurova, T. 2017. 'Framing the Problem in Arctic Offshore Hydrocarbon Exploitation.' In *Governance of Arctic Offshore Oil and Gas,* edited by C. Pelaudeix and E.M. Basse, Chapter 2. London: Routledge.
Langhelle, O. and K.F. Hansen. 2008. 'Perceptions of Arctic Challenges: Alaska, Canada, Norway and Russia Compared.' In *Arctic Oil and Gas: Sustainability at Risk?* edited by A. Mikkelsen and O. Langhelle, 317–349. London: Routledge.
Langhelle, O., B.T. Blindheim and O. Oygarden. 2008. 'Framing Oil and Gas in the Arctic from a Sustainable Development Perspective.' In *Arctic Oil and Gas: Sustainability at Risk?* edited by A. Mikkelsen and O. Langhelle, 15–44. London: Routledge.
Mikkelsen, A. and O. Langhelle, eds. 2008a. *Arctic Oil and Gas: Sustainability at Risk?* London: Routledge.
Mikkelsen, A. and O. Langhelle. 2008b. 'Introduction.' In *Arctic Oil and Gas: Sustainability at Risk?* edited by A. Mikkelsen and O. Langhelle, 1–12. London: Routledge.
Scrivener, D. 1996. *Environmental Cooperation in the Arctic: From Strategy to Council.* Oslo: North Atlantic Committee.
Young, O.R. 1996. *The Arctic Council: Marking a New Era in International Relations.* Washington DC: Twentieth Century Fund.
Young, O.R. 1998. *Creating Regimes: Arctic Accords and International Governance.* Ithaca, NY: Cornell University Press.

4 The EU's role as a facilitator in the development of maritime environmental law in the Arctic

With focus on offshore hydrocarbon activities

Ellen Margrethe Basse

Introduction

This chapter addresses the European Union's (EU's) possible role in the development of the Arctic marine environmental governance. Marine governance is understood as the interaction between different actors at several levels and in different positions, sharing competences and capability in order to govern maritime activities and control their consequences for the environment.[1] After the *Erika* accident in 1999 and the *Prestige* accident in 2002, the EU has undertaken larger responsibilities on the protection of the marine area. The chapter is focused on the role that the EU is playing in respect to filling out gaps in regional environmental law by the use of its 'internal' regulatory power, as well the use of its competence as an 'international personality' developing standards and principles with effects inside and outside the territorial jurisdiction of the EU. Environmental law is seen in this chapter as an important tool providing both stability and a high degree of flexibility and responsiveness to changes in ecosystems, to the understanding of those marine systems, and to the maritime activities – including the offshore hydrocarbon activities – that have impact on the ecosystems.[2]

The chapter focuses on the importance of the Treaty of Lisbon[3] and the Agreement on the European Economic Area (the EEA Agreement)[4] – both of which are distinct legal orders in their own right. Focus is also on the importance of the EU's environmental directives and the judgments of the European Court of Justice (EUCJ) in its development of case law. The European Free Trade Association (EFTA) Court[5] is – as stated in this chapter – respecting the EUCJ case law as binding in the member states covered by the EEA Agreement. It is the hypothesis of the writer of this chapter that the just-mentioned sort of 'top-down' Europeanisation combined with the EU's participation in international and regional agreements on marine governance makes it possible for the EU to have an impact on the development of maritime environmental Arctic law.

Five of the eight Arctic states have special relations with the EU. Sweden, Finland and Denmark are EU member states, Norway and Iceland are EEA/EFTA member states, and all five are EEA member states. The EU's direct or indirect impact on the legislation of the Kingdom of Norway and the Kingdom of Denmark is of special interest in the context of Arctic marine governance, as Norway and Denmark are also Arctic coastal states. Consequently, it is important to look at these relations when assessing a possible role for the EU in the development of Arctic maritime governance.

The special legal order of the EU, based on the Treaty of Lisbon,[6] and the principles of loyalty and cooperation laid down in the Treaty are briefly described in section one of the present chapter. In this section, it is illustrated that an extraterritorial effect of EU standards and principles has been accepted in the case law of the EUCJ with potential consequences for the interpretation of EU's ecosystem-based standards and principles in the Arctic marine area. The description is supplemented with information about the EEA Agreement, which is based on the same environmental principles. Section two covers international and regional cooperation in the Arctic, which, directly or indirectly, involves the EU and the EEA member states. The fulfilment of the EU's political agenda is the subject of agreement between the EU and the third parties concerned.[7] The Convention for the Protection of the Marine Environment of the North-East Atlantic (the OSPAR Convention) is mentioned here as the most important regional cooperation forum. Section three focuses on the EU's internal marine and maritime legislation, its use of an ecosystem management approach and the importance of the EUCJ's case law. The Court has consistently used functional criteria and has hereby held that the geographical scope of the application of EU law follows that of member states' territorial jurisdiction, an approach that potentially makes EU's legislation, directly applicable to the Arctic marine area.[8] The EEA's Offshore Safety Directive[9] is briefly described, in section four, as a new and ambitious marine protection regime with a clear relationship to the ecosystem-based management legislation described in section three. In section five, Norway is examined as the EEA/EFTA member state most relevant to the EU's role in Arctic maritime governance. As one of the five Arctic coastal states, Norway is also one of the largest oil producers.[10] Section six focuses on the Danish Realm (Denmark and its Arctic region), which includes the Faroe Islands and Greenland. These Arctic areas are not included in Denmark's EU membership but are overseas countries and territories (OCTs) associated with the EU. While Greenland is without doubt part of the Arctic, the Faroe Islands are not always included in the definition of the Arctic[11]; while issues concerning offshore hydrocarbon activities have a high priority in Greenland, this is not the case in the Faroe Islands. Section six, therefore, focuses on the special question of Danish competences in the Greenlandic marine areas and on the relevance of this to the EU's role in the Arctic governance of maritime activities.

Drawing on the analyses presented in sections one to six, it is the conclusion, in section seven, that the EU's position makes it possible for it to play an important role in the maritime Arctic governance of hydrocarbon activities.

The EU's legal order and its effect on member-states' international relations

The Treaty of Lisbon formulates the principles and objectives of the EU's external actions and confirms the legal personality of the Union, which is in effect an international personality.[12] Based on the Treaty, the aim is to establish the internal market. The EU's institutions shall work for the sustainable development of Europe based on balanced economic growth and a high level of environmental protection.[13] The principle of conferral is a fundamental principle of EU law.[14] Under this principle, the EU is a union of member states that voluntarily confer some of their competence on the Union. Within the areas of the environment, the Treaty of Lisbon contemplates 'shared competences' between the member states and the EU institutions.[15] Shared competence implies that both the EU and its member states may legislate and adopt legally binding rules. The EU institutions must pass two tests, when they are regulating. *First*, they have to demonstrate that the objectives of the initiatives cannot be sufficiently achieved at the national level, and *second,* they should demonstrate that the actual initiative, by reason of its scale or its effects, can be better, more effective, consistent with the internal market and/or more environmentally friendly achieved at EU level than at national level. On the other hand, the member states shall only exercise their competence to the extent that the EU has not exercised, or has decided to exercise, its competence. Transposition of the EU's environmental standards and principles into the national legislation is to be undertaken within the context of the principle of loyalty.[16] Based on this principle, member states must take all appropriate measures to ensure fulfilment of the obligations arisen out of the Treaty or resulting from action taken by the EU institutions, including the international and regional obligations accepted by the Council.[17] The member states must abstain from any measure that might jeopardise the attainment of the objectives of the Treaty.[18] The Commission has the competence to oversee the application of EU law in the member states. It can bring infringement cases before the EUCJ to control national implementation. The Court can use economic sanctions, too, if the member states are not loyal to the EU.[19]

According to settled case law of the EUCJ, the need for a uniform application of EU law and the principles of equality and effectiveness require that the standards be given an autonomous and uniform – some times as a minimum – interpretation throughout the member states.[20] Therefore, the interpretation at the national level must take into account the aims, the environmental principles stated and the context of the provision in question.[21]

While recognising the governing international principle that the EU cannot take measures on the territory of third states by means of enforcement of EU law without the consent of the relevant third state, the EUCJ has in its recent interpretation of directives and regulations approved the EU's standards and principles with important extraterritorial effects. In its judgement of 21 December 2011, the Court concluded that the 2008 amendment of the ETS Directive that included CO_2 emissions from all flights by the EU as well as non-EU carriers to and from an airport in the territory of the EEA member states is not in conflict with the territorial principle stated in international law.[22] The Court pointed out that the EU policy on the environment aims at a high level of protection.[23] In its judgement of 23 April 2015, the Court stated – with reference to the principles laid down in the Treaty on protection of animal welfare as a legitimate object in the public interest – that the EU's regulation must include the stages of the journey which are to take place in the territory of third countries to ensure compliance with the EU's standards and principles.[24] Another illustration of the extraterritorial effects of the EU's principles and standards accepted by the Court is the judgement of 21 September 2016 on the regulation on cosmetic products.[25] The Court stated that the attainment of the objective of the regulation that promotes the use of non-animal alternative methods would be seriously compromised, if it was possible to circumvent the prohibition of animal testing laid down in the regulation by carrying out the prohibited testing outside the EU. The three judgments just mentioned might be read as a concession to global pluralism by which the Court is balancing the respect for the territorial principle of international law and the 'external dimension' of the EU's standards and principles.

The EU legal order differs from traditional international law due to its body of autonomous law-making institutions, and especially due to the role played by the EUCJ. The institutions of the EU are, in their relations with the wider world, obligated to do all that lies in their power to enhance the international legal order, and to do this under the guidance of the principles that inspired the creation of the Union and its subsequent development.[26] The EU is required to define and pursue common policies and actions and to work for a high degree of cooperation in all fields of international relations.[27] This obligation is also important for the role of the EU in the Arctic – an area of active cooperation between major regional and global actors.[28] In the EU's seventh Environment Action Programme, entitled *Living well, within the limits of our planet*, for the period 2013–2020, objective 9 highlights that:

> ... particular emphasis should be given to the... Arctic regions, where there is a need for intensified cooperation and increased Union involvement. ... [29]

Within their respective competences, the EU and its member states shall cooperate with third countries and with the competent regional or international organisations.[30]

The EU acquires external competence (i.e. the capacity to take part in international agreements on behalf of, or together with, its member states). The external environmental competence grew in an indirect way through the case law of the EUCJ, which created the doctrine of parallelism between internal and external competences.[31] Based on the Treaty, the EU has now[32] exclusive competence in all areas as to the conclusion of an international or regional agreement when its conclusion is provided for in a legislative act of the EU, or is necessary to enable the EU to exercise its internal competence, or in so far as its conclusion may affect common rules or alter their scope. In environmental matters, the EU ratifies regional and international agreements as 'mixed agreements,' with both the EU and its member states as parties.[33]

It is the European Commission that is negotiating, and the European Council (Council) that makes the final decision on international and regional commitments. Once the Council has concluded a multilateral agreement, its legal effects are twofold: the EU, as well as its member states, are bound.[34] All subject matters of such secondary law fall within the scope of the exclusive external EU power, including in situations in which the EU adopts internal rules on the same subject matter discussed within the conventions of the IMO, to which the EU is not accepted as a party (see section below).[35] The multilateral agreements ratified by the EU – as well as the IMO's agreements ratified by EU member states – are transformed by the EU into Union and national law by strategies, and secondary EU legislation (directives or regulations). The international norms automatically start to form 'an integrated part' of EU law, and the interpretation of secondary EU legislation in the national legislation has to be in harmony with the international obligations, ensuring vertical harmonisation.[36] It has been stated in the case law of the EUCJ that the member states as well as the EU institutions have to apply a convention conform interpretation of the EU's secondary legislation in areas covered by a convention ratified by the Council.[37] The reasoning behind this vertical harmonisation is to show third parties that the EU is a reliable international partner.[38] Conflicts concerning the correct understanding and use of the international norms in EU member states are handled only by the EUCJ.[39]

The goal of the EEA Agreement, on the other hand, is the harmonisation of market conditions, extending the EU's single market to the EFTA member states (with some exceptions).[40] The EEA brings together the EU member states and three of the EFTA member states (Iceland, Liechtenstein and Norway).[41] The depth of integration ensured by the EEA Agreement is less far-reaching than the Treaty of Lisbon, but the scope and objective go beyond what is usual for an international or regional convention.[42] The competences of the EEA/EFTA institutions are described in the EEA Agreement. That agreement essentially states that the EFTA Surveillance Authority (ESA)[43] and the EFTA Court are required to follow the European Court of Justice (ECJ) case law from the period before signing the EEA Agreement (titled 'old ECJ case law') and to take due account of new EUCJ case law. Together the EUCJ and the EFTA Court in many aspects have ensured a uniform legal order in situations covered by the EEA Agreement.[44]

The Norwegian courts, too (without being legally bound by the judgments of the EFTA Court and the EUCJ) have in praxis interpreted Norwegian law as far as possible in conformity with the judgments of these two European courts. Therefore, the development of the legal order under the EEA Agreement has in many ways been similar to that just described, making it possible to ensure vertical harmonisation of norms from the international or regional levels to the national level. In the following text, the term 'member states' will be used also in the description of the EEA member states.

A picture of the vertical harmonisation of international and regional norms of special importance for the marine governance in the Arctic will be presented in the following parts of this chapter.

International and regional cooperation involving the EU

Several conventions establish obligations for the parties concerning cooperation on the prevention of oil spills, as well as responsibilities for the parties in respect to economic liability for the damages caused by such spills in the Arctic.[45] The most important convention is the UN's Law of the Sea Convention (UNCLOS), which covers all activities. It is the constitution of the sea.[46] The EU, EU member states and EEA member states have all ratified UNCLOS, which gives coastal states the exclusive right to regulate and give licences for extraction in their exclusive economic zone (EEZ) and on the continental shelf. These rights are combined with state responsibility.[47] UNCLOS also establishes the competences to manage marine protected areas (MPAs) under other conventions, respecting at the same time the right of other states to enjoy innocent passage.[48] It imposes duties of cooperation on information, planning and research programmes as part of the environmental obligations, including special obligations in the Arctic ice-covered waters.[49] It is also mandatory for the parties to UNCLOS to cooperate directly or indirectly through competent international organisations. This cooperation relies on national, EU and regional legislation on offshore activities. The EU is strengthening its efforts in the international maritime and marine areas by pushing for more ambition in resolutions on oceans that promote global membership of maritime governance instruments, such as UNCLOS.[50]

The EU and all its EEA member states are also parties to the UN's Convention on Biological Diversity (the Biodiversity Convention), which aims to conserve biological diversity.[51] The implementation of the ecosystem approach in this international convention is also part of the Convention for the Protection of the Marine Environment of the North-East Atlantic (OSPAR). OSPAR is a regional convention of special importance for cooperation between the EU and its EEA member states on the protection of the Atlantic marine area. It establishes the concept of MPAs as areas of seawaters that are given special protection through legal provisions because of their significance in a number of respects. The ministerial meeting of

September 2010 adopted the North-East Atlantic Environmental Strategy for 2010–2020, which has as its overarching objective the implementation of an ecosystem approach. This approach has been used under OSPAR since 2003.[52] The OSPAR agreement on the strategy of the OSPAR Commission for the Protection of the Marine Environment of the North-East Atlantic 2010–2020[53] is an example of the harmonisation of OSPAR and EU standards. This cooperation is important, as it often prepares the presentation of new approaches and principles that afterwards support the EU directives, once they 'take over' and make the soft law 'harder'.

The EU's role in the OSPAR cooperation has indirect impacts on regulatory action within IMO, as the parties to the OSPAR can raise the need for new initiatives in the IMO. The Convention for the Prevention of Pollution from Ships (MARPOL 1973/78), with its protocols and guidelines, is the primary international instrument for preventing pollution from ships, including some parts of offshore hydrocarbon activities.[54] Further important instruments are the IMO's Convention on Oil-Pollution Preparedness, Response and Cooperation (the OPPRC Convention) and the Protocol on Preparedness, Response and Cooperation to Pollution Incidents by Hazardous and Noxious Substances (the OPPRC–HNS Protocol), which involves obligations of emergency planning on oil pollution and cooperation between the parties on such issues.[55] The OPPRC Convention, which was concluded after the *Exxon Valdez* accident, is another important convention that is based on the 'precautionary approach,' as well as on the 'polluter pays' principle.[56] Under the International Convention on Civil Liability for oil-pollution damage (CLC), a scheme of strict liability in combination with compulsory insurance is also established by the IMO.[57] This convention applies in cases of accidental oil spills at sea. The international convention on the establishment of an international fund (the IOPC Fund Convention) supplements the last-mentioned convention. The aim of the Fund Convention is to provide 'full and adequate' compensation to any person suffering pollution damage, as defined by reference to the CLC, or to provide costs for measures to prevent or minimise such damage. The International Convention on Limitation of Liability for Maritime Claims (the LLMC 76), as amended by the 1996 Protocol, is also relevant in respect to protection of the Arctic marine areas.

The EU is not a party to these IMO conventions, as the IMO accepts only sovereign states as party to them. It is therefore not possible for the EU to act as a party in the IMO.[58] When the EU as mentioned supra does not have the status of a party in a regional or international regime, the member states are obliged to act jointly in the Union's interest on the basis of the duty of loyal cooperation. Therefore, the EU has authorised its member states to ratify these conventions in the interest of the Union so as to respect the principle of loyalty.[59] In 2005, the Commission drafted a procedural framework for the adoption of common EU positions for IMO-related issues and rules governing their expression in the IMO.[60] The EU institutions as well as the member states in the IMO bargaining situations follow it. The Commission frequently issues several reasoned opinions to member states before the meetings in the IMO. It does not hesitate to force the member states to accept that it is not accepted, if they themselves act as parties to IMO conventions not loyal to the EU. The EUCJ is explicitly stating in one of its judgments that the fact that EU is not a member of the IMO does not prevent its external competence being, in fact, exercised, in particular through the member states acting jointly in the EU's interests.[61] The Court stated that by submitting a proposal to the IMO, the member state doing this has failed to fulfil its 'duty of loyalty'. All the conventions and connected agreements on state control, ship inspections, classification societies, rules on double-hull tankers, etc. have been implemented into EU law with binding effects on the member states with the consequences of vertical harmonisation described supra in section one.

The Convention on Environmental Impact Assessment in a Trans-boundary Context (the Espoo Convention of 1991) is an important UNECE convention that has been ratified by the EU and by its member states.[62] Parties to the conventions shall take the necessary legal, administrative or other measures to ensure an environmental impact assessment (EIA) procedure that permits public participation in projects related to offshore hydrocarbon extraction in the Arctic. The EU has passed the EIA Directive making these rules binding on all member states and directly applicable also in member states with a dualistic legal tradition (such as Denmark and Norway).[63] The Protocol on Strategic Environmental Assessments (the SEA Protocol) under the Espoo Convention,[64] which has been ratified both by the EU and by its EEA member states is implemented into EU legislation by the SEA Directive.[65] This instrument is related to plans, programmes and legislative acts that are also of relevance to Arctic offshore extraction, and it is applicable in the member states.

The 'Northern Dimension' policy is an additional important factor in determining the EU's impact on the governance of maritime activities in the Arctic.[66] This is a common policy shared by four equal partners (the EU, Russia, Norway and Iceland) and serving as an umbrella for regional cooperation to be carried out in Northern Europe with other participants such as the Arctic Council, the Barents Euro-Arctic Council, and the Nordic Council of Ministers. This partnership has brought together the principal EU and international financial institutions in different sectors to support the development and implementation of environmental standards in the Arctic. It is the opinion of the Council of EU that the EU can make a significant contribution not least in regional and multilateral cooperation bodies, which deal with Arctic matters.[67]

The ecosystem and an integrated approach in the EU's marine management

The EU's Integrated Maritime Policy (IMP) has set the development of a coherent policy approach to the marine areas as the objective for the EU, with the aim of achieving a comprehensive understanding and taking economic, environmental and social issues into account.[68] As part of this policy, the EU has taken an active role in developing offshore hydrocarbon extraction safety management: a role that may have both direct and indirect positive consequences for Arctic marine governance.

The EU legislation of importance for the protection of the marine environment and maritime activities comprises several directives and policy papers. It is based on a holistic, ecosystem-based approach, as an important part of a functionally oriented policy of sustainable development.[69] This approach is a consequence of the EU's implementation of the ecosystem approach to secondary legislation and policy taken by the Biodiversity Convention and by OSPAR.

The Habitats Directive[70] and the Wild Birds Directive[71] are both key pieces of the EU's ecosystem-based legislation. These directives – which are EEA-relevant – safeguard environmental quality in the EU and, as such, are vital to ensure that maritime activities are developed sustainably.[72] They are implementing the Biodiversity Convention, the Bern Convention and the Bonn Convention into EU legislation ensuring a vertical harmonisation.[73] The directives require member states to take appropriate steps to avoid the deterioration of the special protected species in the protected areas (named Natura 2000 sites). The EUCJ has, by its judgments, ensured the application of these rules in member states' respective exclusive economic zones (EEZs) and on the continental shelf.[74] The Court has judged that if the appropriate assessment of a project under these directives concludes that adverse effects on the habitats protected by the relevant Natura 2000 sites cannot be ruled out, there are strong restrictions on the national authorities.[75]

The EIA Directive[76] – mentioned supra in section two – establishes procedural obligations of importance in any cases of approval of offshore hydrocarbon projects, in harmony with the Espoo Convention. This directive makes it mandatory for the EEA member states to ensure that decision-making is based on public participation, and that the published description of a planned project includes information on the site, design and size of the project, as well as a description of the measures envisaged in order to avoid, reduce and, if possible, remedy significant adverse effects of such a project. The Strategic Environmental Assessment Directive (SEA Directive)[77] supplements this with obligations on the EEA member states to prepare SEAs as part of the preparation of plans and programmes in view of the likely effect on Natura 2000 sites. For all other plans and programmes that set the framework for future development content of projects, the SEA is optional. The decision-making in member states on plans, programmes and legislative acts relating to any measure, which establishes, by defining rules and procedures for scrutiny applicable to the sector (e.g. the energy sector), a significant body of criteria and detailed rules for grant and implementation of one or more projects likely to have effects on the environment (e.g. hydrocarbon extraction), have to follow the strategic environmental assessment rules.[78] These procedural rules are also vertical harmonisation as described supra in section one.

The Marine Strategic Framework Directive (MSFD)[79] together with the Framework Directive for Maritime Spatial Planning (FMSP)[80] establish an integrated approach to marine policy, covering different maritime-sector policy areas. Both directives have broad appeal in addressing ocean crises.[81] The national implementation of these directives is guided by eleven key principles, especially the ecosystem approach obligation and cross-border cooperation and consultation.[82] Where possible, the member states shall also cooperate with third countries. Four regions are established under the MSFD on the basis of geographical and environmental criteria, each of which has to be managed as one 'basin'. The north–east Atlantic Ocean (already regulated by OSPAR) is one of these basins, ensuring coordination between OSPAR and EU standards.

The above-mentioned directives are all relevant to the EEA member states. The joint declaration by the parties to the EEA Agreement made a decision in addition to the MSFD, which implies that the parties are of the opinion that it will apply to the regulation of activities taking place on the continental shelves of the EEA states.[83] The directive was adopted with the ambition of achieving 'good environmental status' across the EU by 2020 and of protecting the resource base for marine-related economic and social activities. National implementation, for instance, in Denmark and Norway, must take into account, where appropriate, those standards applicable under the existing EU legislation, as well as, where relevant, knowledge and approaches developed in the framework of OSPAR and other regional sea conventions. In this manner, the marine management has to be horizontally and vertically well coordinated.

The FMSP respects member states' prerogative to use national legal traditions in the design of plans and strategies, taking into account their economic, social and environmental priorities as well as their sectoral policy objectives. It is not, however, based on its publication in the *Official Journal*, relevant to the EEA. The EU and EEA member states are required to establish management measures that influence where and when offshore hydrocarbon extraction is to occur, and are required to use coordination measures to ensure that the various sectoral measures at different institutional levels are coordinated. The marine environment must be protected, deterioration prevented or, where practicable, marine ecosystems restored in areas in which they have been adversely affected. The FMSP provides the opportunity to complete current efforts to identify and designate marine protected areas under the Habitats Directive, the Wild Birds Directive, and the OSPAR Network of Marine Protected Areas. The development of targets and associated indicators must be carried out in the framework of the requirement for regional cooperation, keeping in mind the objective of coherence of frameworks within the various marine regions (including the area covered by OSPAR), as well as coherence across the EU. In 2017, the Commission will start working with all relevant actors to develop proposals for internationally accepted guidelines on MSP by partner countries and at international level, in particular in the United Nations.[84]

As described above, there are several examples of the vertical harmonisation of standards and principles on environmental protection. It can be supplemented by the fact that the FMSP is inspired by the UNESCO's 2009 guidelines on MSP that set out a number of criteria that support the development of best practice on governance by a public process of analysing and allocating the spatial and temporal distribution of human activities in marine areas to achieve ecological, economic and social objectives that have been specified through a political process.[85] The ambition of the EU is – as mentioned – to make this approach part of the international marine governance by new initiatives in 2017. These ecosystem-based EU directives on the protecting of the ecosystems are not only relevant in the marine territory of the EU as the just mentioned initiative of the Commission as well as the cooperation in the OSPAR makes it possible to ensure that the standards and principles have extraterritorial effects. In the Arctic – where active cooperation between major international, regional, and local actors is an important part of marine governance – such an initiative is of importance for the protection of the environment and its ecosystems.

EU's maritime management by the Offshore Safety Directive

As already stated in section two, the EU has implemented all IMO's standards on maritime activities through secondary legislation in the form of directives and regulations. The EU has also established the European Marine Safety Agency (EMSA) to ensure effective implementation. The EMSA works with EU and EEA member states to develop technical solutions and provide technical assistance in satellite monitoring, etc. The EMSA CleanSeaNet satellite service offers all these member states a near-real-time marine-oil-spill and vessel-detection service. The service is a recognised global monitoring for environment and security (GMES) service, integrated within the national and regional oil-pollution surveillance and response chains. Each coastal state has access to this service.

The Offshore Safety Directive,[86] already discussed above, is based on the integrated approach used in modern EU law. The design of the directive is based on the recognised high standards applying in the North Sea.[87] It comprises rules on best global practice to be used by licensees, operators and owners taking the 'polluter pays principle' into account. The directive contributes to ensuring the protection of the marine environment by reference to ecosystem-based management.[88] It also involves public participation obligations in accordance with international conventions and declarations.[89] The preparation of the directive was not only focused on 'extending EU standards overseas,' but

> … It also proposes the creation of a voluntary code of conduct in which European companies commit to apply the same safety standards to their operations abroad, as they do in Europe.[90]

The directive includes references to OSPAR decision 98/3 on the disposal of disused offshore installations, regarding the obligations of private actors economically involved in the hydrocarbon activities.[91] This decision is based on the common approach that marine governance of offshore hydrocarbon extraction must involve all stakeholders.[92] Under the directive, operators must ensure that their capacity is backed up by independent verification as a necessary assurance system. It is clarified by the directive that holders of authorisation are the strictly liable 'operators' within the meaning of the Environmental Liability Directive.[93] National authorities are required to ensure that the licensee is financially liable for the prevention and remediation of environmental damage caused by offshore hydrocarbon operations carried out by, or on behalf of, the licensee or the operator.

The Offshore Safety Directive also has extraterritorial effect, as it is stated in the directive that EU and EEA member states must ensure that operators domiciled in their jurisdiction and responsible for operations outside the Union on request must report any circumstances of major accident in which they have been involved. If a Danish company such as, e.g., Maersk commences drilling activities in the Arctic beyond the Danish/Greenlandic EEZ and continental shelf, the Danish authorities are thus required to accept the relevance of these rules.

The EU and EEA member states are required to cooperate with their offshore neighbours on emergency response planning and emergency preparedness and response, and they must also establish mechanisms for reporting safety concerns. These EU/EEA obligations make the international obligations established by the IMO's OPPRC Convention more precise and legally binding – including the emergency response plans, taking into account the risk assessment undertaken as part of the major hazardous reporting. These elements of the directive significantly contribute to the extraterritorial effect of the standards and principles codified by it.

The Offshore Safety Directive amended the scope of the Environmental Liability Directive, which now includes all marine areas of EU and EEA member states. The Liability Directive avoids duplication with the international liability legislation that is effective in the EU and respects the supremacy of the international conventions with relevance to civil liability.

If the EUCJ is requested for a preliminary ruling in a case on the protection of the marine environment against hazardous pollution, the aims of the Offshore Safety Directive on effective response to emergencies and the support to best global practice that requires licensees, operators and owners to take primary responsibility for controlling the risks they create by their operations, will inspire the Court to a broad interpretation of the safety standards and environmental principles laid down in the Treaty and the secondary legislation to be interpreted. As illustrated in section one, the Court is balancing the respect for the territorial principle of international law and the 'external dimension' of EU's standards and principles.

Do the EU directives regulate offshore hydrocarbon activities in the Norwegian Arctic area?

The EEA Agreement includes the EU Hydrocarbon Licensing Directive.[94] This directive is designed to deal only with competitive aspects of member states' licensing producers, ensuring equal access to national binding rounds for entities in the entire EU and all EEA member states.[95]

Norway is currently arguing (as it has done since at least the implementation of the Hydrocarbon Licensing Directive)[96] that the scope of the EEA Agreement extends only to Norway's land territory, internal waters and territorial waters (a span of four nautical miles from land). Its argument is that the continental shelf falls outside the sphere of application of the EEA Agreement.[97] The general position of Norway is that it is only the content of EU legislation (and not its geographical scope) that is relevant.[98] The Norwegian position in the current debate concerning the relevance of the marine environmental directives described supra in section three is based on the same environmental arguments as those used in the EU directives. Since 2006 Norway itself has deployed an integrated management planning approach in its legislation covering the Arctic marine area.[99]

The current non-incorporation of the MSFD into the EEA Agreement was decided with reference to Norway's position. The other EEA members do not support Norway in this position,[100] accepting that the directive is of EEA relevance (as stated in its published form in the European *Official Journal*). The ESA, which is controlling the EEA/EFTA member states' loyalty to the EEA Agreement, has adopted a functional approach, following EUCJ practice. Currently, it states that the geographical scope of the EEA Agreement follows the territorial jurisdictions of the EEA/EFTA member states, including the EEZ and the continental shelf. The ESA has, however, not yet challenged the position of Norway in court.[101] The Norwegian position does not, however, constitute a situation in which the EU's marine and maritime policy has no impact on the Norwegian Arctic marine area. In 2011 Norway decided to strengthen the already close cooperation with the EU on the management of the marine environment further.[102] It is also the official policy of Norway as an EEA/EFTA member state to support the EU's foreign policy and maintain a close dialogue with the EU on developments in the High North. The Norwegian government highlights that the 'Northern Dimension' – along with Iceland and Russia – enables it to maintain a close dialogue with the EU in High North policy.[103] UNCLOS, together with the Treaty concerning Maritime Delimitation and Cooperation in the Barents Sea and the Arctic Ocean, which entered into force in 2011, are also important examples of cooperation between Norway and the EU on marine and maritime issues. The cooperation in OSPAR is – as already indicated in section two – of special importance for the common approach to an ecosystem-based sustainable management of Arctic marine areas. The reality of the Norwegian approach to the EU's marine and maritime legislation is – in many respects – the same as if this legislation was incorporated into the EEA Agreement.

On this basis, it is not a problem to conclude that the EU does have an impact on Norwegian Arctic marine governance of offshore hydrocarbon activities. The fact that Norway's EEA membership is formulated with reservations for Svalbard in certain respects is not relevant in this connection. It is the position of Norway – a position accepted by the commission on the limits of the continental shelf (CLCS)[104] – that the Svalbard Treaty covers only land territory, internal waters and territorial waters within a distance of approximately four nautical miles. There are no offshore activities within this area, which is protected by strong environmental legislation, and the sea areas beyond four nautical miles of Svalbard are covered by Norwegian legislation.

Do the EU directives regulate offshore hydrocarbon activities in the Danish Arctic area?

How far the EU may rely on the Kingdom of Denmark's jurisdiction in the Arctic as its basis for taking a more active role in the governance of Arctic offshore hydrocarbon activities is unclear. The Faroese authorities, unlike those of Greenland, have responsibility for the marine environment and search-and-rescue responsibilities. The Danish Act on Greenlandic Self-government[105] gives powers to the Greenlandic authorities. The competence in offshore extraction has been taken over by Greenland, and the Greenlandic Mineral Resources Act now regulates such activities.[106] The Greenlandic Government (Naalakkersuisut) and the Bureau of Minerals and Petroleum requires operators granted licences to ensure that safety and emergency response measures are taken both outside and inside the territorial waters. The competence and responsibility to protect the marine areas from three to two hundred nautical miles from the shore to the boundary between Greenland and Canada and Iceland is still under the competence of the authorities of the Kingdom of Denmark.[107] The Danish Ministry of Defence,[108] the Ministry of Business,[109] the Ministry of Justice[110] and the Ministry of Environment and Agriculture share the responsibility of marine monitoring and marine environmental emergency response. It is the last-mentioned ministry that holds legislative responsibility for the protection of the just-mentioned marine waters. The Danish Marine Environmental Protection Act[111] covers the environmental protection of the Greenlandic marine area without protection of special habitats.[112] Denmark's implementation of the EU directives mentioned above in sections three and four does not cover the Arctic area.

The EU has a clear interest in the Arctic, and a policy on ecosystem-based marine management, including in extraterritorial waters that it wishes to promote:[113]

> … EU Member States' overseas territories give a worldwide dimension to European Maritime Policy.

As described in section one, the Danish authorities have loyalty obligations and a narrow discretionary power in issues of relevance for EU's international relations. One could therefore argue that, based on the EU's legal order, Denmark has the power to use its legal competences and responsibilities on the protection of the Greenlandic Arctic marine area only in so far as they do not harm EU interests.[114] There is no strong Greenlandic interest that could constitute a reason for Denmark not to respect the principle of loyalty to and cooperation with the EU on the Arctic marine management. On this basis, it is possible to conclude that the EU may have impact upon the Danish Arctic marine governance of offshore hydrocarbon activities.

The joint declaration of 19 March 2015 between the EU and Greenland/Denmark established a new basis for relations between the parties, comprising several common objectives, including the sustainable management of the marine environment.[115] To achieve their common goals and develop their partnership, the relation established by this partnership aims to facilitate consultation and policy dialogue on issues of common interest and any other areas within the declaration. The EU has also offered various funding opportunities for Greenlandic projects that can promote a sustainable development.[116]

It is also stated in the Kingdom of Denmark's Strategy 2011–2020. A joint strategy between Denmark, Greenland and the Faroe Islands that it is of importance for the realisation of this strategy to ensure a close partnership with the EU.[117]

Conclusion

As described earlier in sections one and two, the EU uses both its internal and external regulatory power to drive the international negotiations on new measures, both through its member states, its own legal personality and its internal regulatory power. The effectiveness of the EU's role as an important actor in the marine governance of the Arctic is based partly on EU implementation of regional and international conventions and principles within its own environmental marine legislation, and partly on the principles and doctrines developed by the EUCJ (followed by the EFTA Court),[118] which together have developed a vertical harmonisation of international/regional, EU and national environmental law. The EU directives described above in sections three and four are increasingly interrelated and reflect the EU's role in multilateral agreements. The EU directives support the international and regional conventions, making it mandatory for the EU and EEA member states concerned to cooperate with other states.

The principles and doctrines elaborated by the EUCJ are also very important for the EU's internal and external competences, as the Union promotes the Europeanisation of Arctic environmental policy and law.[119] It is explained above, how EUCJ as well as EU legislation are currently working on filling in the gaps.

EU environmental law is increasingly interrelated, reflecting, as well, its role in multilateral agreements and its use of its internal regulatory power ensuring a vertical harmonisation of standards and principles.

As the EU's standards on maritime and marine management are harmonised with international and regional standards – especially with the OSPAR standards – the EEA member states can be pushed to respect both direct and indirect input from the EU membership on EU Arctic responsibilities.[120] The EU's directives create the basis for a merged approach to the open marine system in which the OSPAR also covers sea areas outside the jurisdictions of the EU and EEA member states. The shared membership in OSPAR of the EU and the states concerned – Sweden, Finland, Iceland, Norway and Denmark – also affects the indirect impact of the EU's marine environmental legislation on all parts of their Arctic marine areas. The initiative of the Commissions on MSP mentioned in section three is just one of several examples of the role that the EU is playing in its cooperation with other global regulatory actors. On this basis, the EU can be described as an Arctic actor, to the extent that it is in[121]

> … constant flux, fragmented, balancing somewhere between intergovernmental bargaining and multi-level governance, the institutional structure of marine governance should, then, be understood as the interconnection of intergovernmental, supranational and transnational arenas.

The EU also acts when exercising its extraterritorial effects, by effectively imposing its standards and criteria on all companies under its EU and EEA member states' jurisdiction acting in the Arctic by means of the Offshore Safety Directive. It is an approach well-known from several international and regional instruments that marine governance of offshore hydrocarbon extraction must involve cooperation and responsibility, including also private actors.[122] In its 2001 resolution on 'The High North: Opportunities and Policy Challenges, the EEA Joint Parliamentary Committee stated'[123] that it welcomes the European Parliament's resolution on a sustainable EU policy for the High North, acknowledges the EU's role as a major contributor to Arctic research, and supports the EU's request for observer status in the Arctic Council. The resolution also stresses that the natural resources of the Arctic are of utmost importance not only for the nations in the area, but also for Europe as a whole (including the EEA) and beyond. As mentioned above, the Nordic Arctic countries – Denmark, Norway, Sweden, Finland and Iceland – are all members of the EEA Agreement.

The combination of the EU's external commitments as a party to regional and international agreements and the principles of sincere cooperation and loyalty contribute to the extraterritorial effect of EU's standards and principles on environmental protection.[124] The development of case law in respect to the territorial relevance of EU's directives covering the EEZ as well as the continental shelf, the possibility of having secondary legislation with extraterritorial effects and the broad application of the 'duty of loyalty' ensures the EU a strong position as a facilitator in the development of Arctic maritime environmental law. While recognising the primary responsibility and competences of the Arctic states, the legal competence of the EU described in this chapter is a basis for the future 'joined-up' action, as this action is presented in the proposal of the Commission and the High Representative.[125]

Notes

1 Kern and Gilek 2015, 3f.; van Tatenhove 2015, 37 and Stoessel et al. 2014, 45ff.
2 Riedel 2014, 37f; and Bohman and Langlet 2015, 53.
3 European Union, 2007.
4 EEA Agreement (1994).
5 There are also special institutions and services that are important for EU's possibilities e.g. financial support to research, and capacity building, see European Maritime Safety Agency 2010, 29ff.
6 The Lisbon Treaty consists of the Treaty on the European Union (TEU), the Treaty on the Function of the European Union (TFEU) and some protocols.
7 Article 191 (4) TEUF.
8 Arnesen, 20.
9 European Parliament and Council, 2013a. Directive 2013/30/EU of 12 June 2013 on safety of offshore oil and gas operations and amending Directive 2004/35/EC Text with EEA relevance. (OJ L 178, 28.6.2013, 66).
10 Deloitte and Stevens and Bolton LLP, 39. Iceland is not recognised as such by the five Arctic coastal states.
11 There is no generally accepted definition, see Molenaar et al. 2014b, 4.
12 Article 47 TEU. Concerning the express and implied competences under the Lisbon Treaty, see Eeckhout 2011, 120ff.
13 Article 3 TEU states these goals of the Lisbon Treaty. It includes other goals, such as a balanced economic growth, a high competitive social market economy, full employment and social progress in Europe.
14 Articles 4 (1) and 5 (1)-(2) TEU and Article 4(1) TFEU.
15 Article 4 (2) TFEU.
16 Article 4(3) TEU.
17 Article 288 TEUF.
18 Article 4(3) TEU.
19 Articles 258 and 260 TEUF.
20 Environmental standards are normally minimum standards based on Articles 192–193 TEUF.
21 See *inter alia*, the EUCJ C-204/09 *Flachglas Torgau*, paragraph 37.
22 See Case C-366/10 *The Air Transport Association of America and others,* on extraterritorial effects of the European Parliament's and Council's directive 2008/101/EC of 19 November 2008, amending Directive 2003/87/EC so as to include the aviation activities in the scheme for greenhouse gas emission allowance trading within the Community (the EU ETS Directive), published in OJ L 8/2008, 3. Concerning this case and other examples of EU directives with extraterritorial effects, see Basse, 2016.
23 Article 191 TFEU.
24 See Case C-424/13 *Zuchtvieh-Export GmbH.* It is the preliminary ruling on the interpretation of Regulation(EC) no. 1/2005 on the protection of animals during transport and related operations.

25 C-592/14 *European Federation for Cosmetic Ingredients v. Secretary of State for Business, Innovation and Skill.* The marketing ban on cosmetics containing ingredients was established by the Regulation (EC) no. 1223/09 on cosmetic products.
26 Article 21 TEU.
27 Article 21(2) litra f) TEU.
28 Council of the EU, 2016.
29 European Parliament and Council 2013b.
30 Article 191(4) TEUF.
31 Delreux 2014, 1029.
32 The exclusive competence is stated in Article 3 TEU.
33 See Article 191(4) TFEU and Delreux 2014, 1029.
34 Articles 216(6) and 288 TFEU.
35 Developed by the ECJ in Case C-22/70 *Commission* v. *Council* (the AETR case).
36 The ECJ's judgment in Case C-181/73 *Haegeman* v. *Belgium*.
37 The importance of the UNECE Convention on Access to Information, Public Participation in Decision Making and Access to Justice in Environmental Matters (Aarhus Convention) in the application of the EU secondary legislation on environmental quality as well as the procedural rules – see e.g. C-237/07 *Janecek*; C-260/11 *Edwards*, and 404/13 *ClientEarth*– is an example on this case law.
38 See Case C-6/04 *Commission* v. *United Kingdom and Northern Ireland*; and a more general analysis of this by von Rossem 2013, 20.
39 See Case C-459/03 *MOX Plant* concerning the provisions of UNCLOS that have become part of the EU's legal order and are therefore within the exclusive jurisdiction of the ECJ.
40 Baudenbacher 2013, 9.
41 It is in other words based on a two-pillar structure in which the EU forms the one pillar, and EEA/EFTA the other.
42 Article 3 (5) TEU, concerning this see Baudenbacher 2010.
43 Concerning this institution and its competence, see the Norwegian Ministry of Foreign Affairs 2012, 23.
44 Graver 2004, 22ff. and Baudenbacher, 2005, 387ff.
45 Percival 2010.
46 Rothwell and Stephens 2010; and Molenaar 2014a, 133ff.
47 Koivurova 2011.
48 Jakobsen 2014, 218ff.
49 UNCLOS Article 234 gives the Arctic coastal states the competence to protect such ice-covered areas against damage caused by human activities.
50 Commission and the High Representative, 2016, 6; see European Commission 2016; and Commission COM(2012) 491 final, 10; see European Commission 2012.
51 The Habitat directive described infra in section three is a very strong and effective implementation of this convention by the EU. For the targets in the new biodiversity strategy, see European Commission 2011a.
52 Annex 5. Statement on: 'Towards an Ecosystem Approach to the Management of Human Activities.'
53 Agreement 2010–03.
54 Stoessel et al. 2014, 50f.
55 Hossain et al. 2014, 172f.
56 Rothwell and Stephens 2010, 363.
57 EU has implemented the obligations by the European Parliament and Council Directive 2009/20/EC on the insurance of ship-owners for maritime claims, OJ L 131, 28 May 2009, 128–121.
58 The Convention on the Maritime Organization from 1948 that sets out the establishment of the International Maritime Organisation (IMO) limiting the circle of accepted parties to national states. In 1974 the Commission and the IMO

Secretary-General signed an agreement on cooperation by which the Commission was accepted to participate in meetings with the status as an observer.

59 Article 4 (3) TEU.
60 European Commission, 2005.
61 This is concluded by the Count in the Case C-45/7 *Commission v. Greece.* In this case a proposal on monitoring the compliance of ships and port facilities with the requirements of the International Convention for Safety of the Life at Sea (SOLAS Convention), and the International Ship and Port Facility Security Code (ISPS Code) could not be presented by Greece to the IMO Maritime Safety Committee.
62 Concerning the importance of this convention in the Arctic, see Lesser and Koivurova 2014, 179ff.
63 European Parliament and Council directive 2011/92/EC of 13 December 2011 on the assessment of certain public and private projects on the environment (OJ L26/2011, 1), as amended by Directive 2014/52/EU of 16 April 2014 (OJ L124/2014, 1).
64 It was adopted in 2003 and came into force in 2010.
65 European Parliament and Council directive 2001/42/EC of 27 June 2001 on the assessment of the effects of certain plans and programmes on the environment (OJ L197/2001, 39).
66 ESPON 2013, 16ff. and 29ff.
67 Council of EU, 2016.
68 European Commission 2006a, 2007b, 2007c and 2014a, and Council of EU, 2016.
69 Borja et al. 2010, 4ff.; and Josefsson 2015, 26 and 78.
70 Council Directive 92/43/EEC of 21 May 1992 on the Conservation of natural Habitats and the Wild Fauna and Flora, OJ L 206, 22 July 1992, 7–10.
71 European Parliament and Council Directive 2009/147/EC of 30 November 2009 on the conservation of wild birds, OJ L 20, 26 January 2010, 6–25.
72 Commission staff working document *Ocean Energy*, 16: European Commission 2014b.
73 The UN Convention on Biodiversity from 1992, Council of Europe's Convention on Conservation of European Wildlife and Natural Habitats (the Bern Convention) from 1979, and the UNEP Convention on Migratory Species (the Bonn Convention) from 1979.
74 See also the Commission's *Guidelines for the Establishment of the Natura 2000 Network in the Marine Environment. Application of the Habitats and Birds Directive* in European Commission 2007a.
75 See the judgment in the Case C-127/02 *Waddenzee.*
76 European Parliament and Council Directive 2011/92/EU of 13 December 2011 on the assessment of the effects of certain public and private projects on the environment, as amended by Directive 2014/52/EU of 16 April 2014, (OJ L26, 28 January 2012, 1 and OJ L 124, 25 April 2014, 1).
77 European Parliament and the Council Directive 2001/42/EC of 27 June 2001 on the assessment of effects of certain plans and programmes on the environment, OJ L 197, 21 July 2001, 30–37.
78 C-290/15 *Patrice D'Oultremont and Others.*
79 European Parliament and the Council Directive 2008/56/EC of 17 June 2008 establishing a framework for community action in the field of marine environmental policy, OJ L 164 of 25 June 2008, 19ff. Concerning the new approach in EU's marine environmental protection introduced by this directive, see Long 2011.
80 European Parliament and the Council Directive 2014/89/EU of 23 July 2014 establishing a framework for maritime spatial planning, OJ L 257, 135–145. Concerning the concept of marine spatial planning, see Ehler 2014, 199ff.

81 Jentoft and Chuenpagdee 2015, 21.
82 van Tatenhove 2015, 47.
83 Arnesen 2010, 23.
84 Commission and the High Representative, 2016, 13; see European Commission 2016.
85 UNESCO, 2009 and UNESCO 2014.
86 The European Parliament and of the Council directive 2013/30/EU of 12 June 2013 on safety of offshore oil and gas operations and amending Directive 2004/35/EC Text with EEA relevance. (OJ L 178, 28.6.2013, 66).
87 E.g. the Oil and Gas UK, see Trevisanut 2014, 659.
88 This relation to the MSFD is stated in the preamble and in article 8 of the Offshore Safety Directive.
89 Articles 4–6 of the directive concern the involvement of such an approach with reference to the UNECE Convention on Access to Information, Public Participation in Decision-Making and Access to Justice in Environmental Matters (the Aarhus Convention) and Principle 10 of the Rio Declaration. Concerning this aspect of governance, see Trevisanut 2014, 662f.
90 European Commission, 2011b, 49.
91 Trevisanut 2014, 647f.
92 Citations from Trevisanut 2014, 648.
93 European Parliament and Council Directive 2004/35/EC of 21 April 2004 on the environmental liability with regard to the prevention and remedying of environmental damage (OJ L 143, 30 April 2004, 56), as amended the last time by the Offshore Safety Directive.
94 Arnesen 2010, 19ff.
95 European Commission, 2011b, 64.
96 The European Parliament and Council directive 94/22/EC of 30 May 1994 on the conditions for granting and using authorizations for the prospection, exploration and production of hydrocarbons (OJ L 164/1994, 3).
97 Norwegian Ministry of Foreign Affairs 2012, 13, concerning the understanding of Article 126 EEA.
98 It is stated by the 'ALT Law Firm' in a Memo of 13 March 2013.
99 Sjafjell and Halvorsson, 2014, and Ehler 2014, 200.
100 EEA Joint Parliamentary Committee 2012, 9.
101 See e.g. EFTA Surveillance Authority 1999; and more generally Arnesen 2010, 26.
102 Norwegian Ministry of Foreign Affairs 2012, 43.
103 Norwegian Ministry of Foreign Affairs 2012, 30ff.
104 CLCS is the authority that can recommend rights on the outer continental shelf based on the criteria mentioned in article 76 to UNCLOS, concerning this see Molenaar et al. 2014b, 6; on the Norwegian case, see Byers and Baker 2013, 21.
105 Danish Act No. 473 of 12 June 2009 on Greenlandic Self-Government.
106 Inatsisartut Act No. 7 of 7 December 2009.
107 Greenland has only taken over the marine environmental tasks within its internal waters sand territorial sea, ie, the internal waters and the waters extending up to three nautical miles from the baseline.
108 Since 2000, the Ministry of Defence has been responsible for monitoring the marine environment, checking compliance with the provisions of the Danish legislation.
109 The Ministry of Business has the responsibility for the security of ships.
110 The Ministry of Justice has the responsibility is responsible of enforcement issues.
111 Danish Royal Decision No. 1035 of 22 October 2004 on the Marine Environmental Act, coming into force in Greenland with effect on the area beyond three nautical miles of the coast of Greenland. The very unclear division of

responsibility between the Greenlandic and Danish authorities has been criticized by the Danish Rigsrevisionen, 2013.
112 It is the Danish military authorities that act in situations of oil spill in this Arctic area to fulfil the international obligations of the Kingdom of Denmark.
113 European Commission 2006b, 44. See also Tedsen and Cavalieri 2014, 241f.
114 This right for Denmark to act in the interest of its OTCs was ensured by Declaration No. 25 of the treaty on European Union attached to the earlier Maastricht treaty from 1992. The declaration is not appended to the Treaty of Lisbon.
115 The declaration is made with reference to Council of Europe (2014).
116 Pelaudeix 2015.
117 Ministry of Foreign Affairs 2011, 52.
118 The drafters of the EEA Agreement formulated homogeneity rules, which essentially bind the EFTA Court to follow relevant ECJ case law; see Baudenbacher 2004.
119 von Rossem 2013, 20.
120 Concerning the special challenges related to a sustainable hydrocarbon development in the Arctic, see Koivurova and Hossain, 2012, and Luszczuk 2014.
121 Citation from van Tatenhove 2015, 37.
122 Citations from Trevisanut 2014, 648.
123 At its 36th meeting on 13 April 2011 in Longyearbyen, Svalbard.
124 It is both a legal issue and an indirect diplomatic tool; see the European Parliament 2012, 15ff. and 39.
125 Commission See and the High Representative of the Union for Foreign Affairs and Security Policy, 2016.

References

ALT Law Firm. 2013. 'Offshore Safety Directive: EEA Relevance and Geographical Application.' Memo of 13 March 2013, Oslo.

Arnesen, F. 2010. 'The EEA Agreement and Activities Offshore.' In *Scandinavian Institute of Maritime Law Yearbook*, 19–26. Marius No. 400. Oslo: Oslo University.

Basse, E.M. 2016 (in press). The European Union's Role in the Development of Global Environmental Law. In *Globalization: Strategies and Effects*, edited by B.J. Christensen. Berlin, Springer.

Baudenbacher, C. 2004. 'The EFTA Court: An Actor in the European Judicial Dialogue.' *Fordham International Journal* Vol. 28, No. 2: 353–391.

Baudenbacher, C. 2005. 'The Implementation of Decisions of the ECJ and the EFTA Court in Member States' Domestic Orders.' *Texas International Law Journal* Vol. 40: 383–416.

Baudenbacher, C. 2010. 'The EFTA Court Fifteen Years on.' www.eftacourt.int/fileadmin/user_upload/Files/News/2009/15_Years_EFTA_Court.pdf.

Baudenbacher, C. 2013. *The Judicial Dimension of the European Neighbourhood Policy*. EU Diplomacy Paper 08/2013. Bruges: College of Europe.

Bohman B. and D. Langlet. 2015. 'Float or Sinker for Europe's Seas? The Role of Law in Marine Governance.' In *Governing Europe's Marine Environment: Europeanisation of Regional Seas or Regionalisation of EU Policies?* edited by M. Gilek and K. Kern, 53–73. King's College London Corbett Centre for Maritime Policy Studies Series. Farnham: Ashgate.

Borja, A., M. Elliott, J. Carstensen, A.S. Heiskanen and W. van de Bund. 2010. 'Marine Management: Towards an Integrated Implementation of the European Marine Strategy Framework and the Water Framework Directives.' *Marine Pollution*

Bulletin, doi:10.1016/j.marpolbul.2010.09.026. Epub 2010 Oct 20. Available at www.mosam.org/documents/Borja%20et%20al,%202010%20MPB%20WFD-MSFD.pdf (accessed 26 November 2015)

Byers, M. and J. Baker. 2013. *International Law and the Arctic*. Cambridge Studies in International and Comparative Law. Cambridge: Cambridge University Press.

Council of the EU. 2014. Council Decision 2014/137/EU of 14 March 2014 on Relations between the European Union on the one hand and Greenland and the Kingdom of Denmark on the other. *Official Journal* L 76, 15 March 2014: 1–5. Brussels: Council of the European Union.

Council of the EU. 2016. Council conclusions 10400/16 of 20 June 2016 on the Arctic. Foreign Affairs Council. Brussels: Council of the European Union.

Delreux, T. 2014. 'EU Actorness, Cohesiveness and Effectiveness in Environmental Affairs.' *Journal of European Public Policy* Vol. 21, No. 7: 1017–1032. doi: 10.1080/13501763.2014.912250.

EEA Agreement. 1994. Agreement on the European Economic Area. *Official Journal* L 1, 3 January 1994: 3ff.

EEA Joint Parliamentary Committee. 2012. *The Future of the EU Energy Policy and its Implications for the EEA*. Brussels the 27 November 2012: ref. 11183389. Available at www.efta.int/advisory-bodies/reports-resolutions-opinions/eea-jpc-resolutions (accessed the 26 November 2015).

Eeckhout, P. 2011. *EU External Relations Law*. 2nd edn. Oxford European Union Law Library. New York: Oxford University Press.

EFTA Surveillance Authority. 1999. Letter of formal notice: Failure to ensure compliance with Council Regulation (EEC) No. 1408/71. Brussels: European Free Trade Area Surveillance Authority.

Ehler, C.N. 2014. 'Pan-Arctic Marine Spatial Planning: An Idea Whose Time Has Come.' In *Arctic Marine Governance: Opportunities for Transatlantic Cooperation*, edited by E. Tedsen, S. Cavalieri and R.A. Kraemer, 199–213. Berlin: Springer.

ESPON (European Observatory Network Territorial Development and Cohesion). 2013. *Governance Case Studies: Arctic Ocean*. Luxembourg: ESPON European Seas and Territorial Development, Opportunities and Risks (ESaTDOR). Annex 8 to the Scientific Report. Applied Research 2013/5/1, Version 16 January 2013.

European Commission. 2005. Commission staff working document: Procedural framework for the adoption of Community or common positions for the IMO related issues and rules governing their expression in the IMO. SEC(2005) 449. Brussels: European Commission.

European Commission. 2006a. *Halting the Loss of Biodiversity by 2010 and Beyond: Sustaining Ecosystem Services for Human Well-Being*. Communication from the Commission to the Council, the European Parliament, the European Economic and Social Committee and the Committee of the Regions of 22 May 2006: COM (2006) 216 final. Brussels: European Commission.

European Commission. 2006b. *Towards a Future Maritime Policy for the Union: A European Vision for the Oceans and Seas: How Inappropriate to call This Planet Earth When it is Quite Clearly Ocean*. Green Paper. Communication from the Commission to the Council, the European Parliament, the European Economic and Social Committee and the Committee of the Regions of 7 June 2006: COM (2006) 275 final. Brussels: European Commission.

European Commission. 2007a. *Guidelines for the Establishment of the Natura 2000 Network in the Marine Environment: Application of the Habitats and Birds Directive*. Brussels: European Commission.

European Commission. 2007b. *An Integrated Maritime Policy for the European Union.* Communication from the Commission to the Council, the European Parliament, the European Economic and Social Committee and the Committee of the Regions of 10 October 2007: COM (2007) 575 final. Brussels: European Commission.

European Commission. 2007c. *An Integrated Maritime Policy for the European Union.* Communication staff working document accompanying document to the Communication from the Commission to the European Parliament, the Council, the European Economic and Social Committee and the Committee of the Regions of 10 October 2007: SEC (2007) 1278. Brussels: European Commission.

European Commission. 2011a. *Our Life Insurance, Our Natural Capital: An EU Biodiversity Strategy to 2020.* Communication from the Commission to the Council, the European Parliament, the European Economic and Social Committee and the Committee of the Regions of 3 March 2011: COM (2011) 244 final. Brussels: European Commission.

European Commission. 2011b. *Impact Assessment Annex I.* Commission Staff Working Paper. Accompanying the document 'Proposal for a Regulation of the European Parliament and of the Council on safety offshore oil and gas prospection, exploration and production activities' of 27 October 2011: SEC (2011) 1292 final. Brussels: European Commission.

European Commission. 2012. *Progress of the EU's Integrated Maritime Policy.* Report from the Commission to the Council, the European Parliament, the European Economic and Social Committee and the Committee of the Regions of 11 September 2012: COM (2012) 491 final. Brussels: European Commission.

European Commission. 2014a. *Civil Liability, Financial Security and Compensation Claims for Offshore Oil and Gas Activities in the European Economic Area.* Brussels: European Commission, DG Energy.

European Commission. 2014b. *Ocean Energy: Action Needed to Deliver the Potential of Ocean Energy By 2020 and Beyond.* Commission Staff Working Document Impact Assessment. Accompanying the document 'Communication' of 20 January 2014: SWD (2014) 13 final. Brussels: European Commission.

European Commission and the High Representative of the Union for Foreign Affairs and Security Policy. 2016. *International Ocean Governance: An Agenda for the Future of Our Oceans.* Joint Communication to the European Parliament, the Council, the European Economic and Social Committee and the Committee of the Regions. JOIN (2016) 49 final. Brussels: European Commission.

European Maritime Safety Agency. 2010. *Pollution Preparedness and Response Activities.* Lisbon: European Maritime Safety Agency.

European Parliament. 2012. *The Extraterritorial Effects of Legislation and Polices in the EU and US.* AFET. Brussels: European Parliament. Directorate-General for External Policies. Policy Department.

European Parliament and Council. 2013b. *Living Well, Within the Limits of Our Planet.* Decision No. 1386/2013/EU of 20 November 2013 on a general Union Environmental Action Programme to 2020. Seventh EU Environment Action Programme. *Official Journal* L 354, 28 December 2013: 171–200.

European Union. 2007. Treaty of Lisbon amending the Treaty on European Union and the Treaty establishing the European Community, signed at Lisbon, 13 December 2007. Official Journal C 306, 17 December 2007: 1–271.

Graver, H.P. 2004. *The Effects of EFTA Court Jurisprudence on the Legal Orders of the EFTA States Arena.* Oslo: Oslo University Centre for European Studies. Working Paper 04/18.

Hossain, K., T. Koivurova and G. Zojer. 2014. 'Understanding Risks Associated with Offshore Hydrocarbon Development.' In *Arctic Marine Governance: Opportunities for Transatlantic Cooperation*, edited by E. Tedsen, S. Cavalieri and R.A. Kraemer, 159–176. Berlin: Springer.

Jakobsen, I.U. 2014. 'Marine Protected Areas as a Tool to Ensure Environmental Protection of the Marine Arctic: Legal Aspects.' In *Arctic Marine Governance: Opportunities for Transatlantic Cooperation*, edited by E. Tedsen, S. Cavalieri and R.A. Kraemer, 215–233. Berlin: Springer.

Jentoft, S. and R. Chuenpagdee. 2015. 'The 'New' Marine Governance: Assessing Governability.' In *Governing Europe's Marine Environment: Europeanisation of Regional Seas or Regionalisation of EU Policies?* edited by M. Gilek and K. Kern, 15–34. King's College London Corbett Centre for Maritime Policy Studies Series. Farnham: Ashgate.

Josefsson, H. 2015. 'Good Ecological Status: Advancing the Ecology of Law.' Ll. D. diss., Uppsala University.

Kern, K. and M. Gilek. 2015. 'Governing Europe's Marine Environment: Key Topics and Challenges.' In *Governing Europe's Marine Environment: Europeanisation of Regional Seas or Regionalisation of EU Policies?* edited by M. Gilek and K. Kern, 1–12. King's College London Corbett Centre for Maritime Policy Studies Series. Farnham: Ashgate.

Koivurova, T. 2011. 'The Actions of the Arctic States Respecting the Continental Shelf: A Reflective Essay.' *Ocean Development and International Law* Vol. 42, No. 3: 16. doi:10.1080/00908320.2011.592470.

Koivurova, T. and K. Hossain. 2012. 'Hydrocarbon Development in the Offshore Arctic: Can it be Done Sustainably?' *Oil, Gas and Energy Law Intelligence* Vol. 10, No. 2: 1–29.

Lesser, P. and T. Koivurova. 2014. 'Impact Assessments and the New Arctic Geo-Environment.' In *Arctic Marine Governance: Opportunities for Transatlantic Cooperation*, edited by E. Tedsen, S. Cavalieri and R.A. Kraemer, 179–198. Berlin: Springer.

Long, R. 2011. 'The Marine Strategy Framework Directive: A New European Approach to the Regulation of the Marine Environment, Marine Natural Resources and Marine Ecological Services.' *Journal of Energy and Natural Resources Law* Vol. 29, No. 1: 1–44.

Łuszczuk, M. 2014. 'Developing Oil and Gas Resources in Arctic Waters.' In *The Strategic Assessment of Development of the Arctic: An Assessment Conducted for the European Union*, edited by A. Stępień et al. Brussels: European Union. Accessible at www.arcticinfo.eu/images/pdf/SADA_report.pdf.

Ministry of Foreign Affairs. 2011. *Denmark, Greenland and the Faroe Islands: Kingdom of Denmark Strategy for the Arctic 2011–2020*. Copenhagen: Ministry of Foreign Affairs.

Molenaar, E.J. 2014a. 'Status and Reform of International Arctic Shipping Law.' In *Arctic Marine Governance: Opportunities for Transatlantic Cooperation*, edited by E. Tedsen, S. Cavalieri and R.A. Kraemer, 127–157. Berlin: Springer.

Molenaar, E.J., T. Koivurova, E. Tedsen, A. Reid and K. Hossain. 2014b. 'Introduction to the Arctic.' In *Arctic Marine Governance: Opportunities for Transatlantic Cooperation*, edited by E. Tedsen, S. Cavalieri and R.A. Kraemer, 3–19. Berlin: Springer.

Norwegian Ministry of Foreign Affairs. 2012. 'The EEA Agreement and Norway's Other Agreements with the EU.' *Meld. St. 5 (2012–2013)* Report to the Storting (White Paper). Oslo: Norwegian Ministry of Foreign Affairs.

Pelaudeix, C. 2015. 'EU–Greenland Relations and Sustainable Development in the Arctic.' In *Global Challenges in the Arctic Region: Sovereignty, Environment and Geopolitical Balance*, edited by Elena Conde and Pérez Sara Iglesia. Farnham: Ashgate.

Percival, R.V. 2010. 'Liability for Environmental Harm and Emerging Global Environmental Law.' *Maryland Journal of International Law* Vol. 25: 37–63.

Riedel, A. 2014. 'The Arctic Marine Environment.' In *Arctic Marine Governance: Opportunities for Transatlantic Cooperation*, edited by E. Tedsen, S. Cavalieri and R.A. Kraemer, 21–43. Berlin: Springer.

Rigsrevisionen. 2013. Report of September 2013 to the Public Accounts Committee on Denmark's performance in the Arctic. Copenhagen: Rigsrevisionen.

Rothwell, R. and T. Stephens. 2010. *The International Law of the Sea*. Oxford: Hart Publishing.

Sjafjell, B. and A. Halvorssen. 2014. 'The Legal Status of Oil and Gas Exploitation in the Arctic: The Case of Norway.' In University of Oslo Faculty of Law Legal Studies Research Paper Series No. 2015–17. Version of 6 August 2015.

Stoessel, S., E. Tedsen, S. Cavalieri and A. Riedel. 2014. 'Environmental Governance in the Marine Arctic.' In *Arctic Marine Governance: Opportunities for Transatlantic Cooperation*, edited by E. Tedsen, S. Cavalieri and R.A. Kraemer, 45–69. Berlin: Springer.

Tedsen, E. and S. Cavalieri. 2014. 'EU-US Cooperation to Enhance Arctic Marine Governance.' In *Arctic Marine Governance: Opportunities for Transatlantic Cooperation*, edited by E. Tedsen, S. Cavalieri and R.A. Kraemer, 237–262. Berlin: Springer.

Trevisanut, S. 2014. 'The Role of Private Actors in Offshore Energy: Shifting Models of Participation.' *International Journal of Marine and Coastal Law* 29: 645–665.

UNESCO, 2009. Marine Spatial Planning. A step-by-step approach towards Ecosystem – based management, IOC Manuals and Guides, No. 53, the Intergovernmental Oceanographic Commission.

UNESCO, 2014. A guide to evaluating marine spatial plans, IOC Manuals and Guides, No. 70, the Intergovernmental Oceanographic Commission.

van Tatenhove, J.P.M. 2015. 'Marine Governance: Institutional Capacity-building in a Multi-level Governance Setting.' In *Governing Europe's Marine Environment: Europeanisation of Regional Seas or Regionalisation of EU Policies?* edited by M. Gilek and K. Kern, 35–52. King's College London Corbett Centre for Maritime Policy Studies Series. Farnham: Ashgate.

von Rossem, J.W. 2013. 'The Autonomy of EU Law: More or Less?' In *Between Autonomy and Dependence*, edited by R.A. Wessel and S. Blockmans, 13–46. The Hague: Asser Press.

Yang, T. and Percival, R. 2009. 'The Emergence of Global Environmental Law.' *Ecology Law Quarterly* Vol. 36: 615–664.

5 Indigenous rights in the marine Arctic

Rachael Lorna Johnstone[1]

Introduction

Because of the nature of the marine environment, with its constantly shifting water column and the living species within it, offshore hydrocarbon activities have impacts that can be felt by Arctic communities living hundreds of miles from the site of origin. Indigenous communities that rely on traditional subsistence activities are more vulnerable than most other populations. At the same time, indigenous peoples are also more extensively protected by international law than non-indigenous communities. Hydrocarbon developers in the marine Arctic must, therefore, remain cognisant of the possible consequences of their projects for indigenous communities, the potential legal issues that might arise and the measures they can take to uphold indigenous rights and prevent violations. This is not only a matter of social responsibility but also a pragmatic concern. If an activity is found to be unlawful, it may be halted, and compensation will be payable to affected parties. Even a possibility of illegality can lead to time-consuming litigation with major costs for industry in terms of direct legal expenses, manpower hours, inactive hardware and idle employees.[2]

International law is usually binding only on states and rarely directly specifies obligations for corporations. However, states must exercise due diligence to ensure that corporations (and other non-state actors) do not encroach upon or otherwise impede human rights and the rights of indigenous peoples. States are also required to facilitate remedies under domestic law. Therefore, although the state is almost always the respondent in a human rights application, an international finding can require it to amend or even halt activities of hydrocarbon corporations. The mechanisms available under international law through which indigenous individuals and communities can seek redress are relatively weak and sometimes result in only recommendations or views that the state is not obliged to follow to the letter.[3] However, the Arctic states are all keen to be seen upholding their international obligations in good faith and therefore tend to respond to adverse findings.

This chapter will demonstrate that hydrocarbon development in the marine Arctic can be undertaken in a manner compatible with indigenous rights, and it identifies the key considerations that help to ensure that activities are compliant with international law. It explores the rights of indigenous peoples in light of the UN Declaration on the Rights of Indigenous Peoples (UNDRIP), treaty law, and jurisprudence of human rights courts and monitoring committees. At the core is the principle of the right of indigenous peoples to self-determination and governance over their natural resources. These rights are manifested more concretely through land claims and property rights; cultural expression and continuity; rights to privacy, the home and family life; and the highest attainable standard of health. These substantive rights are protected by procedural safeguards, which, for reasons of space, will be summarised only briefly towards the end of this chapter.

Sources of indigenous rights in the Arctic

United Nations Declaration on the Rights of Indigenous Peoples

The most influential contemporary instrument in any discussion of indigenous rights is the aforementioned UNDRIP. Agreed by the General Assembly with a thumping majority of 143–4 (11 abstentions), the four states that voted negatively have since each endorsed UNDRIP.[4] Russia abstained, and has since indicated that it will take UNDRIP into account in its domestic affairs but only to the extent that it is compatible with the Russian constitution.[5] In sum, all the Arctic states have indicated their support in principle for UNDRIP and a political willingness to pay heed to it.

A General Assembly resolution can never of itself constitute customary international law, but it may be evidence of *opinio iuris*.[6] However, the comments of the states' representatives when UNDRIP was adopted and the careful wording of the four latecomers to the fold indicate that states are not willing to accept UNDRIP as a binding document *per se*. Instead, it is referred to as 'aspirational' and 'non-binding'.[7] In any case, *opinio iuris* must always be complemented by state practice in order to form customary law; while some states, particularly in Latin America, have taken steps to incorporate UNDRIP into domestic law, this is not sufficiently widespread from which to deduce any general conclusions.[8] It is a form of 'soft law.' Soft law is 'not law and [does] not need to be in order to influence conduct in the desired manner'.[9]

Support for UNDRIP is strong in the Nordic countries, with the Kingdom of Denmark, Finland and Norway even proselytising the reluctant Canada in 2009 during the latter's Universal Periodic Review at the Human Rights Council.[10] Canada's endorsement the following year was cautious and conditional with the erstwhile government emphasising its non-binding nature.[11] Canada was the only state that refused to endorse the Outcome Document of the 2014 World Conference on Indigenous Peoples and reiterated that neither the Outcome Document nor UNDRIP had legal force.[12]

The Trudeau campaign and election in Canada in 2015 put UNDRIP centre-stage in a newfound commitment to reconciliation between mainstream and indigenous communities. In direct contrast to his predecessor, Trudeau promised to implement UNDRIP in its entirety into Canadian law. His government's position is that UNDRIP constitutes 'international minimum standards'.[13] Carolyn Bennett, Minister of Indigenous and Northern Affairs, declared that Canada is 'now a full supporter of the Declaration without qualification. We intend nothing less than to adopt and implement the declaration in accordance with the Canadian Constitution.'[14] The caveat was not lost on Canada's indigenous communities: the Canadian constitution will apparently take precedence.

Across the border, UNDRIP was at first recognised as having 'both political and legal force' but not legal authority when the United States first expressed its support.[15] In 2016, the United States justified its rejection of the new American Declaration on the Rights of Indigenous Peoples (ADRIP, see below) by declaring 'its longstanding belief that implementation of the United Nations Declaration on the Rights of Indigenous Peoples should remain the focus of the OAS and its Member States' – an important example of *opinio iuris* in support of UNDRIP.

Many of the principles that UNDRIP contains are reaffirmations of customary law and treaty law. Further, the very existence of the Declaration is influencing state practice, and as this happens, customary international law may crystallise.[16] The UN human rights monitoring committees are beginning to use UNDRIP as a baseline in their constructive dialogue with states' parties (see below), and it is increasingly being cited in domestic proceedings and has even found its way into debates of the International Whaling Commission.[17]

ILO Convention 169

Of the Arctic states, only Denmark and Norway are parties to the sole treaty devoted to the rights of indigenous peoples.[18] The Indigenous and Tribal Peoples Convention, known also as ILO Convention 169, promises general human rights to indigenous persons but goes beyond the individual rights of most human rights treaties by ensuring their collective rights, especially to culture and identity, land and natural resources. It replaced the earlier Convention 107 from 1957 which had taken an assimilationist approach.[19] ILO Convention 169 does not go as far as UNDRIP, requiring only consultation but not free, prior and informed consent, before decisions are taken with consequences for indigenous rights.[20]

Trade unions and industrial organisations can submit representations to ILO's Governing Body if they believe a state is not acting in compliance with an ILO Convention.[21] The governing body then establishes a three-person committee to review such representations and make recommendations as appropriate. One such representation has been brought under ILO Convention 169 in respect of Greenland.[22]

United Nations human rights treaties

The International Covenant on Economic, Social and Cultural Rights (ICESCR) and the International Covenant on Civil and Political Rights (ICCPR) together implement the Universal Declaration of Human Rights.[23] The Convention on the Elimination of Racial Discrimination (CERD) also provides important protections for indigenous peoples.[24] All eight Arctic states are parties to the ICCPR and CERD, and all but the United States are parties to the ICESCR. Each of these treaties has a monitoring committee that is tasked with reviewing states' performance through periodic reports. They can also review communications from persons or groups that claim their rights have been violated, although states must either join an additional protocol to this effect or give explicit consent.[25] At the time of writing, the United States was the only Arctic state not to allow persons under its jurisdiction to send communications to the Human Rights Committee under the ICCPR, and only the United States and Canada do not allow communications under the CERD. The process under the ICESCR is much more recent, coming into force only in 2013; so far in the Arctic, only Finland has accepted the procedure. Nevertheless, views on communications from around the world are instructive in clarifying the legal obligations of all states parties to the parent treaties, irrespective of those states' positions on the communications processes. The monitoring committees have also been prolific in their development of general comments that are detailed explanations of points of treaty law addressed to all states parties.

Regional mechanisms for the protection of indigenous rights

Without addressing indigenous rights directly, both the European Convention on Human Rights (ECHR) and the American Convention on Human Rights (ACHR) have triggered relevant case law on indigenous rights under rights to property, the home, family, freedom of information and culture.[26] All six European Arctic states are parties to the ECHR and, *ipso facto*, allow applications to the European Court of Human Rights.

Across the Atlantic, neither Canada nor the United States are parties to the ACHR, and so petitions cannot be brought in respect of either state before the Inter-American Court of Human Rights. Canada and the United States are, however, both members of the Organisation of American States (OAS) and are monitored by the Inter-American Commission on Human Rights, which holds them to the standards of the American Declaration of the Rights and Duties of Man (ADRDM).[27] Individuals, groups and NGOs can send petitions to the commission for an investigation.[28] Much of the ACHR and the ADRDM overlap, so jurisprudence from the Court, especially regarding the Latin American states in the OAS, clarifies the obligations of the North American Arctic states in the OAS system. In June 2016, the OAS adopted by consensus the ADRIP.[29] It follows much of UNDRIP (including on free, prior and informed consent) but includes a few additional provisions, such as an explicit prohibition of genocide 'in any form' and the right of peoples in voluntary isolation to remain free from outside contact.[30] Both Canada and the United States objected to the text, indicating their preference to focus their attentions on UNDRIP. While the ADRIP may influence developments in Latin America (and perhaps even customary international law) it cannot be expected – yet – to have much impact in the Arctic.[31]

Human and indigenous rights in the middle of the ocean: *Ratione Loci*

The concept of indigenous 'land' in international law is not limited to *terra firma* but extends to 'the total environment of the areas which the peoples concerned occupy or otherwise use.'[32] This includes not only land which they permanently occupy but also areas 'to which they have traditionally had access for their subsistence and traditional activities' including coastal and ocean spaces used for hunting and fishing.[33] UNDRIP recognises indigenous peoples' rights 'to maintain and strengthen their distinctive spiritual relationship with their traditionally owned or otherwise occupied and used lands, territories, waters and coastal seas and other resources.'[34]

In the *Ominayak* case before the Human Rights Committee, the origin of the complaint was a pulp mill some 50 miles from the site of impact.[35] The petition of the Inuit Circumpolar Council (ICC) to the Inter-American Commission on Human Rights in respect of climate change challenged industrial developments and policy decisions thousands of miles from those protesting the impacts.[36]

The substantive rights of indigenous peoples

Scholars trained in Western legal method are encouraged to break down social situations into a number of legal categories and claims, to sift legally relevant and non-legally relevant facts, and to attribute each legally relevant fact, so isolated, to a particular claim. International human rights law also operates on this basis: claims must indicate which right or rights are the subject of the alleged violation and provide factual evidence to support each claim. Yet trying to break down indigenous experience in this way (and, indeed, any human experience) distorts the reality of that experience: life is not lived one right at a time. The ICC petition on climate change demonstrates the connections between changes to ice, permafrost, coastal erosion, flora and fauna, weather patterns, human health, food management, travel, property and culture.[37] Nevertheless, in order to bring a *legal case*, the ICC petition specifies individual rights that are threatened or violated. Consequently, the petition names rights to culture; to use and enjoy traditional lands collectively held; personal and intellectual property; health;

life, physical protection and security; subsistence; residence and home.[38] At the same time, it illustrates how these rights are interwoven. The rest of this chapter will take a similar approach: it will use Western legal methods to identify individual rights, but the examples selected inevitably show the connections between different rights in practice.

The right to self-determination

There is no longer any doubt that indigenous peoples enjoy the right to self-determination, but there is much uncertainty as to what the right entails. While, on the one hand, there are no legal authorities that support a right of indigenous peoples, outside of the colonial context, to independence, on the other hand, simple rights for indigenous individuals to vote or stand for government within the central institutions of the state on the same basis as other citizens are not adequate.[39]

The starting point is to recognise an indigenous people as an independent legal person, more than the sum of its individual members. This community should enjoy 'autonomy or self-government in matters relating to their internal and local affairs' (unless it decides otherwise).[40] This includes governance over land historically occupied and resources traditionally relied upon.[41] These rights do not necessarily prevent industrial development, including hydrocarbon activities offshore, but development should be led by the indigenous community.[42]

In general, it is the duty of the home state to fulfil indigenous peoples' rights to self-determination, but other states that exercise jurisdiction over activities that have transboundary impacts must ensure that those activities do not infringe on indigenous rights.[43] This means that a state must exercise due diligence to ensure that activities on its own continental shelf do not negatively impact the land and resource rights of an indigenous community in a neighbouring state.

The Human Rights Committee has declined to review communications pertaining to self-determination because it is a collective right and the communication process allows only individual communications.[44] It has, instead, reviewed communications in light of the right to culture, which will be discussed further below and has suggested (only once) that it might consider the right to self-determination as a tool of interpretation (i.e., giving context) in its interpretation of the other substantive rights of the ICCPR, in particular, the right to culture.[45] It is possible that the Committee on Economic, Social and Cultural Rights will accept a group communication on the right to self-determination but they may prefer to avoid this.[46] In the meantime, it is probably most useful to conceive of the right to self-determination as an overarching principle that colours the interpretation of the many more precise rights that flow from it – such as the rights to land and resources, property and culture; and procedural rights to participation and benefit-sharing.

The right to land and property

Indigenous rights to land and property are closely linked to indigenous rights to culture. The 'distinctive spiritual relationship' between indigenous peoples and their 'lands, territories, waters and coastal seas and other resources' is identified in UNDRIP and their rights to use, own, develop and control the same promised.[47] This, in turn, reflects the requirements of ILO Convention 169.[48]

Within the Inter-American system, the right to property which appears in both the ACHR and the ADRDM has been key to protecting indigenous land and resources.[49] It includes communally held as well as individual property rights. The Inter-American Court of Human Rights has been open to culturally sensitive demonstrations of land rights in the absence of a legally recognised title.[50] The European system has been less open, with the European Commission on Human Rights insisting on a 'traditional' (meaning Western/legal/written) title.[51] The European system also permits a wider margin of appreciation in property cases compared to protection of the home or privacy.[52]

In *Awas Tingni*, the Inter-American Court accepted the cultural and spiritual importance of land rights for the indigenous community concerned and has followed this approach in later jurisprudence.[53] The Court has also recognised that dispossession is a continuing wrongful act, as the ILO have done but the European Court of Human Rights generally fails to do.[54] In cases where legal title and control over historical indigenous territory has since gone into private ownership, the state must still prevent development in a manner that would damage it irreparably or the natural resources thereon on which the indigenous community has traditionally depended.[55] The Inter-American Court has also found it impossible to distinguish between rights to territory, the resources thereon (or there*in* in the case of offshore resources), rights to culture and rights to religion and spirituality, and the right to exist *qua* people.[56]

It is unlikely that states will be keen to recognize indigenous title claims to the continental shelf on which oil and gas is extracted in the Arctic, and obviously there is no traditional or cultural practice of hydrocarbon exploitation by indigenous peoples. However, an activity does not need to directly target the resource that is central to the indigenous community in order to violate land, property and resource rights.[57] From the indigenous rights perspective, the question is not about whether an indigenous community has 'traditionally' drilled for offshore oil and gas but about whether drilling for oil and gas will have negative impacts on the resources on which the neighbouring indigenous communities *have* traditionally depended – i.e., marine mammals and fish.

A negative impact does not foreclose development. However, it does complicate the decision-making process: a full pre-project evaluation must be conducted (either integrated into, or alongside, the environmental impact assessment), the indigenous community must be involved in the decision-making process, and it must be compensated for any losses and/or entitled to share in the benefits of the project.[58]

The right to culture

Cultural survival is both a prerequisite and an aim of self-determination. Cultural expression is also closely connected to land and resource rights, as shown in the previous section. However, the right to culture is also a stand-alone right for all individuals under the ICESCR and is protected for 'persons belonging to minorities' (including indigenous minorities) under the ICCPR.[59] The right to indigenous culture is addressed in UNDRIP (especially articles 8, 11, 15 and 31) and ILO Convention 169.[60]

The Human Rights Committee has evaluated a number of cases from indigenous authors based on article 27. *Kitok* was the first case on indigenous rights evaluated under article 27. The Human Rights Committee accepted that economic activities, even if now conducted on a for-profit and not a pure subsistence bases, could be 'an essential element in the culture of an ethnic community' and hence be protected by article 27.[61] *Ominayak* was decided shortly afterwards. The province of Alberta had expropriated land from the Lubicon Lake Band and allocated it to private developers for the extraction of oil and gas. Ominayak claimed that this violated the Lubicon Lake Band's right to self-determination as a people under international law, a claim the Human Rights Committee declined to assess because it necessitated a 'group' claim.[62] However, the committee then considered the facts of the case in light of article 27 and held that Alberta's (Canada's) conduct constituted a violation of Ominayak's and others' rights to culture as members of a minority group.[63]

More Saami cases followed: three from Finland and one from Norway.[64] Again, the Human Rights Committee accepted that traditional occupations such as reindeer herding were covered by article 27's right to culture. Although the applicants lost these cases on the facts, they remain important in establishing that traditional economic activities are a manifestation of minority culture for indigenous peoples and that industrial developments that effectively prevent the indigenous (or other minority) individual from practising his or her culture would violate the Covenant. This is neither a simple balancing test nor a margin of appreciation. Industrial activities can be compatible with traditional indigenous activities if they 'have a certain limited impact on the way of life of persons belonging to a minority'.[65] The committee has recognised that cumulative impacts from ostensibly unrelated developments (e.g., logging and stone quarrying in the same area) could constitute a violation, even if each project alone had less than significant impact.[66] It also accepted that the use of modern methods and technology does not deprive an activity of its traditional or cultural aspect if there is historical continuity.[67] Procedural elements (participation of representatives of the minority group concerned in the authorisation process) and substantive considerations (the scale of the activity and its impacts) are both key to the committee's conclusions in these cases.

The connection between fishing as a traditional activity and way of cultural life was recognised in *Mahuika*, where the committee confirmed again that traditional activities are not static but evolve over time and that they can have both subsistence and commercial elements.[68] In this case, the committee on balance found that there had not been a violation because there had been extensive involvement of Maori representatives in the development of the fishing quota system and most of the Maori communities concerned were supportive of the state's plan.[69] Furthermore, the process had been culturally sensitive and took into account the cultural and religious aspects of fishing for the Maori.[70]

Indigenous rights were further examined in *Poma Poma*, a case based on the diversion of water from the indigenous communities in the Andes towards the industrialised regions of the Pacific Coast. The committee considered that llama-raising is 'an essential element' of the Aymara community's culture, showing once more that economic activities may be intrinsic to minority, *a fortiori*, indigenous culture.[71] However, the committee accepted that states have a degree of discretion and a right to pursue economic development, which may in some cases justify (limited) interference with minority rights.[72] Interference is justifiable if it is proportionate, the affected community participates in decision-making and grants its free, prior and informed consent.[73] In *Poma Poma*, Peru had complied with none of these conditions.[74] Informed by these communications, the Human Rights Committee consolidated these interpretations in a General Comment.[75]

That so many of these cases were won by the state respondents is confirmation that indigenous rights do not preclude industrial activities. States can promote developments in such a way as to take adequate account of indigenous culture, including traditional economic activities that are now profit-making enterprises. It does not matter if the drilling takes place off- or onshore: the site of origin of the industrial activity is not as important as the site of impact. Procedural rights become crucial in preventing violations and avoiding the lawsuits that accompany them.

The Committee on Economic, Social and Cultural Rights has yet to issue views on any communications and it may be some time before they have opportunity to pronounce upon the right to culture. The ICESCR's protection of culture differs in two respects from article 27: first, the ICESCR recognises the rights of *everyone* to culture (not just members of minorities), and second, the Optional Protocol to the ICESCR explicitly permits group communications. The committee issued a General Comment on the right to culture in 2009, which, with reference to UNDRIP and ILO Convention 169, refers repeatedly to indigenous peoples' rights.[76] The section on indigenous peoples recognises the 'communal dimension' of cultural life and quotes, approvingly, the UNDRIP approach to rights over lands, territories and resources, irrespective of written legal title.[77] The committee also supports the principle of free, prior and informed consent in matters affecting indigenous rights.[78]

Neither the ECHR nor the ACHR explicitly protect a right to culture. As was shown in the previous section, in the Inter-American system, the right to property has been interpreted to protect land and resource rights which have in turn protected traditional activities. The European Commission on Human Rights rejected minority rights under the ECHR though more recently, the European Court of Human Rights considered the collective, cultural experience of the Sorb minority.[79]

The right to private and family life, home and correspondence

The right to privacy and the right to inviolability of the home and family life are protected under the ICCPR, the ECHR, the ADRDM and the ACHR. Whereas the right to property has been successfully argued to protect indigenous groups in the Americas, claims based on interference with home and family life have had more impact in the European institutions. To establish a violation, an applicant must prove that a development interferes with his or her own home, private or family life.[80] It is rather unlikely that the Court would accept that offshore hydrocarbon developments dozens of miles from the coast interfere with the private, home or family life of residents in general. However, if there are significant impacts on living marine resources and a connection can be drawn to traditional subsistence activities, which are transmitted in indigenous communities through family relationships, there may be grounds to argue that this interferes with the right to respect for family life.

The right to food

In many parts of the Arctic, the sea is by far the most important source of protein. In the event of pollution – either from seepage or from an offshore accident – the consequences cannot be contained to the vicinity of a spill. Not only may any oil itself be transported by the ocean's currents and winds into coastal zones used by indigenous peoples, but some of the living creatures injured, killed or displaced by pollution are also key food sources. However, violations of the right to food do not pivot on the high drama of an oil spill. The impacts of offshore industry on living marine resources are not fully known but there is already enough evidence to indicate that seismic testing can injure marine mammals and possibly fish and noise pollution is known to trigger behavioural changes in singing, movement and mating.[81] These impacts in turn disrupt the rights of indigenous communities that rely on these species. This is not only an issue of the right to food, which, even alone, would be of grave concern, but also impacts the right to culture and the right to health. Furthermore, the right to food is not a mere matter of sufficient calories but is a right to 'adequate food': the Committee on Economic, Social and Cultural Rights interprets this as requiring food that it is of adequate quantity and quality, 'free from adverse substances, and acceptable within a given culture'.[82] If an indigenous community considers the ocean's bounty contaminated by hydrocarbon activities, even in the absence of scientific evidence of contamination, it may cease to be culturally appropriate. External perceptions of contamination can also be devastating for an Arctic indigenous community that relies on fisheries exports: the premium price for Arctic fish is contingent on confidence among purchasers that the Arctic Ocean and its contents are clean.[83]

Other substantive rights

The ICESCR and the ADRDM both protect economic and social rights to the highest attainable standard of health, freedom of choice of work, and housing. For Arctic indigenous communities, these rights are all closely interconnected and tied to self-determination, land, resources and culture. Any interference with traditional hunting can have repercussions for the right to culture, and choice of work; it will even impact the right to the highest attainable standard of health, as substitute foods in the Arctic are of inferior quality and may be unaffordable. In extreme cases – fortunately rare in offshore hydrocarbon activities – the right to life can also be under threat from environmental contamination.[84] The duty of states to prevent environmental conditions that threaten human life and obligations to fulfil the conditions necessary for life to thrive are obligations of due diligence.[85]

The right of indigenous peoples to the highest attainable standard of health not only requires protection of individual health and provision of adequate healthcare services, but it must also address community health and well-being. This means responding to disparities in life-expectancy, suicide rates, and communicable and non-communicable disease rates between indigenous and non-indigenous communities.[86] Indeed, industrial development is often touted as a crucial source of revenue and expertise to make this happen. Aside from cash injections, industrial developments can draw professional healthcare workers to a remote area. However, hydrocarbon activities, even offshore, can have impacts on health if they interfere with a trusted food supply; they can also have psychologically negative impacts on communities, in particular, if indigenous people feel excluded from both the decision-making process and the economic returns.

Procedural rights of indigenous peoples

Only a short summary of procedural rights follows owing to space constraints but the present author has explored this issue in depth elsewhere.[87]

Information, participation, and free, prior and informed consent

The Aarhus Convention, to which the Kingdom of Denmark (excluding Greenland), Finland, Iceland, Sweden, Norway and the European Union are all parties, grants everybody a right to receive environmental information but only the 'public concerned' has a right to participate.[88] Under the ECHR, the right to freedom of expression is a right to impart information but has not been interpreted as a right to receive information, i.e., it is not a right to public information. Owing in part to the broader wording of the ACHR, the Inter-American Court has interpreted the right to 'seek, receive and impart information' as including a right to freedom of public environmental information and the person or NGO seeking it need not show any personal interest.[89] None of these three instruments covers Canada or the United States but freedom of expression (though possibly not information) is protected by the ADRDM.

Emerging from the principle of self-determination, indigenous peoples have much stronger rights to participation in decision-making than the general public. Indigenous peoples must be consulted before any developments take place that impact upon their territories or resources, and there is now an emerging principle of free, prior and informed consent.[90]

The precise requirements of free, prior and informed consent are ambiguous and contested. One of Canada's longstanding objections to UNDRIP was based on a reading of free, prior and informed consent that created a veto for indigenous communities regarding developments on and of their land and resources.[91] In 2014, the same government claimed that UNDRIP's requirements for free, prior and informed consent, if interpreted as a veto, are incompatible with Canadian law.[92] The Trudeau administration's wholehearted endorsement of UNDRIP embraces the free, prior and informed consent provisions. However, Minister Bennett expressed the view that the Canadian constitution already complies with UNDRIP, including free, prior and informed consent.[93] These positions can only be reconciled if one accepts Bennett's view that the principle of free, prior and informed consent requires only good faith negotiations with indigenous peoples and their participation in decision-making but does not give them a veto power.[94]

The International Finance Corporation's Environment and Social Performance Standards also require free, prior and informed consent and interpret this quite explicitly as a requirement *to obtain* consent (not just to seek it in good faith).[95] This has important implications in Arctic Russia where the Standards must be upheld in any World Bank supported activities, such as the Yamal LNG project.[96]

The *degree* of impact likely from offshore activities on Arctic indigenous communities is probably still relevant to determine whether the threshold is one of good faith consultation and participation or of veto-wielding free, prior and informed consent. In order to determine the degree of impact, a full environmental, social and human rights impact evaluation is necessary and must include opportunities for indigenous and other representatives to receive, review and reply to proposals.[97] This is no simple matter in the Arctic where developers must overcome challenges of distance, language and poor communications infrastructure.

Even if the principle of free, prior and informed consent is not (yet) a legal requirement in every case, the uncertainty regarding the status of this principle, its requirements and the speed in which the law can evolve gives cause for developers and the states governing them to pursue free, prior and informed consent and reduce the potential for legal liability.

Compensation and benefit-sharing

Compensation is payable for any damage or human rights violation irrespective of profits, and benefit-sharing is necessary irrespective of damage. The right of indigenous peoples to share in the benefits of development is now widely accepted.[98]

Compensation, being a form of reparation, does not pivot on the profitability or otherwise of the industrial development. In the event of significant interference with living marine resources and repercussions for human rights and indigenous rights, restitution (e.g., returning the environment to its prior condition) is likely to be impossible and compensation due in lieu. Should there be a more dramatic incident such as a spill, restitution, at least partial, would be preferred to the extent possible but will never be perfect so compensation will also be necessary. The risks of a blowout are highest at the earlier stages of exploration; once an oil well is operational, the pressure is reduced and an explosion becomes much less likely.[99] Robust insurance coverage is therefore a must.

Conclusion

The impacts of offshore hydrocarbon development cannot be contained to the immediate vicinity of activities. Even normal operations create changes that can trigger violations of the rights of indigenous peoples who have long-standing connections to the ocean and its bounty. Developers, and the states that grant them licences to explore and exploit offshore Arctic oil and gas, should consider the risks not only as a matter of corporate social responsibility or of human development, but in order to forestall protracted and expensive legal claims.

The key consideration is the right of indigenous peoples to self-determination – control over their own affairs and resources. Responsibility to facilitate self-determination is borne by states, but private operatives should also seek to understand its implications to avoid getting caught up in disputes. Land rights (including rights to coastal and marine areas traditionally used), resource governance, rights to property, culture, food and health are the main substantive rights at stake. They are complemented by procedural rights to information; consultation and participation (as a minimum) or free, prior and informed consent; compensation; and benefit-sharing.

To date, there is inadequate consistency and universality to declare UNDRIP as customary law in its entirety but even its most progressive provisions, such as on free, prior and informed consent, are influencing governmental approaches to resource development and campaigns of indigenous groups seeking to control the use of their lands and waters. Even the most hard-hearted developer, motivated only by profit, needs to understand UNDRIP and seek to uphold it to eliminate unnecessary legal risk. UNDRIP can be seen as a process rather than a final destination for indigenous rights. Whether or not it leads to a binding treaty, the increasing deference paid to it by states in the Arctic and elsewhere is evidence of *opinio iuris*, and commitments to its implementation are evidence of state practice, i.e. the two necessary conditions to create customary international law. Regulatory frameworks are more complex than ever as they recognise the indigenous partners at the decision-making table, alongside states and corporations.

Notes

1 Revisions to this paper were made in light of recent changes to Canadian policy. Thanks to Professor Nigel Bankes and JD Student Amy Matychuk, both University of Calgary, for sharing their research on this topic.
2 E.g. Montgomery 2015.
3 The exception to this is the European Convention on Human Rights.
4 Australia 2009; Canada 2010; New Zealand 2010; United States President 2010.
5 Bankes and Koivurova 2015, 233.
6 Öberg 2005, 898–889, 903–904.
7 United Nations General Assembly, Record of the 108th Plenary Meeting, 13 September 2007, UN Doc. A/61/PV.108; Australia 2009; Canada 2010; New Zealand 2010; United States President 2010.
8 United Nations Permanent Forum on Indigenous Issues, *Study on National Constitutions and the United Nations Declaration on the Rights of Indigenous Peoples,* UN Doc. E/C.19/2013/18, 2013.
9 Shelton 2006, 322.
10 United Nations Human Rights Council Working Group on Universal Periodic Review 2009, paragraphs 24, 48 and 76.
11 Canada 2010.
12 *Ad hoc* coalition on the UN Declaration on the Rights of Indigenous Peoples 2014.
13 Wilson-Raybould 2016.
14 Fontaine 2016.
15 United States President 2010.
16 Koivurova 2011, 32.
17 Bankes and Koivurova 2015, 234.
18 ILO Convention 169 1989.
19 ILO Convention 107 1959.
20 ILO Convention 169 1989, article 6.
21 ILO Constitution, 1919, article 24.
22 *SIK* v. *Denmark* 2001.
23 ICESCR 1966; ICCPR 1966; UDHR 1948.

24 CERD 1965.
25 ICCPR-OP1 1966; OP-ICESCR 2008; CERD 1965, article 14.
26 ECHR 1950; ACHR 1969.
27 ADRDM 1948.
28 Inter-American Commission on Human Rights 2013, article 23.
29 ADRIP 2016.
30 Ibid, articles XI and XXVI.
31 ibid, notes 1 and 2.
32 ILO Convention 169 1989, article 13 (2).
33 Ibid., article 14 (1).
34 UNDRIP, 2007, article 25.
35 *Ominayak* v. *Canada* 1990.
36 ICC Petition, 2005.
37 Ibid., Chapter IV.C.
38 Ibid., Chapter V.B.
39 UNDRIP 2007, paragraphs 3, 4 & 46; ICESCR 1966 article 1; ICCPR 1966, article 1.
40 UNDRIP 2007, article 4.
41 UNDRIP 2007; ICESCR 1966, article 1; ICCPR 1966, article 1.
42 UNDRIP 2007, article 32.
43 Human Rights Council 2009, paragraph 86; Human Rights Committee 1984, paragraphs 4–6.
44 *Kitok* v. *Sweden* 1988, paragraph 6.3; *Ominayak* v. *Canada* 1990, paragraphs 13.3 & 32.1; Human Rights Committee 2008, paragraph 3.1.
45 *Mahuika* v. *New Zealand* 2000, paragraph 9.2; Möller 2011, 31.
46 Johnstone 2015, 75.
47 UNDRIP 2007, articles 25 & 26.
48 ILO Convention 169 1989, articles 13–15.
49 ADRDM 1948, article XXIII; ACHR 1969, article 21.
50 *Sawhoyamaxa* v. *Paraguay* 2006, paragraph 131.
51 *G and E* v. *Norway* 1993, 'The Law' paragraph 2.
52 *Connors* v. *United Kingdom* 2004 (European Court of Human Rights, First Section, Application No. 66746/01), paragraph 82; Bankes 2011, 87.
53 *Awas Tingni Community* v. *Nicaragua* 2001 (Inter-American Court of Human Rights, Petition 11577, Judgment, Series C No. 79), paragraph 148; see also: *Maya Indigenous Community of the Toledo District* v. *Belize* 2004 (Inter-American Court of Human Rights, Petition 12053, Report No. 40/04), paragraph 115; *Sawhoyamaxa* v. *Paraguay*, 2006, paragraph 131; *Saramaka* v. *Suriname*, 2007, paragraphs 80–82.
54 *Sawhoyamaxa* v. *Paraguay* 2006, paragraph 132; *Xákmok Kásek* v. *Paraguay*, paragraph 291; *SIK* v. *Denmark*, 2001, paragraph 29; *Hingitaq 53* v. *Denmark* (European Court of Human Rights, First Section, Application No. 18584/04, 2006); Bankes, 2011, 95–100. But see: *Loizidou* v. *Turkey 1995* (European Court of Human Rights, Application No. 15318/89, Preliminary Objections), in which the European Court of Human Rights recognised dispossession of Greek Cypriots in Northern Cyprus as a continuing wrongful act.
55 *Xákmok Kásek* v. *Paraguay* 2010, paragraph 291.
56 *Saramaka* v. *Suriname* 2007, paragraph 121.
57 Johnstone 2015, 78–79.
58 *Saramaka* v. *Suriname* 2007, paragraphs 129, 134 & 140.
59 ICESCR 1966, article 15; ICCPR 1966, article 27.
60 ILO Convention 169, articles 2(2)(b), 5(a), 23 & 27.
61 *Kitok* v. *Sweden* 1988, paragraph 9.2.

62 *Ominayak* v. *Canada* 1990, paragraphs 13.3 & 32.1.
63 Ibid., paragraph 32.2.
64 *Länsman, Ilmari* v. *Finland* 1994; *Länsman, Jouni E.* v. *Finland* 1996; *Jonassen* v. *Norway* 2002; *Länsman, Jouni* v. *Finland* 2005.
65 *Länsman, Ilmari* v. *Finland* 1994, paragraph 9.4.
66 *Länsman, Jouni E.* v. *Finland* 1996; Möller, 2011, 42.
67 *Länsman, Ilmari* v. *Finland* 1994, paragraph 9.3.
68 *Mahuika* v. *New Zealand* 2000, paragraphs 9.3–9.4.
69 Ibid., paragraph 9.6.
70 Ibid., paragraph 9.8.
71 *Poma Poma* v. *Peru* 2009, paragraph 7.3.
72 Ibid., paragraph 7.4.
73 Ibid., paragraph 7.6.
74 Ibid., paragraph 7.7.
75 Human Rights Committee 2008, paragraph 7.
76 Committee on Economic, Social and Cultural Rights 2009.
77 Ibid., paragraph 36.
78 Ibid., paragraph 37.
79 *G and E* v. *Norway* 1993; *Noack and Others* v. *Germany* 2000 (European Court of Human Rights, Fourth Section, Application No. 46346/99).
80 *Kyrtatos* v. *Greece* 2003 (European Court of Human Rights, Application No. 41666/98), paragraph 19.
81 Papanicolopoulou 2011; Van Dyke, Jon M., Emily A. Gardner and Joseph R. Morgan. 2004.
82 Committee on Economic, Social and Cultural Rights 1999, paragraph 8.
83 DeMarban 2014.
84 See, e.g., *Yanomami People* v. *Brazil* 1985 (Inter-American Commission on Human Rights, Petition 7615, Resolution, OEA/Ser.L/V/II.108, Doc. 62); *Sawhoyamaxa* v. *Paraguay* 2006.
85 *Öneryildiz* v. *Turkey* 2004 (European Court of Human Rights, Application No. 48389/99). Which year date is correct, notes v. bibliography?
86 Hild et al. 2004.
87 Johnstone 2015, 86–97.
88 Aarhus Convention 1998 (Convention on Access to Information, Public Participation in Decision-Making and Access to Justice in Environmental Matters. 2161 UNTS 447).
89 *Reyes* v. *Chile* 2006 (Inter-American Court of Human Rights, Petition 12108, Merits, Reparations and Costs, Series C No. 151), paragraphs 76–77.
90 UNDRIP, article 32; ADRIP, article XXIX; Wiessner et al. 2012, 510–511; Committee on the Elimination of Racial Discrimination 1997, paragraph 4(d); Committee on the Elimination of Racial Discrimination 2008, paragraph 29; Committee on the Elimination of Racial Discrimination 2012, paragraph 20; Committee on the Elimination of Racial Discrimination 2013, paragraph 20(d); Committee on Economic, Social and Cultural Rights 2011, paragraph 7(b); Committee on Economic, Social and Cultural Rights 2009, paragraph 37; *Poma Poma* v. *Peru* 2009, paragraph 7.6; *Saramaka* v. *Suriname* 2007, paragraphs 129 & 134; *Endorois* v. *Kenya* 2009, paragraphs 226, 232 & 257–266; Johnstone 2015, 86–90.
91 United Nations General Assembly 2007.
92 Assembly of First Nations 2014.
93 Bennett 2016.
94 O'Neill 2016.
95 International Finance Corporation 2012.

96 Yamal LNG Environmental and Social Impact Assessment 2014.
97 Johnstone 2015, Chapter 7.
98 ILO Convention 169, article 15(2); Committee on the Elimination of Racial Discrimination 2003, paragraph 16; *Saramaka* v. *Suriname* 2007, paragraphs 129 & 140; *Endorois* v. *Kenya* 2009, paragraphs 294–296; Johnstone 2015, 90.
99 Hunter 2015.

References

ACHR. 1969. *American Convention on Human Rights*. 1144 UNTS 123.

Ad hoc coalition on the UN Declaration on the Rights of Indigenous Peoples. 2014. 'Canada uses World Conference to continue indefensible attack on UN Declaration on the Rights of Indigenous Peoples.' *Union of British Columbia Indian Chiefs*, 24 September 2014. Accessed 27 October 2016. www.ubcic.bc.ca/News_Releases/UBCICNews09241401.html#axzz4OHKYt7PM.

ADRDM. 1948. *American Declaration of the Rights and Duties of Man*. OAS Res XXX.

ADRIP. 2016. *American Declaration on the Rights of Indigenous Peoples*. OAS Res AG/RES.2888 (XLVI-O/16) 167.

Assembly of First Nations. 2014. 'Canada's Statement on the World Conference on Indigenous Peoples Outcome Document.' Accessed 27 October 2016. www.afn.ca/en/news-media/latest-news/canadas-statement-on-the-world-conference-on-indigenous-peoples-outcom.

Australia. 2009. *Statement on the United Nations Declaration on the Rights of Indigenous Peoples, 2009*. Minister for Families, Housing, Community Services and Indigenous Affairs. Accessed 15 April 2014. www.un.org/esa/socdev/unpfii/documents/Australia_official_statement_endorsement_UNDRIP.pdf.

Bankes, Nigel and Timo Koivurova. 2015. 'Legal Systems.' In *Arctic Human Development Report: Regional Processes and Global Linkages*, eds. Joan Nymand Larsen and Gail Fondahl, 221–252. Copenhagen: Nordic Council of Ministers.

Bennett. 2016. *Speech Delivered at the United Nations Permanent Forum on Indigenous Issues*. New York, 10 May 2016. Accessed 27 October 2016. http://news.gc.ca/web/article-en.do?nid=1064009.

Canada. 2010. *Statement of Support on the United Nations Declaration on the Rights of Indigenous Peoples*. Aboriginal Affairs and Northern Development Canada.

CERD. 1965. *Convention on the Elimination of Racial Discrimination*. 660 UNTS 195.

Committee on Economic, Social and Cultural Rights. 1999. General Comment No. 12. *The Right to Adequate Food*. UN Doc. E/C.12/1999/5.

Committee on Economic, Social and Cultural Rights. 2009. General Comment No. 21. *The Right of Everyone to Take Part in Cultural Life*. UN Doc. E/C.12/GC/21.

Committee on Economic, Social and Cultural Rights. 2011. *Concluding Observations: Russian Federation*. UN Doc. E/C.12/RUS/CO/5.

Committee on the Elimination of Racial Discrimination. 1997. *General Recommendation XXIII on the rights of indigenous peoples*. UN Doc. A/52/18, Annex V.

Committee on the Elimination of Racial Discrimination. 2003. *Concluding Observations: Ecuador*. UN Doc. CERD/C/62/CO/2.

Committee on the Elimination of Racial Discrimination. 2008. *Concluding Observations: United States*. UN Doc. CERD/C/USA/CO/6.

Committee on the Elimination of Racial Discrimination. 2012. *Concluding Observations: Canada*. UN Doc. CERD/C/CAN/CO/19-20.
Committee on the Elimination of Racial Discrimination. 2013. *Concluding Observations: Russian Federation*. UN Doc. CERD/C/RUS/CO/20-22.
DeMarban, Alex. 2014. 'Alaska North Slope Communities Divided as Arctic Drilling Delayed.' *Alaska Dispatch*, 23 February 2014. Accessed 23 July 2015. www.adn.com/article/20140223/alaska-north-slope-communities-divided-arctic-drilling-delayed.
ECHR. 1950. *Convention for the Protection of Human Rights and Fundamental Freedoms*. ETS 005.
Endorois v. *Kenya*. 2009. *Endorois Welfare Council (Centre for Minority Rights Development, Kenya, and Minority Rights Group International, on behalf of)* v. *Kenya*. African Commission on Human and Peoples' Rights. Communication 276/2003 (25 November 2009). AHRLR, 75.
Fontaine, Tim 2016. Canada officially adopts UN declaration on rights of Indigenous Peoples'. *CBC News*, 10 May 2016. Accessed 27 October 2016.www.cbc.ca/news/indigenous/canada-adopting-implementing-un-rights-declaration-1.3575272.
G and E v. *Norway*. 1993. European Commission of Human Rights. Applications Nos. 9278/81 and 9415/82. Decision on Admissibility.
Hild, Carl M. et al. 2004. 'Human Health and Well-being.' In *Arctic Human Development Report*, ed. Joan Nymand Larsen. Akureyri, Iceland: Stefansson Arctic Institute.
Human Rights Committee. 1984. General comment No. 12. *Article 1: Right to self-determination*. UN Doc. UN GAOR A/39/40 Annex VI.
Human Rights Council. 2009. *Report of the Office of the High Commissioner for Human Rights on the Relationship between Climate Change and Human Rights*. UN Doc. A/HRC/10/61.
Hunter, Tina. 2015. 'Regulating Petroleum Activities to Protect Fragile Arctic Environments: Are Current Preventative Measures Enough to Prevent Oil Spills?' Paper presented at University of Akureyri, Iceland. 7 April 2015.
ICC Petition. 2005. *Petition to the Inter-American Commission on Human Rights Seeking Relief from Violations resulting from Global Warming Caused by Acts and Omissions of the United States, submitted by Sheila Watt-Cloutier, with the support of the Inuit Circumpolar Conference, on behalf of all Inuit of the Arctic regions of the United States and Canada*. Petition No. P-1413–05. 7 December 2005.
ICCPR. 1966. *International Covenant on Civil and Political Rights*. 999 UNTS 171.
ICCPR-OP1. 1966. *First Optional Protocol to the International Covenant on Civil and Political Rights*. 999 UNTS 171.
ICESCR. 1966. *International Covenant on Economic, Social and Cultural Rights*. 993 UNTS 3.
ILO Convention 107. 1959. *Convention concerning the Protection and Integration of Indigenous and Other Tribal and Semi-Tribal Populations in Independent Countries*. 328 UNTS 247.
ILO Convention 169. 1989. *Indigenous and Tribal Peoples Convention*. 28 ILM 1382.
Inter-American Commission on Human Rights. 2013. *Rules of Procedure of the Inter-American Commission on Human Rights*.
International Finance Corporation (IFC) *Performance Standards on Environmental and Social Sustainability*, 1 January 2012.

Johnstone, Rachael L. 2015. *Offshore Oil and Gas Development in the Arctic under International Law: Risk and Responsibility*. Leiden: Brill.
Kitok v. *Sweden*. 1988. Human Rights Committee Communication No. 197/1985. 27 July 1988. UN Doc. CCPR/C/33/D/197/1985.
Koivurova, Timo. 2011. 'Jurisprudence of the European Court of Human Rights Regarding Indigenous Peoples: Retrospect and Prospects.' *International Journal on Minority and Group Rights* 18: 1.
Länsman, Ilmari et al. v. *Finland*. 1994. Human Rights Committee. Communication No. 511/1992 (8 November 1994). UN Doc. CCPR/C/52/D/511/1992.
Länsman, Jouni E. et al. v. *Finland*. 1996. Human Rights Committee. Communication No. 671/1995 (30 October 1996). UN Doc. CCPR/C/58/D/671/1995.
Länsman, Jouni E. et al. v. *Finland*. 2005. Human Rights Committee. Communication No. 1023/2001 (17 March 2005). UN Doc. CCPR/C/83/D/1023/2001.
Mahuika et al. v. *New Zealand*. 2000. Human Rights Committee Communication No. 547/199 (15 November 2000). UN Doc. CCPR/C/70/D/547/1933.
Montgomery, Marc. 2015. 'Appeal to Start on Arctic Seismic Testing.' *Alaska Dispatch*, 23 February 2015.
Möller, Jakob. 2011. 'Case Law of the UN Human Rights Committee Relevant to Members of Minorities and Peoples in the Arctic Region.' *Yearbook of Polar Law* 3: 27.
New Zealand. 2010. *Statement, Ninth session of the United Nations Permanent Forum on Indigenous Issues, Opening Ceremony*. Accessed 23 July 2015.www.beehive.govt.nz/release/supporting-un-declaration-restores-nz039s-mana.
Ominayak and the Lubicon Lake Band v. *Canada*. 1990. Human Rights Committee. Communication No. 167/1984 (10 May 1990). UN Doc. CCPR/C/38/D/167/1984.
O'Neil, Đ. 2016. 'UN Declaration Doesn't Give Canadian First Nations a Veto: Minister.' *Vancouver Sun*, 30 June 2016. Accessed 27 October 2016. http://vancouversun.com/news/politics/un-declaration-doesnt-give-canadian-first-nations-a-veto-minister.
OP-ICESCR. 2008. *Optional Protocol to the International Covenant on Economic, Social and Cultural Rights*. 48 ILM 262.
Öberg, Marko D. 2005. 'The Legal Effects of Resolutions of the UN Security Council and General Assembly in the Jurisprudence of the ICJ.' *European Journal of International Law* 16 (5): 879.
Papanicolopoulou, Irini. 2011. 'On the Interaction between Law and Science: Considerations on the Ongoing Process of Regulating Underwater Acoustic Pollution.' *Aegean Review of the Law of the Sea and Maritime Law* 1 (2): 247.
Poma Poma v. *Peru*. 2009. Human Rights Committee. Communication No. 1457/2006 (27 March 2009). UN Doc. CCPR/C/95/D/1457/2006.
Saramaka People v. *Suriname*. 2007. Inter-American Court of Human Rights. Petition 12338. Preliminary Objections, Merits, Reparation and Costs. Series C No 172.
Sawhoyamaxa Indigenous Community of the Enxet People v. *Paraguay*. 2006. Inter-American Court of Human Rights. Petition 0322/2001. Merits, Reparations and Costs. Series C No. 146.
Shelton, Dinah. 2006. 'Normative Hierarchy in International Law.' *American Journal of International Law* 100 (2): 291.
SIK v. *Denmark*. 2001. Report of the Committee set up to examine the representation alleging non-observance by Denmark of the Indigenous and Tribal Peoples Convention, 1989 (No. 169), made under article 24 of the ILO Constitution by the

National Confederation of Trade Unions of Greenland (Sulinermik Inuussutissarsiuteqartut Kattuffiat–SIK). GB.277/18/3; GB.280/18/5.
UDHR. 1948. *Universal Declaration of Human Rights 1948*. UNGA Res 217 (A) (III), 10 December 1948.
UNDRIP. 2007. *United Nations Declaration on the Rights of Indigenous Peoples*. UNGA Res 61/295. 13 September 2007.
United Nations General Assembly. 2007. Official Records, 107th plenary meeting, 13 September 2007. UN Doc. A/61/PV.107.
United Nations Human Rights Council Working Group on Universal Periodic Review. 2009. *Canada*. UN Doc. A/HRC/11/17.
United States President. 2010. *Announcement of US Support for the Declaration on the Rights of Indigenous Peoples*. Accessed 23 July 2015.www.state.gov/s/tribalconsultation/declaration.
Van Dyke, Jon M., Emily A. Gardner and Joseph R. Morgan. 2004. 'Whales, Submarines, and Active Sonar.' *Ocean Yearbook* 18: 330.
Wiessner, Siegfried et al. 2012. 'Rights of Indigenous Peoples: Committee Report.' In International Law Association, *Report of the Seventy-Fifth Conference*.
Wilson-Raybould, J. Canada, House of Commons Debates, 42nd Parl, 1st Sess, Vol 148, No 37 (12 April 2016) at 2010.
Xákmok Kásek Indigenous Community v. *Paraguay*. 2010. Inter-American Court of Human Rights. Petition 12420. Merits, Reparations and Costs. Series C No. 214.
Yamal LNG Environmental and Social Impact Assessment, Environ, October 2014. Accessed 27 October 2016. http://yamallng.ru/403/docs/ESIA%20ENG%20.pdf.

Part II

National perspectives on offshore regulations

6 Alaska and offshore hydrocarbon extraction

A legal and socio-economic review

Edward T. Canuel[1]

Introduction

The US Arctic comprises northern Alaska and parts of the Beaufort and Chukchi Seas, an area of nearly 41,000 mile^2. The US Arctic Ocean consists of the Beaufort, Bering and Chukchi seas, extending south to the Aleutian Islands and north to 200 nautical miles from the northern coast of Alaska.[2] Estimated offshore hydrocarbon potential in the US Arctic Outer Continental Shelf (OCS)[3] is vast: the Bureau of Ocean Energy Management (BOEM) estimates that the Chukchi Sea Planning Area contains 15.38 billion barrels of oil and 76.77 trillion cubic feet of gas and that the Beaufort Sea Planning Area holds 8.22 billion barrels of oil and 27.64 trillion cubic feet of gas.[4] To understand US Arctic offshore hydrocarbon extraction, one must navigate the various complex federal, state and substate legal interests in Alaska affecting the 53,000 Alaskans living in the Arctic region,[5] the state and the country itself. Alaska Natives [including two groups of Inuit (Inupiat and Yuit), Aleuts, Athabascans, Tlingit, Haida and Tsimshian] additionally play a crucial role in the decision-making process.[6]

This chapter analyses, from an US perspective, the different legal mechanisms affecting, if not influencing, Arctic hydrocarbon development, providing a roadmap of issues useful for diverse Arctic constituencies. For example, business, environmental and legal considerations are reviewed, including state and federal laws contending with offshore Alaskan hydrocarbon extraction, such as the Outer Continental Shelf Lands Act (OCSLA) and the National Environmental Policy Act (NEPA). Related issues include the implementation of the Alaska National Interest Lands Conservation Act (ANILCA), affecting and shaping Alaskan land use law. Additionally, the impact and importance of native Alaskan rights is discussed through an introduction of US state and federal tribal law. In addition to a survey of key issues affecting multiple stakeholders, this chapter suggests that increasing Arctic interest has created enhanced cooperative opportunities.

Overview: legal considerations

The complex regulatory framework concerning OCS development has sought to balance public and private interests, while legal challenges supporting/

constraining OCS development have occurred over the years from a variety of diverse stakeholders. The development of tribal law has also affected OCS extraction projects, addressing issues such as the rights of Native Alaskans to exploit, and hold title to, natural resources. While the private sector is responsible for discovering, developing and producing hydrocarbons from the OCS, companies lease from the federal government 'the rights to perform these activities.'[7] Over 20 federal agencies and bureaux contend with Arctic-related missions, with Arctic Ocean resources addressed by agencies including the BOEM, the Bureau of Safety and Environmental Enforcement (BSEE) and the Environmental Protection Agency (EPA).[8] Note that following the Deepwater Horizon blowout, the Minerals Management Service (MMS) was split into the Bureau of Ocean Energy Management, Regulation, and Enforcement (BOEMRE) and the Office of Natural Resources Revenue.[9] On 1 October 2011, BOEMRE was itself replaced by BOEM and BSEE.

The separation sought to promote efficiencies, including allowing inspectors more budgetary autonomy and strengthening environmental review/analysis through structural/organisational mechanisms, and ensured that potential environmental effects of proposed operations were given appropriate weight. Offshore drilling regulatory enforcement came under the purview of BOEM and the BSEE, with the Office of Natural Resources Revenue responsible for revenue collection and residing under the jurisdiction of the Department of Interior (DOI)'s Office of Policy, Management and Budget.[10] BOEM and BSEE are subject to permitting any other authority that resides in a number of federal agencies. Unlike the Bureau of Land Management (BLM), which manages federal lands under DOI's purview, BOEM and BSEE are not directed by a statute. There is no statutory companion for ocean management agencies, which, as a result, are left solely with the direction provided in the OCSLA. The DOI – through BOEM and BSEE – plans and authorises offshore hydrocarbon development, exploration and leasing.[11]

State law

From the state perspective, Article 8 of the Alaskan constitution notes several concepts crucial to Arctic natural resource extraction, including the sale or grant of state lands[12] and the grant of leases for oil, gas and oil shale.[13] The bifurcation of federal and state jurisdiction over continental shelf hydrocarbon resources took root in 1945, when President Truman declared that the US government had jurisdiction and control over continental shelf subsoil and seabed natural resources beneath the high seas and contiguous to the US coasts.[14] The US Supreme Court held[15] that – on the basis of commercial, defence and international relations considerations – the federal government had jurisdiction over all submerged lands extending from the coast.[16] Specifically, under the 'paramountcy doctrine,' the federal government must have paramount power to regulate seabed and ocean exploitation to defend the United States and regulate international commerce.[17]

Alaska has jurisdiction over subsea resources from zero to three nautical miles offshore under the Submerged Lands Act of 1953 (SLA).[18] That Act modified California, granting states' title to submerged lands, starting at the state's coastline, beneath a three-mile swathe of territorial sea.[19] Alaska thus makes decisions about offshore oil and gas resources under those waters. The federal government manages the OCS from three nautical miles to the Exclusive Economic Zone 200 nautical miles offshore.[20]

Federal law: the OCSLA

The Outer Continental Shelf Lands Act (OCSLA) of 1953 granted authority to the Department of the Interior Secretary to lease and manage mineral resources in the submerged lands seaward of a state's three-mile zone.[21] The Secretary of the Interior's general guidelines and directives to manage OCS resources came under scrutiny as issued leases increased during the early 1970s, with OCSLA characterised by Congress as effectively delivering 'carte blanche authority' to the Interior Secretary.[22] To provide clear policy guidance to govern OCS leasing, Congress enacted the OCSLA Amendments of 1978, authorising the Interior Secretary to undertake a competitive bid lease sale.[23] The Amendments require the Secretary of the Interior to maintain a proper balance between the potential for environmental damage, resource discovery and adverse impact on the coastal zone in determining the selection and timing of lease sales to be made available from the various OCS areas. It has been noted that the

> OCS oil and gas resources are to be preserved, protected, and developed so as to: (1) make OCS petroleum resources available for domestic use as rapidly as possible; (2) provide for a balance of development with protection of the environment; (3) insure the public a fair and equitable return on the resources of the OCS that are leased to private industry; and (4) maintain free enterprise competition among firms bidding for OCS oil and gas leases.[24]

Under the OCSLA, federal offshore oil and gas activities are governed.[25] The DOI must balance twin OCSLA objectives: expeditious offshore hydrocarbon resource development subject to environmental safeguards.[26]

Under OCSLA, the Interior Secretary develops a national leasing programme, including a five-year proposed lease schedule.[27] The BOEM drafts the plan, which indicates the size, timing and leasing activity location that will 'best meet national energy needs.'[28] Such a five-year leasing programme must balance potential for hydrocarbon discovery, potential environmental damage, and potential adverse impact on the coastal zone.[29] The DOI considers a series of factors when balancing the economic, social and environmental values of the OCS natural resources against the possible impact of hydrocarbon exploration on other natural resource values of the OCS 'and the marine, coastal and human environments.'[30] If it proceeds with a sale, then BOEM conducts a comprehensive analysis related to the specific sale, and the leases are sold through a competitive leasing process with conditional rights to explore, develop and produce hydrocarbons.[31] The BOEM evaluates exploration plans submitted by lessees, and the BSEE must also approve safety and spill response-planning approvals for any well drilling.[32] The BOEM and BSEE must evaluate and approve development and production proposals.[33] OCSLA provides requirements concerning development and production plans, and operators must carry out their activities in conformance with approved development and production plans.[34] With respect to exploration and development phases, provisions concerning spill prevention or preparation are derived from the Clean Water Act.[35] The DOI has been delegated authority for implementing such response-plan approval with respect to offshore hydrocarbon drilling, and DOI has in turn delegated such authority to BSEE[36] by signing the Memorandum of Understanding between the Bureau of Safety and Environmental Enforcement–US Department of Interior and the US Coastguard–US Department of Homeland Security.[37] The BOEM and BSEE also comply with the Endangered Species Act (ESA), the Marine Mammal Protection Act, the Clean Water Act discharge requirements administered by the EPA, the National Pollutant Discharge Elimination System (NPDES) for exploration permits,[38] and its Arctic Oil and Gas Exploration General Permits.[39]

Federal law: NEPA, the OPA and the Magnuson–Stevens Act

NEPA also plays a role in contending with OCS development.[40] Under NEPA, federal officials must balance gained benefits from exploiting a natural resource with possible harm that may then result in another.[41] BOEM and BSEE are subject to additional statutory requirements, including OCSLA's requirements that the NEPA applies at all stages.[42] Accordingly, BOEM prepares Environmental Impact Statements (EIS) to accompany decisions about 'Five-Year Leasing Programs, lease sales and development plans.'[43]

The Oil Pollution Act of 1990 (OPA)[44] requires a responsible party to pay all cleanup costs, while limiting additional liability to $75 million for third-party injuries.[45] This liability cap is not an absolute. For example, the cap is not applicable if additional federal regulations were violated or such release is caused by gross negligence of wilful misconduct.[46] The OPA does not preempt oil-spill liability and compensation laws on the state level.[47] The *Exxon Valdez* spill demonstrates how the OPA's cap was not limited. The federal government filed criminal charges after the *Exxon Valdez* release, based on violations of the Migratory Bird Treaty Act.[48] The spill killed protected birds and dumped refuse into navigable waters, violative of the statutes.[49]

The Magnuson–Stevens Act seeks to protect fisheries. Under the Act, the Department of Commerce is responsible for its implementation.[50] The Secretaries of Commerce and Interior must equally consider the OCSLA and

Magnuson–Stevens Act policies in order to minimise possible conflicts, balancing the interests of developing hydrocarbon and fishery resources and thus reading, to the extent possible, both statutes in harmony with each other.[51] In *Massachusetts v. Andrus*,[52] the Commonwealth of Massachusetts and conservation groups focused upon proposed offshore oil drilling in then-productive fishing grounds of Georges Bank.[53] The court held that the Secretary was 'under a duty to see that gas and oil exploration and drilling is conducted without unreasonable risk to the fisheries. The Interior Secretary's duty includes the obligation not to go forward with a lease sale in a particular area if it would create unreasonable risks in spite of all feasible safeguards.'[54]

In considering an EIS, courts balance threats and harms. For example, the *Andrus* court held that if the threat to fisheries[55] 'is relatively small, and the damage posed to fishing would be of no major consequence, the Secretary may determine that leasing should proceed.' The *Dubois* court further noted that 'The question whether a particular deficiency or combination [in an EIS] is sufficient to warrant holding it legally inadequate, or constitutes merely a 'fly speck,' is essentially a legal question, reviewable de novo.'[56]

Tribal law

Native tribes in the United States maintain certain sovereign powers, such as the authority to establish tribal governments and justice systems.[57] Native American jurisdictions are effectively sovereign nations that are 'separate but dependent' on the United States.[58] Accordingly, while tribes retained rights to use and occupy their territory (established through the tribes' prior exclusive use), such rights were subject to federal sovereignty.[59] Aboriginal title permits tribes to exploit natural resources on land and in the water. In a case involving the Shoshone tribe, the court held that[60] '... aboriginal title included the right to exploit natural resources above and below surface (timber and minerals), given aboriginal title established through "undisturbed possession of the soil from time immemorial".'

While only Congress may extinguish aboriginal title, Congress is not required to compensate tribes when extinguishing title, as: '... congressionally unrecognized aboriginal title is not a 'property right' protected by the Fifth Amendment.'[61]

The US government's interaction with tribes is similar to a trust relationship.[62] For example, the EPA maintains a consultative relationship with Alaskan tribes.[63] The EPA Region 10 Tribal Consultation and Coordination procedures dated 5 October 2012 require that each EPA office in this region (an area which includes Alaska) interact with tribes on a government-to-government basis.[64] Accordingly, federal agencies consider tribal interests in planning and decision-making processes.[65] The EPA's Tribal Trust and Assistance Unit, for example, is identified as a resource for Alaskan tribes interested in designing a community energy plan.

Indigenous-person proprietary rights have a different focus in Alaska as compared to any other US state. The Alaska Native Claims Act of 1971 (ANSCA) eliminated aboriginal title and claims on land and water.[66] In order to create the Trans-Alaska Pipeline System (TAPS), lingering real property claims concerning Native Alaskans – and resulting uncertainty – needed finality.[67] Under ANSCA, Alaska Natives received over 40 million acres of land and approximately one billion dollars.[68] ANSCA created twelve for-profit regional corporations and 200 village native for-profit corporations. An additional regional corporation was created for Alaska Natives who no longer resided in Alaska. With ANSCA, the 800-mile-long TAPS was constructed – beginning in Prudhoe Bay on Alaska's North Slope and extending to Valdez – the most northern ice-free port in the United States.[69] Alaska Natives thus became regional corporation shareholders. Where village corporations controlled the surface estate, the subsurface estate would be controlled by the regional corporations.[70] Additionally, under ANILCA,[71] a series of factors (not including native status) are considered in setting non-wasteful subsistence uses for the taking of fish and wildlife over federal public lands.[72] ANILCA affected over 100 million acres of federal lands in Alaska, doubling the size of the country's national park and refuge systems and tripling the amount of land designated as wilderness. Following ANILCA,[73] Alaska Natives do not have treaties with the federal government concerning explicit subsistence rights.[74]

Native legal challenges to hydrocarbon development have challenged certain links within the complex OCS regulatory scheme, or built upon growing US case law recognising the effects of climate change. For example, in *Massachusetts v. Envtl. Prot. Agency,*[75] the Supreme Court recognised harmful impacts from climate change affecting Massachusetts' citizens. The Court held that the EPA's refusal to regulate human-made emissions contributed to the state's injuries.'[76] In another case, a federal court noted that it possessed neither the expertise nor the authority to evaluate the policy judgments that EPA offered as justification for refusing to regulate motor-vehicle emissions.[77]

In *Native Village of Kivalina v. ExxonMobil,*[78] an Alaskan Inupiat village claimed that global warming resulting from defendants that included oil companies negatively impacted Arctic sea ice and threatened the village's very existence.[79] Alleged federal and state law breaches included public and private nuisance and civil conspiracy.[80] The federal court dismissed the public nuisance claim as a political, not legal question, holding that the court would otherwise have an impossible duty of balancing the social utility as compared to the harm flowing from the defendants' acts.[81] The court specifically noted that climate change was 'a matter appropriately left for determination by the executive or legislative branch in the first instance.'[82] The court further found that the '[P]laintiffs essentially concede that the genesis of global warming is attributable to numerous entities which individually and cumulatively over the span of centuries created the effects they are now experiencing.'[83] The court ultimately held that the village could not show that any of the defendants' conduct caused its injuries.[84]

Balancing subsistence needs was also discussed in *North Slope Borough v. Andrus*.[85] In *North Slope Borough*, the Interior Secretary was held to have discretion to balance subsistence needs of the Alaskan Inupiat people against other conflicting public interests. The *North Slope Borough* court studied the Secretary's trust responsibilities within the context of the ESA and affirmed tribal considerations. Specifically, the Court held that the Secretary was aware of drilling's[86] 'cumulative impacts and assimilate[d] within his decision-making any synergistic threats to the environment.' The Court further held that the Secretary complied with the ESA[87] requirements, stating:

> But the Secretary, even aside from his imputed role of trustee, does not have a free hand to neglect the environment. All of the environmental statutes, particularly ESA, structure and prescribe for the Secretary a solicitous stance toward the environment. Hence, where the Secretary has acted responsibly in respect of the environment, he has implemented responsibly, and protected, the parallel concerns of the Native Alaskans.

The North Slope Borough court concluded that when an agency complies in good faith with NEPA requirements and issues an EIS indicating that the agency closely examines the relevant environmental questions, its decision should be afforded great deference.[88]

Conclusion

OCS development raises a complex series of economic, political and social issues bound together by legal questions. The multiplicity of federal agencies, bureaux and offices contending with the OCS (such as BOEM, BSEE, the Office of Natural Resources Revenue or ONRR, the Environmental Protection Agency and, via the National Marine Fisheries Service, the Department of Commerce) evidence the recognition that offshore development is complex and must weigh several factors, including jurisdictional questions, compliance with multiple regulations, following tribal law, and whether such development is commercially/socially feasible. Recognising the stewardship of offshore resources with regulating offshore extraction opportunities requires significant resources and a diversity of stakeholders including Native Alaskans. The vexing issue is how to ensure that a multiplicity of regulations – and actors – work together, share information and perform efficiently.

Yet, an emerging trend indicates that growing communication involving industry, federal/state government and tribes creates opportunities for dialogue. Broadening the decision-making process while simultaneously mandating increasing inter-agency coordination advances an inclusive approach that fosters buy-in. The Obama administration has moved in this direction, creating a National Policy for the Stewardship of the Ocean, Our Coasts and the Great Lakes and the establishment of the National Ocean Council in 2010.[89] The Council issued a National Ocean Policy Implementation Plan in April, 2013, envisioning, among other things, that the plan[90]: '[P]rovides clear direction to Federal agencies and increased specificity to stakeholders. The Plan reflects a commitment to develop and apply the latest science and information, conduct the business of government more efficiently and collaborate more effectively with State, tribal, and the local authorities, marine industries and other stakeholders.' The National Plan pledges that improving the stewardship and health of the oceans will affect multiple stakeholders, including states and tribes benefiting from improved coordination with federal agencies, improved information for decision-making and support for regional priorities/solutions.[91] Broadening and deepening multi-party coordination is also described in a 2013 report issued through the US interagency, *Managing for the Future in a rapidly changing Arctic: A Report to the President*.[92] The report noted that coordinated stakeholder engagement 'can provide a foundation for a more holistic, integrated approach to management in the region.'[93] In addition, a 21 January 2015 Executive Order was issued (Enhancing Coordination of National Efforts in the Arctic) seeking to strengthen a cohesive approach to federal efforts.[94]

Recognising the multiplicity of stakeholders with Alaskan Arctic equities will ensure a balanced approach to the opportunities and challenges flowing from Arctic OCS development. Building this dialogue will allow multiple voices and perspectives to shape the world's last frontier, considering a myriad of social, environmental and commercial factors.

Notes

1 The author recognises the significant contribution of West Point graduate Second Lieutenant Sean McQuade. Note: This chapter does not reflect the views of the US government.
2 US Coastguard 2013, 15; LeVine, Van Tuyn and Hughes 2014, citing Arctic Research and Policy Act, 15 U.S.C. § 4111 (2012).
3 The OCS is defined in the Outer Continental Shelf Lands Act, section 1331 (a) as 'all submerged lands lying seaward and outside of the area of lands beneath navigable waters as defined in section 1301 of this title, and of which the subsoil and seabed appertain to the United States and are subject to its jurisdiction and control.' 43 U.S.C. § 1331 et. seq. (2012).
4 US Bureau of Ocean Energy Management 2015b.
5 Alaska Arctic Policy Commission 2014. For additional information on Alaskan Arctic efforts, *see, generally*, Alaska Arctic Policy Commission 2015.
6 Osherenko and Young, 1989, 80–81; Ogunwole 2006.
7 Jones 1987, 589.
8 LeVine, Van Tuyn and Hughes 2014, 1277.
9 For additional discussion on the MMS restructuring see Hogue 2010.
10 US Bureau of Ocean Energy Management 2011.
11 US Department of Interior 2011.

12 Alaska Const. Art. VIII, § 9.
13 Ibid. § 12. [Ditto]
14 Jones 1987, 593, citing Proclamation No. 2667, 10 Fed. Reg. 12, 303 (1945).
15 *United States* v. *California* 1947.
16 *United States* v. *Texas* 1950 and *United States* v. *California* 1947.
17 Ibid.
18 Act of 1953, 43 U.S.C. §§ 1301(a) (2), 1311(a) (2012).
19 Alaska Statehood Act § 6(m). Alaska follows the Submerged Lands Act.
20 Fishery Conservation and Management Act of 1976, Pub. L. No. 94–265, 90 Stat. 331, renamed Magnuson–Stevens Fishery Conservation and Management (Magnuson) Act, Pub. L. 104–208, 110 Stat. 3009 (codified as amended at 16 U.S.C. 1801–1883 (2000).
21 Jones 1987, 594.
22 H.R. Rep. No. 590, 95th Cong., 1st Sess. 74 (1977), reprinted in 1978 *United States Code Congressional & Administrative News* 1461, 1464 and 1507.
23 See 43 U.S.C. § 1337(a) (1) (1982).
24 Jones 1987, 596.
25 See 43 U.S.C. § 1331, et. seq. (2012).
26 43 U.S.C. § 1332(3).
27 Hartsig 2011, 273.
28 Pursuant to 43 U.S.C. § 1344(a) (2012).
29 43 U.S.C. § 1344(a) (1), (a) (3) (2012).
30 Ibid. § 1344(a) (1), Ibid. § 1344(a) (2)(g).
31 LeVine, Van Tuyn and Hughes 2014, citing 43 U.S.C. § 1336(a), 43 U.S.C. § 1337(b) (4) (2005).
32 See § 1340(a) (1) and § 1348(b) (1)–(3).
33 See 43 U.S.C. § 1351(a) (1) (2014) and §§ 1351(c) (1)–(6), 1351(b).
34 See 43 U.S.C. § 1351(a) (1) (2014).
35 Ibid. § 1321(j) (5) (A) (i) and § 1321(j) (5)(D)(iii).
36 43 U.S.C. § 1321(j) (5) (D)(iii); Executive Order No. 12,777, 56 Fed. Reg. 54757 (Oct. 18, 1991).
37 Memorandum of Understanding 2012.
38 See 16 U.S.C. §§ 1531–1544 (2014), 16 U.S.C. § 1362(12)(A) (2012) and § 1532(15); 33 U.S.C. § 1311 (2012).
39 US Environmental Protection Agency 2013.
40 National Environmental Policy Act of 1969, 42 U.S.C. § 4321 §§ 4321–4370 (1982).
41 42 U.S.C. § 4331(b).
42 See 43 U.S.C. Ibid. § 1351(e) (1)–(2) and § 1331(p).
43 LeVine, Van Tuyn and Hughes 2014, citing 43 U.S.C. § 1351(f).
44 Oil Pollution Act 1990, Pub. Law Nos. 101–380, 104 Stat. 484. Codified as amended at 33 U.S.C. 2701–2761 (2006 & Supp. III 2009).
45 33 U.S.C. § 2701–61 (2012) and, with respect to third-party liability, § 2704(a) (3). See Torrant 2011, 10–13.
46 33 U.S.C. § 2704(c) (1) (2012); see Unger 2014.
47 Unger 2014, citing Richardson 2010.
48 16 U.S.C. §§ 703–712, July 3, 1918, as amended and the Refuse Act, 33 U.S.C. §407 (1899).
49 Unger 2014, citing Richardson 2010 at p. 4. For a further description of the Exxon Valdez spill, see U.S. Environmental Protection Agency 2015.
50 16 U.S.C. § 1802(20).
51 See *Massachusetts* v. *Andrus*. 1979, 594 F.2d at 890–891. 'Allowing oil and gas exploitation to take absolute priority over fishing would be to sanction a schizophrenic national policy, in which one hand was busily at work undoing what the other was seeking to accomplish.'

52 594 F.2d 872, 888–891 (1st Cir. 1979).
53 In *Massachusetts* v. *Andrus*, 594 F.2d 872, 874 (1st Cir. 1979).
54 Ibid. at 889.
55 Ibid.
56 *Dubois et al.* v. *United States Department of Agriculture et al.* 1996, citing *Oregon Environmental Council* v. *Kunzman*, 817 F.2d 484, 493 (9th Cir. 1987).
57 See Ristroph 2010, 66–80.
58 Reinhard 2010, 538.
59 *Felix S. Cohen's Handbook of Federal Indian Law 1982 edition*. 1982, 491, citing Santa Fe, 314 US 339; *Washington* v. *Washington State Commercial Passenger Fishing Vessel Association*, 443 US 658, 670 n.15, 687 (1979).
60 *United States* v. *Shoshone Tribe* 1938.
61 Richards 2003, 945, citing Santa Fe, 314 US at 347; *Tee-Hit-Ton Indians* v. *United States* 1955; see also *United States* v. *Shoshone Tribe* 1938.
62 For a discussion of US tribal law, see Canuel 2015, 746–748; Flynn and Parsons 2001, 271; Wood 1995, 735.
63 US Environmental Protection Agency 2011.
64 Ibid.
65 US Environmental Protection Agency 2012.
66 43 U.S.C. § 1601 *et seq.*
67 Busenberg 2001. Discusses the pipeline as a case-study.
68 Lindsay 1999, 270.
69 Alyeska Pipeline Service Company 2015.
70 Ibid., 171.
71 Alaska National Interest Lands Conservation Act. 1980. U.S.C. 16 (1980), §§ 410hh-3233 (1980), U.S.C 43, §§ 1602–1784 et seq.
72 Ristroph 2010. For an interesting discussion of tribal cultural viewpoints concerning proprietary rights, see Osborne 2004, 203.
73 Mauer 2014.
74 A court action demonstrating the tension between Alaska and the federal government is discussed in Mauer 2014. See also Ristroph 2010. In March, Alaska Governor Parnell sued the Department of Interior for the right to run its own $50 million oil-scouting programme over ANWR's 1.5-million-acre coastal plain. The DOI holds that such exploration would be illegal and has refused to grant Alaska a permit when it applied in 2013. The DOI concluded its own exploration of the plain in the 1980s, and has maintained a position that any additional work could only be authorised by an act of Congress. The Obama Administration (and those of Republican and Democratic administrations since the Eisenhower era) has consistently opposed drilling the refuge and its predecessor-in-interest.
75 *Massachusetts v. Environmental Protection Agency* 2007.
76 Ibid.
77 *Comer et al.* v. *Murphy Oil USA*, Inc., 2012, citing Massachusetts, 549 US at 533.
78 663 F. Supp. 2d 863 (N.D. Cal. 2009).
79 663 F. Supp. 2d 868–869 (N.D. Cal. 2009).
80 Ibid.
81 Ibid. 872.
82 Ibid.
83 Ibid. 880.
84 Ibid. 881.
85 642 F.2d 589, 612–613 (D.C. Cir. 1980).
86 Ibid. 691. Ibid. 612.
87 7 U.S.C. § 136 (1996), 16 U.S.C. § 1531 (2014).
88 Ibid. 599. See *Northern Alaska Environmental Center* v. *Kempthorne* 2006.
89 Executive Order 2010.

90 National Ocean Council 2013, 3.
91 National Ocean Council 2013, 3.
92 Interagency Working Group 2013.
93 Interagency Working Group 2013, 2.
94 Executive Order 2015.

References

Alaska Arctic Policy Commission. 2014. 'Alaska Arctic Policy Commission Preliminary Report to the Alaska Legislature.' 30 January 2014. www.akarctic.com/wp-content/uploads/2014/02/AAPCpreliminaryReportV13final.pdf.

Alaska Arctic Policy Commission. 2015. 'Alaska Arctic Policy Commission Final Report and Implementation Plan, January 30, 2015 Executive Summary.'

Alyeska Pipeline Service Company. 2015. 'Overview of TAPS.' Last reviewed 21 June 2015. www.alyeska-pipe.com/TAPS.

Bureau of Ocean Energy Management. 2011. Chukchi Sea Planning Area, Oil and Gas Lease Sale 193 in the Chukchi Sea, Alaska, Final Supplemental Environmental Impact Statement, Vol. I, Appendix A (2011).

Busenberg, George J. 2001. 'Learning in Organizations and Public Policy.' *Journal of Public Policy* 21:2, 173–189.

Canuel, Edward T. 2015. 'The Four Arctic Law Pillars: A Legal Framework.' *Georgetown Journal of International Law* 46, 735–764.

Comer et al. v. *Murphy Oil USA, Inc.* 2012. 839 F. Supp. 2d 849, 851.

Dubois et al. v. *US Department of Agriculture et al.* 1996. 102 f.3d 1273, 1287.

Executive Order. 1991. Executive Order No. 12777 of October 18, 1991, 56 Fed. Reg. 54757.

Executive Order. 2010. Executive Order No. 13547 of July 19, 2010: Stewardship of the Ocean, Our Coasts, and the Great Lakes. www.whitehouse.gov/files/documents/2010stewardship-eo.pdf.

Executive Order. 2015. Executive Order – Enhancing the Coordination of National Efforts in the Arctic.

Felix S. Cohen's Handbook of Federal Indian Law 1982 edition. 1982. Eds. Rennard Strickland et al. Charlottesville, VA: Michie.

Flynn, Roger and Jeffrey C. Parsons. 2001. 'The Right to Say No: Federal Authority over Hardrock Mining on Public Lands.' *Journal of Environmental Law and Litigation* 16, 249, 271.

Hartsig, Andrew. 2011. 'Shortcomings and Solutions: Reforming the Outer Continental Shelf Oil and Gas Framework in the Wake of the Deepwater Horizon Disaster.' *Ocean and Coastal Law Journal* 16, 269, 273.

Hogue, Henry B. 2010. Congressional Research Service, R41485, Reorganization of the Minerals Management Service in the Aftermath of the Deepwater Horizon Oil Spill. www.fas.org/sgp/crs/misc/R41485.pdf.

Interagency Working Group on Coordination of Domestic Energy Development and Permitting in Alaska, 2013. Managing for the Future in a rapidly changing Arctic: A Report to the President.

Jones, Kevin G. 1987. 'Harvesting the Ocean's Resources: Oil or Fish?' *Southern California Law Review* 60, 587, 589, 593, 594 & 596.

LeVine, Michael, Peter Van Tuyn and Layla Hughes. 2014. 'Oil and Gas in America's Arctic Ocean: Past Problems Counsel Precaution,' *Seattle University Law Review* 37.

Lindsay, Britt. 1999. 'Tribal Land Quarrels in Alaska.' *Public Land & Resources Law Review* 20, 169, 270.
Massachusetts v. *Andrus*. 1979. 594 F.2d 872, 874 (1st Cir. 1979).
Massachusetts v. *Environmental Protection Agency*. 2007. 549 US 497, 523 (2007).
Mauer, Richard. 2014. 'State Suing over the Arctic National Wildlife Reserve, but is it Trying to Prove what's already been Proven?' *Alaska Dispatch News*, 25 March 2014.
Memorandum of Understanding. 2012. Memorandum of Understanding between the Bureau of Safety and Environmental Enforcement-US Department of Interior, and the US Coastguard-US Department of Homeland Security. 2012.
National Ocean Council. 2013. 'National Ocean Implementation Plan.' April 2013.
Northern Alaska Environmental Center v. *Kempthorne*. 2006. 457 F.3d 969, 977 (2006).
Ogunwole, Stella U. 2006. 'We the People: American Indians and Native Alaskans in the United States.' Washington, DC: US Census Bureau. February 2006. www.bia.gov/cs/groups/public/documents/text/idc-001819.pdf.
Osborne, Stephen D. 2004. 'Protecting Tribal Stories: The Perils of Propertization.' *American Indian Law Review* 28, 203.
Osherenko, Gail and Oran R. Young. 1989. Arctic Homelands: Native Interests in the Age of the Arctic, Hot Conflicts and Cold Realities Cambridge: Cambridge University Press.
Reinhard, Taylor. 2010. 'Advancing Tribal Law through "Treatment as a State" Under the Obama Administration.' *Tulane Environmental Law Journal* 23, 537, 538.
Richards, Andrew P. 2003. 'Aboriginal Title or the Paramountcy Doctrine? *Johnson* v. *Mcintosh* Flounders in Federal Waters Off Alaska in *Native Village of Eyak* v. *Trawler Diane Marie, Inc.*' *Washington Law Review* 78, 939, 945, 956.
Richardson, Nathan. 2010. 'Deepwater Horizon and the Patchwork of Oil Spill Liability Law,' *Resources for the Future* 4. www.rff.org/files/sharepoint/WorkImages/Download/RFF-BCK-Richardson-OilLiability.pdf.
Ristroph, Elizabeth Barrett. 2010. 'Alaska Tribes' Melting Subsistence Rights.' *Arizona Journal of Environmental Law & Policy* 1: 1, 47–91.
Tee-Hit-Ton Indians v. *United States*. 1955. 348 US 272, 279, 284–85 (1955).
Torrant, Andrew J. 2011. 'The Oil Pollution Act Of 1990: A Year in the Spotlight: Why the Act is still a Viable Method for Handling Spill-Related Claims.' *Houston Lawyer* 48, 10–13.
Unger, Jacob D. 2014. 'Regulating The Arctic Gold Rush: Recommended Regulatory Reforms to Protect Alaska's Arctic Environment from Offshore Oil Drilling Pollution,' *Alaska Law Review* 31, 263, 270, 275–276.
United States v. *California*. 1947. 332 US 19 (1947).
United States v. *Shoshone Tribe*. 1938. 304 US 111, 117 (1938).
United States v. *Texas*. 1950. 339 US 707, 719 (1950).
US Bureau of Ocean Energy Management. 2011. 'The Reorganization of the Former MMS,' Bureau of Ocean Energy Management.' www.boem.gov/About-BOEM/Reorganization/Reorganization.aspx.
US Bureau of Ocean Energy Management. 2015b. 'Alaska OCS Leasing Strategy – Factsheet.
US Coastguard. 2013. 'United States Coastguard.
US Department of Interior. 2011. 'Fact Sheet: The BSEE and BOEM Separation.' 19 January 2011.

US Environmental Protection Agency. 2011. 'EPA Policy on Consultation and Coordination with Indian Tribes.' 4 May 2011. Last reviewed 5 November 2014. www.epa.gov/tribal/pdf/cons-and-coord-with-indian-tribes-policy.pdf.

US Environmental Protection Agency. 2012. 'Outreach: 2012 Sustainable Energy Opportunities: Best Practices for Alaska Tribes.'

US Environmental Protection Agency. 2013. 'Arctic Oil and Gas Exploration General Permits.'

US Environmental Protection Agency. 2015. 'Exxon Valdez Spill Profile.' Last reviewed 21 June 2015.

Washington v. *Washington State Commercial Passenger Fishing Vessel Association*. 1979. 443 US 658, 670, nos. 15, 687 (1979).

Wood, Mary Christina. 1995. 'Symposium on Clinton's New Land Policies: Fulfilling The Executive's Trust Responsibility Toward the Native Nations on Environmental Issues: A Partial Critique of The Clinton Administration's Promises and Performance.' *Environmental Law Review* 25, 733, 735.

7 Governance of offshore hydrocarbon activities in the Arctic and energy policies

A comparative approach between Norway, Canada and Greenland/Denmark

Cécile Pelaudeix

Introduction

In recent years, there has been an increase in exploration and exploitation activities by extractive industries in the Arctic, particularly in the offshore sector. The rise in global demand for energy,[1] combined with the pressure for economic development in the North and the challenges of offshore activities, has led Arctic countries to adapt their legislation and regulatory frameworks.[2] Arctic countries face similar technical and environmental challenges drilling in the fragile and harsh environment of the Arctic marine areas, even if the various seas concerned – for instance, the Beaufort Sea and the Barents Sea – show geographical differences in terms of depth and sea ice. Still, the design of regulatory governance does not seem to follow the same pattern in these states. The question thus arises as to what extent these countries regulate differently and how to understand such differences. Do the differences in regulation derive only from geographical factors? The hypothesis I will test in the present chapter is that the dominant characterisations of a state impact the energy policies which themselves shape regulatory responses.

This chapter therefore presents a comparative analysis of governance of offshore hydrocarbon activities in Norway, Canada and Greenland. The choice of these three regulatory systems, two being designed by states and one designed by a self-government,[3] relies on their sharing relatively similar approaches to offshore regulations (based on a mainly goal-setting approach, rather than the mainly prescriptive approach of the United States[4] and Russia[5]) as well as space constraints. The chapter will show that a correlation exists between energy policy and offshore regulation. The first part compares the regulatory features of Canada, Norway and Greenland/Denmark with a focus on three criteria: economic incentive, environment protection and public – in particular, indigenous – participation. Drawing on the results of the first part, part two analyses the extent to which the differences in regulatory responses are related to the energy policies of Canada, Norway and Greenland/Denmark, which consider oil and gas as a commercial good, a public good or a strategic good.[6] Ultimately, it is shown that the dominant characterisations of the country/territory as a neoliberal state, a social democracy and a territory in transition to independence shed light on the regulatory responses of each country/territory.

Regulatory features

Offshore hydrocarbon activities and comparison criteria

In Canada, offshore drilling in the Beaufort Sea began in the early 1970s. The National Energy Board (NEB) has regulatory responsibilities for oil and gas exploration and development on frontier lands and in offshore areas not covered by provincial or federal management agreements.[7] The NEB operates under the Canada Petroleum Resources Act,[8] which governs the lease of federally owned oil and gas rights on 'frontier lands' to oil and gas companies under the Canada Oil and Gas Operations Act.[9] One hundred and forty-two Canadian Arctic offshore wells have been drilled, 92 of them in the Beaufort Sea region, since the early 1970s.[10] The industry operates in an extremely harsh environment, yet in shallow waters, with a maximum depth of 68 m. Still, the production has been minimal. Of the 152 exploration licences recorded as active in Arctic Canada, only 16 concern the Beaufort Sea, and only one production licence has been issued so far.[11] No drilling activity took place between 1990 and 2006. Exploration licences have been issued in the Beaufort Sea in 2007 and 2008 for deep waters up to 1500 m in the Ajurak and Pokak fields,[12] but no drilling activity is taking place at the moment. Seismic tests have been envisaged in Baffin Bay, raising opposition from Inuit associations. In 2010, seismic tests in Lancaster Sound were stopped by a decision of the Nunavut Court of Justice; other seismic tests planned in Baffin Bay were approved in 2014 by a decision of the Federal Court of Appeal which have been challenged before the Supreme Court of Canada.[13]

In Norway, exploration of the Barents Sea has been under way for more than 30 years. Offshore production begun in 2007 in the Snøhvit field, with an offshore installation based on seabed facilities. The authority regulating offshore oil and gas drilling lies with the Petroleum Safety Authority, but there are two other regulators with independent authority over aspects of health, safety and environmental regulation of the industry (the Petroleum Safety Authority and the Norwegian Environment Agency). The oilfield Goliat, a bit farther south, is currently being developed by ENI Norge A/S. In March 2016, production started from a traditional surface platform. The two new important oil discoveries by Statoil in the Barents Sea north of Snøhvit – Skrugard in April 2011 and Havis offshore oil fields in January

2012, renamed the Johan Castberg field – are expected to enter into exploitation by 2020. The legislation regulating such activities is the Norwegian Petroleum Act of November 1996.[14] The responsible administrative authority is the Ministry of Petroleum and Energy.

In Greenland, exploration started in 1975 with five wells drilled offshore. The Mineral Licence and Safety Authority (MLSA) is the administrative authority for mineral (including oil) resources. Cairn Energy recently completed an exploration campaign, but no commercially viable oil has been found so far. Considering that about 20 years' time is required between discovery and exploitation and that only 15 wells have been drilled in Greenland, the government (Naalakkersuisut) is continuing its strategy of exploring for commercially viable oil. In the period from 2014 to 2018, Naalakkersuisut will conduct licensing rounds for various areas around the island.[15]

Comparing the economic incentive systems: liability, taxation and licensing

Offshore activities in the Arctic are costly ventures due to limited geological information, significant technical and environmental challenges and lack of infrastructure. These constraints come in addition to the growth in investment and operating costs in recent years in the petroleum industry,[16] as well as falling oil prices. Arctic governments promote investment in the offshore hydrocarbon sector through various incentives pertaining to taxation, liability and licensing conditions.

Considering the potential cross-border consequences of an oil spill, liability issues have been discussed at the international and supranational levels. Liability for oil pollution resulting from a platform is not regulated by any international convention. Offshore activities take place in the territorial sea or in the EEZ or on the continental shelf of Arctic coastal states, where, under UNCLOS, states enjoy sovereign rights over their resources (Articles 56 and 77) and are entitled to exercise respective legislation. These sovereign rights carry with them the duty of due regard for the rights and duties of other states (Article 56), as well as minimum standards to protect and preserve the marine environment (Articles 192 and 193). In addition to domestic law, many international rules and international or regional agreements apply to the EEZ in the Arctic region when it comes to pollution at sea. Existing conventions, however, fail to adequately cover issues of civil and environmental liability for pollution resulting from activities from a platform.[17] In the aftermath of the Deepwater Horizon blowout, discussions have taken place at the IMO about an international convention covering offshore oil and gas activities, and the EU has adapted its legislation with the Offshore Safety Directive, which includes rules on strict environmental liability. The EU is working on increasing the compliance requirements binding on companies for both equipment standards and financial guarantees.[18]

The Offshore Safety Directive has extended the scope of the Environmental Liability Directive, which now also includes all the marine areas of EEA member-states.[19]

In 2015, Canada passed legislation – the Energy Safety and Security Act – to increase the liability caps in the offshore industry.[20] The principle of strict liability applies in Canada: persons who cause oil spills are generally liable for damages caused to third parties even absent proof of fault or negligence. The liability is limited, though, and the caps, even raised from 40 million to 1 billion Canadian dollars, remain low if one considers that responding to the 2010 oil-well blowout in the Gulf of Mexico cost the operator more than 40 billion US dollars (52 billion Canadian dollars) within less than two years.[21] The upper limit of compensation available from the International Convention on the Establishment of an International Fund (the IOPC fund convention) is 1.1 billion US dollars: this will apply only to 'no fault' liability. If operators are found to be at fault or negligent, they will continue to face unlimited liability, but it is considered difficult to prove fault or negligence, and taxpayers can be picking up the bill. In allowing investors without sufficient funds to pay for the cleaning-up and reparations for a large-scale environmental disaster, the cap is considered as essentially a transfer of risk to the public sector to encourage investment.[22]

The attribution of licences is decided after a bid made by companies, which engage in spending a certain sum on exploration. Section 27 of the Canada Oil and Gas Operations Act (COGOA) provides that companies who apply for exploration or production permits or licences must provide proof of financial responsibility in the form of a letter of credit, a guarantee or indemnity bond or in any other form satisfactory to the National Energy Board (NEB), in an amount satisfactory to the Board. This relative level allows flexibility. In 2012, British-based Franklin Petroleum secured leases over 9,060 km^2 in the Beaufort Sea after committing to spending only $7.5 million on exploration, an amount that includes spill response and prevention.[23] As a comparison, in 2008, BP Exploration Company Limited committed to spend $1.18 billion on exploration activity for large blocks in the Beaufort Sea.[24] Regarding taxation, Canada has a Petroleum and Gas revenue Tax levied since 1981 at an effective rate of 12 percent on gross income and a fix 10 percent royalty. In 1982, the Petroleum Incentive Program introduced the reimbursement of Canadian-owned companies for up to 80 percent, and foreign companies for up to 25 percent of eligible exploration costs.

By contrast, in Norway the Petroleum Act imposes unlimited and strict liability for pollution damage,[25] and the Environmental Liability Directive – mentioned above – is implemented into Norwegian law. Norway, instead, proposes reduced taxation as an incentive for companies to invest in the offshore sector, aware that for all companies cost is increasingly problematic. Revenues from petroleum produced on the Norwegian continental shelf are subject to the high marginal profit tax rate of 78 percent, which comprises a 28 percent corporate tax (the same income tax that is charged on all businesses) and a 50 percent special petroleum tax.[26] In the early 2000s, Norway introduced an incentive system for the offshore sector, including annual refunds of 78 percent of all direct exploration costs and other generous deductions for investments. As the Snøhvit field is exploited with an offshore installation having a shore base, the operating company – Statoil – benefits from exemption from the additional 50 percent tax on profits from offshore production.[27]

In another difference from Canada, the licensing procedure uses a tender process (with a tender evaluation committee) in combination with a grant system, under which the licence is granted to the best offer, rather than the highest bidder.[28] Production licences are awarded on the basis of objective, non-discriminatory and published criteria. The most important criteria are: relevant experience and technical expertise; satisfactory financial capacity; and geological evaluation of the area in question.[29] There is no signing fee, but a fee to cover the cost of processing the application.[30] The process is intended to prevent speculation.

In principle, Greenland applies the principle of strict liability, with no liability limits indicated. Liability terms are formulated in a vague way in the Greenlandic Mineral Resources Act[31] without any effects on the licensee, as the addressee of the relevant article is Naalakkersuisut, which designs the licence: "The license may stipulate that the licensee's liability must be covered by insurance or another type of security."[32] Unlike the Norwegian Act on Petroleum Activities, the Greenlandic Mineral Resources Act does not provide a specific clause for compensation for fishermen, either. In addition, liability issues in the marine areas around Greenland are complicated by the fact that the respective responsibilities of Greenland and of the Kingdom of Denmark when it comes to pollution at sea in the exclusive economic zone (EEZ) and the continental shelf remain a complex issue.[33] Licences are granted on the basis of similar criteria as in Norway, i.e. expertise, financial background, and performance of the activities (e.g. in relation with safety, health and the environment).[34]

A significant economic incentive provided by the Greenlandic self-government to facilitate investment in its 'frontier area' relates to taxation, which is in relation with cumulated expenditures. The corporate tax for oil and mineral is 30 percent, with a 2.5 percent royalty on turnover. Yet, royalties are progressive: they are 7.5 percent, 17.5 percent and 30 percent, which will be payable when accumulated revenues exceed accumulated expenditure by 35 percent, 45 percent and 55 percent, respectively.[35]

Comparing the environment protection systems

Significant differences arise between Canada, Norway and Greenland/Denmark when it comes to environmental protection. Environmental impact assessments (EIAs) are required in all three countries/territory. In contrast to this, strategic environment assessments are required only in Norway, though they have been implemented in the Greenlandic offshore planning since 2006.[36] The management system, which includes rules to promote safety and environmental protection, does not require risk analysis in Canada,[37] but the Norwegian rules do.[38] In Greenland a management system is not required under the Mineral Resources Act.[39] The Act uses only a very general formulation to address environmental and safety issues.[40]

As the drilling of a relief-well is increasingly demanded internationally – particularly in the aftermath of the Deepwater Horizon blowout – such a technique is also required in Norway, Canada and Greenland, but the legislation in Canada contains an exemption clause. The current Canadian regulation allows the possibility of replacing the 'same-season relief-well standard' – that is, an old standard requiring companies to secure backup relief-well rigs for all drilling projects – by an equivalent measure. On 11 July 2014, the NEB accepted the request of Imperial Oil (for a consortium with Exxon and BP) to consider a review and ruling on 'equivalent approach to satisfy same season relief well.'[41] This decision, which looks somehow paradoxical considering the international context of tightening regulatory requirements and imposing the 'same-season relief-well standard' as a basic standard, has sparked concern in Canada.

Oil spill preparedness requires a contingency plan in Canada; but only Norway recommends that such plans be tested.[42] In Greenland, the legislation is less strict: no contingency plan is required and there is no minimum requirement for response capacity. Additional requirements can still be added, however, by supplementing with additional impact benefit agreements (IBAs)[43] and/or licences.[44]

Comparing the participative democracy and consultation processes

Decisions over offshore activities can involve public consultation in two circumstances. The first is the consultation of indigenous peoples, which is required by the Indigenous and Tribal Convention under the International Labour Organisation – ILO 169 (1989). The Convention, which recognises the rights of indigenous peoples to culture and identity, land and natural resources, is ratified in the Arctic only by Norway and Denmark.[45] The (non-binding) United Nations Declaration on the Rights of Indigenous Peoples (UNDRIP) goes further and contains provisions on obtaining a free, prior and informed consent from indigenous peoples for any project affecting their lands or territories and other resources.[46] The second circumstance relates to access to information, public participation and access to justice, which are regulated by the UNECE Aarhus convention.[47] The convention focuses on interactions between the public and public authorities in a democratic context: it establishes that sustainable development can be achieved only through the involvement of all stakeholders. It also links government accountability and environmental protection. Norway is the only one of the three countries/territory covered by this comparative analysis that has ratified this convention. Denmark has ratified it only with reservation for Greenland.

In the Canadian Arctic, the NEB keeps the above-mentioned competences over the administration of the offshore sector even when devolution over resources has been granted to a territorial government such as the Northwest Territories. The Crown has a duty to consult indigenous peoples, but this does not mean a duty for the NEB to follow the comments received – as several judges have ruled recently.[48] Canada did endorse the UNDRIP in 2010, but announced it would do it 'in a manner fully consistent with Canada's constitution and laws.'[49] This conditional endorsement has been analyzed by law scholars as undermining 'the status of this vital instrument' and preventing its application, whereas the 'Declaration can be effectively used in litigation in Canadian courts.'[50] After the 2010 ruling of the Nunavut Court of Justice, which required to stop the seismic tests in Lancaster Sound, Nunavut,[51] it would appear that the Inuit, arguing that such tests could impact marine mammals on which they rely for subsistence, had a strong position under Canadian law. The judgment was not based on the issue of consultation: the judge considered that the true nature or value of the consultations that did take place could not be determined; the decision to block seismic testing was made on the consideration that the potential for significant harm that the testing posed to the Inuit was greater than the losses that would be incurred if the injunction was granted and the testing was not completed as scheduled.[52] The last court judgment, emanating from the Federal Court in July 2015, dismissed the application of Nunavut plaintiffs hoping to reverse a decision to allow seismic tests in Baffin Bay and Davis Strait: the judge also reminded that the duty to consult was not a veto right, and, in that case, deemed that the NEB had concluded reasonably on the unlikeliness of significant environmental damage.[53] The full endorsement of UNDRIP – as proposed by Prime Minister Trudeau in 2016 – could lead to a notable change in the Canadian position vis-à-vis the principle of free, prior and informed consent as a politically accepted principle.[54]

In Norway, the offshore industry is in competition with the fisheries sector, which has always played a key social and economic role. The government has consequently prohibited drilling around the Lofoten Islands, but allowed drilling further north. Consultations involve the public population, including the Sámi people. Strategic Environment Assessments (SAE) which are required in Norway imply public consultation and offer an opportunity for engagement and influence at the strategic tier. In the case of the Goliat project in the Barents Sea, participation has been assessed as beneficial for the proponent who could explain the consistency of project mitigation actions.[55] With regard to indigenous peoples, an agreement has been signed between the Norwegian government and the Sámi parliament regarding how such consultations will take place.[56] But, the Sámi claim that their historical fishing rights in marine areas are not recognised by the current practice. The Norwegian Ministry of Petroleum and Energy endeavours to comply with international law and refers to rights as defined in the International Covenant on Civil and Political Rights (ICCPR) Article 27,[57] stating that ethnic minorities shall not be denied the right to enjoy their own culture, but considers that "the wild living marine resources belongs to the community of the country as a whole."[58] However, an amendment made in 2012 to the Norwegian Participation Act has allocated additional fishing quotas to the Sámi. But the Standing Committee of Justice (SCJ) recognised that Sámi rights were not legally protected in a reliable way. This is, among other factors, a concern when it comes to compensation for the Sámi people's economic losses in case of an oil spill.[59]

In Greenland, the regulation related to mineral (including oil) resources does not contain any rule on SEA nor any specific provision or protection of indigenous rights. SEA have been implemented in the Greenlandic offshore planning since 2006, but formal public hearing periods were only introduced later using the governmental hearing portal.[60] It is also the opinion of Naalakkersuisut that it represents the interests of the Inuit. However, the content, form and practice of consultation processes regarding projects affecting the environment have been criticised for lack of proper available public information, lack of transparency in the decision of approval of activities and inadequate inclusiveness of the general public.[61] In that context, the reservation that Denmark made for Greenland when ratifying the Aarhus Convention is currently being questioned in the Greenlandic parliament (Inatsisartut).[62] In addition, in June 2014, as a consequence of new rules related to the involvement of the Ministry for the environment in mineral extractive activities, Naalakkersuisut presented a bill amending the 2009 Mineral Resources Act in order to prevent public access to previously confidential documents. Finally, after much concern in Greenland about the issue, the restriction of access has been removed from the proposed amendments on pre-consultation and consultation.

Significant differences

Although the three regulatory frameworks bear common features, significant differences arise from the analysis. The main economic incentives are related to liability caps and licensing bids in Canada, whereas in Norway and Greenland, taxation is an important leverage. Important differences arise when it comes to regulation of the environment. Greenland does not incorporate many provisions in its legislation on raw material extraction, leaving possibilities for additional requirements to be added by supplementing agreements (IBAs) and licences. In Canada, a flexible regulation on safety measures introduces the possibility of providing an equivalent measure to the 'same season relief well' (SSRW). Regarding the participation of indigenous peoples, there is room in all three regulatory systems to fully comply with international law as formulated in the UNDRIP.

Energy policies and regulatory frameworks

To explain why the regulatory responses differ significantly, this section presents a comparative analysis of energy policies in Canada, Norway and Greenland, with a focus on oil and gas. It is shown that regulatory responses are shaped by energy policies. Energy is an ambivalent good,[63] and in the three cases studies, energy appears to be an asset of differing value for each government. In Canada, which is a net exporter, oil and gas energy is mainly a commercial good. In Norway, where the economic importance of oil and gas exports is related to the welfare system, and where profits are put in a public fund, energy mostly stands as a public good. In Greenland, where economic revenues from oil and gas are needed to support a political agenda on independence from Denmark, energy stands as a strategic good. The dominant political economy characterisations of the country/territory as a neoliberal state, a social democracy and a territory in transition to independence shed light on the regulatory responses of each country/territory.

Canada and the neo-liberal model: energy as a commercial good

For Canada, energy appears to be considered above all as an economic activity, carried out by the private sector and including an important part of its exports. Canada has vast energy resources, including hydropower, biomass, coal, conventional and unconventional oil and natural gas, wind, solar, uranium, and tidal and wave energy, which makes it one of the world's five largest energy producers. It is in fact the fifth-largest natural gas producer in the world, and the sixth-largest producer of petroleum in the world.[64] Over the next 20 years, energy production levels have become increasingly greater than domestic needs, resulting in growing amounts of energy available for export,[65] mainly to the United States. The new energy strategy (2015) renews the objective to promote exports of energy, expertise, and innovation.[66] Indeed, the energy sector has been a primary driver of Canada's economy for many decades.[67] In its 2015 energy strategy, Canada develops a vision according to which the country is a global leader in providing a secure, sustainable and reliable supply of energy, and defines objectives insisting on achieving a balanced approach between the provinces and the territories, strengthening its economy, maintaining the highest environmental standards, and promoting energy exports.

In its Arctic strategy, Canada defines itself as an Arctic power, a qualification to which energy makes a contribution.[68] In addition to onshore exploration and development there is renewed interest in the offshore possibilities, including a new area of oil and gas exploration in the deeper waters of the Beaufort Sea.[69] Canada deems that the huge potential of energy resources in its Arctic region, including the resources in the ocean, needs to be unlocked:[70] for that purpose, the government has launched a massive geo-mapping campaign (the Geo-mapping for Energy and Minerals programme) consisting of two plans of 100 million Canadian dollars each (2008–2013 and 2013–2020) to identify areas of mineral and petroleum potential and to lead to more effective private-sector exploration investment.[71] This objective is consistent with and related to another important objective of the Canadian federal government: 'exercising its sovereignty' in the region, which is the first objective of its Arctic foreign policy. Canada understands the exercise of its sovereignty as, first, resolving boundary issues and, second, exercising sovereign rights over the resources of the seabed and subsoil.[72] In that perspective, the Arctic stands as a region of huge potential, in which Canada is additionally pursuing a political agenda revolving around sovereignty issues.

Canada's mechanism of licensing and the attractiveness of liability caps (even after the passing of the Energy Safety and Security Act in 2015), the flexibility of environment regulation (alternatives to the same-season relief-well standards) in the time-consuming operations context of the Arctic, as well as little participation of indigenous peoples as a mean to influence decisions[73] are in relation with energy conceived as a commercial good.

Norway and the "state centred" model: energy as a public good

Petroleum activities have been key to the development of Norway's current welfare state.[74] The Norwegian petroleum industry has over the last 40 years evolved to become Norway's most important industry. Norway's GDP per capita is one of the highest in the world and the country has a very high standard of living compared with other European countries. Petroleum accounts for 30 percent of the government's revenues,[75] and Norway exports most of its oil and gas production.[76] Almost no natural gas is consumed in the country:[77] the nation relies nearly entirely on hydroelectric power for its electricity (it is the sixth-largest producer in the world) and for 26 percent of its heat. Norway is the third-largest exporter of energy in the world.[78]

Norway does not pay dividends to shareholders, but deposits 100 percent of its oil and gas revenues into its sovereign wealth fund. Maximum 4 percent a year is withdrawn and goes into the state budget. The economy of Norway is a developed mixed economy, in which the state has ownerships in strategic areas of the economy. The state invests in leases through its special oil investment company Petoro, which does not operate oil fields; it merely takes an equity stake in the leases that the government wants. The state also has a majority stake in Statoil, which operates more as a regular commercial company.

Norway has two major national strategies for energy: oil and gas in the twenty-first century (OG21) and Energi21. Energi21 focuses on enhancing technology for renewable energy and carbon capture and storage, while OG21 aims at sustaining profitability and resource optimisation on the Norwegian continental shelf, as well as increasing exports of technology and knowledge. Norway believes that the remaining potential resources, especially in the form of gas and new discoveries, indicate growth potential and a long-term future on the continental shelf. The remaining resources, including the resources in the Arctic, are less accessible and more challenging.[79] Norway has defined the Barents Sea as a new energy province and the first out of seven development trends that will shape the initiatives and priorities of Norwegian High North policy.[80] The importance of facilitating new development projects in the oil and gas sector in the High North is renewed in the 2014 Arctic strategy of the Norwegian government, which also emphasises the need to meet world energy demand.[81]

In Norway, the petroleum activities are much in focus. The petroleum industry is by far the most important industry of the last 40 years and, as a welfare state, Norway has dedicated the revenues of its hydrocarbon resources to the benefit of the country through a public fund. Norway has built its reputation on high environmental standards, and, indeed, its legislation includes unlimited and strict liability, risk management, well control and a granting system based first and foremost on expertise, experience and financial capacity. It therefore does not come as a surprise that Norway manoeuvres with taxation, instead of protection of the environment, to offer attractive investment opportunities. Regarding participation, Norway has not granted specific rights to the coastal Sámi, and it is deemed that they only enjoy a weak protection of their historical rights.[82]

Greenland and the "independence building model": energy as a strategic good

Greenland's oil and gas strategy is based on securing investment for exploration and development of viable production. As mentioned above, no commercially viable oil has been found so far, but relying on exploitation experience in Canada and Norway, Naalakkersuisut deems that patience is in order as few wells have been drilled so far and the territory's offshore potential is ranked as third (East Greenland) and fifth (West Greenland) most prolific of the resource provinces in terms of oil (out of 33).[83]

As fisheries and shellfish represent almost 90 percent of Greenlandic exports, the territory's economy is vulnerable to international price fluctuations[84] and needs to be diversified. Securing a stronger economic basis is not only required to lessen the economic dependence on Denmark, but also to provide extra income, as it is expected that by the year 2040 economic aid from Denmark will not be able to cover the public expenditure.[85] Denmark provides €470 million in economic aid to Greenland each year, representing approximately 40 percent of Greenland's GDP. The petroleum industry is thus considered one of the most important areas for creation of the basis for a self-sustaining economy.[86] Greenland's Oil and minerals strategy highlights Naalakkersuisut's goal of furthering the chances of making a commercially viable oil find.[87]

The objective of the government of Greenland is to find commercial oil and to start exploitation. As stated by Kuupik Kleist, when he was premier of Greenland, the decisions ahead are not costless:

> Economic, social and political realities make it imperative that Inuit develop a clear position on resource development, especially on the timely, political and environmentally sensitive matter of offshore [...]. If Inuit want greater political and economic freedom, then the paramount question we must ask ourselves is, what price are we prepared to pay?[88]

In a competitive international market, the main challenge is to attract companies.[89] The incentives to invest in offshore exploitation need to be strong, particularly when the infrastructure available is limited, e.g. onshore chemical storage facility. Naalakkersuisut has tried to come up with a 'balancing act' to achieve objectives that are recognised as 'contradictory to some extent': to provide a framework attractive for oil companies to invest, to ensure that Greenland society benefits financially from the activities and, finally, to prevent irreversible damage to the environment.[90] Greenland's legislation has taken inspiration from the Norwegian experience but varies in several respects, as rather than incorporating requirements into its legislation, Greenland proposes instead a general framework, leaving detailed and constraining provisions to be potentially incorporated in the licences, agreements (IBAs) and guidelines.

In the end, differentiated responses between the three regulatory systems with regard to economic incentive, protection of the environment and participation can all be explained by the respective energy policies defined in the context of specific political economy models. The relation between regulatory framework, in terms of economic incentives, environment and participation, and energy policies can be summarized in the table below.

Table 7.1 Regulation and energy policies

	Canada (Neo-liberal model)	*Norway (State-centred model)*	*Greenland (Independence Building Model)*
	Energy value *Commercial good*	Energy value *Public good*	Energy value *Strategic good*
Regulation *Economic Incentives*	Strong (weak liability)	Strong (low taxation)	Strong (progressive taxation)
Regulation *Environment Requirement*	Low	Strong	Middle
Regulation *Public Participation*	Low	Middle	Low

Conclusion

The characteristics of the regulation of Arctic offshore oil and gas activities derive from more factors than the solely technical challenges of sea ice, depth and remoteness. The extreme natural-climate conditions (icing, icebergs, ice floes, high winds, darkness), the remoteness of the region from basic infrastructure and the low sustainability of the region's ecosystems are not all that accounts for the regulatory framework. This analysis has shown that there is a relation between the energy strategies of Canada, Norway and Greenland and their regulatory framework with regard to the hydrocarbon offshore sector, whether that relation concerns the economic incentive system, environmental protection or indigenous peoples' and public participation. None of the three regulatory systems under scrutiny has taken steps to fully fulfil the provisions of the UNDRIP, which remains endorsed in a non-binding way. Regarding economic incentive and environmental protection, Canada, which has an economic and a political agenda in the Arctic, has taken measures that diverge from international standards and best practices (relief-well requirements, liability caps and licensing criteria). Norway looks to its taxation system to offer an attractive investment environment and keeps high environmental standards for its primary industry, which fuels a public fund. Greenland has adopted a general framework so as to retain flexibility to implement (or not) stricter provisions in licences or guidelines and yet maintain attractiveness in a competitive international market, with a view to creating the basis for a self-sustaining economy.

Neither in Canada nor in Norway or Greenland are offshore oil and gas activities aimed at energy self-sufficiency. Although energy is an ambivalent good which can serve several goals, it appears to be conceived of primarily as a commercial good in Canada, a public good in Norway and a strategic good in Greenland. Energy strategies and related regulatory governance reflect the main characterisations of the three authorities as, respectively, a neo-liberal state, a social democracy and an autonomous territory in transition to independence. Regulation of offshore oil and gas activities therefore not only reflects technical rationality, but is also based on political choices. While future research extending to the United States and Russia could shed additional light on this issue, the results of this analysis show the need for a reflection on the drivers of offshore oil and gas exploitation, in order to balance them with environmental and social costs, and to inform decision and regulatory processes in accordance with risk acceptance.

Notes

1 The demand is expected to rise by more than a third by 2035. International Energy Agency 2012.
2 Pelaudeix 2015; Baker 2012.
3 Since the Act on Greenland Self Government in 2009 (cf. the Danish Act No. 473 of 12 June 2009 on Greenland Self-Government), Greenland has exercised

jurisdiction in areas including mineral resources. Greenland is still part of the Kingdom of Denmark.
4 See Chapter 6.
5 See Chapter 8.
6 Gupta 2012; Edwards 2015.
7 In onshore areas of Canadian provinces, regulatory power over energy policy lies with the provinces.
8 Canada Petroleum Resources Act, c. 36, 1985. http://laws-lois.justice.gc.ca/eng/acts/C-8.5/index.html.
9 Canada Oil and Gas Operations Act c. 0–7, 1985. http://laws-lois.justice.gc.ca/eng/acts/O-7/FullText.html?term=response.
10 Callow 2012. See also Henderson and Loe 2014, 18.
11 Henderson and Loe 2014, 19.
12 Imperial Oil Resources Ventures Limited 2013.
13 Federal Court of Appeal 2015. The Supreme Court will issue its decision in 2017.
14 Act 29 November 1996 No. 72 relating to petroleum activities, as supplemented by regulations laid down with Royal 27 June 1997. www.npd.no/en/Regulations/Regulations/Petroleum-activities/.
15 Government of Greenland 2014.
16 Tormodsgard 2014, 14.
17 For the issue of civil liability, cf. Scicluna 2011. According to Scicluna, 'Little success was obtained when trying to assimilate the civil liability regime applicable to the shipping industry [the 1992 CLC and 1992 Fund, applicable to tanker vessels] to offshore operations. This is said in the light of the various dissimilarities, which exist between ships and offshore installations. For instance while it may be difficult to estimate the potential severity of future uncontrolled blowouts of offshore installations, the maximum storage capacity of ships is known and the potential risk is calculable' (54–55). Thus the need, according to Scicluna, for a comprehensive and binding global instrument that addresses *liability* for oil pollution damage caused by offshore activities. Scicluna 2011, 40. For the issue of civil and environmental liabilities, see also Basse 2015, para. 334–336.
18 Directive 2013/30/EU of the European Parliament and of the Council of 12 June 2013 on safety of offshore oil and gas operations and amending Directive 2004/35/EC Text with EEA relevance. *OJ* L 178, 28.6.2013, 66–106. The national authorities are required to ensure that the licensee is financially liable for the prevention and remediation of environmental damage caused by offshore hydrocarbon operations carried out by, or on behalf of, the licensee or the operator. See Chapter 4.
19 Environmental Liability Directive (2004/35/EC), 2004, as amended by the Offshore Safety Directive (2013/30/EU).
20 Energy Safety and Security Act, adopted in 2015.
21 Porta and Bankes 2011, 6.
22 Emmerson and Lahn 2012, 41.
23 Byers and Stoller 2013.
24 Dagg et al. 2011, 8.
25 Norwegian Petroleum Act, section 7(3). See Chapters 4 and 11.
26 Henderson and Loe 2014, 42.
27 A significant incentive for oil exploration, the Norwegian tax system is albeit on less favourable terms since 2013. Ibid., 42–43.
28 Persily 2011.
29 Cf. Regulations to Act relating to petroleum activities. Laid down by Royal Decree 27 June 1997 pursuant to Act 29 November 1996 no 72 relating to petroleum activities, section 10–18 and Act 10 February 1967 relating to procedure in cases concerning the public administration, section 13 c third paragraph and

section 19 third paragraph. Last amended by Royal Decree 2 July 2012 No 729.) Available at www.npd.no/en/Regulations/Regulations/Petroleum-activities/#3. See also Norwegian Ministry of Petroleum and Energy 2013.

30 The fee amounts to 109,000 Norwegian kroner (in 2014), around €12 000. See Svensen et al. 2014.

31 Inatsisartut Act No. 7 of 7 December 2009 on Mineral Resources and Mineral Resource Activities, with later amendments. 'A licensee must compensate damage caused in connection with operations or activities under the license even if the cause of damage is accidental.' Article 92.

32 Article 92(3).

33 See Chapter 4. Greenland is bound by Denmark's ratification of IMO's International Convention on Civil Liability for Oil Pollution Damage (CLC), its Oil Pollution Compensation Funds, but not to its International Convention on Civil Liability for Bunker Oil Pollution Damage (Denmark made a reservation), nor is Greenland covered by EU's Environmental Liability Directive (not being a member of the EU).

34 Mineral Resources Act, art. 24–1.

35 Government of Greenland 2014, 10–11.

36 For Greenland, see Chapter 15. There are no legal rules on strategic environmental assessment in the Greenlandic legislation. The Greenlandic rules on EIA are only framework rules supplemented by guidelines, and they are not in harmony with the UNECE's Espoo Convention (which has been ratified by Denmark without reservation for Greenland). The United States, Iceland and Russia have signed but not yet ratified the Espoo convention. Johnstone deems that a binding treaty among the eight Arctic states to govern environmental impact assessments remains 'a distinct possibility': Johnstone 2015, 274.

37 Dagg et al. 2011, 46.

38 Section 11, entitled 'Risk Reduction Principle' of the Norwegian Regulations relating to health, safety and the environment in the petroleum activities and at certain onshore facilities ('The framework regulations'). (Last amended 24 May 2013.) www.psa.no/framework-hse/category403.html.

39 Dagg et al. 2011, 46 and 52.

40 'Best international practices' are required, and 'activities must be performed appropriately as well as in a sound manner as regards safety, health, the environment, resource utilisation and social sustainability,' cf. the Mineral Resources Act, article 83(1). Such obligations cannot be enforced, as they are not clear enough. The Mineral Resources Act (Article 84(1)) also provides for a general competence of Naalakkersuisut to make administrative binding obligations in the form of '... provisions on technical matters, matters relating to health and safety in connection with offshore activities as well as environmental matters, resource utilisation and social sustainability.' This competence has not been used, however.

41 Request for Review and Ruling on Equivalent Approach to Satisfy Same Season Relief Well (SSRW) Policy for the Imperial Oil Resources Ventures Limited (IORVL) Beaufort Sea Exploration Joint Venture Drilling Programme (Project).

42 Dagg et al. 2011, 161 and 162

43 Concerning the IBAs, see Chapter 14.

44 Section 53 (2) in Part 13 (on the general rules on environmental protection) of the Greenlandic Mineral Resources Act reads: 'Anyone who wishes to commence, commences or performs activities that may cause pollution must take measures that can prevent such pollution and plan the establishment, organisation and performance of the activities in a manner so that the activities cause the least possible pollution. In connection with the choice, establishment and

arrangement of the facilities, etc. for the activities, including machinery, equipment and any accommodation facilities and in connection with the organisation of operations, including the choice of exploration, exploitation, application or working processes, raw materials, substances and materials for use in connection with the operations as well as emergency and pollution abatement procedures, it must be ensured that pollution, emissions, the generation of waste and the use of resources will be reduced in the best possible manner.'

45 See Chapter 5.
46 See Article 32 of the Declaration.
47 UNECE Convention on Access to Information, Public Participation in Decision-making and Access to Justice in Environmental Matters, 1998.
48 See Pelaudeix 2015.
49 Canada Governor General 2010, 19.
50 Joffe 2010.
51 Nunavut Court of Justice 2010.
52 The legal argument for the injunction relied on the Supreme Court of Canada's 1997 *Delgamuukw* decision, which acknowledged an inherent aboriginal right to land, plus the two rulings (*Haida* in 2004 and *Mikisew* in 2005), which require the Crown to consult first nations even if a treaty is settled.
53 Federal Court of Appeal 2015. See also Pelaudeix 2015 and Chapter 10.
54 See Chapter 5.
55 Fidler and Noble 2012.
56 Norwegian Ministry of Petroleum and Energy 2011, 145.
57 International Convention on Civil and Political Rights. An amendment made in 2012 to the Participation Act has allocated quotas.
58 Marine Resources Act s. 2. See Chapter 11.
59 See Chapter 11.
60 See note 36.
61 Olsen and Hansen 2014.
62 See Pelaudeix 2015.
63 Westphal 2006.
64 Clarke 2010.
65 National Energy Board 2013.
66 Canada's Premiers 2015, 11.
67 Ibid., 3.
68 Government of Canada 2010, 5.
69 Government of Canada 2009, 16.
70 Ibid.
71 Government of Canada 2013.
72 Government of Canada 2010, 9.
73 In the Rio Tinto and Little Salmon Carmack decisions, the Supreme Court of Canada has further explained that the duty to consult is a constitutional duty.
74 Tormodsgard 2014.
75 Ibid., 12.
76 International Energy Agency 2011, 14. In 2010 it contributed nearly 50 percent of Norwegian exports and 26 percent of the government's income.
77 Persily 2011.
78 International Energy Agency 2011.
79 Research Council of Norway 2012.
80 Norwegian Ministry of Foreign Affairs 2011, 14.
81 Norwegian Ministry of Foreign Affairs 2014, 20.
82 See Chapter 11.
83 US Geological Survey 2008, 4.

84 Government of Greenland 2015.
85 Economic Council 2013.
86 Kielsen 2007. Preface.
87 Government of Greenland 2014, Preamble.
88 ICC Alaska 2011.
89 Interview conducted by the author with Greenlandic minister of industry and mineral resources, Jens-Erik Kirkegaard, 19 June 2014, Nuuk.
90 Mineral Resource Committee 2009.

References

Baker, B. 2012. 'Offshore Oil and Gas Regulation in the Arctic: Room for Harmonisation?' *The Yearbook of Polar Law* IV: 475–504.

Basse, E.M. 2015. *Environmental Law in Denmark.* Copenhagen: DJØF [Danmarks Jurist- og Økonomforbund]; Alphen aan den Rijn: Wolters Kluwer.

Byers, M. and M. Stoller. 2013. 'What Small Teeth You Have: Arctic Oil Spill Response Agreement Weakened by Conflicting Interests.' EU Arctic Information Centre. Available at www.arcticinfo.eu/en/features-what-small-teeth-you-have.

Callow, L. 2012. Oil and Gas Exploration & Development, Activity Forecast: Canadian Beaufort Sea 2012–2027, Beaufort Regional Environmental Assessment. Government of Canada Aboriginal Affairs and Northern Development Canada.

Canada Governor General. 2010. A Stronger Canada: A Stronger Economy Now and for the Future: Speech from the Throne. Ottawa, Ontario: 3 March 2010.

Canada's Premiers. 2015. *Canadian Energy Strategy.* Ottawa, Ontario: Council of the Federation. July 2015.

Clarke, S.F. 2010. *Oil Spill Liability and Regulatory Regime: Canada.* Washington, DC: Library of Congress. www.loc.gov/law/help/oil-spill-liability/canada.php.

Dagg, J., P. Holroyd, N. Lemphers, R. Lucas, and B. Thibault. 2011. *Comparing the Offshore Drilling Regulatory Regimes of the Canadian Arctic, the US, the UK, Greenland and Norway.* Drayton Valley, Alberta: Pembina Institute.

Economic Council. 2013. *The Economy of Greenland.* Nuuk: Government of Greenland Economic Council. http://naalakkersuisut.gl/~/media/Nanoq/Files/Attached%20 Files/Finans/DK/Oekonomisk%20raad/ Rapport%202013FINAL2%20GR%20 ENG%203.pdf.

Edwards, D.V. 2015. 'The Promise of Constructivism as a Method for Studying the Policy Process.' Paper presented at the Second International Conference on Public Policy, Milan. July 2015.

Emmerson, C. and G. Lahn. 2012. *Arctic Opening: Opportunity and Risk in the High North.* Chatham House-Lloyd's Risk Insight Report. London: Royal Institute of International Affairs and Lloyd's. www.chathamhouse.org/publications/papers/ view/182839.

Fidler, C. and B. Noble. 2012. 'Advancing strategic environmental assessment in the offshore oil and gas sector: Lessons from Norway, Canada, and the United Kingdom', *Environmental Impact Assessment Review* 34: 12–21.

Government of Canada. 2009. Canada's Northern Strategy: Our North, Our Heritage. Ottawa, Ontario.

Government of Canada. 2010. Statement on Canada's Foreign Policy: Exercising Sovereignty and Promoting Canada's Northern Strategy Abroad. Ottawa, Ontario.

Government of Canada. 2013. *GEM: Geo-Mapping for Energy and Minerals.* Ottawa, Ontario. www.nrcan.gc.ca/earth-sciences/resources/federal-programs/geomapping-energy-minerals/10904.

Government of Greenland. 2014. *Greenland's Oil and Mineral Strategy 2014–2018.* Nuuk: Government of Greenland. FM 2014/133 IASN-2013–093824: pp. 10–11.

Government of Greenland. 2015. *Economy and Industry in Greenland.* Nuuk: Government of Greenland. http://naalakkersuisut.gl/en/About-government-of-greenland/About-Greenland/Economy-and-Industry-in-Greenland.

Gupta, K. 2012. 'Comparative Public Policy: Using the Comparative Method to Advance Our Understanding of the Policy Process.' *Policy Studies Journal* 40(S1): 11–26.

Henderson, J. and J. Loe. 2014. *The Prospects and Challenges for Arctic Oil Development.* Oxford: Oxford Institute for Energy Studies. OIES Paper: WPM 54.

International Energy Agency. 2011. *Energy Policies of IEA Countries: 2011 Review.* Paris: International Energy Agency. www.iea.org/publications/freepublications/publication/norway2011_web.pdf.

International Energy Agency. 2012. *World Energy Outlook 2012.* Available at www.iea.org/publications/freepublications/publication/world-energy-outlook-2012.html.

ILO (International Labour Organisation). 2009. *Indigenous and Tribal Peoples' Rights in Practice: A Guide to ILO Convention No. 169.* Geneva: International Labour Organisation, International Labour Standards Department.

ICC (Inuit Circumpolar Council) Alaska. 2011. *Inuit Declaration on Resource Development Principles.* Anchorage, Alaska: Inuit Circumpolar Council Alaska. *Drum* (ICC Alaska Newsletter) 4, no. 2, June 2011.

Imperial Oil Resources Ventures Limited. 2013. *Beaufort Sea Exploration Joint Venture, Drilling Programme, Project description*, Calgary, September. www.neb-one.gc.ca/pplctnflng/mjrpp/archive/mprlssrw/prjctdscrptn-eng.pdf.

Joffe, P. 2010. 'UN Declaration on the Rights of Indigenous Peoples: Canadian Government Positions Incompatible with Genuine Reconciliation.' *National Journal of Constitutional Law* 26(2): 121–229.

Johnstone, R. 2015. Offshore Oil and Gas Development in the Arctic under International Law. Leiden: Brill.

Kielsen, K. 2007. *Annual Report 2007.* Preface. Nuuk: Government of Greenland Bureau of Minerals and Petroleum. www.govmin.gl/images/stories/about_bmp/publications/annual_report_2007.pdf.

Mineral Resource Committee. 2009. 'The analysing report of 21 November 2009 from the Committee on the Naalakkersuisut's bill on the Greenlandic Mineral Resources Act presented for Inatsisartut under its second reading of the bill.' Nuuk: Government of Greenland Mineral Resource Committee. J. No. EM2009/1020.

National Energy Board. 2013. *Energy Supply and Demand Projections to 2035: Canada's Energy Future.* Calgary, Alberta: National Energy Board.

Norwegian Ministry of Foreign Affairs. 2011. *The High North, Vision and Strategies.* Oslo: Ministry of Foreign Affairs.

Norwegian Ministry of Foreign Affairs. 2014. *Norway's Arctic Policy.* Oslo: Ministry of Foreign Affairs. www.regjeringen.no/globalassets/departementene/ud/vedlegg/nord/nordkloden_en.pdf.

Norwegian Ministry of Petroleum and Energy. 2011. *An Industry for the Future: Norway's Petroleum Activities.* Oslo: Ministry of Petroleum and Energy. Meld. St. 28 (2010–2011): Report to the Storting (white paper).

Norwegian Ministry of Petroleum and Energy. 2013. *Invitation to Apply for Petroleum Production Licence: Art. 4: Conditions for the Award.* Oslo: Ministry of Petroleum and Energy. www.npd.no/Global/Engelsk/2-Topics/%5BLicence-awards%5D/22-round/Announcement/Invitation_22round.pdf.

Olsen, A.-S.H. and A.M. Hansen. 2014. 'Perceptions of Public Participation in Impact Assessment: A Study of Offshore Oil Exploration in Greenland.' *Impact Assessment and Project Appraisal* 32 (1): 72–80. doi:10.1080/14615517.2013.872842.

Pelaudeix, C. 2015. *Governance of Arctic Offshore Oil and Gas Activities: Multilevel Governance and Legal Pluralism at Stake.* Akureyri: Northern Research Forum. *Arctic Yearbook 2015*, 214–233. www.arcticyearbook.com/images/Articles_2015/11.Governance-of-Arctic-Offshore.pdf.

Persily, L. 2011. 'Oil and Gas Development: Does Norway Do a Better Job than Alaska?' *Alaska Dispatch News,* 9 September.

Porta, L. and N. Bankes. 2011. Becoming Arctic-Ready: Policy Recommendations for Reforming Canada's Approach to Licensing and Regulating Offshore Oil and Gas in the Arctic. Philadelphia, Pennsylvania: Pew Environmental Group.

Research Council of Norway. 2012. OG21: Oil and Gas in the 21st Century: Norway's Technology Strategy for the 21st Century Strategy Document. Lysaker: Research Council of Norway.

Scicluna, N. 2011. 'A Legal Discussion on the Civil Liability for Oil Pollution Damage Resulting from Offshore Oil Rigs in the Light of the Recent *Deepwater Horizon* Incident.' LL.M. dissertation, IMO International Maritime Law Institute, Msida, Malta.

Svensen, T.K., S. Simonsen, and K.M. Lind. 2014. 'Oil and Gas Regulation in Norway: Overview,' *Practical Law Multi-jurisdictional Guide 2014.* Energy and Natural Resources. London: Practical Law.

Tormodsgard, Y., ed. 2014. *Facts 2014: The Norwegian Petroleum Sector.* Oslo: Ministry of Petroleum and Energy.

US Geological Survey. 2008. *Circum-Arctic Resource Appraisal: Estimates of Undiscovered Oil and Gas North of the Arctic Circle.* US Geological Survey Fact Sheet 2008–3049. Reston, Virginia: US Geological Survey. Available at http://pubs.usgs.gov/fs/2008/3049/.

Westphal, K. 2006. 'Energy Policy between Multilateral Governance and Geopolitics: Whither Europe?' *Internationale Politik und Gesellschaft* 4: 44–62.

8 The Russian offshore oil and gas regime

When tight control means less order

Roman Sidortsov

Introduction

The story of 30 Greenpeace protesters detained in Russia after attempting to scale the Prirazlomnaya oil rig in the Pechora Sea in September 2013 captured the attention of millions around the world.[1] In addition to rekindling the discourse about dangers of oil and gas development in the Arctic, the story reaffirmed the perception of tight control exercised by the Russian government over the sector that it considers most strategically important for the national economy. According to the US Energy Information Agency, hydrocarbons accounted for 70 percent of Russia's export and 52 percent of its budget revenue.[2] The oil and gas sector is also responsible for Russia's re-emergence as a major global economic power.[3]

Based on Russia's policy since Vladimir Putin's return to the state's helm, there is little doubt that the leadership intends to strengthen the country's position as a major oil and gas producer and exporter. However, these intentions may soon run into the serious obstacle of oil-reserve depletion. According to the BP *Statistical Review of World Energy*, Russia saw the largest oil-reserve decline of all states in 2014, losing 1.9 billion barrels. The problem is compounded by the fact that the vast majority of Russian hydrocarbon revenue comes from oil proceeds.

To replace the declining legacy oil fields in Western Siberia, Russian policy-makers designated several areas, with Arctic offshore being the most important of them all.[4] The Russian government has taken steps to attract foreign and domestic capital and expertise to its Arctic province. The amendments to the tax code dated as of 30 September introduced a zero mineral extraction tax (MET) rate for the Arctic offshore fields currently under development, lower MET rates for undiscovered fields, export-duty exemptions for some Arctic offshore fields and lower tax rates on corporate assets located on the Arctic continental shelf.[5] In addition, the Russian government appears more than willing to provide subsidies on an individual basis, as it wiped the financial slate clean for Gazprom in the Prirazlomnoe project.[6]

However, the effective tax rate and the promise of hydrocarbon riches are only two parts of a complex equation. Oil and gas companies want a stable and transparent legal and regulatory environment in which they can make multi-billion dollar investments in capital-intensive offshore projects. Yet, this does not mean a complete *carte blanche* for the industry. A well-balanced system with appropriate and legitimate environmental and socioeconomic checks indicates a society that is capable of deciding complex issues in a discursive manner and, most importantly, knowingly accepting the risks that come with these types of decisions.

The principal thesis of this chapter is that despite the seemingly tight control over offshore oil and gas development in the Arctic, Russia lacks such balance.[7] To support this thesis, I review the applicable policy, legal and regulatory framework, with an emphasis on the access to offshore hydrocarbon resources and the conditions (checks) of their development.

Applicable policy, legal and regulatory framework

Policy discourse

It would only be appropriate to start the discussion of the policy, legal and regulatory framework governing offshore Arctic oil and gas development in the Russian Federation where it is captured in the broadest terms. It is important to clarify that the Russian oil and gas vernacular lacks the term 'offshore'.[8] Russian law distinguishes between 'territorial sea' and 'continental shelf'. Thus, the conventional meaning of 'offshore' includes both the territorial sea of the Russian Federation, a 12-nautical-mile zone extending from the shore,[9] and the continental shelf of the Russian Federation, a 200-nautical-mile zone extending from the shore. The outer boundary of the continental shelf may exceed the 200-nautical mile-mark if it "corresponds with the outer subsea boundary of the continent as delimited in accordance with international law."[10] It is important to note that, during the writing of this chapter, Russia submitted an application for extension of its Arctic continental shelf to the Commission on the Limits of the Continental Shelf (CLCS).[11]

It is common for high-ranking Russian officials to make statements on various matters of domestic and international policy. Oil and gas, by virtue of being the lifeblood of the Russian economy, occupy a considerable portion of these statements. Government officials, including the two most highly ranked, the president and the prime minister, offer their remarks at various forums while pursuing a most diverse set of goals. For example, in May 2014, President Vladimir Putin, in a shrewd public relations move, declared Russian oil companies to be world leaders in offshore safety and environmental protection.[12] In a meeting with energy-sector leaders, President Putin attempted to convince (if not coerce) the Russian company Novatek's CEO, Leonid Mikhelson, into having his company join a consortium with three large state-controlled companies that would be Russia's main manufacturer of equipment for offshore oil and gas operations.[13] Yet, such lobbying goes both ways. At a 13 February 2013 meeting of the Presidential Commission on the Strategic Development of the Fuel and Energy Sector and Environmental Security (the Presidential Energy Commission), the Russian companies Rosneft and Novatek secured President Putin's support for reforms to the Russian liquefied natural gas (LNG) export regime, which opened many offshore natural gas fields for development.[14]

At meetings akin to that of the Presidential Energy Commission, business leaders differ as to who should get access to offshore fields, and government officials argue as to whether the state should provide financial subsidies for the development. However, there is little disagreement regarding the role that the Russian leadership envisions for the Arctic region in terms of the country's economic and geopolitical growth.[15] The Arctic continental shelf represents a critically important area for this expansion.

Before the collapse of the Soviet Union, the government invested sizable resources into oil and gas prospecting and exploration. Exploratory drilling was widespread but often wasteful, as the Soviet Ministry of Energy set quantity of wells completed, not quality, as the main goal. However, quantity at times resulted in quality, and drillers made new discoveries. Thus, the vast majority of the current production comes from legacy fields, and the vast majority of recently and soon commissioned fields originate from 'legacy discoveries'.[16] For example, Russia's only Arctic offshore field, Prirazlomnoe, was discovered in 1989.[17]

After the Soviet Union's breakup, the oil and gas industry went into survival mode, and exploration activities came to a halt. Despite oil and gas production reaching Soviet levels in the 2000s, exploration is yet to do so. For example, according to Sergey Kudryashov, a former deputy Energy Minister and, as of the writing of this chapter, the head of state-owned oil company Zarubezhneft', only six or seven wells are drilled on the Russian continental shelf each year, as compared to 19 per year during the Soviet period.[18]

The majority of the planned resource base expansion is projected to occur in the Arctic, particularly the Arctic continental shelf. This is the area that, according to Vladimir Putin, will be responsible for the growth of Russia's wealth:

> Lomonosov once said that Russia will grow through Siberia – he was right, it is already happening. However, it will certainly grow through the Arctic. And not just because of its gigantic – global, I would say – all-planet mineral resources. I am talking about oil, gas, and metals also, because this region is very suitable for developing a transportation infrastructure.[19]
>
> (President, 29 August 2014)

Russia made its Arctic intentions clear in 2007 when it placed a plaque on the North Pole's ocean floor.[20] The Kremlin was quick to scorn any speculation about potential land claims. A foreign journalist asked President Putin whether Canada needs to worry about Russia's plans to appropriate the North Pole; the President jokingly replied that such concerns would be similar to concerns over the United States declaring ownership of the moon after placing its flag there.[21] Putin's comment was only a half-joke. As noted above, Russia recently submitted a claim to extend the boundaries of its Arctic continental shelf beyond 200 nautical miles. Sergey Donskoy, Russia's current environment minister, described it as 'the most important, largest and most economically valuable'.[22]

In practical terms this means that Russia will likely continue offering more areas of its Arctic continental shelf for prospecting, exploration, development and production, soliciting foreign financial and technical participation in Arctic offshore projects and investing domestic resources to make such projects more viable.

Programmatic policy statements

However, statements by government officials made at various meetings, press-conferences, and events are not the only sources from which one can learn about Russia's offshore Arctic plans. The Russian leadership appears to have a strong interest in having in place a programmatic statement on virtually every area of public policy. Although Russian policy-makers never created a stand-alone programme or strategy for the Artic continental shelf, the Ministry of Natural resources and the Environment has written several drafts of the continental-shelf strategy since 2006.[23] The document entitled 'The Strategy of Exploration and Exploitation of Oil and Gas Potential of the Russian Continental Shelf for the Period Ending in 2020' was not approved by the government of the Russian Federation (henceforth the RF government).[24] Instead, the RF government incorporated provisions related to continental-shelf development (including the Arctic continental shelf) in various energy and/or Arctic-related programmatic statements.

The most important document among the programmatic statements related to energy policy is 'The Energy Strategy of the Russian Federation for the Period ending in 2030.' The strategy designates oil and gas development in the Arctic continental shelf as one of the key elements of the Russian economic future, or, as the document puts it, 'new economic infrastructure.'[25] In fact, the strategy mentions the Arctic continental shelf (*schelf arkticheskih morey*) 26 times.[26] Two other documents, 'The Comprehensive Scheme for the Development of the Gas Sector for the Period Ending in 2030' and 'On the Main Measures of Strengthening Russia's Positions in the Global Energy Sector for the Period Ending on 1 January 2016', are further examples of programmatic and policy documents that underscore the importance of the Arctic continental shelf for Russia's economic development.[27]

'The Foundations of the National Policy of the Russian Federation in the Arctic for the Period Ending in 2020 and Beyond' and the more specific 'Strategy of the Arctic Zone Development and Ensuring National Security for the Period Ending in 2020' are the two main official policy statements noting the utmost importance of the Arctic continental shelf to the Russian Federation.[28] Both documents identify the Arctic offshore as one of the main areas for replenishing Russia's hydrocarbon reserves and for large-scale economic development.[29]

Another document entitled 'Strategic Action Programme for Protecting the Environment of the Arctic Zone of the Russian Federation', which was developed as part of a UN Environmental Programme project by the RF government, focuses on environmental dangers of hydrocarbon development in the Arctic. It lists sobering facts, including increased pollution in the region, and warns about environmental and socioeconomic impacts (including climate change) of oil and gas exploration and extraction.[30]

Statutes (zakony)

The Russian legal system has a robust *de jure* hierarchy of sources of law. The constitution of the Russian Federation sits atop, with constitutional statutes (*konstitutsionnye zakony*) and statutes (*zakony*) cascading down the legal authority ladder.[31] Next in line are the so-called sub-statutes (*podzakonnye akty*). The main difference between the former and latter categories is that the constitution, constitutional statutes, and statutes are enacted and amended by the people via a referendum or, far more frequently, by the legislature. Sub-statutes, on the other hand, are promulgated by various agencies of the executive branch of the Russian government, generally (but not always) under an enabling statute.[32] Thus the closest functional equivalent of sub-statutes is what is generally referred to in the Western legal regimes as 'rules and regulations'.

Eleven articles in the constitution have direct relevance to environmental, regulatory, and jurisdictional aspects of the offshore exploration and extraction of oil and gas.[33] Perhaps the most important and, in light of the recent increase of federal control over mineral resources, controversial provisions are Articles 15, 67, 71, 72, and 76 concerning regulatory and jurisdictional issues. Article 72 lists matters within the joint jurisdiction of the Russian Federation and the territorial entities of the Russian Federation (*subjekty federatsii*).[34] This list includes: "issues of the possession, utilisation and management of land and of sub-surface, water and other natural resources and 'protection of the environment and provisions for ecological safety'". This could be interpreted to mean that both federal and regional governments have an arrangement analogous to the concept of cooperative federalism utilised under the Outer Continental Shelf Lands Act (OSCLA) in the United States. However, pursuant to the pre-emption doctrine under Article 76, concerning all matters set forth in Articles 71 and 72, "[l]aws and other normative legal acts of the constituent entities of the Russian Federation shall not conflict with federal laws. In the event of a conflict, 'the federal law shall prevail." The policy of strengthening of the vertical power employed by President, turned prime minister, turned President Vladimir Putin left regions with no authority on a great deal of matters, including offshore oil and gas development.[35] As I elaborate below, due to changes in the federal legislation, regions were virtually cut off from the decision-making process regarding the Russian Arctic continental shelf by 2008.[36]

Russia appears to be in a state of perpetual reform regarding its mineral resource extraction legislation, including its legislation on offshore oil and gas development. For example, 'On Continental Shelf of the Russian Federation' ('On Continental Shelf'), one of the two main statutes governing offshore oil and gas activities, has been amended 23 times since its enactment in 1995.[37] The other main statute, Law on Subsoil Resources, has been amended 50 times since the Russian president signed it into law in 1992.[38] Yet the quantity of amendments and revisions has not necessarily translated into quality. Many statutory provisions still contradict one another, and the constant revising of the statutory framework has impaired what investors and the industry covet most – stability. On the other hand, because US and EU economic sanctions have limited the opportunities for foreign investment and technology transfer, the need for a predictable, transparent and coherent legal framework is not as acute as it was prior to Russia's annexation of Ukraine in March 2014.

The statutes relevant to offshore oil and gas development are numerous. This is hardly surprising, as the statutory framework governs a complex set of jurisdictional, environmental, health and safety, licensing and other issues. In the United States, for example, over 40 statutes are involved in governing offshore hydrocarbon exploration and extraction.[39] As mentioned above, two statutes dominate the statutory framework: 'On Continental Shelf' and 'On Subsoil Resources', with the former having pre-emptive authority over the latter by virtue of being a more specific statute. The most pertinent statutes covering jurisdictional matters include, 'On Inland Sea Waters, Territorial Sea and Adjacent Zones of the Russian Federation' ('On Inland Sea Waters') and 'On the Exclusive Economic Zone of the Russian Federation'.[40] 'On Environmental Review', 'On Environmental Protection', and 'On Guarantees of the Rights of Numerically Small Indigenous Peoples of the Russian Federation' govern environmental matters as well as matters of indigenous participation in decision-making.[41] 'On Production Sharing Agreements' offers an alternative to the currently prevalent method of issuing oil and gas licences, and 'On Technical Regulating' establishes a framework for operational, health, safety and environmental, search and rescue and other standards for offshore oil and gas operations.

I elaborate on the most relevant aspects of these statutes in the ensuing sections. However, it is important to note two common features of the law-making process in Russia that have hindered its legal system, including the aforementioned statutes. A careful analysis of amended legislation often reveals that the Russian parliament has made changes to fit the needs of a specific group or sometimes a few individual actors. This practice is especially prevalent in the offshore oil and gas sector, as the RF government maintains a firm grip on access to the development of the resources. For example, as explained in more detail in section three of this chapter, 'On Subsoil Resources' was amended in April 2008 so as to impose a rather curious set of requirements on companies allowed to access mineral resources located on the continental shelf of the Russian Federation.[42] Although the amending legislation did not name Rosneft and Gazprom as the only such companies, it might as well have done so, as the legislation appears to have been crafted to fit the credentials that only these two companies possessed.

The other feature is the irrelevance of the checks and balances system in the Russian legislative process. In practical terms, this means that if a legislative initiative has Kremlin backing, it will likely become law. The April 2008 amendments did not encounter any opposition in the Russian parliament because of the support from President Medvedev and Deputy Prime Minister Igor Sechin.[43] The latter combined his government post with that of Rosneft's head of board of directors from 2004 until 2011.[44]

Contrary to the view popularly portrayed in the Western media, the Kremlin's domination over the legislative process does not mean that President Putin exercises absolute control over all facets of political life in the country. Based on my analysis of over 100 transcripts of presidential meetings and opinions expressed by commentators closely tracking political discourse in Russia, President Putin's influence is best described as 'first among equals'.[45] According to Gregory Yavlinsky, a former presidential candidate and leader of an opposition to the Kremlin party, Vladimir Putin is an effective representative of the Russian power elite capable of negotiating among often divergent interests.[46] Thus, an initiative must gather enough support from the vested interests to translate into law, which in the context of the LNG export amendments meant that Rosneft and Novatek's effort has been successful and Lukoil's has not.[47]

Under the vast powers granted by the Russian Constitution, the President has the capacity to not only make oil and gas policy but also to implement and enforce it. Article 90 of the Constitution gives the President the power to issue executive orders (*ukazy*) that subordinate to statutes but supersede all rules and regulations. With the national legislature, the Federal Assembly (*Federal'noe Sobranie*), under Kremlin's political control, both Vladimir Putin and Dmitry Medvedev could have opted for an even more streamlined rulemaking process implementing Kremlin's energy agenda.[48] Yet both have displayed surprising commitment to exercising their powers through the legislative process. It is unclear whether the Kremlin would have gone outside this process if the Federal Assembly refused to cooperate. For many Russians, this commitment creates an impression that the government manages mineral resource development in a transparent and deliberate manner pursuant to the public interests.

Another factor that further legitimizes Kremlin's tight control over the oil and gas sector is the fact that the Russian state has never given up its legal rights to exercising such control. Gustafson, describes this dormant during 1990s power of the Russian state as follows:

> Despite the weakening of the state control in the first half of the 1990s and the appearance of near-total privatization that followed, the state never fully exited from ownership and control of the oil industry. It retained legal rights over every part of the system: from ownership of oil in the ground to ownership of the pipeline systems; from licensing of exploration and development to regulation of reserves and field development plans; from control over the allocation of export quotas and access to export capacity, to control (by municipal governments) over much of domestic distribution and sales.
>
> ...
>
> What was built in the first half of the 1990s, in other words, was a system of quasi-private property that restricted the ownership rights of the companies to junior roles vis-à-vis the state. This was not apparent at the time. Indeed, so weak and disorganized was the state at all levels – especially at the centre – that it appeared to contemporary observers, even to the major players themselves, as though the oil industry had genuinely escaped from state control. But it had not. All that had happened was that the system of state controls had gone dormant. It retained large power over the industry in theory, but in practice that power became largely latent, present mainly as an invitation to evasion.[49]

This explains the rapid return to near-absolute state control over the oil and gas sector when the current regime spearheaded by President Putin came to power.[50] The manner by which private actors obtained rights to oil and gas assets aided the current leadership in justifying its case for reclaiming them. For example, the infamous 'loans for shares' program by which Roman Abramovich and Mikhail Khodokovsky, among others, acquired much of their oil and gas assets was more of a divvying up of loot by gang members than a privatization auction, the principal official objective of which was getting the most financial return for the struggling Russian state.[51]

Regulations (podzakonnye akty)

Russia employs a prescriptive regulatory model for governing offshore oil and gas activities.[52] This means that a regulator needs to spell out every substantive and procedural requirement, from the thickness of steel at a certain installation to the steps that need to be taken to operate the installation.

Given the high complexity of offshore oil and gas technology, the regulator must have an extensive arsenal of rules and standards. As I elaborate in section four, the Russian regulatory arsenal has many gaps, and generally remains a work in progress. However, despite those significant gaps, the legal and regulatory framework concerning matters of offshore mineral resource use and environmental protection includes over 800 documents.[53]

Some parts of the regulatory framework are disconnected from the overarching statutory framework. Thus, as I noted in the preceding subsection, some sub-statutes are not promulgated under an enabling statute, and a sub-statute has pre-emptive authority on a particular issue. An example of this category of regulations would be the expired 2003 Oil and Gas Industry Safety Rules. Because 'On Technical Regulating' replaced the enabling statute, the implementing agency had to reaffirm the rules in order for them to remain mandatory.[54]

The standards for environmental protection constitute an example of how sub-statutes interact with enabling statutes. The law 'On Environmental Protection' sets forth the general legal framework for environmental standards in Articles 1 and 19–29. Article 1 establishes general concepts of environmental protection and the pertinent types of standards and regulations. Environmental quality standards establishing maximum allowable concentrations of pollutants are described in Article 21. Article 22 discusses procedural standards, which, in turn, set forth environmental-impact standards. Article 23 covers air and water emission/discharge standards. It is important to note that the statute does not actually set the standards; rather, it defers to the administrative agencies to develop individual provisions containing concentrations, limits and other specific measurable requirements.[55]

Sub-statutes come under various names, with various degrees of legal authority. They range from the aforementioned presidential orders to letters (*pisma*) and instructions (*instruktsii*) by an administrative agency's structural unit. To determine the pre-emptive authority of a document, one should examine the place of the issuing agency or unit in the hierarchy of the executive branch of the Russian government.[56] Documents issued by government special agencies and research institutions, as well as industry and corporate standards, supplement the decrees, orders, letters, and instructions enacted by official government ministries and agencies. For example, it is not uncommon for an agency to utilise a research arm of a corporate entity, such as Gazprom's Natural Gases and Gas Technologies Research Institute, to develop mandatory technical regulations.[57]

Requirements for access to offshore mineral resources

As noted above, under Russian law, the term 'offshore' includes the areas of territorial seas and the continental shelf of the Russian Federation. This bifurcation is significant, as Article 9 of 'On Subsoil Resources' creates two different legal regimes: one for areas that are at least in part located on the continental shelf, and another for areas situated entirely within the territorial seas. Only entities formed under the laws of the Russian Federation, with five years of experience operating on the Russian continental shelf and with the Russian state controlling more than 50 percent of their voting stock, are allowed to have access to the areas forming the first group.[58] The provisions of 'On the Continental Shelf' to the second group do not apply, thereby eliminating the five-year operational experience requirement, which broadens the scope of entities allowed to access resources located therein.[59] Access to the second group of areas (located exclusively within the territorial sea) is nonetheless restricted to entities formed under Russian laws. In addition, pursuant to the aforementioned April 2008 amendments to 'On Subsoil Resources', mineral deposits located in both groups of areas are deemed of federal significance.[60] This effectively means that: (1) the RF government can unilaterally decide who can access such areas for development (all other deposit categories are disposed via tenders); and (2) the RF government can further restrict access to such areas to entities with foreign participation.[61]

Because the set of requirements set forth in Article 9 of the Subsoil Resources Act was tailored to the credentials possessed by only two companies, Rosneft and Gazprom, other companies have failed to gain access to the Arctic continental shelf as licence-holders on substantively insignificant grounds. For example, Zarubezhneft, a state-owned company, has more than five years of operating experience on foreign, but not the Russian, continental shelf. As a result, this company has been unsuccessful in gaining access to the Russian continental shelf and the Arctic part of it in particular.[62] The company went so far as to acquire another state company, Artikmoreneftegazrazvedka, which held licences to the Russian continental shelf in the 2000s for over five years.[63] Yet despite the support from the Minister of Natural Resources and the Environment, the RF government remains unconvinced.

Another example of a company running into the Article 9 obstacle is Lukoil. The company has been operating offshore since 1999 in several parts of the world, including the Black, Baltic, and Caspian seas. Yet none of these offshore areas formally qualify as Russian and/or continental shelf.[64] Lukoil also has experience in the Russian Arctic, operating the Varandey offshore oil loading terminal.[65] However, this experience is not in exploration, development and extraction. Finally, the company acquired a licence to develop the onshore part of the East Taymyr deposit, which extends into the territorial sea and Arctic continental shelf.[66] Yet, because Lukoil acquired rights to the onshore part of the deposit, it fell short of expanding to the continental shelf.

Under Russian law, acquisition of the right to offshore mineral resources is a two-step process. The first step involves the RF government deciding on the recipient of the right, either as the result of a tender or on an ad hoc basis.[67] The tender process is similar to the process employed by some other

Arctic nations, whereby a government opens an area for competitive bidding to entities interested in leasing blocks within it. The ministry of natural resources and the environment (Minprirody) plays the lead role in organising and conducting tenders, including setting the tender criteria.[68] Such criteria comprise the quality of the proposed development programme, recovery rate, contribution to the socioeconomic development of the surrounding area, proposed duration of the development and production, effectiveness of the measures aimed at mitigating and preventing environmental damage, and national security considerations.[69]

The ad hoc process, and the criteria used for bestowing the right thereunder, are far less clear. The applicable provision of 'On Subsoil Resources' added on 18 July 2008 simply states that the RF government bestows such right without 'conducting an auction or tender'.[70] During his first term as Russian prime minister, Dmitry Medvedev defended the legislative change in the following remark:

> Continental shelf is our national treasure. For this reason, this is a special law that contains special procedures. It does not have tenders and auctions that are a common practice; instead we have a targeted solution. It is done consciously, to exploit the national treasure in a rational manner.[71]

Vladimir Putin also defended the ad hoc approach, charging the tenders and auctions process with not being sufficiently transparent.[72] His remark is especially puzzling because little is known about the ad hoc decision-making process, whereas the auctions and tenders have requirements set forth in the aforementioned regulations. In addition, as evidenced by Rosneft's suit against Lukoil regarding the East Taymyr deposit tender, the selection criteria are available to the general public, which is not the case in the ad hoc decisions.[73]

The second step is issuing a licence. The Federal Agency for Mineral Resources (Rosnedra), which is part of Minprirody, plays the lead role during this process. Pursuant to Article 6 of 'On Subsoil Resources' and Article 7 of 'On Continental Shelf', the four types of subsoil deposit use for which an offshore licence is required are regional prospecting, prospecting, exploration and extraction.[74] Accordingly, Rosnedra can issue the following main types of licences in connection with offshore oil and gas activities: (1) for regional prospecting; (2) for prospecting; (3) for exploration and extraction; and (4) for prospecting, exploration and extraction (the so-called 'combined' licence).[75] It is important to note that a combined licence does not automatically give the right to explore and extract hydrocarbons upon completion of the prospecting stage. As mentioned above, in an apparent effort to increase control over exploration and exploitation activities occurring on the continental shelf, Article 6 of 'On Subsoil Resources' was amended on 28 April 2008. Pursuant to the amendment, a separate authorisation by the

RF government is required to proceed with such activities upon completing the prospecting phase, even in the case of a combined licence including all three phases.[76]

It might appear that the issue of a licence is a purely formal step because the RF government has already decided under the tender or the ad hoc basis described above to allow access to offshore deposits. However, this is not the case, as a licence captures important economic and environmental requirements, including the term within which the licensee must complete the allowed activities. A licence normally allows for several activities associated with the principal phase for which the licence is issued. For example, a licence issued for exploration and extraction is likely also to allow for reinjection of associated water and gas.[77] Article 9 of 'On the Continental Shelf' distinguishes the process for issuing permits for drilling operations from the licensing procedure related to the types of subsoil uses outlined above. Thus, some activities essential to oil and gas development, such as drilling and waste disposal, are subject to a separate permitting process. I will briefly touch on some of the permits in the next section.

The law 'On Production Sharing Agreements' was enacted prior to the aforementioned amendments to 'On Continental Shelf' and 'On Subsoil Resources' that gave rise to the RF government as the principal decision-maker in matters concerning the country's major oil and gas deposits. Although the RF government enters on behalf of the Russian Federation into a production-sharing agreement (PSA) with the licensee, the Russian parliament determines which areas may be licensed pursuant to PSAs.[78] However, the statute has been largely dormant, as the only three PSAs had been reached before it was enacted in 1995.[79]

Environmental assessment and operating requirements

This final section briefly covers the conditions upon which access to offshore oil and gas resources is granted. Pursuant to this designation, environmental assessment should be part of the foregoing section on requirements for access to mineral resources, as the results of an environmental assessment should in theory influence the decision whether to proceed with oil and gas development. However, because the 'no-action option' in reality is all but never considered, the results of an environmental assessment act as de facto operational requirements.

It is also important to note that Russian law uses the term '*ekologicheskaya ekspertiza*' (ecological review) to describe the process that amounts to environmental assessment. As noted below, under Russian law this is a two-step process consisting of the preparation of an environmental-impact assessment (EIA) and an official government review of the EIA. Thus, to avoid confusion, I refer to the principal statute governing environmental assessment as 'On Environmental Review'; I retain the Russian acronym for the preparation of an environmental-impact assessment, OVOS (*otsenka vozdeystviya na okruzhaiyschuiy sredu*); and I retain English acronyms for the second step of the process, state environmental review (SER), and for the entire process, environmental assessment (EA).[80] Pursuant to Article 46 of 'On Environmental Protection', "construction and operation of oil and gas production, processing, transportation and storage facilities" located within the offshore areas of the Russian Federation are subject to environmental assessment. Article 31 of 'On the Continental Shelf' and Article 34 of 'On Inland Sea Waters', which largely mirror one another, contain the most important provision regarding environmental assessment of offshore oil and gas activities. Both articles state that no offshore activity can take place absent a positive finding of an EA. This is especially important because since the enactment of 'On Environmental Review' in 1995, the EA's reach in Russia has eroded[81] to what some estimated to be approximately 5 percent of the activities originally covered by the statute.[82]

The responsibility to conduct an OVOS lies with the proponent of the activity. The 16 May 2000 Order of the Committee of the Russian Federation on Protection of the Environment[83] identifies three stages of an OVOS. During the first stage, the proponent prepares and submits to the authorities a notice of the planned activity, along with preliminary information about the planned OVOS. During the following research stage, the proponent conducts all the necessary studies and gathers all the necessary information. 'On Environmental Review' and Order 372 require the developer to solicit public opinion to inform about the proposed activity and identify public preferences.[84] The scarce evidence of public participation in OVOS regarding Arctic offshore projects raises serious concerns about the impact of such participation on the outcome of EAs. For example, both the RF government and the proponent (Gazprom) ignored significant apprehensions regarding the safety of the Prirazlomnoe development.[85]

The final stage of the process consists of finalising the OVOS documentation, which becomes the subject of the SER. During the SER, the Federal Service for Oversight of Natural Resources (Rosprirodnadzor), the same agency under Minprirody that finalises offshore licences, appoints an 'expert commission' that reviews the submitted documentation and renders either a 'positive' or 'negative' conclusion. The documentation reviewed by an expert commission also includes an oil-spill contingency plan.[86] Under the most notable recent addition to the Russian legal and regulatory regime governing offshore hydrocarbon activities, an operator must have an approved oil-spill contingency plan before commencing such activities.[87]

In addition to SER, 'On Environmental Review' establishes a public environmental review.[88] This type of review is initiated by citizens, a local government or an NGO. It is not mandatory, but creates a pathway for a developer to gain a social licence to operate, as in the case of Sakhalin Environmental Watch assessing the Exxon Negtegaz Limited project in Sakhalin Island's Piltun Bay.[89] On the other hand, a lack of cooperation on the developer's side, as in the case of Gazprom during the Prirazlomnoe project, may derail the process and elevate public anxieties about the proposed activity.[90] If allowed, the results of a public environmental review must be considered during the SER.

As mentioned above, in addition to the operating requirements specified in a licence, offshore oil and gas operations require several permits. Some permits require input and approval from different agencies. For example, a drilling permit requires consultations with ten different ministries and agencies including the Ministry of Economic Development, and the Federal Service for Environmental, Technological, and Nuclear Oversight (Rostekhnadzor).[91]

Finally, operating requirements are set in a great number of sub-statutes, promulgated by federal administrative agencies. Of central importance are the "Federal Industrial Safety Regulations 'Offshore Oil and Gas Safety Rules'" approved by order of Rostekhnadzor on 18 March 2014 (the 'Offshore Safety Rules'). This regulation covers a wide range of issues, from requirements for designing and operating offshore installations to employee qualifications. The 'Offshore Safety Rules' are an example of prescriptive regulations, as some provisions contain the finest details of processes that an operator must follow.[92] Although the regulation does not feature an Arctic-specific section, the document has a number of provisions on operating in ice and cold-weather conditions.[93]

'On Technical Regulating', enacted in 2002, was supposed to bring much-needed clarity and structure to the disjointed and often conflicting realm of operating requirements. The statute introduced technical regulations (*tekhnicheskie reglamenty*) that were supposed to organise detailed and technical standards into coherent groups.[94] However, the RF government overestimated its ability to understand and control fast-moving complex technologies and consequently failed to promulgate such regulations in many sectors and subsectors critical to the Russian economy, including most of the oil and gas sector.[95]

Conclusion

The Kremlin's tight control over access to Russia's Arctic offshore oil and gas resources has created a great deal of tension in the country's energy sector. Because the current Rosneft/Gazprom two-horse race is a result of creative lobbying and de facto legislative permitting, the present order may disappear rapidly, should the political winds change. However, because so much emphasis has been placed on the access to Arctic offshore resources, other, perhaps more important, aspects have not received due attention. Notwithstanding Vladimir Putin's jubilant pronouncement on the state of safety and environmental controls in the Russian offshore oil and gas sector, the situation is far from perfect. In fact, when Dmitry Medvedev, during his 'place-holding' presidency, opened the issue of environmental protection adequacy for discussion, he received a flood of the most critical comments from high-ranking Russian government officials. These comments painted a vivid picture of disorder in environmental affairs. For example, one highly ranked Russian government official described the state of environmental assessment in Russia as complete disintegration, and labelled 'On Technical Regulating' a total failure.[96] Moreover, judging by the to-do list in the aftermath of the 29 June 2014 presidential meeting on Arctic issues, the Russian leadership is in the preliminary stages of commissioning research on such critical topics as ecosystem protection and sustainable development.[97] Thus for a nation that plans to maintain its current economic status by betting on Arctic offshore development, Russia needs more aspects of its policy, legal, and regulatory system to be in working order.

Notes

1 BBC 2013.
2 EIA 2015.
3 Paik 2012, 21.
4 See section two for more discussion on the Russian leadership's plans for oil and gas development in the Arctic.
5 Federal Law Dated as of 30 September 2013 N. 268-FZ On Amending Parts I and II of the Russian Federation Tax Code and Some Legislative Acts of the Russian Federation in Connection with the Tax and Custom Duty Stimulus Measures Regarding Hydrocarbon Production on the Continental Shelf of the Russian Federation, accessed 1 September 2015 http://pravo.gov.ru/ (hereinafter, Federal Law N. 268-FZ).
6 Lunden and Fjaertoft 2014, 1.
7 As I elaborate in the remainder of the chapter, the process through which companies gain access to offshore oil and gas deposits lacks transparency and inclusiveness. As a result, critical stakeholder groups such as indigenous communities are often left out of the decision-making.
8 In fact, this term is often used in the context of moving capital out of Russia to 'offshore' financial institutions.
9 Federal Law Dated as of 31 July 1998 N. 155-FZ On Inland Sea Waters, Territorial Sea and the Adjacent Zone of the Russian Federation, as last amended on 13 July 2015, Article 2, accessed 1 September 2015 http://pravo.gov.ru/ (hereinafter, On Inland Sea Waters).
10 Federal Law Dated as of 30 November 1995 N. 187-FZ On the Continental Shelf of the Russian Federation, last amended on 2 May 2015, Article 1, accessed 1 September 2015 http://pravo.gov.ru/ (hereinafter, On Continental Shelf) With reference to the UN Convention on the Law of the Sea (LOS Convention) Article 76.
11 It was submitted in accordance with LOS Convention Article 76(8): concerning this see Staalesen, 2015.
12 The President of Russia, Speech at the Security Council Meeting Concerning the Protection of National Interests in the Arctic, 17 September 2008, accessed 1 September 2015 http://news.kremlin.ru/transcripts/1433 (hereinafter, Presidential meeting transcript, 17 September 2008).
13 The President of Russia, Videoconference with the West Alpha Platform in the Kara Sea, 9 August 2014, accessed 1 September 2015 http://news.kremlin.ru/news/46421(hereinafter, Presidential meeting transcript, 9 August 2014).
14 The President of Russia, Meeting of the Commission on the Strategy of Fuel and Energy Sector Development Environmental Security, 13 February 2013, accessed 1 September 2015, http://news.kremlin.ru/news/17511/print. (hereinafter,

Presidential meeting transcript, 13 February 2013. Concerning this see Sidortsov 2014. See also Letter from Dmitry Medvedev, the Prime Minister of the Russian Federation, to the State Duma, 6 November 2013, accessed 1 September 2015 http://asozd2.duma.gov.ru/main.nsf/(SpravkaNew)?OpenAgent&RN=378656–6&02.

15 There are multiple remarks by the Russian leadership that affirm these statements. See e.g. The President of Russia, All-Russia Youth Forum "Seliger", 29 August 2014, accessed 1 September 2015 http://news.kremlin.ru/news/46507 (hereinafter, Presidential meeting transcript, 29 August 2014).

16 Gustafson 2012.

17 Gazprom 2016.

18 Presidential meeting transcript, 13 February 2013.

19 The Russian President slightly misquoted Mikhail Lomonosov, the 'father' of Russian science, who is believed to once have said: 'The *wealth* of Russia will grow through Siberia.' [emphasis added]

20 Parfitt 2007.

21 The President of Russia, Annual Big Press-Conference, 14 February 2008, accessed 1 September 2015 http://kremlin.ru/events/president/transcripts/24835 (hereinafter, Presidential meeting transcript, 14 February 2008).

22 Presidential meeting transcript, 4 April 2014).

23 Ministry of Natural Resources and the Environment, Strategy for Exploration and Exploitation of Oil and Gas Potential of the Russian Continental Shelf for the Period Ending in 2020, 2006, accessed 1 September 2015 https://www.mnr.gov.ru/regulatory/list.php?part=1571.

24 The Government of the Russian Federation (*or Pravitelstvo Rossiyskoy Federatsii) is* a mega-agency that consists of many sub-agencies. For the sake of clarity, in this chapter the term 'RF government' refers to this mega-agency.

25 The Government of the Russian Federation, The Energy Strategy of Russia for the Period Ending in 2030, 13 November 2009, at 12, accessed 1 September 2015 http://minenergo.gov.ru/ (hereinafter, the Energy Strategy).

26 *Id.*

27 The Government of the Russian Federation, On the Main Measures of Strengthening Russia's Positions in the Global Energy Sector for the Period Ending on January 1, 2016, 2012, accessed 1 September 2015 http://pravo.gov.ru/; The Ministry of Energy of the Russian Federation, The Comprehensive Scheme for the Development of the Gas Sector for the Period until 2030, 2008, accessed 1 September 2015 http://pravo.gov.ru/.

28 The Strategy of the Arctic Zone Development and Ensuring National Security for the Period Ending in 2020, 2013, accessed 1 September 2015 http://pravo.gov.ru/.

29 The Foundations of the National Policy of the Russian Federation in the Arctic for the Period Ending in 2020 and Beyond, 18 September 2008, accessed 1 September 2015 http://www.scrf.gov.ru/documents/98.html (hereinafter, the Foundations of the National Arctic Policy and the Strategy of the Arctic Zone Development).

30 The Government of the Russian Federation, The Strategic Action Program for Protecting the Environment of the Arctic Zone of the Russian Federation, 2009, accessed 1 September 2015 http://pravo.gov.ru/ (hereinafter, the Programme of the Russian Federation for Protecting the Environment of the Arctic Zone).

31 Constitution of the Russian Federation, 1993, Article 15.

32 IEE 2011. Because this subsection is devoted to legislatively enacted sources of law, I will on the applicable sub-statute in the following section.

33 Ibid., 3.

34 Because Russia is an asymmetrical federation that consists of several types of territorial entities with divergent legal statuses and names, I will refer collectively to them as 'regions'.

35 Nysten-Haarla and Kotilainen 2009, 18; See Federal Law 'On Subsoil Resources' Federal Law dated as of 29 December 2004 N. 199-FZ On Incorporation of Changes in Certain Legislative Enactments of the Russian Federation in Connection with Broadening the Role of the States of the Russian Federation in the Matters of Joint Jurisdiction of the Russian Federation and the States of the Russian Federation, as well as with the Broadening of the Local Matters of Municipalities, as last amended on 27 May 2014, accessed 1 September 2015 http://pravo.gov.ru/.

36 It is important to note that recent revisions allow the federal government to delegate the authority to regulate matters of mineral resource use to regions. Whether such authority will actually be granted remains to be seen. See Federal Law dated as of 13 July 2015 N 233-FZ On Amending the Federal Law On General Principles of Regional Legislative and Executive Government Organisation and Various Legislative Act of the Russian Federation and Affirming Cancellation of Certain Provisions of Legislative Acts of the Russian Federation, accessed 1 September 2015 http://pravo.gov.ru/.

37 See On Continental Shelf.

38 See Federal Law of the Russian Federation Dated as of 21 February 1992 N 2395-I On Subsoil Resources, last amended on 29 June 2015, accessed 1 September 2015 http://pravo.gov.ru/ (hereinafter, On Subsoil Resources).

39 Baker & Sidortsov, 2014, 12.

40 This statute has little to do with offshore and gas development under Russian law, but it is mentioned here as related to jurisdictional matters regarding other (e.g. fishing) activities.

41 Federal Law dated as of 30 April 1999 N 82-FZ On Guarantees of the Rights of Indigenous Peoples last amended on 13 July 2015, accessed 1 September 2015 http://pravo.gov.ru/.

42 On Subsoil Resources, article 9.

43 The President of Russia, Working Meeting with the Deputy Prime Minister Igor Sechin, 18 July 2008, accessed 1 September 2015, http://news.kremlin.ru/news/825 (hereinafter, Presidential meeting transcript, 18 July 2008).

44 Igor Sechin became Rosneft's CEO in 2012 upon leaving the RF government. Rosneft, 2017.

45 Yavlinsky 2014.

46 Yavlinsky 2014.

47 Barsukov 2013.

48 The Federal Assembly comprises two houses, the State Duma (*Gosudarstvennaya Duma*) and the Federation Council (*Sovet Federatsii*).

49 Gustafson 2012 pp. 96–97. Wheel of Fortune: The Battle for Oil and Power in Russia. London: The Belknap Press of Harvard University Press.

50 Id. pp. 95–96.

51 Hoffman 2011.

52 However, due to numerous regulatory gaps, certain areas are left to self-regulation. Thus, de facto, Russia has a mix of the prescriptive and self-regulation model.

53 IEE 2011 at 43.

54 Federal Environmental, Technological and Nuclear Oversight Service. Decree dated 5 June 2003 N 56. On Affirmation of Oil and Gas Industry Safety Rules. As reaffirmed by Order N 435, dated 28 June 2011. Accessed 1 September 2015 http://pravo.gov.ru/ (hereinafter, Safety Rules, 2003).

55 IEE 2011 at 49.

56 The Russian Government – referring to the entire executive apparatus.

57 The Federal Agency for Technical Regulating and Metrology, Order Dated as of 30 November 2009 N 4347 On the Establishment of Technical Committee on

Standardisation of Natural and Liquefied Gas accessed 1 September 2015 http://pravo.gov.ru/ (hereinafter, Order N 4347).

58 On Subsoil Resources Article 9.

59 Ibid.

60 On Subsoil Resources Article 2.1.

61 On Subsoil Resources Article 9.

62 Zarybezhneft 2017.

63 OilCapital.ru 2013.

64 Lukoil even received praise from President Putin for its exemplary environmental record at its offshore installations in the Caspian Sea. The President of Russia, Meeting with the Business Leaders Participating in the Summit, 23 May 2014, accessed 1 September 2015 http://kremlin.ru/events/president/news/21078.

65 Lukoil 2015.

66 Kommersant 2015. Interestingly, Rosneft appealed the results of this tender in court: Terentyeva 2015.

67 Ibid.

68 The Ministry of Natural Resources, Decree Dated as of 14 November 2002 N 457-r On Methodological Recommendations on Conducting Auctions and Tenders to Receive the Right to Use Subsoil Resources, as amended on 21 March 2015,§ 1.3, accessed 5 September 2015 http://www.rosnedra.gov.ru/article/116.html (hereinafter, Methodological Recommendations N 457-r).

69 Ibid. § 3.20.

70 'On Subsoil Resources' Article 10.1.

71 Presidential meeting transcript, 18 July 2008.

72 The President of Russia, Meeting of the Commission on the Strategy of Fuel and Energy Sector Development and Environmental Security, 10 July 2012, accessed 1 September 2015, http://news.kremlin.ru/news/15912 (hereinafter, Presidential meeting transcript, 10 July 2012).

73 Terentyeva 2015.

74 The principal difference between regional prospecting and prospecting is that the latter has a smaller spatial scale and a higher degree of invasiveness.

75 'On Subsoil Resources' Articles 6 and 10.1, and On Continental Shelf Article 7.

76 'On Continental Shelf' Article 6.

77 'On Subsoil Resources' Article 11.

78 Federal Law dated as of 30 December 1995 N 225-FZ On Production Sharing Agreements, last amended on 29 June 2015, article 2, accessed 1 September 2015 http://pravo.gov.ru/ (hereinafter, On PSAs).

79 Mazkov 2008.

80 This is consistent with the approach that my co-authors and I took in *IEE* 2011.

81 The 22 August 2004 amendment was especially detrimental to environmental assessment in Russia. See Federal Law dated as of 22 August 2004 N 122-FZ On Amending Legislative Acts of the Russian Federation and Deeming Invalid Certain Legislative Acts of the Russian Federation Due to the Enactment of Federal Laws 'On Amending and Supplementing Federal Law on the General Principles of Regional Legislative and Executive Government Organisation' and On General Principles of Local Self-Governance in the Russian Federation,' art. 62, accessed 5 September 2015 http://pravo.gov.ru/ (hereinafter, Federal Law N 122-FZ).

82 The President of Russia, Transcript of the State Council's Presidium Meeting on Improving Government Regulation of Matters Concerning Environmental Protection, 27 May 2010, accessed 1 September 2015, http://kremlin.ru/events/president/transcripts/7872 (hereinafter, Presidential meeting transcript, 27 May 2010).

83 State Committee of the Russian Federation on Protection of the Environment, Order Dated as of 16 May 2000 N 372 On Affirmation of the Regulations for Environmental Impact Assessments, accessed 1 September 2015 http://pravo.gov.ru/ (hereinafter, Order No. 372).
84 Federal Law dated as of 23 November 1995 N 175-FZ Environmental Review, last amended on 13 July 2015, article 3, accessed 1 September 2015 http://pravo.gov.ru/ (hereinafter, On Environmental Review); the 'Order 372' Articles 1 and 3.
85 WWF.
86 'On Continental Shelf' Article 31 and 'On Inland Sea Waters' Article 34.
87 'On Continental Shelf' Article 22.2 and 'On Inland Sea Waters' Article 16.1.
88 'On Environmental Review', Article 4.
89 IEE 2011.
90 WWF.
91 The Government of the Russian Federation, Decree Dated 2 October 2009 N. 783 On Some Aspects of Implementation of the Federal Statutes 'On the Continental Shelf of the Russian Federation' and 'On the Exclusive Economic Zone of the Russian Federation,' para b, accessed 5 September 2015 http://pravo.gov.ru/ (hereinafter, Decree N. 783). Also see Federal Law dated as of 17 December 1998 N 191-FZ On the Exclusive Economic Zone of the Russian Federation, last amended on 14 October 2014, 1 September 2015 http://pravo.gov.ru/.
92 Federal Environmental, Technological and Nuclear Oversight Service, Order Dated as of 18 March 2014 N-105 On Affirmation of Federal Industrial Safety Regulations 'Offshore Oil and Gas Safety Rules,' Part III, accessed 1 September 2015 http://pravo.gov.ru/ (hereinafter Offshore Safety Rules).
93 See e.g., 'Offshore Safety Rules 'Part II.
94 Federal Law dated as of 10 January 2002 N 7-FZ On the Protection of the Environment, last amended on 13 July 2015, accessed 1 September 2015 http://pravo.gov.ru/.
Federal Law dated as of 27 December 2002 N 184-FZ On Technical Regulating, last amended on 13 July 2015, article 2, accessed 1 September 2015 http://pravo.gov.ru/ (hereinafter, On Technical Regulating).
95 Rosstandart.
96 Presidential meeting transcript, 27 May 2010.
97 The President of Russia, Transcript of the State Council's Presidium Meeting on Improving Government Regulation of Matters Concerning Environmental Protection, 27 May 2010, accessed 1 September 2015, http://kremlin.ru/events/president/transcripts/7872.

References

Baker, Betsy and Roman Sidortsov. 2014. The Legal and Regulatory Regime for Offshore Hydrocarbon Resources in the U.S. Arctic, ABA-SEER.

Barsukov, Yurij. 2013. 'Lukoil Aims at LNG Exports.' *Kommersant.ru,* 20 November 2013. Accessed 1 September 2015. www.kommersant.ru/doc/2348143.

BBC. 2013. 'Russia Drops First Greenpeace Arctic 30 Case.' *BBC News,* 24 December 2013. Accessed 1 September 2015. www.bbc.com/news/world-europe-25504016.

EIA (Energy Information Administration). 2015. 'Russia: International Energy Data and Analysis.' *EIA Beta,* 28 July 2015. Washington, DC: US Department of Energy/Energy Information Administration. Accessed 1 September 2015. www.eia.gov/beta/international/analysis.cfm?iso=RUS.

Gazprom. 2016. *Prirazlomnoe Oil Field.* Accessed 27 November 2016. www.gazprom.com/about/production/projects/deposits/pnm/.
Gustafson, Thane. 2012. *Wheel of Fortune: The Battle for Oil and Power in Russia.* London: The Belknap Press of Harvard University Press.
Hoffman, David. 2011. *The Oligarchs.* New York: Public Affairs.
IEE (Institute for Energy and the Environment). 2011. *Arctic Offshore Oil and Gas Guidelines in Greenland and the Russian Federation.* Arctic Offshore Oil and Gas Guidelines White Paper No. 5, February 2011. South Royalton, Vermont: Vermont Law School Institute for Energy and the Environment, for Inuit Circumpolar Council.
Kommersant. 2015. 'Lukoil Won the East Taymyr Bloc Tender.' *Kommersant,* 11 August 2015. Accessed 5 September 2015. www.kommersant.ru/doc/2786534.
Lukoil. 2015. *Offshore Projects.* Moscow: Lukoil. Accessed 5 September 2015. www.lukoil.com/materials/doc/Library/Offshore_Projects_eng.pdf.
Lunden, Lars Petter and Daniel Fjaertoft. 2014. *Government Support to Upstream Oil & Gas in Russia: How Subsidies Influence the Yamal LNG and Prirazlomnoe Projects.* Geneva, Oslo, Moscow: International Institute for Sustainable Development; Global Subsidies Initiative; Sigra Group; World Wide Fund for Nature. July 2014. Accessed 1 September 2015. www.iisd.org/gsi/sites/default/files/ffs_awc_russia_yamalprirazlomnoe_en.pdf.
Mazkov, Evgeniy. 2008. 'Legal Regulation of Geological Exploration and Extraction of Oil and Gas in the Continental Shelf of the Russian Federation.' Cand. Legal Studies dissertation, Moscow State Law Academy.
Nysten-Haarla, Soili and Juha Kotilainen. 2009. 'Institutions, Interest Groups and Governance of Natural Resources in Russia.' In *The Changing Governance of Renewable Natural Resources in Northwest Russia,* edited by Soili Nysten-Haarla. London: Ashgate.
OilCapital.ru. 2013. 'The Environmental Ministry Agrees to Allow Zarubezhneft to the Shelf.' *OilCapital.ru,* 3 June 2013. Accessed 5 September 2015. www.oilcapital.ru/industry/209570.html.
Paik, Keun-Wook. 2012. *Sino-Russian Oil and Gas Cooperation: The Reality and Implications.* Oxford: Oxford Institute for Energy Studies.
Parfitt, Tom. 2007. 'Russia Plants Flag on North Pole Seabed.' *The Guardian*, 2 August 2007. Accessed 30 November 2016. www.theguardian.com/world/2007/aug/02/russia.arctic.
Rosneft. 2017. 'Rosneft: Board of Directors.' Accessed 28 February 2017. www.rosneft.ru/governance/corpboard/.
Rosstandart. nd. *Current Technical Regulations.* Moscow: Rosstandart (Federal Agency on Technical Regulation and Metrology). Accessed 1 September 2015. http://gost.ru/wps/portal/pages/directions/techreg?WCM_GLOBAL_CONTEXT=/gost/GOSTRU/directions/TechnicalRegulation/TechnicalRegulationses.
Russian Government. nd. *The Russian Government: Structure, Ministries and Agencies.* Web page. Accessed 1 September 2015. http://government.ru/en/ministries/.
Sidortsov, Roman. 2014. 'The Myth of Liberalisation: The 2013 Changes in the Russian LNG Export Regime.' *The Energy Law Journal* 35 (2): 323–43.
Staalesen, Atle. 2015. 'Russia submits claim for North Pole.' *Barents Observer,* 4 August 2015. Accessed 1 September 2015. http://barentsobserver.com/en/arctic/2015/08/russia-submits-claim-north-pole-04-08.

Terentyeva, Aleksandra. 2015. 'Rosneft Appealed the East Taymyr Bloc Tender.' *Vedomosti,* 18 August 2015. Accessed 5 September 2015. www.vedomosti.ru/business/articles/2015/08/18/605273-rosneft-osporila-konkurs.

WWF (World Wide Fund for Nature). nd. *Gazprom: Actions Taken to Deploy Drilling Rig Prirazlomnaya on the Pechora Sea Shelf.* Moscow: World Wide Fund for Nature. Accessed 1 September 2015. www.wwf.ru/about/what_we_do/oil/full_list/gazprom/doc2831/page1.

Yavlinsky, Grigoriy. 2014. 'Russia and Ukraine: Causes of Crisis and Prospects.' Unpublished lecture. Cambridge: Cambridge University, 10 June 2014.

Zarybezhneft. 2017. *Zaruberzhneft History.* Accessed 27 Feburary 2017. www.zarubezhneft.ru/en/about_company/history/.

9 The Arctic offshore hydrocarbon hiatus of 2015

An opportunity to revisit regulation around the pole

Betsy Baker

Introduction

For once, regulators of offshore oil and gas operations have the chance to improve their rules not in response to disaster but to a deliberate downturn in drilling.[1] Since 2012, operators exploring for hydrocarbons in the Arctic Ocean have slowed or suspended offshore operations, or surrendered offshore lease interests, in Alaska, Canada, Greenland, Norway's high Arctic and Russia.[2] In October 2015, citing the dramatic decline in the global oil market, US regulators canceled remaining lease sales scheduled for 2012–2017 and declined to extend other leases.[3] Norway's Barents Sea remains the one active Arctic offshore oil lease area: Although Statoil postponed operations at its Johan Castberg find in the high Arctic in March 2015,[4] operator interest has been keen in Norwegian lease blocks closer to Russia that Statoil opened for bidding in November 2015.[5]

This hiatus in offshore oil and gas activity in the Arctic offers a prime opportunity to consider how best to strengthen the relevant regulatory regimes around the North and connect them more directly to national energy and climate related policies and opportunities. Such examination can help ensure better regulatory outcomes for such time as market and other forces render exploration in the Arctic offshore financially feasible and clarify which risks politically and economically acceptable, and which are not.

A flurry of useful comparative studies of offshore regulations in the Arctic states globally followed the 2010 Macondo Deepwater disaster in US waters of the Gulf of Mexico.[6] Three chapters in this volume complement those studies with recent regulatory developments for offshore Arctic regions in the five Arctic Ocean coastal States: Cécile Pelaudeix reports on Canada, Denmark/Greenland, and Norway; Roman Sidortsov covers the Russian Federation; and Edward T. Canuel surveys the United States regulatory structure.

The present chapter offers an overview of trends in offshore regulation around the Arctic by stepping back to consider more broadly the detailed discussions of national regulatory systems by Pelaudeix, Sidortsov and Canuel. This chapter neither summarizes nor critiques their contributions but identifies the highlights and recurring themes that emerge from reading the three chapters as a whole. The present chapter is not a work of original research; instead, it simply observes common elements and connections across the five legal systems surveyed by the three authors. It also touches on international and bilateral mechanisms which other chapters do not address, focusing on tools developed in the Arctic Council.

The chapter concludes by proposing ways to revisit Arctic offshore regulatory regimes under three general headings: the Drilling Downturn, Climate Change, and Integrated Management. It encourages countries (1) to ensure that the relative lull in activity leads not only to diverting attention from the Arctic but also to focusing on regulatory lessons learned from activity there to date, so as to be better prepared for activity if and when it resumes; (2) to consider how climate change already does, or has the potential to, reshape offshore regulation by tying permitting more closely to potential climate impacts of the activity permitted; and (3) to better integrate offshore hydrocarbon activity into their national regulatory structures in ways that address the fact it is only one of multiple uses of ocean space, each of which is often regulated as a separate sector.

National approaches to regulating Arctic offshore oil and gas activity

Pelaudeix, in comparing offshore regulatory polices in Canada, Greenland and Norway, argues that a correlation exists between national energy policy and offshore regulation. She concludes that

> In Canada, which is a net exporter, oil and gas energy is mainly a commercial good. In Norway, where the economic importance of oil and gas exports is related to the welfare system, and where profits are put in a public fund, energy mostly stands as a public good. In Greenland, where economic revenues from oil and gas are needed to support a political agenda on independency from Denmark, energy stands as a strategic good. The dominant characterizations of the country/territory as [respectively] a neo-liberal state, a welfare state, and an independence looking territory, shed light on [their] regulatory responses.[7]

Pelaudeix plausibly infers that the economic incentives and environmental requirements for Arctic offshore operations in each country reflect not only the energy policies but also the basic principles of the respective political system in which they are nested. For example, she points out that Canada, Greenland and Norway all require oil spill contingency plans of operators but only Norway requires that they be tested in advance.[8] This difference might reflect the historical influence of the Norwegian legal and social systems, which promote tripartite collaboration between companies, unions and government regulators. In the offshore context, this means greater involvement of oil industry workers (through the unions) in designing, among other things, offshore operational regulations.[9]

The relative openness of the regulatory process to the public, especially indigenous peoples, is one of Pelaudeix's three comparative focal points, the other two being economic incentive and environmental protection. She concludes that national mechanisms (the constitution and land claims agreements) are the main driver of Canada's accommodation for indigenous peoples' rights, whereas in Norway the drivers are international obligations (given its membership in the International Labor Organization Convention 169 and the International Covenant on Civil and Political Rights). Also according to Pelaudeix, Greenland has no special legislative protections for indigenous peoples as such, because its self-government status is premised on 'the people of Greenland being a people pursuant to international law', and the government considers itself to represent all Greenland Inuit.

The title of Sidortov's chapter – *The Russian Offshore Oil and Gas Regime: When Tight Control Means Less Order* – and indeed its very format, reflect the highly prescriptive and multilayered offshore regime in the Russian Federation. Sidortsov provides several examples to demonstrate the complex interactions of numerous responsible ministries with constitutional, statutory and sub-statutory provisions. In one case, he highlights how multiple sources of operational requirements interact by singling out the permitting process that follows the grant of an exploration license (itself a complex, multistep process and a source of operational requirements). He describes the latter permitting process as follows:

> In addition to the operating requirements specified in a license, offshore oil and gas operations require several permits. Some permits require input and approval from different agencies. For example, a drilling permit requires consultations with ten different ministries and agencies including Ministry of Defence, the Federal Security Service, the Ministry of Economic Development, and the Federal Service for Environmental, Technological, and Nuclear Oversight. Finally, operating requirements set in a great number of sub-statutes promulgated by federal administrative agencies.[10]

Sidortsov acknowledges that complexity is not unique to the Russian offshore regulatory world, pointing to the multiple statutes and agencies governing US offshore operations.[11] By providing detailed insights into Russia's multiple Energy and Arctic policies and strategies, however, as well as its internal politics, he makes clear that some of the regulatory intricacies are unique to existing political and power structures and national aspirations.[12] This result is not unlike what Pelaudeix suggests in her observation that, for example,

> For Canada, energy appears first as an economic activity, carried out by the private sector, and having an important part of its exports; in that

> perspective, the Arctic stands as a region of huge potential where Canada also pursues a political agenda based on asserting its sovereignty and exercising sovereign rights.[13]

Finally, political and power structures and national aspirations play a role not only in Russia. A US government investigative report released in December 2015 identifies substantial pressure on federal offshore regulators, from Alaska's U.S. congressional delegation and others, to expedite the agency's final review of the Environmental Impact Statement for Shell's 2015 drilling season in the Chukchi Sea.[14]

Canuel introduces the key federal laws and agencies that govern the US offshore in Alaska, and the actors that participate in the regulatory process, discussing extensively the unique situation of Alaska Native tribes.[15] He also describes how the agencies responsible for implementing the Outer Continental Shelf Lands Act (OCSLA) were reorganized after the Macondo – Deepwater Horizon disaster to separate functions previously joined in one bureau. Creating the US Bureau of Ocean Environmental Management (BOEM) and the Bureau of Safety and Environmental Enforcement (BSEE) allowed 'inspectors more budgetary autonomy and strengthening environmental review'.[16] Tellingly, however, regulations specific to 'Exploratory Drilling on the Arctic Outer Continental Shelf' proposed in February 2015 have still not been issued. If and when they are issued, they will be the first regulations specific to Arctic offshore operations issued by BOEM and BSEE post-Deepwater Horizon.[17]

As Sidortsov does for the Russian system, Canuel spells out the regulatory complexities unique to the United States. The complexities are presented as deriving from different sources in each country. Whereas Sidortsov sketches a Russian regulatory system that is in many ways dependent on the political figures behind the national strategies and policies and less systematically open to engaging stakeholders, Canuel focuses on the interchange between regulators, industry, Alaska Natives and other stakeholders. Canuel concludes that 'an emerging trend indicates that growing communication involving industry, federal/state government and tribes creates opportunities for dialogue. Broadening the decision-making process while simultaneously mandating increasing inter-agency coordination advances an inclusive approach that fosters buy-in'.[18]

Canuel thus touches on some of the same principles that undergird an influential US Arctic policy document from 2013: *Managing for the Future in a rapidly changing Arctic: A Report to the President*, produced by the US Interagency Working Group on Coordination of Domestic Energy Development and Permitting in Alaska.[19] Two of the report's five guiding principles are 'whole-of-government coordination to improve efficiency and operational certainty' and 'direct and meaningful partnership with stakeholders'.[20] The Report identifies the Open Water Season Conflict Avoidance Agreement (CAA) between the Alaska Eskimo Whaling Commission and oil and gas companies as 'another example of integrating cultural, environmental economic needs'.[21] That the government characterizes CAAs as a 'promising' approach reflects the regulators' openness to incorporating practical solutions proposed outside the formal regulatory process into integrated management of the Arctic offshore.[22]

International and bilateral mechanisms

Non-binding international mechanisms

Many binding and non-binding international instruments are available to inform national regulators responsible for their government's oversight of Arctic offshore oil and gas operations.[23] This section focuses on recent developments in non-binding Arctic Council mechanisms,[24] in part because many good analyses already exist of the binding treaty regimes most significant for offshore hydrocarbon activity.[25] Those regimes include the United Nations Convention on the Law of the Sea, numerous International Maritime Organization conventions, and the Oslo-Paris Convention for the Protection of the Marine Environment of the North-East Atlantic (OSPAR).[26] Also well covered in the literature,[27] and thus not discussed further here, are the first two binding agreements to emerge from the Arctic Council, the 2011 Agreement on Search and Rescue in the Arctic and the 2013 Agreement on Cooperation on Marine Oil Pollution Preparedness and Response in the Arctic.[28]

The 2009 Arctic Council Offshore Oil and Gas Guidelines (AOOGG) grew out of, and laid a foundation for, information sharing between national offshore hydrocarbon regulators in each of the Arctic Council member states.[29] The AOOGG aim 'to define a set of recommended practices and outline strategic actions for consideration by those responsible for regulation of offshore oil and gas activities' and 'to assist regulators in developing standards, which are applied and enforced consistently for all offshore Arctic oil and gas operators'.[30] Greenland expressly models its Guidelines for preparing environmental impact assessments on the PAME AOOGG,[31] but most Arctic Ocean coastal states do not appear to refer explicitly to the AOOGG. So what is their value?

The 2009 Guidelines have led to at least two further practical outcomes:

- A 2014 *Systems Safety Management and Safety Culture Report, Avoiding Major Disasters in Arctic Offshore Oil and Gas Operations*. The report supplements the 2009 AOOGG by suggesting tools for and approaches to 'reducing the threat of catastrophic effects of major oil and gas related accidents'. Among its recommendations are to use leading and lagging indicators for systems safety.[32] Notable here is a subsequent academic study delving deeper into the use of indicators in Arctic offshore operations, albeit in the context of environmental safety.[33]

- A web-based information sharing portal, *Arctic Offshore Oil and Gas Management, Regulation and Enforcement*, launched in 2014 as a collaboration between the PAME Working Group and the International Regulators Forum. The portal is also known as the *Arctic Offshore Oil and Gas Regulatory Resource or AOOGRR.*[34]

  The extent to which national regulators make use of these new tools is unclear, beyond the fact that many states have sent representatives of their regulatory bodies to the workshops that developed the tools. The Arctic hydrocarbon hiatus of 2015 presents a chance to focus regulators' attention on the availability of these tools and to begin to assess and improve their usefulness.

The Arctic Ocean Review (AOR) Final Report is another non-binding product of the Arctic Council, which its ministers endorsed in 2013 at the Kiruna Ministerial. In the Final Report, the Arctic Council working group on the Protection of the Arctic Marine Environment (PAME) surveyed international instruments relevant not only to oil and gas but to multiple actors and activities that affect the Arctic Ocean.[35] Two of the Report's four recommendations for offshore hydrocarbon activity focus on interactions between regulators and industry. Under Recommendation 1, 'The Arctic Council should urge its members to support, as appropriate, efforts in the ISO and other processes to develop standards relevant to Arctic oil and gas operations'[36] while Recommendation 4 provides that 'Arctic states should further engage industry and regulator involvement, as appropriate, in PAME and EPPR initiatives on offshore oil and gas activity by utilizing existing industry forums, or by convening an Arctic-specific oil and gas dialog for industry and contractor groups'. [37]

The AOOGRR web-based portal introduced above is in line with the kind of information sharing proposed by AOR Recommendation 4 for oil and gas in that it connects Arctic Council member states with the broader International Regulators Forum to share best practices. As for Recommendation 1 and the use of industry standards, different Arctic states incorporate standards for safety and environmental systems differently. For example, the United States incorporates standards explicitly by reference into the relevant regulation while Canada no longer does so.[38] These distinct national approaches to industry standards in offshore oil and gas regulation suggest value in examining how industry standards are used in other activities that pose potentially high risks to the public, such as the nuclear, pharmaceuticals and financial sectors. One US study of government-administered and industry-administered regulatory programs – voluntary and mandatory alike – identifies

> specific design features that lead to successful programs and effective utilization of industry input, including (1) clear, measurable program goals, (2) up-to-date industry performance standards, (3) performance standards created with input from a diverse group of stakeholders,

(4) accurate, independent verification of the regulated entity's performance, (5) robust enforcement mechanisms, and (6) combining of industry resources with government oversight.[39]

To the extent the Arctic Council resources discussed in this section contain recommendations or guidance endorsed by the Arctic Council Ministers, they constitute non-binding international mechanisms that can be used to improve communication between the different regulatory systems of the Arctic States. Further engagement with these resources by academics, regulators and other stakeholders need not lead to harmonization of offshore regulation around the North but can promote increased understanding among regulators as to how best practices compare in each country.[40]

Binding bilateral and regional mechanisms

The 2010 *Treaty Concerning Maritime Delimitation and Cooperation in the Barents Sea and the Arctic Ocean*[41] between the Russian Federation and the Kingdom of Norway is rightly hailed as a significant diplomatic success. Among other achievements, the Agreement resolves a forty-year disagreement and sets a single maritime boundary for the continental shelf and exclusive economic zones alike. Less obvious from the agreement's formal title is the fact that it also establishes procedures for exploiting trans-boundary hydrocarbon deposits. Because the Norway-Russia agreement has been suggested as a possible model for the still unresolved Beaufort Sea maritime boundary between Canada and the United States,[42] it is worth considering how such agreements can contribute to more robust and complementary regulation of offshore oil and gas activity in a shared maritime region.

Some of the Norwegian lease sale blocks offered in November 2015 and mentioned in the introduction to this chapter lie along the previously disputed maritime boundary now settled by the 2010 Agreement between Russia and Norway.[43] Strong industry interest in the 2015 lease sale, which counters the otherwise downward trend currently observed in Arctic offshore oil and gas activity, not only indicates the region's geophysical promise,[44] but it may also be a sign that the 2010 Agreement increases confidence in the regulatory regime that would apply to any joint development in the region.

The 2010 Norway-Russia umbrella agreement does not detail how the two national regulatory bodies would interact in case of joint development of a trans-boundary deposit.[45] It does, however, require the Parties to enter into a separate cross-border unitization and development agreement on allocation and exploitation if a deposit extends to the continental shelf of the other party and its exploitation is impossible without affecting that party's rights. A joint operating agreement would regulate the exploitation of the joint hydrocarbon deposit, giving each party the right to conduct inspections of hydrocarbon installations. The 2010 umbrella agreement provides that, under any cross-border unitization and development agreement signed, the parties would have to ensure 'continuous consultation and exchange of information' through a Joint Commission and include the duty grant licenses and permits as allowed by law.[46] Beyond these general provisions, little is said about what a cross-border joint unitization agreement must specify about the level of contact required between the two countries' regulators.

It is beyond the scope of this chapter to examine whether the existence of umbrella bilateral or regional agreements on exploiting trans-boundary hydrocarbons – such as the 2010 Norway-Russia agreement – strengthens the respective national regulatory regimes even for events that play out exclusively in national waters. Still, it is worth asking whether each national regulatory regime would be improved by having to systematically compare regulations across maritime boundaries as part of an umbrella agreement. Without further research into the kind of regulatory exchange that umbrella bilateral or regional hydrocarbon agreements generate (as distinct from separate unitization and development agreements for individual trans-boundary deposits), any attempt to draw connections between the existence of such agreements and more effective regulation would be inconclusive.

For example, neither the 1988 Piper Alpha disaster that killed 167 people in UK waters of the North Sea nor the 2010 BP Macondo-Deepwater disaster that claimed 11 lives in the US Eastern Gulf of Mexico involved trans-boundary deposits or trans-boundary spills. The UK and Norway had signed an umbrella delimitation agreement for the North Sea in 1965[47] and a cross-border unitization agreement for the separate Frigg deposit in 1976[48] (the Alpha Piper platform delivered gas to the Frigg Platform in Norwegian waters[49]). The Frigg Agreement, however, did not apply directly to the Piper Alpha, nor is it clear what systematic regulatory review the UK undertook, if any, as part of either the North Sea or the Frigg Agreement.[50] In the Eastern Gulf of Mexico, no umbrella agreement was in place when the Macondo well blew out, but the accident spurred US interest in drilling safety in Cuba and Mexico.[51] The 2012 *Agreement Between the United States of America and the United Mexican States Concerning Transboundary Hydrocarbon Reservoirs in the Gulf of Mexico* applies to the Western Gulf.[52]

For now, more concrete recommendations for rendering two different countries' offshore regulations more compatible can be seen in Barents 2020, a systematic regulatory review of Russian, Norwegian and global standards of potential relevance to Arctic offshore operations.[53] The Norwegian Foreign Ministry requested the Barents 2020 project, which Det Norske Veritas launched in 2006 and concluded in 2012, 'to seek industry cooperation with Russia to harmonize and agree HSE standards to be used in the Barents Sea'.[54] While independent of the 2010 Agreement between Russia and Norway, Barents 2020 was complementary and responsive to the fact that the two countries needed to prepare for Arctic offshore operations in extreme conditions. Barents 2020 is a model for bilateral and regional regulatory comparisons, inviting input from industry, regulators, and other key stakeholders and recommended standards specific to the Barents region in which either country might eventually license offshore operations.

Opportunities for regulatory information exchange

Taken together, Pelaudeix, Sidortsov and Canuel's pieces suggest that all five Arctic Ocean coastal states are working to address at least three common situations in their regulation of Arctic offshore hydrocarbon activity.

1 *Integrated Regulation:* How to integrate the actions of numerous national regulatory authorities with responsibility for Arctic offshore hydrocarbon activity into a congruent, more efficient regulatory whole;
2 *Regulatory-Economic Consistency*: How to synchronize regulatory outcomes with the role of hydrocarbons in their respective economies; and
3 *Indigenous Participation:* How to better incorporate input from actors that are subject to regulation, especially the Arctic's indigenous peoples.

The five national systems may well face other common regulatory challenges in the Arctic offshore, especially on a bilateral basis. However, these are the three themes that emerge from a review of the material Pelaudeix, Sidortsov and Canuel choose to cover in their contributions to this volume.[55]

This concluding section suggests that Arctic offshore regulators should work nationally and collectively to address these and any other common themes in light of three developments across the North: the Drilling Downturn, Climate Change, and the move toward Integrated Management.

Drilling downturn

National regulators and policy makers should take advantage of the relative lull in Arctic offshore oil and gas activity to assess the state of regulation and compare best practices. They should ensure that this hiatus leads not to diverting attention from the Arctic but is instead used to convene experts to parse lessons learned from regulatory and operator activity in the Arctic in the last five years. By remaining focused on the Arctic, regulators can be better prepared for offshore hydrocarbon activity if and when it resumes. Indeed, the substantial interest in Norway's November 2015 leases in the Barents Sea indicates that the pause may be short-lived at least in parts of the Arctic.

More specifically, regulators from Canada, Greenland and the United States could use the relative downturn in activity to study the results of the Norwegian-Russian Barents 2020 study and consider adapting its approach to create operating standards more tailored to their respective areas of the Arctic Ocean. In addition, the conclusion of the public comment period in May 2015 for the US Arctic-specific regulations for offshore operations[56] offers an opportunity to share information domestically and internationally.

That information could be usefully shared whether or not the regulations are adopted in final form in the near future. By showcasing both the draft regulations and lessons learned from Shell's Alaska drilling seasons in other international forums and workshops, US regulators, industry and advocacy groups have a unique opportunity to present the information not as a victory or defeat for any particular interest group but as an opportunity to build upon experience to improve regulatory outcomes for any future operations.

Climate change

Another lens through which regulators will soon have to focus their attention even more closely is the effect of domestic and global climate change policy on offshore oil and gas activity. This perspective dovetails with one of the common regulatory challenges across the five Arctic states, as presented in the chapters by Pelaudeix, Sidorstov and Canuel: How to synchronize regulatory outcomes with the role of hydrocarbons in their respective economic, climate, and energy polices. National regulators of Arctic offshore activity should exchange information on how climate change already does, or has the potential to, reshape offshore regulation by tying permitting more closely to potential climate impacts of the activity permitted. The following suggestions identify tools already available to regulators to do so.

This chapter was submitted for publication just days after 195 countries signed a historic climate agreement at the 21st meeting of the Conference of the Parties to the Framework Convention on Climate Change in Paris. The Paris Agreement calls for 'holding the increase in the global average temperature to well below 2°C above pre-industrial levels'.[57] In January 2015 the journal *Nature* published one of the more visible pieces in a growing body of literature discussing the option of leaving Arctic resources in place.[58] It concluded that 'development of resources in the Arctic and any increase in unconventional oil production are incommensurate with efforts to limit average global warming to 2°C'.[59]

The movement urging nations and industries that produce hydrocarbons to 'keep it in the ground' will be debated long and hard.[60] Rather than respond to broad national and international policy debates, national regulators of Arctic offshore activity can direct their efforts more narrowly. One such focus could come through exchanging information about how climate change affects the national policies, laws and regulations that create their regulatory mandates.

> The Arctic Council Arctic Offshore Oil and Gas Guidelines discussed in the section *Non-binding international mechanisms* include 'Sustainability' as one of their four guiding principles.[61] The Guidelines define a key component of sustainability as the need 'to maintain hydrocarbon production rates in keeping with sound conservation practices as

a means of minimizing environmental impacts'. National constitutions and offshore legislation around the Arctic take varying approaches to balancing environmental protection and resource development. A comprehensive survey of those differences exceeds the scope of this paper. A few examples, however, suggest national approaches that may prove useful models as each country's energy policies adapt to reflect commitments made at the Paris 2015 climate conference that, in turn, could lead to possible changes in national rules governing offshore hydrocarbon resources.

Part 13 of the 2009 Greenland Mineral Resources Act (MRA)[62] specifically addresses Environmental Protection (sections 51–54), Climate Protection (sections 55–58) and Nature Conservation (sections 59–62), in order to 'help to protect the environment so that society can develop on a sustainable basis respecting human conditions of life and respecting preservation of animal and plant life'. The 2015 Paris Climate agreement could, in theory, play a role because, under the MRA the government may establish rules on any of these matters, including the applicability of provisions of 'national or international rules, agreements, or guidelines' relevant to each area. The Explanatory Notes to the MRA view these provisions as indicating how the entire MRA is intended to balance economic development with the need to limit environmental and social impacts. Through the MRA provisions on Environmental Protection, the Greenland Parliament, or *Inatsisartut*, aims to 'prevent, limit, and combat pollution and other impacts on the climate from activities' that may directly or indirectly 'endanger human health', 'damage animal or plant life or natural or cultural values', 'limit the use of … resources', and 'impair human conditions of life', amongst other things. The MRA rules on Climate Protection aim to reduce the discharge of CO_2 and other greenhouse gases and only allow activities that enable society to develop on a sustainable basis.

Greenland's Mineral Resource Act is the product of a different era than, for example, the US Outer Continental Shelf Lands Act (OCSLA), originally enacted in 1953. As Canuel explains, under the 1978 amendments to OCSLA, the Department of the Interior 'must balance twin OCSLA objectives: 'expeditious and orderly development, subject to environmental safeguards, in a manner which is consistent with the maintenance of competition and other national needs'.[63] While climate is not specified in the legislative text, there is room to include climate considerations in the regulatory process, a step that has already begun in how Environmental Impact Statements are prepared.

Exchange of information between Arctic regulators regarding the changing role that climate considerations play in permitting offshore activity could be a strategically important contribution to national energy and climate policy. Promoting such a discussion could offer a practical response to voices on all sides of the debate, whose positions can range from demanding a complete ban of offshore hydrocarbon exploration and exploitation to advocating unlimited development of those resources.

Integrated management

A third challenge common to national offshore regulatory authorities around the Arctic as derived from Pelaudeix, Sidortsov and Canuel's chapters in this volume, is the need to better integrate offshore hydrocarbon regulation into each national regulatory structure. Such integration would ideally consider hydrocarbon exploration and exploitation as just one of multiple uses of ocean space, each of which often has a separate, sectoral regulatory regime. Here, too, an exchange of best practices on how integrated management is practiced around the Arctic could strengthen regulation of offshore hydrocarbon activity.

The Greenland Mineral Resource Act discussed in the preceding section is 'based on a holistic view of man's interaction with nature'[64] and includes measures to protect the environment and the climate. Combining such protections in an act that governs mineral resource activity reflects the Act's integrated approach to mineral resource development and lays the groundwork for environmental, climate and resource policies to work closely together, whether the resources are developed or conserved.

In Norway, integrated ecosystem management has been successfully applied in the Barents Sea-Lofoten area by 'translating ecological values and vulnerability ... into a boundary infrastructure, which was consequently distilled into a user-oriented grid that provided a temporary framework for oil and gas activities'.[65] Hydrocarbon exploration and exploitation are only one set of activities covered by the integrated plan for the area. Also relevant to the Barents Sea, the president of the Russian Federation issued directive Pr-1530 on 5 June 2014 ordering the Government to 'Draft a pilot project on integrated management of marine resources in the Arctic seas for following implementation in the Russian part of the Barents Sea'.[66] This pilot project can be seen as falling under 'integrated socio-economic development of the Arctic zone of the Russian Federation', which is the first of five Priority areas identified in the 2013 *Strategy of the Arctic Zone Development and Ensuring National Security for the Period Ending in 2020.*[67]

In the Canadian Arctic, the Beaufort Sea Integrated Management Planning Initiative has also met with success, drawing in part on structures established by law under the Inuvialuit Land Claims Agreement and on years of cultivating working relationships between subsistence hunters, industry, government and other actors.[68] Specific integrated management projects are not yet well established in the US Arctic but an interagency working group on Coordination of Domestic Energy Development and Permitting in Alaska, has defined Integrated Management as 'a science-based, whole-of-government approach to stewardship and planning in the U.S. Arctic that integrates and balances environmental, economic, and cultural needs and objectives. It is an adaptive, stakeholder-informed means for looking holistically at impacts and sensitivities across the U.S. Arctic and generating sustainable solutions'.[69]

The extent to which the offshore regulatory regime for hydrocarbons plays a role in each of these integrated approaches is another potentially fruitful area in which national regulators could exchange best practices. Revisiting the energy policies that Pelaudeix studies in her review of Canada, Greenland, and Norway for a better understanding of how climate change informs those policies, if at all, is one potential avenue for beginning to draw closer links between national energy policies and climate change impacts on offshore regulation around the Arctic.

An essential component of integrated management is engaging stakeholders and rights holders in the regulatory process. Pelaudeix, Sidortsov and Canuel all touch on this central topic, especially as it relates to the rights of indigenous peoples in each of the five Arctic Ocean coastal states. Their three chapters reflect how inseparable the question of indigenous rights is in each country from its respective legal system and underlying constitutional values and history. Pelaudeix in particular makes clear, however, that such differences between legal and regulatory systems neither prevent sensible comparison of best practices nor preclude domestic rules from invoking international instruments such as the UN Declaration on the Rights of Indigenous Peoples.

Conclusion

Climate change and integrated management have the potential to reshape how offshore oil and gas are regulated in the Arctic. As this paper has demonstrated, tools already exist both in each country and internationally for regulators, industry and stakeholders to exchange and learn from their nascent experience in the Arctic offshore. Using the Arctic hydrocarbon hiatus of 2015 for such exchange is not only prudent, it is critical to ensure the continued availability and productivity of all Arctic resources for the benefit of the Arctic and its people for generations to come.

Notes

1 Regulatory reform and reports proposing reform proliferated after the 1988 Alpha Piper disaster in the North Sea and the 2010 BP Macondo well blowout in the Gulf of Mexico. See e.g. United Kingdom, 1990; National Energy Board, 2011, and National Commission, 2011. This note was submitted for publication in December 2015 and does not cover developments after that date, beyond cross-references to chapters in this volume dated 2016.
2 Park 2015; Kay and Thorup 2014.
3 Department of Interior, Press Release 2015.
4 Kavanagh 2015.
5 Milne 2015. Shnøvit is producing gas but no oil is currently produced in the Norwegian Arctic.

6 Among these, the National Energy Board of Canada's comprehensive circumpolar comparisons included in its Arctic-specific national review process are notable for the range of useful studies it commissioned and the ease of access it provides to offshore drilling reviews by industry groups and other countries. See National Energy Board, 2011, including its webpage devoted to studies by other countries and groups. https://www.neb-one.gc.ca/nrth/rctcffshrdrllngrvw/dcmnt-eng.html#s7. See Baker 2012, Appendix for additional post-Macondo reviews and studies.
7 Pelaudeix 2016, text following note 79.
8 Pelaudeix 2016, text preceding note 40.
9 See e.g. Petroleum Safety Authority Norway 2011 at 8 and 9 on the importance of this tripartite collaboration.
10 Sidortsov 2016, at note 82.
11 Referring at his note 32, e.g.to the more than 40 US statutes relevant to offshore hydrocarbon exploration and extraction. Canuel's chapter provides even more detail on the complexity in the US regulatory system
12 See, e.g. Sidortsov's discussion of the role of the Prime Minister and President at his notes 17 and 18. This follows his presentation of six different and overlapping strategies and policies: 'The Energy Strategy of the Russian Federation for the Period ending in 2030', 'The Comprehensive Scheme for the Development of the Gas Sector for the Period Ending in 2030,' 'On the Main Measures of Strengthening Russia's Positions in the Global Energy Sector for the Period Ending on January 1, 2016', 'The Foundations of the National Policy of the Russian Federation in the Arctic for the Period Ending in 2020 and Beyond', the more specific 'Strategy of the Arctic Zone Development and Ensuring National Security for the Period Ending in 2020', and the 'Strategic Action Program for Protecting the Environment of the Arctic Zone of the Russian Federation'.
13 Pelaudeix, last sentence in the section *Canada.*
14 Department of the Interior 2015, 16.
15 Canuel 2016.
16 Canuel 2016, after his note 7.
17 Department of the Interior 2015 (Federal Register). http://www.gpo.gov/fdsys/pkg/FR-2015-02-24/pdf/2015-03609.pdf Public comment ended May 27, 2015.
18 Canuel 2016, first two paragraphs in his section entitled 'The Way Forward'.
19 A 2011 Executive Order 13580 established the US Interagency Working Group on Coordination of Domestic Energy Development and Permitting in Alaska, see http://www.whitehouse.gov/the-press-office/2011/07/12/executive-order-interagency-working-group-coordination-domestic-energy-d
20 Interagency Working Group 2011, 2. The other three principles in the Report are 'science-based decision-making focused on ensuring sustainable ecosystems; adaptive approaches guided by ongoing research and monitoring; a region-wide planning approach that looks across jurisdictional boundaries; and improved understanding and consideration of the cumulative impacts of human activities in the region.'
21 Interagency Working Group 2013, 41–42.
22 On conflict avoidance agreements generally see Lefevre 2013.
23 On the interplay of binding and non-binding international instruments with each other and with domestic law of the Arctic nations for all areas of Arctic law, not just offshore oil and gas regulation, see Canuel 2016.
24 For a full list of all Arctic Council working group outputs (for AMAP, EPPR and PAME) relevant to offshore oil and gas see PAME 2009, 3–4, and PAME 2013, 61, Sidebar 5.1.
25 Spicer and Bath, 2010; Byers 2013; PAME AOR 2013; Shibata
26 See e.g. PAME 2013, Chapter 5.

27 See e.g. Molenaar 2012; Koivurova and Graczyk 2014; Canuel 2015; Rottem 2015.
28 Arctic Council 2011; Arctic Council 2013.
29 PAME 2009, 1, 3.
30 PAME 2009, 4.
31 Danish National Environmental Research Institute et al. 2011, 9.
32 PAME 2014, Systems Safety, e.g. 7, 19.
33 Jacobs and Joroff 2015.
34 PAME undated.
35 PAME 2013. The other topics covered in the AOR are Indigenous peoples and cultures, living marine resources, arctic marine operations and shipping, Arctic marine pollution, Ecosystem-based management and scientific research.
36 PAME 2013, 65.
37 PAME 2013, 66.
38 Baker 2012.
39 Hastings et al. 2012, 6–7.
40 On harmonization as ‘bringing two sets of regulations more in line with each other and making them more complementary’, see Baker 2012, 477.
41 Kingdom of Norway and The Russian Federation 2010.
42 Byers 2013, 88–89; for other models see McDorman 2009, 188–189.
43 Shipping Herald 2015.
44 Reuters 2015.
45 Henriksen and Ulfstein 2011, discuss the Agreement generally.
46 Kingdom of Norway and The Russian Federation 2010, Annex II, Art. 1, Sec. 5.
47 According to Bastida et al. 2007, 378, this 1965 delimitation agreement between United Kingdom and Norway is ‘the first example of an international agreement containing a commitment regarding cooperative development of straddling petroleum reservoirs’.
48 Bastida et al. 2007.
49 Greenhouse 1998.
50 Bastida et al. 2007, op cit.: ‘To mitigate the effect of separate jurisdictions, the Frigg Agreement provided for consultation between the two governments in order to ensure that all installations were subject to uniform safety and construction standards’.
51 Martin and Wood 2013. Garcia Sanchez and McLaughlin 2015, indicate that a joint development agreement may be appropriate for the Eastern Gulf in the future.
52 Garcia Sanchez and McLaughlin 2015, discuss this 2012 agreement in detail.
53 Barents 2020 Assessment of international standards for safe exploration, production and transportation of oil and gas in the Barents sea, Harmonisation of Health, Safety, and Environmental Protection Standards for The Barents Sea, Final Report, Report no 2009–1626. Available at http://www.dnvusa.com/resources/reports/barents2020.asp.
54 DNV and VINNIGAZ 2012, 9.
55 Notably, the three authors did not collaborate on style or content in preparing their contributions to this volume.
56 Department of the Interior 2015.
57 United Nations FCCC 2015, Art. 2(1)(a).
58 McGlade and Ekins 2015.
59 Ibid.
60 In the United States, for example, Senators Jeff Merkely and Bernie Sanders introduced Bill S.2238 – Keep It in the Ground Act of 2015, 114th Congress (2015–2016) on 4 November 2015.
61 PAME 2009.

62 Inatsisartut 2009 (amended 2012, 2014).
63 Canuel 2016.
64 Inatsisartut 2009a.
65 Knol 2011.
66 Hansen et al. 2015.
67 Russian Federation 2013.
68 Fast, H. et al. 2005.
69 Department of the Interior 2013. The White House 2014 *Implementation Plan for The National Strategy for the Arctic Region* also draws on this understanding of integrated management.

References

Arctic Council. 2011. *Agreement on Cooperation on Aeronautical and Maritime Search and Rescue in the Arctic*, 12 May 2011, 50 I.L.M. 1119.

Arctic Council. 2013. *Agreement on Cooperation on Marine Oil Pollution Preparedness and Response in the Arctic*, 15 May 2013, available at www.arctic-council.org/index.php/en/documentarchive/category/425-main-documents-from-kiruna-ministerial-meeting.

Baker, B. 2012. 'Offshore Oil and Gas Regulation in the Arctic: Room for Harmonization?' *The Yearbook of Polar Law* Vol. IV: 475–504.

Bastida, A., et al. 2007. 'Cross-Border Unitization and Joint Development Agreements: An International Law Perspective', *Houston Journal of International Law* Vol. 49: 355–422.

Byers, M. 2013. *International Law and the Arctic*, Cambridge: Cambridge University Press.

Canuel, E.T. 2015. 'The Four Arctic Law Pillars: A Legal Framework', *Georgetown Journal of International Law* Vol. 46: 735–764.

Canuel, E.T. 2016. Alaska and Offshore Hydrocarbon Extraction: A Legal and Socio-Economic Review. In *Governance of Arctic Offshore Oil and Gas*, Pelaudeix, C. and Basse, E. M. (Eds.), Abingdon: Routledge.

Cullen, W. Douglas and Great Britain (Department of Energy). 1990. *The Public Inquiry into the Piper Alpha Disaster* (Chair: Lord Cullen), London: HM Stationery Office.

Danish National Environmental Research Institute, Greenland Institute of Natural Resources, and Bureau of Minerals and Petroleum. 2011. *BMP Guidelines – for Preparing an Environmental Impact Assessment (EIA) Report for Activities Related to Hydrocarbon Exploration and Exploitation Offshore Greenland.*

Department of the Interior. 2015. *Oil and Gas and Sulphur Operations on the Outer Continental Shelf—Requirements for Exploratory Drilling on the Arctic Outer Continental Shelf*, 9916 Federal Register / Vol. 80, No. 36 / Tuesday, 24 February 2015.

Department of the Interior, Office of the Inspector General. 2015. *Investigative Report of Management Interference with Lease 193 EIS*, posted to the web 7 December 2015.

Department of Interior. 2015. *Press Release. Interior Department Cancels Arctic Offshore Lease Sales Beaufort and Chukchi Sea Lease Sales will be Cancelled in Current Five Year Oil and Gas Program*, 16 October 2015.

DNV and VINNIGAZ. 2012. *Assessment of International Standards for Safe Exploration, Production and Transportation of Oil and Gas in the Barents Sea,*

Harmonisation of Health, Safety, and Environmental Protection Standards for the Barents Sea, Final Report Phase 4, Barents 2020 Report no 2012-0690.
Fast, H., et al. 2005. Integrated Management Planning in Canada's Western Arctic: An Adaptive Consultation Process. In *Breaking Ice: Renewable Resource and Ocean Management in the Canadian North,* Berkes, F. et al. (Eds.), Calgary: University of Calgary Press, 95–118.
Garcia Sanchez, G.J. and McLaughlin, R.J. 2015. 'The 2012 Agreement on the Exploitation of Transboundary Hydrocarbon Resources in the Gulf of Mexico: Confirmation of the Rule or Emergence of a New Practice?' *Houston Journal of International Law* Vol. 37: 681–792.
Greenhouse, S. 1988. '165 Feared Dead from Oil Rig Blast', *New York Times*, 8 July 1988, A7.
Hansen, J.R., et al. 2015. 'Norwegian–Russian Environmental Cooperation in the Barents Sea. Toward Development of a Coordinated Ecosystem Based Management', *Barents Observer*, 11 August 2015.
Hastings, D., et al. 2012. *Recommendations for Improved Oversight of Offshore, Drilling Based on a Review of 40 Regulatory Regimes*, Cambridge, MA: Harvard Law School, Emmett Environmental Law & Policy Clinic.
Henriksen, T. and Ulfstein, G. 2011. 'Maritime Delimitations in the Arctic: The Barents Sea Treaty, at 10', *Ocean Development & International Law* Vol. 42: 1–21.
Interagency Working Group on Coordination of Domestic Energy Development and Permitting in Alaska. 2013. *Managing for the Future in a rapidly changing Arctic: A Report to the President.*
Inatsisartut. 2009. *Greenland Parliament Act No. 7 of 7 December 2009 on Mineral Resources and Mineral Resource Activities* (the Mineral Resources Act or MRA), amended in 2012 and 2014. Available at www.govmin.gl/about-bmp/legal-foundation.
Inatsisartut. 2009a. Explanatory Notes to the Bill [Greenland Parliament Act No. 7 of 7 December 2009 on Mineral Resources and Mineral Resource Activities] https://www.govmin.gl/images/stories/faelles/explanatory_notes_to_the_mineral_resources_act.pdf, last visited May 15, 2017.
Jacobs, W.B. and Joroff, A.D. 2015. 'Proposed Indicators to Measure the Environmental Responsibility of Oil and Gas Companies and Regulatory Reforms to Improve Access to Information about Offshore Drilling', *Washington Journal of Environmental Law and Policy* Vol. 5: 101–153.
Kavanagh, M. 2015. 'Statoil delays development of Arctic Oil Field', *Financial Times,* 6 March 2015. www.ft.com/intl/cms/s/0/f9758b84-c40d-11e4-a02e-00144feab7de.html#axzz3tgPn9hz0.
Kay, J. and Thorup, S. 2014. *Oil and Gas in Greenland – Still on Ice? Notes from the Field – An English Law Perspective on the Oil & Gas Market.* AndrewsKurth.com Pressroom, November 2014.
Kingdom of Norway and the Russian Federation. 2010. *Treaty Concerning Maritime Delimitation and Cooperation in the Barents Sea and the Arctic Ocean*, Annex II, art. 1(8), 15 September 2010, 50 I.L.M. 1113. https://www.regjeringen.no/globalassets/upload/ud/vedlegg/folkerett/avtale_engelsk.pdf.
Knol, M. 2011. 'Mapping Ocean Governance: From Ecological Values to Policy Instrumentation', *Journal of Environmental Planning and Management,* Vol. 54 (7): 979–995.

Martin, J. and Wood, D. 'U.S. Should Act Quickly on Transboundary Hydrocarbon Agreement with Mexico', *World Politics Review*, 3 May 2013.

Koivurova, T. and Graczyk, P. 2014. 'The Future of the Arctic Council: Navigating between Sovereignty and Security', In *International Relations and the Arctic: Understanding Policy and Governance,* Murray, R.W. and Nuttall, A.D. (Eds.), Amherst: Cambria Press, 441–481.

Lefevre, J. 2013. 'A Pioneering Effort in the Design of Process and Law Supporting Integrated Arctic Ocean Management', *Environmental Law Reporter* Vol. 43: 10893–10908.

McDorman, T. 2009. *Salt Water Neighbours: International Ocean Law Relations between the United States and Canada*, New York: Oxford University Press.

McGlade, C. and Ekins, P. 2015. 'The Geographical Distribution of Fossil Fuels Unused When Limiting Global Warming to 2°C', *Nature* Vol. 517: 187–190. doi:10.1038/nature14016.

Milne, R. 2015. 'Norway feels the Arctic chill', *Inside Business, Financial Times,* 19 August 2015. www.ft.com/intl/cms/s/0/bfade0cc-466c-11e5-b3b2-1672f710807b.html#axzz3tgPn9hz0.

Molenaar, E.J. 2012. 'Current and Prospective Roles of the Arctic Council System Within the Context of the Law of the Sea', *International Journal of Marine and Coastal Law* Vol. 27 (3): 553–595.

National Commission. 2011. *National Commission on the BP Deepwater Horizon Oil Spill and Offshore Drilling, Deep Water: The Gulf Oil Disaster and the Future of Offshore Drilling*, Report to the President, 2011.

National Energy Board of Canada. 2011. *The Past is Always Present – Review of Offshore Drilling in the Canadian Arctic – Preparing for the Future.* Ottawa, 2011.

PAME. 2009. *Arctic Offshore Oil and Gas Guidelines*, Protection of the Arctic Marine Environment (PAME) Working Group.

PAME. 2013. *The Arctic Ocean Review Project, Final Report, (Phase II 2011–2013), Kiruna, May 2013.* Protection of the Arctic Marine Environment (PAME) Secretariat, Akureyri.

PAME. 2014. *Arctic Offshore Oil and Gas Guidelines, Systems Safety Management and Safety Culture Report, Avoiding Major Disasters in Arctic Offshore Oil and Gas Operations*, Protection of the Arctic Marine Environment (PAME) Working Group.

PAME. Undated [launched 2014]. *Arctic Offshore Oil and Gas Management, Regulation and Enforcement*, A Legal Regime Web-Based Information Resource. www.pame.is/index.php/projects/offshore-oil-and-gas/mre.

Park, G. 2015. 'Arctic Unease Spreads, Shell's Decision in Alaska Compounds Deferral of Canadian Beaufort Exploration', *Petroleum News* Vol. 20, no. 41, Week of 11 October 2015.

Pelaudeix, C. 2016. Governance of Offshore Hydrocarbon Activities in the Arctic and Energy Policies: A Comparative Approach in Norway, Canada and Greenland/Denmark. In *Governance of Arctic Offshore Oil and Gas*, Pelaudeix, C. and Basse, E. M. (Eds.), Abingdon: Routledge.

Petroleum Safety Authority Norway. Undated [2011]. *The Deepwater Horizon Accident – assessments and recommendations for the Norwegian petroleum industy* [sic], Summary.

Reuters. 2015. *Oil Firms Pile in as Norway Moves Exploration Closer to Russia*, 4 December 2015.

Rottem, S.V. 2015. 'A Note on the Arctic Council Agreements', *Ocean Development & International Law* Vol. 46: 50–59.

Russian Federation. 2013. *The Development Strategy of the Arctic Zone of the Russian Federation and National Security for the Period up to 2020*, approved 13 February 2013 by President Vladimir Putin, available in translation at: www.iecca.ru/en/legislation/strategies/item/99-the-development-strategy-of-the-arctic-zone-of-the-russian-federation.

Shipping Herald. 2015. 'Russian Oil Explorers among Bidders for Norway Arctic Blocks', www.shippingherald.com/russian-oil-explorers-among-bidders-norway-arctic-blocks/.

Sidortsov, R. 2016. The Russian Offshore Oil and Gas Regime: When Tight Control Means Less Order. In *Governance of Arctic Offshore Oil and Gas*, Pelaudeix, C. and Basse, E. M. (Eds.), Abingdon: Routledge.

Spicer, W. and Bath, T. 2010. 'The Canadian Arctic: The Changing Seascape of Offshore Oil and Gas Exploration Issues', *48 Alberta Law Review* Vol. 255: 2010–2011.

United Nations FCCC. 2015. *Adoption of the Paris Agreement*, Framework Convention on Climate Change, FCCC/CP/2015/L.9, 12 December 2015, Conference of the Parties Twenty-first session Paris, 30 November to 11 December 2015.

Part III

State-based approach, sub-states entities and indigenous peoples

10 Offshore development and Inuit rights in Inuit Nunangat[1]

Thierry Rodon

Introduction

In the Canadian Arctic, offshore development started in the Mackenzie Delta–Beaufort Sea region in the early 1970s. At that time, Aboriginal rights and title were neither recognised nor taken into account, and the regulatory regime was quite simple. Since then, with climate change creating more favourable conditions for offshore activities and steady demand for oil and gas products, exploration has increased in the Canadian Arctic, and the institutional landscape has correspondingly changed as well. Aboriginal[2] rights have been recognised by the Supreme Court of Canada and enshrined in the Canadian constitution, and all of Canada's Inuit-inhabited regions have signed land claim settlements. In the case of Nunavut, a self-government agreement has led to the creation of the government of Nunavut.

In this chapter, after presenting the Canadian rights-based approach to Aboriginal rights, we will assess what rights the Inuit have with regard to offshore development and contrast them with the principle of free, prior and informed consent (FPIC) that has been enshrined in the United Nations Declaration on the Rights of Indigenous Peoples.

We will then assess the offshore development strategies of Inuit from two regions: Nunavut and the Inuvialuit Settlement Region. In the second region, Inuit organisations have entered into partnerships with oil companies. In Nunavut, they have gone to the courts to challenge seismic testing for offshore development. These two case studies will be used to map the legal challenges and power dynamics created by Inuit land-claim settlements and offshore development projects.

A rights-based approach to indigenous issues: aboriginal rights, land claim settlements, and the duty to consult

Canada, over the years, developed a rights-based approach to Aboriginal issues. Ever since confederation, Aboriginal peoples have been considered to be wards of the state and as such had no special rights. A famous policy document known as the 1969 White Paper argued that their rights were no longer relevant and that the only issue was how better to integrate Aboriginal peoples into Canadian society. It met with strong opposition from them, and following many legal challenges by Aboriginal groups, the Canadian government had to reverse its position.[3]

The first recognition of the existence and persistence of Aboriginal rights came from the Supreme Court of Canada in the 1973 Calder case.[4] Its ruling started a new trend and was followed by many more court decisions over the years. This process was further consolidated when recognition of Aboriginal rights was written into section 35.1 of the Constitution Act of 1982.

Indigenous rights were still poorly defined, and it took another 20 years of court cases for a clearer picture to emerge of what these rights were and how they could be expressed in our contemporary world. The next landmark court case was the Van der Peet trilogy,[5] it has established a test to define Aboriginal rights: according to the Supreme Court, such rights have to be an integral part of a distinctive culture (practice, custom or tradition) and must be of central significance to the Aboriginal society in question. Furthermore, the practices, customs, and traditions that constitute Aboriginal rights are those which have continuity with the practices, customs and traditions that existed prior to contact with Europeans. Such rights therefore vary according to the different Aboriginal groups and their distinct material cultures. Finally, the courts have clearly stressed that such a right must be considered in its original cultural context and that continuity of this right does not mean lack of interruption but rather continuous importance in the culture, even if it has not always been exercised.

The Supreme Court has also established in the Delgamuukw case[6] that Aboriginal title refers to an inherent right to land and territory and, as such, has special features. Aboriginal title is not a fee-simple property right, but rather a collective title that is separate from property rights given under Canadian common law. Establishing such title means showing exclusive and continuous occupation and control of the land. The recent Tsilhqot'in decision[7] has clarified application of this test to semi-nomadic groups by adding that occupation needs only to be sufficient and not necessarily intensive, contrary to what had been argued in a lower court case. So far, the Tsilhqot'in case is the only Canadian court decision where Aboriginal title has been formally recognised. According to the Supreme Court, Aboriginal title means that Aboriginal peoples can decide how the land will be used, and they may economically benefit from this land as long as such use respects their culture.[8] This implies a form of consent. The Supreme Court holds that governments can infringe upon these rights, but the burden is on them to prove that the reasons are valid and that all efforts to accommodate Aboriginal interests have been made.

This new legal environment forced the Canadian government to come up with a landclaims settlement policy for all Aboriginal groups who had not signed a formal treaty and whose rights had not been formally extinguished. The first comprehensive land claims policy was announced in 1973 and has since been updated regularly to reflect new court decisions. The latest policy[9] was adopted in 1986 and proposed to exchange Aboriginal rights, including title, for the rights defined in the treaty.

At first, the Inuit of Canada tried to negotiate a single treaty, but they soon realised the impracticality of trying to negotiate a region-wide treaty with four entities: the federal government, one territorial government and two provincial governments.[10] Treaty negotiation is a very long process, and its pace is controlled by the federal government, which can walk away from the table if Aboriginal positions are deemed unreasonable.[11] Resource development is usually what drives such agreements. The James Bay and Northern Quebec Agreement, signed in 1975 by the Inuit of Nunavik, was negotiated so that the Quebec government could go ahead with major hydro-electric power projects. The Inuvialuit signed their final agreement in 1984, at a time when the Mackenzie Delta was seen as a very promising region for gas production. Finally, the Nunatsiavut Final Agreement was signed in 2005 to allow mining of nickel deposits at Voisey's Bay. The Nunavut Final Agreement, signed in 1993, is a special case, since its main purpose was not so much to make resource development easier as to strengthen Canadian sovereignty over the high Arctic islands.[12]

The Supreme Court of Canada has also established the government's duty to consult and accommodate Aboriginal peoples before making any decision that could affect their rights, as recognised by the courts and the constitution. This duty is in proportion to the strength of these rights and the potential impacts of the decision on them. The Supreme Court has made it clear, however, that the duty to consult and accommodate does not amount to a veto right.[13] The Supreme Court has also recently ruled that consent might be needed when a government decision infringes on a potential Aboriginal title, the strongest of all Aboriginal rights, although governments can dispense with this duty if they demonstrate substantive Aboriginal engagement and a 'compelling and substantial public purpose' that justifies not obtaining consent.[14] Clearly, it is not necessary to obtain consent in order to show that the duty to consult has been carried out. It is more a matter of proving that the consultation has been substantive and meaningful, and the Supreme Court has asserted that Aboriginal rights can be infringed for the greater public good.

Recently, the United Nations Declaration on the Rights of Indigenous Peoples (UNDRIP) has enshrined the principle of free, prior and informed consent as an international standard for resource development on Aboriginal territory. In article 32.2, the UNDRIP establishes that:

> States shall consult and cooperate in good faith with the indigenous peoples concerned through their own representative institutions in order to obtain their free and informed consent prior to the approval of any project affecting their lands or territories and other resources, particularly in connection with the development, utilization or exploitation of mineral, water or other resources.

Clearly, the need for consent is central to the principle of free, prior and informed consent (FPIC). However, the UNDRIP is a non-binding legal instrument and as such cannot be enforced or used in courts. Even though the United Nations General Assembly formally adopted the UNDRIP in 2007, Canada at first refused to sign the declaration because of its potential impact on Canadian Aboriginal policy, and when Canada finally did sign, in 2010, it only gave qualified support and stressed that it did not adhere to the principle:

> Canada's unique constitutional framework recognizes and affirms Aboriginal and Treaty rights. Thus, in Canada, governments have a legal duty to consult Aboriginal Peoples and, where appropriate, accommodate Aboriginal peoples, when the Crown contemplates conduct that might adversely impact potential or established Aboriginal or Treaty rights. Canada interprets the principles expressed in the Declaration in a manner that is consistent with our constitution. Free, prior and informed consent, as it is considered in paragraphs 3 and 20 of the WCIP Outcome Document, could be interpreted as providing a veto to Aboriginal groups and in that regard, cannot be reconciled with Canadian law, as it exists.[15]

The Canadian government position on FPIC has recently changed with the election of a new government more committed to the recognition of Aborignal rights in October 2015. On May 2016, the new Minister of Indigenous Affairs committed her government to the full implementation of the UNDRIP in a statement to the United Nation's Permanent Forum on Indigenous Issues (Canada, 2016). Although, she added that the FPIC will be implemented through the Canadian legal and constitutional framework in a manner consistent with existing practices in Canada (Papillon and Rodon 2016).

Thus, the Canadian approach recognises only rights established by the Supreme Court and protected by section 35.1 of the Constitution. Aboriginal rights are context-dependent and must be negotiated through land claim negotiations. Meanwhile, governments must consult, accommodate and, in the few cases that involve Aboriginal title, seek consent. The Supreme Court has nonetheless insisted that Aboriginal peoples have no right to veto development projects.

Inuit offshore rights

In the test established by the Van der Peet case, the Supreme Court defines Aboriginal rights broadly: "*Activity based on customs, tradition and practices, which are an integral part of a distinctive culture, the activity has to be practised before contact and have a measure of continuity*".

It is well documented that the Inuit way of life is based on the use of marine resources, either on open sea or on sea ice.[16] A good example is provided by the testimony of Vince Teddy, from Tuktoyaktuk, Northwest Territories, during the Inuvik roundtable on the National Energy Board (NEB) review of Arctic offshore drilling:

> The ocean feeds us, the ocean is our road, it's our path. The ocean has a life of its own. The ocean expresses itself differently in different times of the season. The Inuvialuit way of life, traditions, and culture is dependent on the Arctic Ocean.[17]

Clearly, their activities have an offshore component and, as we will see, this argument has been used in court by Inuit groups to oppose seismic testing. This offshore right has been formally recognised in two recent court decisions on seismic testing.[18] Inuit leaders are keenly aware of the need to assert this offshore right, as seen by the recent name change of the Canadian Inuit region from Inuit Nunaat (Inuit land) to Inuit Nunangat (Inuit area), a term that includes not only the land but also the sea, thus better reflecting Inuit use of offshore resources.

The Circumpolar Inuit Declaration on Resource Development Principles in Inuit Nunaat, issued by the Inuit Circumpolar Council, stresses the need for transparency and accountability in order to secure project acceptance:

> 7.5 International standard-setting bodies must seek and secure direct and meaningful input from Inuit. National, regional and local bodies, SUCH as offshore and land management regimes, must be designed and operated to be effective, transparent and accountable, thereby gaining and sustaining the confidence of the Inuit public at all times.

It also clearly invokes the right of the free, prior and informed consent:

> 2.3… No matter what level or form of self-determination the Inuit of any particular region have achieved, resource development in Inuit Nunaat must proceed only with the free, prior, and informed consent of the Inuit of that region.[19]

The Canadian Arctic offshore regulatory system

North of the 60th parallel, offshore oil and gas comes under the jurisdiction of the federal government. This regulatory system is administered primarily by two bodies: Aboriginal Affairs and Northern Development Canada (AANDC) grants commercial rights through an auction system under the *Canada Petroleum Resources Act*; and the NEB regulates offshore exploration and drilling in the Canadian Arctic and operates under the *Canada Oil and Gas Operations Act*. It decides whether a project is acceptable after reviewing it on safety, environmental, conservation and technical grounds.

Projects are also governed by the *Canadian Environmental Assessment Act*, especially in the Beaufort Sea, which falls within the Inuvialuit Settlement Region. This Act also applies to projects outside the *Nunavut Land Claims Agreement* area (beyond the land fast ice zone). The NEB keeps the Nunavut Impact Review Board informed and seeks its comments during the review process (NEB review). Both the Inuvialuit Settlement Region and Nunavut have specific environmental review processes that are set out in their respective land claims agreements. We will discuss the review processes in more detail in the following sections.

The Inuvialuit: a corporate strategy

The Inuvialuit Settlement Region is the most active offshore zone in the Canadian Arctic. Drilling began in 1973, and about 100 exploratory wells were drilled at that time. Due to uncertainty over unsettled Aboriginal rights and the high cost of extracting oil and gas,[20] only one offshore well in the Beaufort Sea was briefly operated in the 1990s.[21] Drilling has been mostly confined to shallow water, but seismic exploration is active with two offshore programmes in 2012. Sixteen offshore exploration licences are currently valid, for a total of about $2 billion in work commitments, and ultimate recoverable oil is estimated at 8 billion barrels. At this time, no authorisations are being sought from the NEB for Arctic offshore drilling but one proposed project is being examined.[22]

The Inuvialuit signed the Inuvialuit Final Agreement (IFA) in 1984, the second modern treaty to be signed in Canada and the first one negotiated under the land claims policy. The Inuvialuit were given title to a total of 91,000 km^2 of land: 13,000 km^2 with surface and subsurface title and 78,000 km^2 without rights to oil, gas, and specified minerals. The Inuvialuit also received $45 million in cash compensation, a $7.5 million Social Development Fund, and a $10 million Economic Enhancement Fund. The IFA also established four co-management boards, half of whose members are appointed by the Inuvialuit. In addition to the Fisheries Joint Management Committee and the Wildlife Management Advisory Council, two co-management boards specifically manage the environmental review process. The Environmental Impact Screening Committee screens the project and, when deemed necessary, sends it on to the Inuvialuit Environmental Impact Review Board, which reviews the project and makes recommendations to the decision-making body.

The IFA has no sections on offshore resource development, even though at the time offshore exploration was very active in the Beaufort Sea – Mackenzie Delta area. Only one section mentions offshore development but only with respect to wildlife management: "*14.(47) The Council shall have jurisdiction in respect of that portion of the Inuvialuit Settlement Region that falls within the Northwest Territories, including the adjacent near shore and offshore waters*".

Nor does the IFA have any provisions for self-government, since that right was not recognised at the time of treaty negotiation. Even without formal self-government, the IFA has allowed the Inuvialuit to create the Inuvialuit Regional Corporation (IRC), which represents the interests of Inuvialuit beneficiaries and administers Inuvialuit land and compensation payments.

The Inuvialuit have clearly chosen a strategy of partnership with the oil and gas industries. In 1985, they used IFA funds to create the Inuvialuit Petroleum Corporation, an Inuvialuit oil and gas company that has been very successful at trading in oil and gas.[23] Through this company, the Inuvialuit organisations have entered into partnership with the oil companies BP, Exxon Mobile, and Imperial Oil Resources Ventures. These companies hold large offshore parcels in the Beaufort Sea, but are still at the exploration stage.[24] The Inuvialuit have also created oil and gas service companies like Akita Equtak Drilling (50/50) and Inuvialuit Oilfield Services. Finally, the IRC was part of the Mackenzie Valley Pipeline Consortium, an economic consortium that called for construction of a pipeline to southern markets. These corporations and businesses have been an economic success, earning the Inuvialuit a combined after-tax profit of $52.5 million in 2000, up from $5.6 million in 1999. The 2000 profit came from revenues of $277.2 million.[25] So clearly, the Inuvialuit Regional Corporation is not opposed to offshore exploration and drilling as long as it respects the environment.

This last point is important. In 2010, following the Deepwater Horizon oil spill, the Inuvialuit Regional Corporation CEO issued a statement saying that the IRC "*has requested a pause in all offshore hydrocarbon drilling activity in the Beaufort Sea until adequate measures have been undertaken to protect the region's sensitive ecosystem*".[26]

The moratorium stemmed from a request from Inuvialuit communities and was supported by Inuit Tapiriit Kanatami (ITK), the national Inuit organisation. The Inuvialuit thus support offshore development but not at all costs.

To reduce the concerns created by the oil spill, the NEB decided to conduct an extensive review of Arctic offshore drilling. To this end, it asked for public feedback, conducted eleven community meetings in the Arctic (Whitehorse, Yellowknife, Aklavik, Inuvik Tuktoyaktuk, Paulatuk, Sachs Harbour and Ulukhaktok in the Western Arctic; and Pond Inlet, Clyde River and Iqaluit in Nunavut), and concluded with an Arctic Review Roundtable in Inuvik.[27] The outcome was the publication in December 2011 of a comprehensive report 'Review of Offshore Drilling in the Canadian Arctic: Preparing for the Future'.[28]

Using the transcript of the five-day roundtable held in Inuvik in September 2011, it is possible to gauge Inuvialuit attitudes towards oil and gas development. The Inuvialuit leadership clearly support oil and gas development as a means to create employment and economic spinoffs for Inuvialuit communities. All of the Inuvialuit organisations stress, however, that it should not compromise the environmental integrity of the Beaufort Sea, which is at the core of Inuvialuit livelihoods:

> And our land brings family and friends closer together, and if anything happens to our lands and we lose our animals and – if we lose our animals and that, like, I don't know how we are going to survive and our culture will be lost. Like – if, like, an oil spill and all that happens, like it's going to be happening in my generation.[29]

Their strategy of partnership notwithstanding, the Inuvialuit are still trying to gain more control over offshore development through ongoing negotiations on self-government. Negotiations were first held with the Gwich'in in order to create a Western Arctic regional government. Now, however, the Inuvialuit are negotiating an agreement for their six communities, and controlling other offshore activities is a central concern, as explained by Nellie Cournoyea, the IRC Chair and CEO:

> The Inuvialuit are a coastal peoples who depend on the sea for subsistence and way of life… The Devolution Agreement sets the stage for offshore negotiations. An offshore agreement can address some of the uncertainty for the Inuvialuit in the future in terms of benefits and risks to offshore development.[30]

The IRC has set for itself four major negotiation objectives: (1) full participation in management of offshore lands and resources; (2) full economic participation in all offshore oil and gas exploration and development activities; (3) preservation of the integrity and intent of the Inuvialuit Final Agreement; and (4) funding so that the IRC can engage meaningfully in this initiative.[31] In short, the goal is not only financial but also to achieve more control over oil and gas development in the region.

Nunavut: trying to enforce consent through litigation

Offshore exploration is not new in Nunavut. 140 exploration wells were drilled since the 1970s in the Sverdrup basin in the high Arctic.[32] There has never been any offshore commercial extraction in Nunavut, however, and estimated reserves are not nearly as large as in the Beaufort Sea, with ultimate recoverable oil estimated at only 0.8 billion barrels.[33] Baffin Bay and Lancaster Sound have been barely explored but are believed to hold reserves, and most of the seismic testing is supposed to be conducted in this region.

Nunavut is the biggest and northernmost Inuit jurisdiction. The Inuit of Nunavut signed the Nunavut Land Claims Agreement (NLCA) with Canada and the Northwest Territories in 1993 and the government of Nunavut was created in 1999. This government serves all Nunavummiut regardless of ethnic origin, but the Inuit represent 85 percent of the population. The NLCA provided for a $1.1 billion settlement fund to be administered through the Nunavut Trust. The Inuit of Nunavut are also supposed to receive 50 percent of the first million dollars of royalties from every oil, gas, and mineral project on Crown land. Finally, the Inuit of Nunavut hold title to the surface rights of 355,842 km^2 of territory (18 percent of Nunavut) and to the subsurface rights of 35,257 km^2 of territory (1.8 percent). The NLCA has also led to the creation of co-management boards, also known as 'institutions of public governance' (IPGs). There are four IPGs: the Nunavut Wildlife Management Board (NWMB), the Nunavut Impact Review Board (NIRB), the Nunavut Water Board (NWB), and the Nunavut Planning Commission (NPC). Half of the IPG members are either directly appointed, as with the NWMB, or chosen by Inuit organisations and appointed by the relevant federal minister, as with the other IPGs. With the exception of the NWMB, which has decision-making power (albeit subject to federal ministerial review), these boards only have recommendation-making power. In practice, however, they hold quasi decision-making power[34] and, as such, play an important role in Nunavut policymaking.

Nunavut encompasses islands in both the Arctic and the High Arctic and therefore has a large marine component. To reflect this situation, the Nunavut Land Claims Agreement (NLCA) has a section on 'marine areas,' which are defined as

> ... part of Canada's internal waters or territorial sea, whether open or ice-covered, lying within the Nunavut Settlement Area, but does not include inland waters. (1.1.1)

There is no Inuit-owned land in marine areas but the government

> ... has to seek advice of the NWMB with respect to any wildlife management decisions in Zones I and II which would affect the substance and value of Inuit harvesting rights and opportunities within the marine areas of the Nunavut Settlement Area. (15.2.3)

The NWMB shall furthermore provide the Nunavut government with relevant information that may assist wildlife management beyond the marine areas of the Nunavut Settlement Area (15.3.4). Article 27 also establishes an obligation for governments to consult Inuit organisations before starting offshore exploration for petroleum or other natural resources. Finally, the NLCA stipulates that the Nunavut regulatory co-management boards can, jointly as a Nunavut Marine Council, or each separately,

> ... advise and make recommendations to other government agencies regarding the marine areas, and government shall consider such advice and recommendations in making decisions which affect marine areas. (15.4.1)

Even though quite a few articles deal with offshore/marine issues, there is only a duty to consult Nunavut co-management boards and Inuit organisations when offshore exploration activities are being considered in the NLCA settlement area.

As we have seen above, offshore exploration is not new in Nunavut, and the first round of exploration left bad memories:

> The Inuit had not yet established their organizations and were basically ignored by the government and the oil companies. No permission was sought, and no consultations took place. The oil companies were allowed to do pretty much what they wanted to do by the Government of Canada. Because the Inuit organizations were not in place, very little information was passed on to Inuit, and monitoring of the exploration was almost non-existent.
>
> It was only years later that Inuit began to see the damage the oil companies had done in the High Arctic. There was a huge blow-out at one of the drilling sites, which lasted about three months. It was fortunate that it spewed only natural gas on water. If it had been oil, it would – there would have been an environmental disaster. There were fires. There was a horrific plane crash, fuel barges sinking. The only reason we found out that a barge with one million litres of diesel fuel had been caught in ice and sank and is still there, and we were never told. Cat trains would go through the ice and sink into the bottom of the ocean, tons of abandoned equipment, garbage and drilling mud left behind.[35]

This quote is important because it shows that trust in oil companies was already at a low level. As we will see, this widespread distrust has led to strong opposition to any offshore exploration.

The first legal dispute arose in 2010 when the federal government hired a German research vessel, *RV Polarstern,* for geological mapping of Baffin Bay by seismic testing. Polarstern applied for a research licence from the Nunavut Research Institute (NRI), the organisation in charge of regulating research in Nunavut. Since the project had an environmental impact, the NIRB had to screen the application. After reviewing the case and inviting public comments, it decided not to submit the project to environmental review but instead asked the minister of natural resources to attach specific conditions to the licence, including a condition that public consultations be held in five North Baffin communities.[36] Most of the Inuit organisations' and communities' submissions to the NIRB asked that the application be denied. For example, the Qikiqtani Inuit Association (QIA) was concerned about the lack of consultation and the possible impact on marine mammals. To deal with these objections, the project proponent organised public consultations in the five communities and discussed possible changes to the project with the Inuit organisations. Once the consultations and amendments had been completed, the NIRB sent the project to the minister for approval, and the NRI was able to issue a research licence.

The approval raised some concerns in the Inuit organisations and the North Baffin communities. Seismic testing is controversial, and many Inuit hunters consider it harmful to marine mammals, the very species they depend upon for their subsistence. As Madam Justice Cooper from the Court of Nunavut noted in her decision: "*There has been considerable controversy about the project. It is fair to say that the communities most likely affected by the activity, Arctic Bay, Grise Fiord, Resolute Bay, Pond Inlet and Clyde River, are opposed to the testing*".[37]

The QIA responded by seeking a temporary injunction against the seismic testing to be conducted by Polarstern. The QIA argued that the consultations were not meaningful and that therefore the governments failed to honour their duty to consult and, if necessary, to accommodate Inuit interests. As we have seen in the first part if this chapter, the duty to consult has been well established by the Supreme Court of Canada. Debate during this case thus focused on the quality of the consultations that were held in the five communities and on the lack of accommodation concerning the possible impact of seismic testing on marine mammals. Madam Justice Cooper, after seeing assessments of the potential for irreparable damage, agreed to grant the QIA a temporary injunction in 2010, and the project had to be cancelled since it would now be too late to start the seismic testing campaign. This case shows clearly that even though the Inuit have no regulatory powers over offshore exploration, they can oppose seismic projects using rights recognised by the Supreme Court, the constitution and the NLCA.

In May 2011, three oil and gas companies applied to the NEB for authorisation to conduct a five-year offshore seismic survey in Baffin Bay and the Davis Strait. The NEB decided to conduct an environmental assessment of the project, and the project proponents held multiple consultations in all of the communities concerned.[38] The communities were still opposed to seismic testing and voiced their opposition during the consultation process. For example, the NEB received a petition from the community of Clyde River, stating their opposition to the project.[39] The community of Pond Inlet also stated its opposition, and the Nunavut Marine Council sent a letter to the NEB asking that a strategic environmental assessment of the marine zone be conducted before any decision is made.[40] Yet despite this widespread opposition, the NEB finally approved the project in 2014.

The mayor of Clyde River decided to appeal the NEB decision and filed for a judicial review at the federal appeal court. This time, only the mayor, the Hamlet of Clyde River, and the Hunters and Trappers Association of Clyde River were appealing the decision. The legal challenge was supported by other Nunavut municipalities and by Greenpeace, but both Nunavut Tunngavik Inc. (NTI), the Nunavut Inuit organisation, and the QIA, the regional Inuit organisation, decided to abstain from the challenge, probably because they were advised that the case was not likely to be won. The challenge was based on two arguments: the Crown had failed to adequately fulfil its duty to consult the Inuit about the project and the Crown had failed to seek the advice of the NWMB as stipulated in article 15.3.4 of the NLCA.

The Clyde River application for judicial review has been dismissed by the federal court of appeal.[41] According to the judge, even though the potential impact of the seismic testing was substantial, the consultation processes were adequate and fulfilled the Crown's duty to consult the Inuit. Finally, the Crown was not obliged to seek the advice of the NWMB. This dismissal confirms that the duty to consult has to be seen as a process and not as a search for consent. The mayor of Clyde River has decided to take the case to the Supreme Court of Canada and at the surprise of many, the Court accepted to hear the Clyde River case. This is an important victory since the Supreme Court only accepts cases that can break new legal ground. This acceptance led the Inuit organizations to regain interest in the case since it could establish new legal standard, and Nunavut Tunngavik Inc., Makivik Corporation and the Inuvialuit Regional Corporation all intervened in the Hamlet of Clyde River vs. Petroleum Geo-Services Inc. when it appeared before the Supreme Court of Canada in the fall of 2016. The Court decision is expected in the spring of 2017 and could break new ground in the matter of Aboriginal consultation.

The litigation process has been based solely on the question of meaningful consultation on the possible impacts of seismic testing but clearly, there is an underlying issue. The NEB delayed the project to allow a second round of community consultations, and the project proponent tried to accommodate the Inuit. So the issue is not lack of consultation, but instead the power to control what kind of development should be allowed in Nunavut.

In fact, Nunavut Inuit communities are generally opposed to seismic testing and to oil and gas offshore exploration and extraction and try to prevent these activities altogether. Their opposition to seismic testing stems mainly from the potential impact on marine mammals and the lack of direct benefits for Inuit in these projects.[42] This is not an easy problem to solve. Seismic testing is an exploration activity that employs relatively few people and creates no monetary returns for the project proponent, so there is little room to share wealth or jobs with Inuit communities beyond a few jobs and, in case of damage, some compensations.

Many Inuit from Nunavut are under the impression that the NLCA has given them back control over what happens on their land[43] as this quote from John Amagoalik, one of the key Inuit negotiators of the NLCA, illustrates clearly:

> But the development of Nunavut's natural resources cannot occur as it unfolded in the 1960s. It must be... it must be done with proper measures in place, and very broadly, there should be an agreement between Inuit and Canada on how exploration and development of oil and gas will be done. I know that's a tall order, but we have to start somewhere.[44]

At this time, the Inuit cannot veto these developments through the oil and gas regulatory system, the NLCA, or court decisions and the constitution. They have only a right to be consulted and, in some cases, accommodated, so there is little recourse for them when they oppose a project, such as the seismic testing campaign. To deal with this shortcoming, Nunavut communities litigate to try to at least delay the seismic activities by invoking the right to be consulted. In fact, it may be that Inuit communities are trying to enforce the principle of free, prior and informed consent of the UNDRIP. The case that will be heard by the Supreme Court of Canada could test this limited interpretation of FPIC.

Conclusion

The land claims settlement agreements that have been signed to date offer Inuit little control over offshore development. Inuit organisations and communities can, through the co-management boards and the different formal and informal consultation processes, participate in decision-making, but the final decision is clearly made by a territorial or federal minister or by a federal regulatory agency. This is far from the free, prior and informed consent principle of the UNDRIP but should not be surprising, since the federal, in spite of having recently endorsed this principle, has argued that it could be implemented through the existing processes.

Nonetheless, both Inuvialuit and Nunavut Inuit are demanding that Inuit consent be part of the regulatory process. For them, this is Inuit Nunangat, the Inuit region, and nothing should be done without the express consent of its original inhabitants. For many Inuit, the land claims settlement and self-government processes are supposed to bring more control over their lives, including choice of livelihood and the right to refuse some activities on their lands and seas. Opposition to seismic testing offers a good example, but this belief is also very apparent in the fight against the Kiggavik uranium mine in Kivalliq region.[45]

Uncertainties do result from this differing comprehension of the respective roles of Inuit organisations and the federal government in decision-making on offshore development. The Nunavut Inuit can delay and even block a project, through litigation, as seen in the cancellation of the Polarstern research programme following the injunction granted by the Nunavut Court of Justice,[46] and in the case of the latest application for seismic testing, the project was delayed a few times so that proper consultations could be carried out with the impacted communities. These extensive consultations did not enable the proponent and the federal government to avoid litigation. The Inuit of Clyde River lost the first round[47] but have been heard by the Supreme Court of Canada, thus maintaining a cloud of uncertainty over the project and maintaining the possibility to have a landmark judgement in a new context where the Canadian government has declared that it will endorse the FPIC principle.[48]

The Inuvialuit have chosen a different strategy. When they signed the IFA in 1984, oil and gas development was already active in their region, and federal policy was more restrictive on what could be negotiated. The Inuvialuit have thus chosen to be part of development, thereby giving themselves a measure of control through partnerships with oil and gas companies while remaining cautious about risk acceptance. They are also trying to acquire jurisdiction over offshore oil and gas development through their negotiations for self-government.

Notes

1 I wish to acknowledge the invaluable contribution of Aude Therrien and Sabrina Bourgeois, who provided expert research assistance to document the Nunavut and Inuvialuit region controversies about offshore exploration and exploitation.
2 In this chapter, the term "Aboriginal" is used to refer to the three constitutionally recognized Aboriginal peoples in Canada: The Indians, the Metis and the Inuit. The term "Indigenous" is mostly used in international documents and has been recently adopted by the Canadian government, although the term "Aboriginal People" is still used in the legal documents.
3 Weaver 1981.
4 *Calder et al.* v. *Attorney-General of British Columbia* [1973], S.C.R. 313.
5 *R.* v. *Van der Peet* [1996], 2 S.C.R. 507.
6 *Delgamuukw* v. *British Columbia* [1997], 3 S.C.R. 1010.
7 *Tsilhqot'in Nation* v. *British Columbia* [2014], 2 S.C.R. 256.
8 *Delgamuukw* v. *British Columbia* [1997], 3 S.C.R. 1010.
9 Canada 1987.
10 Abele and Rodon 2007.
11 Dionne 2004.
12 Abele and Rodon 2007.
13 *Haida Nation* v. *British Columbia* [2004] 3 SCR 511.
14 *Tsilhqot'in Nation* v. *British Columbia* [2014], 2 S.C.R. 256.
15 Canada 2014.
16 For anthropological studies see: Wenzel 1981; Boas 1964; Riewe 1991; Freeman 2011. For a legal analysis see: VanderZwaag and Pharand 1983.
17 National Energy Board 2011b, *Transcripts of the Inuvik Roundtable on Arctic Offshore Drilling.* Vince *Teddy: 421. available from National Energy Board.*
18 *Qikiqtani Inuit Association* v. *Canada (Minister of Natural Resources),* 2010 NUCJ 12 and *Hamlet of Clyde River* v. *TGS–NOPEC Geophysical Company ASA (TGS),* 2015 FCA 17.
19 Inuit Circumpolar Council 2011.
20 AMAP 2010.
21 Hossain et al. 2013.
22 Barnes 2015.
23 Anderson et al. 2004: 643.
24 Social, Cultural and Economic Working Group 2008.
25 Ibid.: 644.
26 'IRC Seeks Pause in all Offshore Drilling in the Beaufort Sea,' IRC, press release, 19 May 2010.
27 National Energy Board 2011a.
28 Ibid.
29 National Energy Board 2011b. *Transcripts of the Inuvik Roundtable on Arctic Offshore Drilling, Divalynn Pokiak: 3543, available from National Energy Board.*

30 Inuvialuit Regional Corporation 2013.
31 Inuvialuit Regional Corporation 2014.
32 Natural Resources Canada 2016.
33 AANDC 2014.
34 White 2008.
35 National Energy Board 2011b. *Transcripts of the Inuvik Roundtable on Arctic Offshore Drilling.* John Amagoalik: 783–787, available from National Energy Board.
36 NIRB (Nunavut Impact Review Board) 2010: Screening decision Report file: 10YN017, available on the NIRB website.
37 *Qikiqtani Inuit Association* v. *Canada (Minister of Natural Resources),* 2010 NUCJ 12.
38 National Energy Board 2014.
39 National Energy Board Public Registry, files 2011–05–31shrgrhrd01-eng and 2011–05–31shrgrhrd02-eng.
40 Nunavut Marine Council. 2014. National Energy Board – Recommendations of the Nunavut Marine Council Regarding Strategic Environmental Assessment of the Baffin Bay and Davis Strait in Advance of the NEB's Consideration of Seismic Surveys and Oil and Gas Development With Potential Impacts on Nunavut's Marine Environment, available from the Nunavut Impact Review Board website.
41 *Hamlet of Clyde River* v. *TGS-NOPEC Geophysical Company ASA (TGS),* 2015 FCA 17.
42 Butler 2015.
43 Rodon 2014.
44 National Energy Board 2011b. *Transcripts of the Inuvik Roundtable on Arctic Offshore Drilling.* John Amagoalik: 795, available from National Energy Board.
45 Papillon and Rodon 2016.
46 *Qikiqtani Inuit Association* v. *Canada (Minister of Natural Resources),* 2010 NUCJ 12.
47 *Hamlet of Clyde River* v. *TGS-NOPEC Geophysical Company ASA (TGS),* 2015 FCA 17.
48 Papillon and Rodon 2017.

References

AANDC. 2014. *Northern Oil and Gas Annual Report.* Quebec: Government of Canada, Aboriginal Affairs and Northern Development Canada. Accessible at www.aadnc-aandc.gc.ca/eng/1431106507542/1431106696195.

Abele, F. and T. Rodon. 2007. 'Inuit Diplomacy in the Global ERA: The Strengths of Multilateral Internationalism.' *Canadian Foreign Policy* 13 (3): 45–63.

AMAP. 2010. *Assessment 2007: Oil and Gas Activities in the Arctic: Effects and Potential Effects.* Vol. 1. Oslo: Arctic Monitoring and Assessment Programme.

Anderson, R., B. Kayseas, L. Dana and K. Hindle. 2004. 'Indigenous Land Claims and Economic Development.' *The American Indian Quarterly* 28: 634–648.

Barnes, P. 2015. 'Industry Perspectives on Offshore Oil and Gas Development and R&D in Canada's Arctic.' *Presentation to Canada's Third Ocean Conference*: Calgary, Alberta, 26 June 2015. Retrieved 31 August from www.capp.ca/publications-and-statistics/presentations-and-speeches.

Boas, F. 1964. *The Central Eskimo.* Lincoln, Nebraska: University of Nebraska Press.

Butler, K. 2015. 'Feast Worth Fighting for: Inuit Appeal Approval of Seismic Testing at Federal Court.' *Indian Country* 20 April 2015.

Canada. 1987. *Comprehensive Land Claims Policy.* Ottawa: Minister of Indian Affairs and Northern Development.

Canada. 2014. *Canada's Statement on the World Conference on Indigenous Peoples Outcome Document.* New York: 22 September 2014. Retrieved August 17, 2015, Accessible at www.canadainternational.gc.ca/prmny-mponu/canada_un-canada_onu/statements-declarations/other-autres/2014–09–22_WCIPD-PADD.aspx?lang=eng.

Canada. 2016. Speaking Notes for the Honourable Carolyn Bennett, Minister of Indigenous and Northern Affairs, delivered at the United Nations Permanent Forum on Indigenous Issues, New York, May 10.

Dionne, P. 2004. 'La reconnaissance et la définition contemporaines des droits ancestraux: négocier ou s'adresser au juge?' In *Droit, territoire et gouvernance des peuples autochtones*, ed. G. Otis. p. 71. Quebec: Presses de l'Université Laval.

Freeman, M.M. 2011. 'Looking Back—and Looking Ahead—35 Years after the Inuit Land Use and Occupancy Project.' *The Canadian Geographer/Le Géographe canadien* 55 (1): 20–31.

Hossain, K., T. Koivurova, and G. Zojer. 2013. 'Understanding Risks Associated with Offshore Hydrocarbon Development.' In *Arctic Marine Governance*, eds. R.A. Kraemer and S. Cavalieri, 159–176. Berlin: Springer.

Inuit Circumpolar Conference. 2011. *A Circumpolar Inuit Declaration on Resource Development Principles in Inuit Nunaat.* Accessible at http://inuit.org/about-icc/icc-declarations/declaration-on-resource-development-principles-2011/.

Inuvialuit Regional Corporation. 2013. *Board Summary* Vol. 18 (3/4). Inuvik, Northwest Territories: Inuvialuit Regional Corporation. 20 p.

Inuvialuit Regional Corporation. 2014. *Board Summary* Vol. 21 (3). Inuvik, Northwest Territories: Inuvialuit Regional Corporation. 20 p.

National Energy Board. 2011a. *The Past is Always Present: Review of Offshore Drilling in the Canadian Arctic: Preparing for the Future.* Calgary, Alberta: Government of Canada, National Energy Board.

National Energy Board. 2011b. *Transcripts of the Inuvik Roundtable on Arctic Offshore Drilling.* Available from the NEB public registry. Calgary, Alberta: Government of Canada, National Energy Board. Accessible at https://apps.neb-one.gc.ca/REGDOCS/File/Download/713542.

National Energy Board. 2014. *Environmental Assessment Report for the Northeastern Canada 2D Seismic Survey.* Baffin Bay/Davis Strait. Accessible at www.neb-one.gc.ca/nrth/dscvr/2011tgs/nvssssmnt/nvssssmnt-eng.pdf.

Natural Resources Canada. 2016. Nunavut's Shale and Tight Resources. Accessible at www.nrcan.gc.ca/energy/sources/shale-tight-resources/17706.

Nunavut Impact Review Board (NIRB). 2010. *Screening Decision Report, NIRB FILE NO.: 10YN017.* 15 p. Accessible at http://ftp.nirb.ca/01-SCREENINGS/COMPLETED%20SCREENINGS/2010/10YN017-GSC-%20ECASE%20-%20Gordon%20Oakey/03-DECISION/100521-10YN017-Screening%20Decision%20Report-OT1E.pdf.

Papillon, M., and T. Rodon. 2016. 'Proponent-Indigenous Agreements and the Implementation of the Right to Free, Prior, and Informed Consent in Canada.' *Environmental Impact Assessment Review* 62 IS: 216–224.

Riewe, R. 1991. 'Inuit Use of the Sea Ice.' *Arctic and Alpine Research* 23 (1): 3–10.

Rodon, T. 2014. 'Le Nunavut: une composition inachevée?' *Études Inuit Studies* 38 (1–2): 1–20.

Social, Cultural and Economic Working Group. 2008. Social, Cultural and Economic Overview and Assessment Report for the Beaufort Sea Large Ocean Management Area, 136 p.

VanderZwaag, D. and D. Pharand. 1983. 'Inuit and the Ice: Implications for Canadian Arctic Waters.' *Canadian Yearbook of International Law* 21: 53.

Weaver, S.M. 1981. *Making Canadian Indian Policy: The Hidden Agenda 1968–1970.* Toronto, Ontario: University of Toronto Press.

Wenzel, G.W. 1981. *Clyde Inuit Adaptation and Ecology: The Organization of Subsistence.* Musée National de l'Homme (Canada): Collection Mercure, Division d'Ethnologie, Service Canadien d'Ethnologie, Dossier Ottawa (77).

White, G. 2008. '"Not the Almighty": Evaluating Aboriginal Influence in Northern Land-Claim Boards.' *Arctic* 61 (Suppl. 1): 71–85.

11 Securing the coastal Sámi culture and livelihood

Øyvind Ravna and Kristoffer Svendsen

Introduction

As the rights of the indigenous Sámi have come under increased scrutiny, the situation of the coastal Sámi has been investigated by, among others, the Sámi Rights Committee and the Coastal Fishing Committee (CFC).[1] The latter was established in 2006 with the mandate to examine the right to fish along the coast of Finnmark (the extreme north-east of Norway, an area that borders Finland to the south and Russia to the east).

This chapter deals with the legal protection of the substantive culture and livelihood of the coastal Sámi. In the aftermath of the work of the CFC, which was not approved by the Norwegian government, two main questions must be asked. First, is the access of the Sámi people to fish and marine resources adequately protected? And second, as increased needs for energy, together with the rapidly changing climate, point toward a more active petroleum industry in the Arctic seawaters, can the threat posed by these activities be controlled relative to the coastal Sámi culture?

The first part of the analysis will elaborate on the current legal situation, examining national and international laws protecting indigenous peoples in general and the Sámi in particular. The second part will analyse the legal protection of the coastal Sámi with respect to the impacts of the oil industry, particularly oil spills. Here the approach will be the law on compensation of damages, rather than the threshold for interventions contradicting international law.

Sámi rights to fisheries and marine resources

Historical backdrop

The earliest historical records

Although the dispute over marine resources in the coastal Sámi areas can be traced back to the early twentieth century, the rights themselves are much older. The first historical record of such resources is the narrative of the Viking chief Ottar, dating from the ninth century.[2] The coastal Sámi culture extended from the coast of Helgeland, Norway, to the Kola Peninsula in Russia. It involved both local home fishing and seasonal fisheries such as cod fishing in the Lofoten archipelago.[3] Until the thirteenth century, only the coastal Sámi used these marine resources. From that point on, the appearance of the European stock fish market resulted in an expansion of Norse settlers northwards.[4]

The fishing gear used by the coastal population was of such nature that it could not possibly have put them at risk of overfishing fish stocks. The competing interests of the well-capitalised pelagic fishing fleet, however, raised disputes as early as the early twentieth century; by the end of the century, with the new Norwegian fishery regulation of 1990, concern had emerged about injustice in the allocation of fishing quotas and rights to catch. Because the new regulation regime granted fishing rights on the basis of historical catch, the coastal Sámi lost a significant proportion of their rights, established over the centuries, because of low 'historical catch' in the three previous years.[5]

The issue of coastal Sámi rights to coastal fishing

The question of the rights of the coastal Sámi to fishing was included in the mandate that the Sámi Rights Committee had been tasked to investigate in 1980.[6] The committee found that the most appropriate way to facilitate Sámi coastal fishing along the Finnmark coastline was to provide administrative priority, including free fishing for vessels less than 10 m.[7] It also proposed that local influence in the management of the coastal fisheries should be increased. The Norwegian government, however, did not approve these proposals.

The issue of Sámi coastal fishing rights was, however, the subject of consultations between the Norwegian government's Standing Committee of Justice (SCJ), the Sámi parliament, and the Finnmark county council prior to the adoption of the Finnmark Act in 2005. In the preparatory work for the Act, the SCJ stated its awareness that coastal fishing is an important part of the livelihood of the Sámi culture, that the Sámi currently suffer from unreliable legal protection and that the Norwegian government should undertake an investigation of these issues.[8]

In acknowledgement of these points, the SCJ required the government to carry out a study of the Sámi rights to fish in the sea along the coast of Finnmark as soon as possible, including a minimum fishing quota for vessels less than 10 m. Under the guarantee that such an independent investigation would be undertaken prior to the adoption of the Finnmark Act, the parties agreed to remove this issue from their negotiations.[9]

The attempt to establish a Finnmark fishing act

The proposal of the coastal fishing committee

Based on the proposal by the SCJ and additional consultations with the Sámi parliament, the Norwegian government in 2006 established the Coastal

Fishing Committee (CFC), with the mandate to investigate the rights of the coastal Sámi and others to fish in the sea off the coast of Finnmark. In February 2008, the committee submitted a unanimous report in which it concluded that the peoples living around the fjords and along the coast of Finnmark have legal rights to fish in the mandated sea waters.[10] The basis for these rights were, first, historical use, and second, the commitments of international law protecting the exercise of culture of indigenous peoples and minorities[11] as codified in the International Convention on Civil and Political Rights (ICCPR) Article 27, stating that ethnic minorities shall not be denied the right to enjoy their own culture. These are rights that apply regardless of governmental fisheries regulations.[12] To support its conclusions, the CFC presented research conducted by Kirsti Strøm Bull. This research documented that fjord fishing has been considered as an exclusive right of the local population. According to Bull

> The use that the Sámi people from olden times exercised in the fjords was by the beginning of 1800s of such a nature that it constituted grounds for established rights. Thus there is no reason to estimate their use differently from the use that reindeer herders and others exercised on the mainland.[13]

In addition, Bull argued that '[i]n accordance with the opinion that there may be local rights to fish in sea waters, this use has been of such a nature that people in the fjords had acquired a right to this fishery.'

The CFC proposed that these rights of fishing, which were named *fjord rights,* should be codified in a new Finnmark Fishing Act in order to ensure their implementation. The committee recommended the inclusion of a right to fish for personal consumption, a right to take up fishing as a livelihood, and a right for professional fishermen to catch in order to provide the financial basis for a household.[14] In relation to the necessary governmental regulations or restrictions on fishery resources, the committee also recommended that the coastal population's right to fish to a sufficient degree should be completed by quotas. In determining such quotas, the committee stated, the substantive basis for the coastal Sámi culture and other coastal cultures in Finnmark must be secured by statutory rules. Notably, the proposed fjord right (comparable to rights in, e.g. Canada[15]) was drafted as a right relative to a geographically defined area. Such a fjord right would mean that all persons living around a fjord have the right to fish in that particular fjord, irrespective of their ethnicity.[16] The committee's report also included a proposal to establish a regional governing body – Finnmark Fisheries Management – to determine the framework of the fjord fishing right in each fjord according to specific terms in the proposed act, including the resource bases.[17] According to the draft, the management should provide necessary fishing permits for implementing the right to sea and coastal fishing.

The ministry's response

Both Sámi and local fishermen's organisations in Finnmark largely approved the CFC's draft for a Finnmark Fishing Act. The position taken by ocean trawlers and the central fishermen's association, however, was that the draft challenged their access to marine resources allocated to them under the government-approved quota system. The government apparatus, including the ministry of fishery and coastal affairs, naturally supported the ocean trawlers, leaning on the doctrine that 'the wild living marine resources belongs to the community of the country as a whole.'[18]

One of the strongest opponents of the CFC's recommendation, and a spokesman for the Norwegian government, was the Attorney-General, who, several months after the deadline of the hearing, filed a negative submission that closed the doors on the draft becoming a law bill.[19] Commenting on the submission, the Attorney-General inquired as to whether ICCPR Article 27 protected fishing with modern gear. This elicited a response from the head of the CFC, Carsten Smith, stating that 'it cannot be required that the coastal Sámi shall continue to use oars and sails in order to enjoy legal protection for coastal fishing.'[20]

Norway fails to recognise Sámi rights to fish in the sea off Finnmark

Despite the position of the local communities of the Finnmark coast and local fishermen's associations, and the recommendations of the UN special rapporteur James Anaya,[21] the Norwegian government rejected the CFC's draft bill. In the later preparatory work for the Marine Resources Act, the ministry emphasised that it did not share the opinion of the CFC that, based on international law and historical usage, there exist fishing rights for the coastal Sámi. Instead, the ministry emphasised that the present regulations are consistent with international legal obligations to the Sámi.[22]

In the final consultations in 2011, the Sámi parliament accepted an agreement with the government in which their historical rights were set aside in return for an annual quota of 3,000 tonnes of cod.[23] However, the agreement did not allay concerns about injustice among the coastal population arising from the fishery regulations of the 1990s, and the Sámi parliament did not consider the consultation as a final resolution of the dialogue in furthering the draft of the CFC.[24]

Current legislation on the rights to fish in the sea off Finnmark

Although the Norwegian government rejected the CFC's draft Finnmark Fishing Act, and consequently failed to recognise the historical rights of the coastal Sámi, it did propose amendments to the Marine Resources Act and the Fisheries Participation Act[25] which were intended to secure the Sámi rights to marine resources.[26] The Norwegian parliament approved the bill in the autumn of 2012.[27]

In these proposals, the ministry declared that it agrees with the CFC that the concept of culture in ICCPR Article 27 covers Sámi coastal fishing rights, particularly for Sámi home-based coastal and fjord fishing built on the use of small vessels and passive gear. In contrast, with its previous position, the ministry acknowledged that this requirement does not present an obstacle to the adoption of modern technology and gear within this framework.[28]

However, the consensus ends here. Unlike the CFC, the ministry considers coastal fishing to be an issue of regional policy rather than an international legal obligation imposed on the government, arguing that the assessments of the CFC extended these rights beyond the scope of international law.[29] Consequently, the ministry does not agree with the opinion of the CFC that there exist particular rights to coastal fishing for the Sámi based on international law and historical usage. Instead, the ministry finds that the fish, as living resources, belong to the community as a whole, and that the current regulation is consistent with international legal obligations to the Sámi.[30]

The amendment to the Fisheries Participation Act includes a right to fish for all persons living in Finnmark, North Troms, and other areas with coastal Sámi settlement and owning a registered vessel less than 11 m. In addition, it includes new provisions intended to raise awareness of international legal obligations to the Sámi.[31] The new Section 1A in the Fisheries Participation Act aims to ensure that the act applies in accordance with international obligations to the Sámi and to all states, declaring that 'The act shall be interpreted in accordance with international law of indigenous peoples and minorities.' However, the provision does not entail any changes to the act beyond showing existing international legal obligations.[32] It is not clear whether the new Section 1A is an implementation of ILO Convention no. 169; but since it establishes that the act is to be applied in accordance with international law on indigenous peoples and minorities, it may be understood in such a way.

The old idea of free fishing for small vessels is partly satisfied in the amendment. Section 21 includes a right to fish cod, haddock and saithe for fishermen living in Finnmark, North Troms and areas with coastal Sámi settlement in the rest of north Norway after further determination, using vessels less than 11 m.

The amendment to the 2008 Marine Resource Act includes the possibility of establishing a Fjord Fishing Committee for Finnmark, Troms, and Nordland through a new provision in the Marine Resources Act Section 8B.[33] In addition, the amendment includes a provision in the Finnmark Act Section 29, allowing claims to rights to fishing grounds to be heard by the Finnmark Commission.

In a weak echo of the CFC's suggestions, the Marine Resource Act also codifies a provision to safeguard the Sámi material culture in the management of the fish resources in Section 7, paragraph 2, letter G, stating: 'In managing wild living marine resources... it shall be emphasised that... the management measure is ensuring the material basis for Sámi culture.'

In the reasoning for this provision, the ministry argued that it is a fundamental consideration that management must safeguard the material basis of the Sámi culture and that the provisions of letter G represent a strengthening of indigenous rights compared with the previous legislation.[34] However, the ministry refused to take a position on the indigenous issues into account in the act before the completion of the ongoing assessments of the CFC.

We have in fact seen how the government clearly took a position on the 'indigenous issues' in the 2012 amendment once the CFC had submitted its report. Despite thorough consultations, the Sámi parliament was not able to meet this position, and the negotiations ended far from meeting the Sámi expectations.

A new provision, based on the governmental rather than the Sámi view, now forms part of the Marine Resource Act. Section 11, paragraph 6, which covers areas with a coastal Sámi population, states: 'By allocation of quotas of wild marine resources, and by other forms of regulation of these resources... there shall be placed considerable emphasis on Sámi use and what the use means for the Sámi local communities.'

The new provision is intended to emphasise Norway's international responsibility towards indigenous peoples and minorities in the management of wild living marine resources, where the ministry refers to ICCPR Article 27.[35] Furthermore, it is argued that the provision adds an additional dimension by emphasising the Sámi use of these resources, and that the Sámi coastal communities should be prioritised in the allocation of quotas. The provisions will consequently be an authority for additional quotas for allocation to vessels participating in the open group, and for new provisions in the Fisheries Participation Act, Section 21.[36] According to the ministry, the provision, in combination with other regulations, is intended to contribute to ensuring that future Norwegian fisheries law will clearly act within the framework of international law.

At present time, it is difficult to say what impact the scattered attempt to acknowledge international law protecting Sámi culture in the two acts mentioned above will have, particularly since independent and historical rights to fishing are not recognised and consequently do not provide independent legal bases for such rights. Although the acts include some statements of principle, local fishermen can be granted increased quotas and the appointment of a Fjord Fishing Committee is proposed, there is no recognition of an enhanced right for the coastal Sámi to participate in the governance of fish resources, which would have been a natural consequence of a recognition of their historical rights. Consequently, the amended acts are very different from the proposals of the CFC for safeguarding the coastal Sámi culture.

The absence of adequate recognition of and safeguards for the coastal Sámi culture has been acknowledged internationally. Recently, the UN

Committee on the Elimination of Racial Discrimination (CERD), in a concluding observation on Norway, expressed its concerns as follows:

> The 2012 amendments to the fisheries legislation (the Marine Resources Act, the Fisheries Participation Act, and the Finnmark Act) did not recognise that the Sámi have established rights to fisheries and other renewable marine resources in the Sámi coastal area, and that the legal frameworks may therefore not be able to withstand future reform.[37]

The CERD therefore recommends that the state party review the fisheries legislation and ensure that it fully recognises the Sámi fishing rights, based as they are on immemorial usage and local customs.[38]

The Sámi rights to legal protection from damage to the marine environment caused by oil spills

The impact of oil spills on the environment

The extent and magnitude of harm inflicted on people, property, environment, and communities caused by petroleum spills from vessels and offshore oil rigs and installations can be tremendous. The *Exxon Valdez* and Deepwater Horizon oil spills demonstrated the environmental and communal effects of large oil spills, while smaller oil spills from vessels and offshore installations in Norway have caused minor damage to the environment. As a result of the *Exxon Valdez* oil spill in the Gulf of Alaska, local herring and salmon stocks were destroyed. The herring population has been so low that there has been no herring fishing during 15 years after 1989.[39] Previous oil spill accidents show that reliance on fishing, clean water and clean beaches for enjoyment and living can be drastically affected by oil spills. In relation to the coastal Sámi, there is particular reason to focus on oil tankers along the Norwegian coast.

Both Norway and Russia are contracting parties to the International Convention on Civil Liability for Oil Pollution Damage (the CLC Convention) and its 1992 replacement Protocol,[40] which regulate liability for oil-pollution damage resulting from maritime casualties involving oil-carrying ships. Both countries have also focused on the consequences of a possible oil spill from platforms in the wake of the Deepwater Horizon accident, either by confirming national legislation or by enforcing their own national regulatory regime, as well as by conducting inquiries into the accident and comparing it to their own national oil industry. Both countries are aware of the risks of oil-pollution damage from both offshore exploration and production and seagoing oil transportation, and of the huge ecological damage that oil spills may cause. There has accordingly been a focus on emergency preparedness, something that possesses its own challenges.[41] However, the

Norwegian government currently argues that the new EU Offshore Safety Directive applies only to Norway's land territory, internal waters, and territorial waters and not to the economic exclusive zone (EEZ), the continental shelf, or the high seas.[42]

Norway has extensively examined the effects of such an accident in the Barents Sea, and its environment agency has warned against low emergency preparedness in the Barents Sea and possible large pollution damage before the oil is removed.[43] Simultaneously, the current clean-up infrastructures are not ideal. Conventional oil booms (floating barriers used to contain an oil spill) do not perform in most sea conditions,[44] and the chemicals used to dissolve oil on water can themselves cause additional damage to marine life.[45] Lack of sound emergency preparedness could have direct consequences for the extent of pollution damage. The growth in exploration and production in the northern parts of Russia has resulted in increased transportation of oil by seagoing vessels in the Barents region, something that, again, increases the risk of oil spills from these vessels in northern Norway.[46]

Precise details of the consequent harm to the environment are generally disputed. The environmental characteristics of sea areas also vary. The report of the Norwegian Forum for Cooperation Concerning Risk[47] points out the very different environmental characteristics in the Barents Sea and in the Gulf of Mexico, and tries to a very limited extent to say something about the vulnerability of these characteristics. The conclusion is that the Barents Sea contains a sensitive ecosystem.

Regulation of compensation for damage to the marine environment caused by oil spills in Norway

Regulation does not assist in defining compensable damage

The Norwegian Maritime Code,[48] adopting the position of the CLC Convention of 1992, contains provisions[49] regulating liability for oil-pollution damage resulting from maritime casualties involving oil-carrying ships, while the Norwegian Petroleum Act[50] regulates liability for pollution damage as a consequence of effluence or discharge of petroleum from a facility.[51] Under the Maritime Code, the owner of the vessel is liable without fault for pollution damage,[52] while the Petroleum Act places no-fault liability on the licensee for pollution damage.[53] A vessel owner's liability is limited, unless intent or gross negligence is proven,[54] while a licensee carries unlimited liability for its pollution damage.[55] The Maritime Code defines 'pollution damage'[56] as:

a Damage or loss caused outside the ship by contamination resulting from the escape or discharge of oil from the vessel. In addition to loss of profit, damage through impairment of the environment nevertheless only compromises the costs of reasonable measures of reinstatement which have been or will be adopted.

b Expenses, damage or loss in consequence of reasonable measures adopted after an event which causes or entails an immediate and considerable risk of damage as mentioned in letter a, and the purpose of which is to prevent or limit such damage.

The Petroleum Act defines 'pollution damage'[57] as:

> Pollution damage means damage or loss caused by pollution as a consequence of effluence or discharge of petroleum from a facility, including a well, and costs of reasonable measures to avert or limit such damage or such loss, as well as damage or loss as a consequence of such measures. Damage or loss incurred by fishermen as a consequence of reduced possibilities for fishing is also included in pollution damage.

Preparatory works to the Petroleum Act give examples of certain types of damage that would qualify as pollution damage. For the purposes of this analysis, it may be noted that harm inflicted to wildlife in the sea and on land, the soiling of beaches and fishing gear, and the closure of a water area as an impediment to fishing are included.[58] The preparatory works confirm that compensable pollution damage must fulfil the prerequisites for every type of damage compensable in delict law, including the prerequisite of economic loss.[59] Neither the main delict statute, the Damage Compensation Act,[60] nor the other instruments of delict legislation notably assist much in defining compensable damage.[61] The concept of 'pollution' in connection to 'damage' must be read in conjunction with the supplementing legislation, the Pollution Control Act.[62] It is inaccurate to state that the core of delict law is that the injured party should not be positioned worse financially with the injury than if it was not inflicted when damage is inflicted to the natural environment.

Damage to the natural environment is often considered as an infringement of non-economic interests. Infringed natural environmental interests enjoy protection in delict law, and are compensable under the Maritime Code and the Petroleum Act. Protection is expressed through the guiding restoration principle, applying compensation for costs of 'reasonable measures' to restore the environment back to its original state without adhering to strict economic delict requirements. However, there is no requirement that the natural environment (the injured party) should be placed in the same position as if the injury had never occurred. This indicates a softening of the economic character prerequisite, to some extent, so as to compensate damage to the environment.[63] It is the economic character of the necessary and foreseeable expenses of the reasonable and appropriate activities to restore, replace or clean the natural resources that is compensable.[64] This view reflects a conversion or commercialisation,[65] which essentially gives the infringement of a non-economic interest an economic value through the execution of measures to avert or limit the infringement of the non-economic value. The measures can be objectively assessed as reasonable and appropriate, and given a specific monetary value.

Furthermore, private property rights generally enjoy a higher level of legal protection than unowned natural sources.[66] Damage inflicted to private property and the consequential loss of economic character are compensable.[67] To illustrate, a hotel may have a beach or beautiful natural skerries in front of it. The property owner of this hotel is compensated for damage to the property based on the reduction in sales value and any loss to the property's commercial activity. The hotel's property may also suffer environmental damage that, in itself, does not reduce the property's sales value, such as damage to trees that as a result must be cut down or waterfront vegetation that must be removed. Damage to the environment that cannot be determined by a measurable reduction in the property's sales value is compensated through necessary environmental restoration or replacement costs.[68] Damage to certain natural resources is harder to valuate due to the absence of individual ownership, which would reflect the human measurement of a monetary value of the damage to the owner. Similarly, compensation of damage to 'un-owned' natural resources is executed based on compensation of necessary costs for reasonable environmental restoration and replacement measures. If restoration or replacement is not possible, then only clean-up costs are compensated. This is the same position taken in the Pollution Control Act, in which the reasonable costs of restoring the general public's rights of commons (*allemannsretter*) for non-commercial purposes, such as angling and the use of uncultivated land for private leisure purposes, are protected and compensated.

Protection of Sámi interests

As a result of oil spills, the Sámi fishermen may experience loss of commercial and community fishing opportunities. Sea areas could be closed for fishing, new fishing licences would be halted, fewer fishing licences would be issued, and/or the caught fish would reflect a quality below the standard required for human consumption. The fishermen are directly injured parties, even though in consequence of harm to the ocean. These types of loss to fishermen are expressly protected in delict law,[69] including losses related to limitations on fishing opportunities and reduction of spawn (resulting, again, in the reduction or loss of fish stock)[70] and loss of complete or partial fishing grounds due to pollution damage.[71] As mentioned above, the preparatory works to the Petroleum Act affirm compensation for '... loss that follows directly from a relevant water area for shorter or longer period of time is damaged, for example that fishing and shipping become hindered....'[72]

In summary, both compensation of loss to income and profits and damage to property (equipment, etc.) lie within the scope of pollution damage covered by the act. That said, documenting losses may become a challenge for Sámi fishermen. The Alaska Native subsistence case, in the aftermath of *Exxon Valdez,* showed how the Alaska Natives documented their losses through lost sales, missing return on capital, and margin calculations to a lesser extent than the ocean fishing fleet.[73] Furthermore, Sámi claims may also be rejected based on legal requirements for documentation of the causation between the oil spill and the economic loss, and by a balance-of-interest exercise made by a Norwegian court, the outcome of which is dependent on the factual circumstances.

Without going into a detailed discussion of the definition of fisherman protection afforded by the Petroleum Act,[74] use of the phrase in its ordinary sense to mean 'a person engaged in fishing' would include most groups in society engaged in fishing as a cultural and traditional part of that society. The coastal Sámi could be directly affected by an oil spill, as the oil could permanently or temporarily destroy traditional Sámi fishing areas. The Sámi (and others) traditionally engage in local fishing in inshore waters with passive equipment and smaller fishing boats and return home every day.[75] This fishing activity is conducted in combination with other types of trade or commerce. Compensability depends on the exercise of use, a defined and limited group of fishermen, a limited geographical fishing area, and dependence on the activity.[76] In the Kåfjord case, which was decided by a small majority,[77] the Norwegian Supreme Court granted compensation for expropriation for the infringement of public interests.[78] The case concerned the question of whether the decision made by the Norwegian authorities in leasing the rights to perform hydropower activities was an expropriation of the local fishermen's rights and of the common interest, which made coastal fishing more difficult. The fishing interest could be considered exclusive due to its strong geographical limitation, because the population engaged in local fishing of cod in the inner part of the fjord arm, and because this fishing interest had, from an early period, constituted a considerable part of the population's household economy. The court confirmed the stand taken in another Supreme Court case: that if a claim for compensation of a loss due to water regulation was not based in a right, the use must be '… so concentrated and specific that it outwards appears essentially as the exercise of a right.'[79]

The court interpreted this to mean that for an interest to be protected, the exercise of the use that was the reason for the protection must have been to some extent exclusive and must have had a significant economic impact on the users.[80]

If the coastal Sámi have indeed suffered an infringement of their local public fishing interests, they may as a consequence have a stronger connection to such fishing interests, as fishing in their local surroundings is a strong part of the coastal Sámi culture – especially in view of the fact that the sea Sámi culture is currently fragile and endangered.[81] Additional ethical, moral, and cultural considerations, as well as international agreement obligations, may also have an impact on this issue.

Protection in delict law of collective rights and rights of common

Previously, only specific or special interests of economic character were protected by the delict rules. A special interest can be seen as an individual right protected by the aim of relevant legislation. Delict law protects individuals' proprietary rights, which include the right and the ability to transfer the property from one person to another and the power to use the property and to exclude others from it. Hence, neither collective rights nor rights of common were protected in delict law. This has changed to some degree with the development of case law.

Rights of common are often considered to be a benefit located in water, ocean or the air, which in delict law are not considered protected, because no private property rights can be identified in these public benefits.[82] Some examples of rights in common are the right to fish in the ocean or in public lakes, the right to collect seaweed and sea tangle beyond the point of where the private property rights end, swimming, and access and berry-picking on uncultivated land.[83] Rights of common are vested in members of the public at large, including Sámi individuals, but not limited only to Sámi individuals.

Collective rights are rights belonging to a collective, which means that the rights can be exercised only by members of the collective.[84] Sámi collective rights are an example of such rights.[85] The collective's interests are protected in delict law, but not the interests of the members of the collective.[86] Members of the collective can be limited by a class of specific individuals or by a geographical area.[87]

Putting these protected rights into perspective, then, rights of common are not limited by an identifiable circle of individuals and hold weaker protection in delict law than collective rights. In other words, protection in delict law can be considered a sliding scale, with the strongest protection for individual rights, somewhat weaker protection for collective rights, and the weakest protection for rights of common.

Conclusion

We have seen above how the Norwegian government rejected the CFC's draft bill safeguarding fishing as the basis for the coastal Sámi culture. Instead, it proposed a far less binding legislation, which has since been approved by parliament. Although these amendments include some statements of principle, it is currently difficult to say what impact they will have in protecting the coastal Sámi culture.

The presentation above shows that both Norwegian and international compensation law is primarily aimed at safeguarding economic, tradable interests and private property. This creates additional challenges for the coastal Sámi communities, who cannot invoke title of their fishing grounds, shorelines or other areas, and are less able than the ocean fishing fleet to document losses through lost sales, missing return on capital, and margin calculations.

The weak protection currently in place for the historical rights of the coastal Sámi in the context of the growing oil industry and increased tanker transport makes it urgent to raise the question whether Norway is complying with its international legal obligations to protect the coastal Sámi culture. This question, in turn, implies that, rather than languishing in the archives of the ministries, this topic should be out in the public eye being addressed by governments, parliamentary representatives, Sámi politicians and local politicians – the latter two of these undoubtedly having coinciding interests.

A tanker accident on the coast of Finnmark could undoubtedly mean the devastation of the basis for the coastal Sámi culture. The emphasis of this provision, which is incorporated into Norwegian law with precedence in case law, seems today, however, to be very far from the realm of applicable legal arguments and case law. ICCPR Article 27, which states that ethnic minorities 'shall not be denied the right… to enjoy their own culture' and which is intended to protect indigenous peoples and, particularly, their access to fishing and harvesting of other natural resources as a material basis for their culture,[88] deserves to receive renewed attention – not only by scholars and Sámi politicians, but, in particular, by the Norwegian government and parliament.

Notes

1 Respectively NOU 1997:4 (Norwegian Official Report, 'Naturgrunnlaget for samisk kultur [The natural basis for Sami culture],' Oslo, 1997), and NOU 2008:5 (Norwegian Official Report, 'Retten til fiske i havet utenfor Finnmark [The right to fish in the sea off Finnmark],' Oslo, 2008).
2 Hansen and Olsen 2004, 67. See also Ravna 2014, 313–321, which Chapter 2 in parts is elaborated on.
3 Sametinget 2004.
4 Pedersen, S., 1994, 'Bruk av land og vann i Finnmark i historisk perspektiv [Use of land and water in Finnmark in historical perspective],' NOU [Norwegian Official Reports] 1994:21, 83.
5 NOU 1997:4, 308, Ravna 2014, 313.
6 NOU 1997:4, 304–318.
7 NOU 2008:5, 40.
8 Innst. O. nr. 80 2004–2005 (Innstilling O nr. 80 fra Justiskomiteen om lov om rettsforhold og forvaltning av grunn og naturressurser i Finnmark fylke [Recommendation of Justice Committee on legal rights and management of land and natural resources in Finnmark county/Parliamentary bill for Finnmark Act]. Oslo), 30.
9 Ibid. 15, 30–31.
10 NOU 2008:5, 13, 14.
11 Ibid. 250.
12 The provisions under ICCPR are paramount to the Norwegian fisheries regulation (see 1999 Human Rights Act section 2 and 3), while the historic rights have a basis in immemorial customary law usage, see the CFC in NOU 2008:5, 250.
13 Ibid. 156.
14 Ibid. 5, 14.
15 Harris and Millerd 2010, 82–107.
16 NOU 2008:5, 14.

17 Ibid. 15.
18 Marine Resources Act 2008 (Lov 6. Juni 2008 nr. 6 om forvaltning av viltlevande marine ressursar [Law of 6 June 2008 No. 6 on the management of wild living marine resources], Oslo), 2.
19 Regjeringsadvokaten 2009.
20 Smith 2010, 22.
21 Anaya 2011, para. 80.
22 Prop. 70 L 2011–2012 (Endringar i deltakerloven, havressurslova og finnmarksloven (kystfiskeutvalet) [Changes in the Participation Act, the Marine Resources Act and the Finnmark Act (Coastal Fishing Committee)], parliamentary bill, Oslo), 7.
23 Sametinget 2011.
24 Ibid.
25 Act 26. March 1999 No. 15 on the Right to take part in Fishing and Hunting (the Participation Act).
26 Prop. 70 L (2011–2012), 7.
27 Amendment 21 September 2012 No 66 of Fisheries Participation Act, Marine Resources Act and Finnmark Act (Lov 21 September 2012 nr. 66 om endringar i deltakerloven, havressurslova og finnmarksloven, Oslo).
28 Prop. 70 L (2011–2012), 88.
29 Ibid. 89.
30 Ibid. 99.
31 Ibid. 8, 126.
32 Ibid. 122.
33 Ibid. 8, 122.
34 Ot.prp.nr. 20 2007–2008 ('Om lov om forvaltning av viltlevande marine ressursar (havressurslova) [On the law on the management of wild living marine resources (Marine Resources Act)],' parliamentary bill, Oslo), 183.
35 Prop. 70 L (2011–2012), 123.
36 Ibid. 124.
37 Committee on the Elimination of Racial Discrimination, 'Concluding observations on the twenty-first and twenty-second periodic reports of Norway,' CERD/C/NOR/CO/21–22 28 August 2015, para. 29 (d).
38 Ibid. para. 30 (f).
39 Kennedy 2010.
40 CLC Convention (International Convention on Civil Liability for Oil Pollution Damage, adopted 29 November 1969, entry into force 19 June 1975; replaced by 1992 Protocol, Entry into force 30 May 1996).
41 Agreement between Norway and the Russian Federation 1994 (On cooperation to combat oil spills in the Barents Sea, Moscow, 28 April 1994).
42 Concerning this issue see Chapter 4, 'The EU's Role as a Facilitator in the Development of Standards for Offshore Hydrocarbon Extraction in the Arctic'.
43 Norwegian Environment Agency 2013.
44 Nilsen 2012, 4–6.
45 NOU 1982:19, 'Generelle lovregler om erstatning for forurensningsskade [General law on compensation of pollution damage]' (Norwegian Official Reports, Oslo), 80.
46 Karlsen 2013, 14 ff.
47 Forum for Samarbeid om Risiko 2010.
48 Act no 39 of 24 June 1994.
49 The Maritime Code's section 191.
50 Act no 72 of 29 November 1996. [Where? This is just the name of Act, location in act in note 51]

51 Chapter 7, Petroleum Act 1996 (Lov om petroleumsvirksomhet, 29 November 1996, No. 72, Oslo).
52 Section 91, Maritime Code 1994 (Lov om sjøfarten 24 June 1994, No. 39, Oslo).
53 Section 7 (3), Petroleum Act.
54 Section 194, Maritime Code.
55 Section 7 (3), Petroleum Act.
56 Maritime Code, 191.
57 Section 7 (1), Petroleum Act.
58 NOU 1981:33, 'Erstatningsansvar for forurensningsskade som følge av petroleumsvirksomhet på norsk kontinentalsokkel [Liability for pollution damage resulting from the petroleum activities on the Norwegian Continental Shelf],' Norwegian Official Reports, Oslo, 35.
59 Ibid.
60 Act No. 26, 13 June 1969.
61 Koch 2010, 250–281.
62 Act No. 6, 13 March 1981. See further Svendsen 2015, 166.
63 NOU 1981:33, 35.
64 Rettens gang 1979, 715 and NOU 1982:19, 143.
65 Askeland 2010, 1–72; Stavang 2007, 38; Monsen 2010, 20–21.
66 Jing 2013, 34–38.
67 Lov om skadeserstatning [Damage Compensation Act], 13 June 1969, No. 26, Oslo), s. 4–1.
68 Norsk retstidende (NRt). 2015, 216
69 Petroleum Act, section 7 (1) and Maritime Code, section 191.
70 Ot.prp.nr. 25 1988–1989 ('Om lov om endringer i lov 22. mars 1985 nr. 11 om petroleumsvirksomhet [On the law amending the law of 22 March 1985 No. 11 relating to petroleum activities], parliamentary bill, Oslo), 26 and 32.
71 Ibid. opposite Hammer, et al. 2009, 534.
72 NOU 1981:33, 35.
73 Duffield, Neher and Patterson. 2014, 53.
74 Petroleum Act, section 7 (1).
75 NOU 2008:5, 383.
76 Skogvang 2012, 197–204.
77 Three out of the five judges; two of the judges did not support the stand of the majority.
78 Norsk retstidende (NRt). 1985, 247.
79 Norsk retstidende (NRt). 1969, 1220 at 1226.
80 Norsk retstidende (NRt). 1985, 247 at 251–252.
81 NOU 2008:5, 393.
82 NOU 1982:19, 81–84; and Aasland 1985, 45.
83 Aasland 1985, 56.
84 Pedersen and Sørheim 2012, 272.
85 Norsk retstidende (NRt). 2001, 769 and 1229.
86 Pedersen and Sørheim 2012, 272.
87 Ibid.
88 Human Rights Committee, General Comment No. 23, Article 27, CCPR/C/21, adopted in 50th Session, 8 April 1994, para. 7.

References

Aasland, B. 1985. 'Fra oljeutblåsning til motorveistøy: erstatningsspørsmål ved forurensning [From blowout to freeway noise: questions of compensation in case of pollution].' *Jussens Venner*: 43–64.

Anaya, J. 2011. Report of the Special Rapporteur on the Rights of Indigenous Peoples: the Situation of the Sami People in the Sápmi region of Norway, Sweden and Finland. A/HRC/18/35/Add.2. Geneva: Human Rights Council.

Askeland, B. 2010. 'Erstatning for preventive utgifter [Compensation for preventive expenses].' *Tidsskrift for Rettsvitenskap* 123: 1–72.

Duffield, J., C. Neher and D. Patterson. 2014. 'Oil Spill in Northern Waters: Trial Outcomes and the Long-Term in case of Exxon Valdez.' *Arctic Review on Law and Politics* 5: 38–74.

Forum for Samarbeid om Risiko. 2010. 'Ulykken i Mexicogulfen: Risikogruppens vurdering [The accident in the Gulf of Mexico: Risk Group assessment].' www.regjeringen.no/nb/dep/kld/dok/rapporter_planer/rapporter/2010/ulykken-i-mexicogolfen.html?id=626552 (accessed 20 August 2015).

Hammer, U., T. Stang, S.B. Bjelland, Y. Bustnesli and A.B. Tørum. 2009. *Petroleumsloven* [The Petroleum Act]. Oslo: Universitetsforlaget.

Hansen, L.I. and B. Olsen. 2004. *Samenes historie fram til 1750* [The history of the Sami to 1750]. Oslo: Cappelen.

Harris, D. and P. Millerd. 2010. 'Food Fish, Commercial Fish, and Fish to Support a Moderate Livelihood.' *Arctic Review on Law and Politics* 1: 82–107.

Jing, L. 2013. Compensating Ecological Damage: Comparative and Economic Observations. Cambridge, Antwerp, Portland: Intersentia and Metro.

Karlsen, E. 2013. 'Hvordan forhindre oljeforurensning fra utenlandsk skipstrafikk i transitt [How to prevent oil pollution from foreign ship- traffic in transit].' PhD diss., University of Tromsø.

Kennedy, S. 2010. 'Expert from Exxon Valdez Accident Saddened by Oil Spill's Effects.' *Bradenton Herald*, 2 June 2010.

Koch, S. 2010. 'Det erstatningsrettslige skadebegrepet – en sammenligning mellom tysk og norsk rett [The tort damage concept: a comparison between German and Norwegian law].' *Tidsskrift for Erstatningsrett, Forsikringsrett og Velferdsrett*, 250–281.

Monsen, E. 2010. 'Om rekkevidden av erstatningsrettslig vern for tap og ulempe som følge av formuesskade [On the scope of protection against liability [Correct?] for loss and inconvenience resulting from asset damage].' *Jussens Venner*, 1–67.

Nilsen, D. 2012. 'Wind-driven Surface Currents: the Death Knell for Conventional Oil Booms?' *Allmaritim*, 4–6.

Norwegian Environment Agency. 2013. 'Advarer mot hastverk i Barentshavet [Against haste in the Barents Sea].' Trondheim: Norwegian Environment Agency. www.miljodirektoratet.no/no/Nyheter/Nyheter/Old-klif/2013/Januar_2013/Klif_advarer_mot_hastverk_i_Barentshavet (accessed 15 August 2015).

NOU 1982: 19 (Norwegian Official Report). 1982. 'Generelle lovregler om erstatning for forurensningsskade [General legal rules for compensation of pollution damage]', Oslo.

NOU 1997: 4 (Norwegian Official Report). 1997. 'Naturgrunnlaget for samisk kultur [The natural basis for Sami culture],' Oslo.

NOU 2008: 5 (Norwegian Official Report). 2008. 'Retten til fiske i havet utenfor Finnmark [The right to fish in the sea off Finnmark],' Oslo.

Pedersen, S. 1994. 'Bruk av land og vann i Finnmark i historisk perspektiv [Use of land and water in Finnmark in historical perspective].' *NOU* 1994: 21.

Pedersen, S. and S.Ø. Sørheim, 2012. 'Hvem kan representere kollektiver i tvistemål ['Who is to represent collectives in litigation]?' *Juss i Nord*: *Hav, Fisk og Urfolk*

[Law in the North: sea, fish and indigenous peoples], eds. T. Henriksen and Ø. Ravna. Oslo: Gyldendal.

Ravna, Ø., 2014, 'The Fulfilment of Norway's International Legal Obligations to the Sámi – Assessed by the Protection of Rights to Lands, Waters and Natural Resources', *International Journal on Minority and Group Rights*, 21 (3): 297–329. doi:10.1163/15718115–02103001.

Regjeringsadvokaten. 2009. NOU 2008: 5 Retten til fiske i havet utenfor Finnmark – Høyring [The right to fish in the sea outside Finnmark: hearing]. www.regjeringen.no/no/id4/ (accessed 25 August 2015).

Sametinget. 2004. Sametingets melding om fiske som næring og kultur i kyst-og fjordområdene [Sami Parliament of Norway's statement on fishing as industry and culture in the coastal and fjord areas]. www.sametinget.no/content/download/540/4881 (accessed 31 August 2015).

Sametinget. 2011. Retten til fiske i sjøsamiske områder 2011 [The right to fish in coastal Sami areas in 2011].

Skogvang, S. 2012. *Retten til fiske i fjorder og kystnære farvann* [The right to fish in fjords and coastal waters]. Oslo: Universitetsforlaget.

Smith, C. 2010. 'Retten til fiske i havet utanfor Finnmark [The right to fish in the sea off Finnmark].' *Arctic Review on Law and Politics* 1: 4–27.

Stavang, E. 2007. *Erstatningsrettslig analyse – med særlig vekt på eiendom og miljø* [Compensation law analysis: with special emphasis on property and the environment]. Oslo: Cappelen.

Svendsen, K. 2015. Compensable damage ex delicto as a result of harm in the Barents Sea caused by petroleum spills from offshore installations. A Norwegian and Russian comparative legal analysis of conflict of laws, the concept of harm, losses suffered by third parties, and environmental damage and its valuation and calculation, caused by petroleum spills from offshore oil rigs and installations in the Barents Sea. Tromsø: PhD thesis at the Faculty of Law, UiT-Arctic University of Norway.

12 Indigenous modes of ownership

Reopening the case for communal rights in Greenland

Pelle Tejsner

Introduction

In the context of the currently ongoing round of licensing applications for on- and offshore oil and mineral operations in Greenland, it is timely to revisit and appraise the historical, yet enduring relationships that continue to grow from and inform Inuit community conceptions of land, coastal and sea tenure. In the Arctic, an area whose future lies uneasily poised between its indigenous communities, the Greenlandic authorities and multinational oil and mining operators, social science approaches that reclaim the specific social and historical contexts of community territorial rights are a uniquely valuable input into the policy debate. They are highly relevant both to the human rights dimension and to the controversies that have arisen in the Arctic in connection with potential extraction sites in areas that are of interest to the indigenous communities, the authorities and the multinational operators. This chapter reviews the historical evidence for the various notions of Inuit territorial rights and, specifically, the community or communal conceptualisations of ownership and property rights, in the context of contemporary field studies. It assesses the cultural differences at work in the various interpretations of the post-colonial encounter between local stakeholders, multinational oil and mineral companies, and the Greenlandic authorities.

Anyone opening a Greenlandic newspaper today will find themselves buffeted by a cacophony of voices, from business executives and the Greenlandic authorities to NGOs and (former or otherwise) Danish politicians, all racing to have their say in the public debate over oil and mineral exploration in the newly carved-out nation. The debate over on- and offshore oil, gas and mineral exploration in Greenland is frequently marked by accusations of social exclusion and the absence of community engagement in the public consultation process. Occasionally, local voices can be discerned. As we move between the Greenlandic authorities and the municipal spheres of interest, community stakeholder interests are frequently stated in the various public forums, ranging from issues of civic participation to concerns about community territorial interests. These developments can be examined as fractured jurisdictional domains, with divisions between the Greenlandic government and the municipal councils occasionally becoming evident. This chapter will review some of the fractures implied by local (or rather customary) conceptions of ownership and user rights as these have been expressed in the unfolding debates, both historical and contemporary, on the future of Greenland's natural resources.

The research presented in this chapter is based on archival source material which has directly or indirectly documented aspects of community territory, as expressed by indigenous informants and scholars during the period prior to the end of Greenland's status as a Danish colony in 1953. The archival material is supported by contemporary fieldwork interviews with local informants, and subsequently appraised in a review of the literature on issues of indigenous ownership, property rights and aspects of territoriality. Fieldwork findings prepared for this chapter are based on a one-year stay in Qeqertarsuaq (from 2007 to 2008) for documenting the seasonal cycle of renewable marine-resource harvesting, with a follow-up study in 2015, together with a more recent stretch of fieldwork at the Nalunaq gold mine and in the adjacent community of Nanortalik, South Greenland. While the many voices to be heard in the ongoing debate in Greenland over exploration licences and drilling activities have in common that they all address equally important aspects of governance, this chapter will focus only on one of these aspects: the community interest sphere. The chapter begins with a brief review of indigenous peoples' rights as these relate to resource extraction. After this, we turn to assess historical and contemporary notions of ownership and territorial rights as made evident from a reading of the source material on Greenland. Finally, a precedent case of conflicting interests in resource use will be reassessed in the light of current developments and discussed with a view to future activities in offshore areas. Throughout the chapter, statements by local stakeholders, whose livelihoods rest on customary conceptions of hunting and fishing territories, have been included to support the findings and the overall argument.

Indigenous peoples' rights in a circumpolar context

On several occasions, Arctic indigenous peoples have been confronted by significant obstacles in their claims to the ownership of traditional lands, territories and resources, particularly in the area of exploration and exploitation activities by multinational mineral and oil companies.[1] Conversely, they have often had to struggle for recognition of their rights at the international human rights level. The International Labour Organisation's Convention 169 (ILO 169), adopted in 1989, establishes a set of minimum standards on behalf of indigenous peoples, while simultaneously calling for the protection of their way of life and culture based upon their own aspirations and priorities. These priorities or aspirations, are spelt out further in Articles 14 and 15 of the convention. They address the following set of provisions that are of particular relevance to indigenous land usage, resource and territorial rights:[2]

1 The rights of ownership and possession of the peoples concerned over the lands which they traditionally occupy shall be recognized [...] measures shall be taken in appropriate cases to safeguard the right of the peoples concerned to use lands *not exclusively occupied by them,* but to which they have *traditionally had access for their subsistence and traditional activities.*[3]
2 Governments shall take steps as necessary to identify the lands, which the peoples concerned *traditionally occupy,* and to guarantee effective protection of their rights of *ownership* and protection [emphasis added].

The role of the state in upholding the rights of its population is at the heart of these articles, since the relevant authorities are not only required to recognise cases of indigenous claims to ownership and possessory interest, but, moreover, remain obliged to identify the extent of such lands, so as to guarantee their effective protection and local users' rights. Since Denmark's ratification of ILO 169 in 1996, it is important to ask to what extent the Greenlandic self-government authorities – Inatsisartut (the parliament) and Naalakkersuisut (the government) – have in fact safeguarded the possessory interest of value, aspiration and priority of the Kalaallit (the Greenlandic Inuit people) in the more geographically remote community spheres of interest.

Article 15 of the convention deals with the rights of indigenous peoples in relation to resource extraction activities, and specifically the duties and responsibilities of the authorities concerning natural resources. In the case of Greenland, where the authorities exercise ownership of mineral or subsurface resources, the convention specifically identifies the responsibilities of the relevant governments, which

> shall establish or maintain procedures through which they shall consult these peoples, with a view to ascertaining whether and to what degree their interests would be prejudiced, before undertaking or permitting any programs.[4]

Article 32 of the UN Declaration on the Rights of Indigenous Peoples (UNDRIP) concerns the relevant state's responsibility to

> consult and cooperate in good faith with the indigenous peoples concerned [...] in order to obtain their free and informed consent prior to the approval of any project affecting their lands or territories.[5]

In the Canadian High Arctic, where the Inuit Nunangat people have often found themselves opposing an otherwise federal government framework with respect to their claims to offshore ownership rights, claims to rights of ownership offshore have been formulated quite explicitly.[6] In the Greenlandic context, however, these rights appear to be embedded in the various levels of civic participation, ranging from public demonstrations in Nuuk to degrees of community participation and engagement, as we move from the larger towns to the smaller outlying villages and settlements.

Article 32 of UNDRIP is especially relevant in the light of recent local experiences and the charge that citizen involvement has been conspicuously lacking. These complaints have specifically targeted the one-way conduct of public hearings, the delays involved, and the highly technical nature of public reports relating to the proposed resource extractions near Narsaq and Cairn offshore test drillings in Disko Bay[7] (to which we will return below). These complaints and stated disagreements relating to them, have now given rise to a memorandum consisting of a series of recommendations, in light of the absent citizen involvement, formulated by the group of volunteer lawyers and citizen activists known as the NGO Coalition for Improved Citizens' Involvement. This memorandum, which was submitted to Naalakkersuisut, addressed several aspects of the outlined above rights, while repeatedly stressing the authorities' continued failure to observe these.

UNDRIP similarly recognises the rights of indigenous peoples. Articles 25 to 32 address various aspects of rights pertaining to lands, territories and resources. In relation to the question of territorial ownership, Article 26 (2) states that indigenous communities have the right to own and control:

> the lands, territories and resources that they possess by reason of traditional ownership or other traditional occupation or use 8 [.]

It states that the state's obligations towards achieving these rights include provisions for granting:

> legal recognition and protection to these lands, territories and resources [...] conducted with due respect to the customs, traditions and land tenure systems of the indigenous peoples concerned.

Knowledge of, and recognition of, customary Greenlandic Inuit systems of tenure is central to recognition of the case for communal territorial boundary conceptions and land rights. As I examine indigenous conceptions of ownership with relevance to ILO Convention 169 and UNDRIP, I wish to discuss these concepts as they have commonly found expression in the local Greenlandic vernacular. The cases explored below are instances in which community-shared concerns about user rights were mobilised accordingly, because developments were seen as a possible threat to livelihoods.

Indigenous conceptions of communal territorial interests

Conceptions of territory and related usage practices can vary not only with the form of extraction involved hunting, fishing or farming but also according to the social integration and community structures that frame the extractions. Any kind of extraction, or subsistence harvesting, inevitably entails a reference to local conceptions of 'territory,' which invokes particular geographical and social dimensions for the local population.[8] Different spheres of reception and negotiation occasionally witness unequal developments of the notion of territory from the micro to the macro level of governance, and this renders the question of social control a key issue in any kind of resource appropriation.[9] Many formerly colonised states in Africa, South America and Asia developed new national territorial associations or 'imagined communities'[10] that significantly complicated the translation of rights for thus marginalised indigenous groups (i.e. loss of control over native lands, resources and territories). The same could be said for the Arctic, as self-governing regions such as Greenland exhibit a number of socioeconomic change processes reminiscent in character of those in developing regions elsewhere in the world. The unequal development experienced in what some have described as the two Greenlands as we move from Nuuk to the smaller towns and settlements was the subject of fiercely contested debate in the run-up to the Greenlandic election of November 2014.[11]

According to Brøsted, there are no authoritative accounts or descriptions of the Greenlandic land tenure system in use before colonisation or during the early colonial period.[12] The existing archival material that refers to the indigenous system of tenure is mostly of variable quality and was usually documented for different purposes, which consequently tend to reflect the given interests of the narrator. In the ethnographic record, we do however find – almost incidental – examples of references to ownership. One hunter from the hamlet of Timerdlit in south-west Greenland states: 'it would be fine to get some fresh meat from the hunting territory of the Kangamiut people.'[13]

Although the example, which Petersen chose to highlight in the reference in the quoted text, may merely have referred to: 'where the people from nearby Kangamiut usually go hunting'. Its phrasing remains indicative of the fact that the hunting territory of a settlement was a commonly recognised concept at that time.

Most accounts of the Greenlandic Inuit version of systems of land tenure can be divided between two significantly divergent conceptions of access: the notion of free and public appropriation (collective rights) versus a communal right of access through demonstrated usage, sharing of resources and so on (individual/family rights). Both versions were originally rooted in the community notion of land access; only the first, however, was chosen for incorporation into the inevitable centralisation by which nation-building is performed. The older, pre-existing model of territorial rights was based on the individual's affiliation to the local community, which in turn ensured access to the community's hunting areas a model in which commonly shared understandings and values about proper hunting methods and patterns of tenure must be observed when access is agreed.

The reason for this divergence in interpretations can be traced back to the juridical expedition sent to Greenland in 1948–1949 to investigate customary law, the Greenlandic Law Committee. The committee's inherently Western focus resulted in a very unsatisfactory interpretation of the sources.[14] Although the expedition essentially had to assess two very different conceptions of rights, ranging from the-public-belongs-to-all to the less evident local communal rights, its report decided upon the prior (inherently more evident interpretation) as the principal rule. The committee originally inserted a provision for compensation to protect existing rights for community occupational pursuits, with a view to potential conflicts between traditional Greenlandic land use and new exploitation interests. However, this provision was subsequently rejected by the Danish legal experts in the planning process, fearing the consequences for the Danish–Greenlandic relationship. The indigenous authority at the time, the Greenlandic provincial council (*Landsrådet*), was quick to emphasise the need to clarify problems of aboriginal rights by demanding relevant consultations of international law standards and practices with due consideration for the 'expropriation of collective hunting and fishing rights.'[15] However, the ministry for Greenland in Copenhagen ignored the demand. Subsequently, the Danish parliament mandated a revision of the Greenlandic Land Use and Planning Act (1977), but this did not pass into an amendment of the Act. The intention of changing the approach to ownership was included in the preparation of the bill for the transfer of the Land Use and Planning Authority in 1980.[16] To give a better grasp of the importance of this misinterpretation (whether deliberate or accidental) and consequent silencing of the older (community and individualised) rights framework, it may be useful to give an account of communal Greenlandic territorial rights as these have been found and documented in the archival evidence and, where applicable, backed by *in situ* empirical research on community territorial interests.

The coastal tenure system of Arctic indigenous peoples is commonly organised and defined by numerous multi-family hunting territories, in which the hunting efforts of each group or family, are typically organised around an older family member or, as described elsewhere in the Canadian Arctic, a family figurehead or senior 'hunting boss.'[17] Although Dahl[18] locates rights of ownership in the community sphere of interest, with access to resources granted through membership as a resident in the community, Petersen's discussion of individual (even private) ownership along the Greenlandic west coast suggests that these, even if perceived as individual rights, remain family expressions of ownership. This concept of ownership, however, hardly resembles the kind of private property rights that are commonly demarcated with signs or fences. It remains more flexible, as 'the boundaries of the four groups [families] are natural ones, and coincide with those of the hunting territories which are not marked out either.'[19]

In the anthropological literature, questions of indigenous land tenure often revolve around the observation that divisions of the landscape into territorial compartments are very different from Western practices of defining zones of exclusive access according to particular holders or owners, but rather serve to 'regulate the exploitation of dispersed resources over a common range'[20] and can thus be interpreted as based on practical cooperation rather than social competition in the global marketplace. This aspect found frequent support in interviews with Qeqertarsuarmiut (the people of Qeqertarsuaq) about household harvesting areas and use patterns during my fieldwork in Disko Bay. Local users were more interested in talking about what actually goes on inside their hunting territories than where any figurative or non-figurative line should be demarcated.

According to Brøsted,[21] Greenlandic customary practices of land use entail the idea that hunters may obtain and hold individual privilege to the use of certain parts of the local communally defined territory. For the individual or family privilege to gain community-wide acceptance and acknowledgement, it must be connected to a process of specification, most often made evident through the maintenance of nets, building of traps or setting up of campsites (i.e. a general reflection of maintenance). The sites involved typically range from familiar fishing spots along the coast to hunting and trapping trails further inland. The privilege is viewed as exclusive and entails aspects of transfer from father to son, uncle to cousin and so on through inheritance.[22] A final practice we find with regard to individual and family usage of a given site revolves around the *transfer* of rights, so that should the use of a place be discontinued, any previously prescribed user rights ideally revert to the community.[23]

In moving beyond the commonly expressed opposition between, on the one hand, a naturalistic view of the land as the empty backdrop merely awaiting the activities of human agency, as the concept of *terra nullius* implies, and on the other hand, a Western-derived interpretation of the land as reduced to the cognitive ordering of space, we may attempt to approach the concept of communal ownership and user rights from the 'dwelling' perspective.[24] The main observation of this approach recognises the enduring interactions between the land and the peoples' usage of it, made manifest 'as an enduring record – and testimony to – the lives and works of past generations who have dwelt within it, and in so doing, have left there something of themselves.'[25] In exploring the grounds of individual autonomy in relation to collective (local) appropriations of the environment, Ingold has also addressed the key differences between the kinds of individualism at work in what are often referred to as 'traditional' societies (or communities) and our own 'Western' conception of individualism.[26] Individualistic conceptions of property are far from unknown among subsistence-based hunting societies, and according to Herskovits, cross-cultural conclusions have ranged from *theirs* being a kind of 'communism in living' to the observation that 'considerations of private property are supreme.'[27] More to the point, Herskovits simultaneously emphasises that the dichotomy between 'communism' and 'private ownership' is meaningless unless those rights that concern property are more specifically spelt out, albeit such rights vary significantly from context to context. But it is also in the very attempt at 'spelling out' claims of ownership to aboriginal lands that indigenous peoples' negotiations with non-indigenous governments and their approach to ownership in the court systems have been met with mixed success. During the legal battles that ensued from the aboriginal land rights campaigns of the 1970s, for example, the Australian courts faced considerable difficulty in interpreting Aboriginal proprietary interests and concepts. In mobilising legal opposition to the Nabalco aluminium company's encroachment upon indigenous territories, the Yolngu people of North-East Arnhem Land strove to gain recognition of their prior title to the land. However, despite testimonies to the contrary, the ruling of the court failed to acknowledge Yolngu conceptions of ownership when:[28]

> His Honour Justice Blackburn in his decision found the system underlying the Aboriginal claim to be a system of law, but he did not accept that the Aboriginal claimants held proprietary interests in the land under Australian law.

In the case reported by Mulrennan and Scott between the Inuit of Nunavik and the Canadian federal government, a similar failure to recognise the interests of the native population is evident.[29] Mulrennan and Scott demonstrate that although the 1975 James Bay and Northern Quebec Agreement remains a significant charter for relations between indigenous and central government parties, providing for ownership and control of fisheries and for environmental and social impact assessments, that agreement does not make provisions for Inuit interests in the offshore, where critical sources of subsistence abound.

In accounting for hunting territories, multi-family hunting domains, netting sites and fishing spots, questions of ownership, access and spatial divisions among local families require further examination. Initially, we find numerous references in the literature to the annual occupational cycle governing local use of land, sea and shorelines.[30] In Greenland, as elsewhere in the Arctic, the right of use to a particular location or fishing spot is, in the traditions of the Inuit, dependent on usage. The following example from Petersen's examination of ownership and property claims helps to shed some light on this issue.[31] According to Petersen, the hunting territory of the family unit was transferred from father to son, and this practice is still in effect today in those parts of Greenland where locals continue to enjoy an enduring relationship with the coastal environment (i.e. in the outlying towns and settlements). Fishing and netting spots were previously accompanied by a set of 'prescriptive rights' concerning access to a camp or netting site. These were commonly 'handed over' if, prior to the arrival of the family, another family was found in the area that was communally understood as holding a vested interest in or a family history commonly associated with the area in question.[32]

One afternoon during fieldwork in Qeqertarsuaq, I joined a senior hunter and his son as they were out scouting around what they (and the rest of the community) understood as being their family's hunting trail. We had hiked up along the mountainside for about a kilometre, when we noticed another hunter on the other side of the ravine we were traversing. My informant was quick to point out that the trails along that side of the ravine were the family trails of the hunter we had encountered.[33] In my experiences of local Inuit (Qeqertarsuarmiut) dealings with aspects of property or ownership of the land and its resources, I would argue that although a hunter will indicate a stretch of land by referring to it as 'my country,' he is by no means in a position to refuse others access. In practice, the said person (if and when community consensus is observed) can expect to be consulted by anyone intent on using it, since he or she is commonly perceived as the holder of knowledgeable insights concerning animals and plants typically found in that place. Here, in contrast to Western notions of ownership, the concept of possession is anything but static. Rather, it is a matter of enduring attendance in the form of practical maintenance of existing resources and the continuous ecological processes unfolding in the said places.

Brøsted, in his analysis of the Greenlandic local community status as a legal entity, similarly notes its flexible character with respect to indigenous territorial rights, as well as its concomitant relatively formal organisation, whereby issues of concrete territorial demarcations are commonly dealt with in an imprecise manner.[34]

Although our own, predominantly Western categories of ownership would designate such usage or users as 'owners', the local logic behind the concept of individual possession is rather grounded in the communal apprehension here. In this equation, that which belongs to all is simply taken to be the individual's exercise of rights, or better, responsibilities under the auspices of the collective. In that sense, all an owner can really own, to the exclusion of others, is the privilege of *custodianship*, rather than what in the Western tradition is *held in custody*.[35] In other or better words, what we might view as 'possession' or 'ownership' is merely that which is reserved by an individual *on behalf of* the community, rather than *as against* all others.[36] This will become clearer as we review Greenlandic modes of tenure in the coastal and sea-ice environments.

Coastal and sea-ice environments

Although significant achievements have been made in the recognition of land claims, with the steady erosion of the old colonial doctrine of *terra nullius* as refuting indigenous rights in property, the concept of *mare nullius* has proved far more ambiguous and continues to lack appropriate investigation. This lack of attention to the (also colonially rooted) doctrine of *mare nullius*, according to which the sea, again, is perceived as empty space or simply vacant of indigenous tenure, continues to feature as an obstacle to the recognition of indigenous ownership. Since sea space is difficult to conceive of as property, the socio-ecological continuums of communal territories continue to be side-lined as indigenous users struggle to gain some element of control over what is locally often stated to be our rightful coastal territories and associated resources.[37]

In Greenland, as elsewhere in the Arctic, we find that since time immemorial each community has been constituted by its own unbound and non-exclusive hunting territory, within which the community has continued to exercise and mobilise its principles of social control. One such expression of community-rights interests became evident in what is now known as the Beluga Conflict.[38] In the early 1990s, this conflict of interest about the harvesting of beluga whales along the west coast of Greenland became a frequent bone of contention between local users, the Greenlandic authorities, and biologists employed by the Greenlandic department of wildlife and fisheries. It began when biologists initially issued a warning about unsustainable harvesting levels, which the then home rule authorities accepted by introducing a new management regime which, as well as imposing regulations on the hunt, removed the otherwise socially regulated control over the beluga resource from the local communities. Dahl[39] notes that the framing of this disagreement as one between differing regimes of knowledge production and authority was merely the 'tip of the iceberg', obscuring more fundamental changes in Greenlandic society and the development of the Greenlandic (imagined) community as a result of a changed notion of territoriality. A closer examination of the conflict revealed what locals felt was an encroachment on and impediment to their expressed interests in the community marine resources found along the coast, sea and ice. There was a clear sense of attempted inroads by outsiders (in this case the larger deep-sea trawlers) into what locals, again, continually expressed as *our* local waters.

On the surface, the Beluga Conflict appeared to be about differing knowledge regimes and the opposing claims of scientists and hunters. But in reality the conflict reflected more fundamental changes in Greenlandic society: rather than regulating harvesting levels more strictly, the then home rule authorities effectively removed the control over access from the locus of the communities. The conflict revealed how as part of the establishment of a new 'Greenlandic' society, imagined and based on a system of politically centralised control, and arguably modelled on the Danish colonial system of administration, community social control continued to be eroded by changing power relations (although it never collapsed altogether).

The development of a Greenlandic society with a new and 'imagined' sense of territoriality has, in turn, sparked what Dahl called a 'concomitant erosion of social control of local communities.'[40] Prior to interventions by the Greenlandic authorities in the form of imposed quota allocations for the categories of occupational and non-occupational hunters, rules and procedures had been grounded in local customary or usufruct rights.[41] Sejersen observes that the Greenlandic authorities' new classification scheme, presumably drawn up in accordance with socioeconomic criteria, has triggered a process of compartmentalisation, based on regulations that most local hunters have found confusing.[42] I have argued elsewhere that not only has the process of compartmentalisation imposed particular prescriptions for discrete groups of otherwise commonly unified hunters, but the increased regulation and quota system, originally intended to regulate animal populations, has resulted in an endless series of restrictions affecting the Inuit users of local renewable resources.[43]

In order to gain a better understanding of how the different layers of society, from individual to community wide level, are interpreted locally, we could examine the ways in which hunting and fishing disputes are typically settled *in situ*. When disagreement arises about an individual's improper conduct in an area that is otherwise commonly acknowledged to be identified with one kin group over another, such as when tracking out ptarmigan or geese, individual or autonomous hunting rights are often invoked. But when the dispute turns on a resource that is genuinely understood to belong in the sphere of common benefit to the general community (such as a larger marine mammal), communal aspects of ownership will concomitantly be raised. These, however, are simultaneously restricted both by international and regional conventions and by Greenlandic legislation (as in the Beluga Conflict). The current slogan is that Greenland is 'open for business,' and oil and mineral concessions and licences are now dealt with solely by the Mineral Licence and Safety Authority (MLSA).[44] Although, as other chapters in this volume explain, local communities are often involved in both the different stages and the final end-products of strategic environmental assessments that involvement has not always been ensured in a proper manner. Here, a previous case will help to shed light on this matter as it concerns the conflicting interests of a multinational operator and a Greenlandic community with a hitherto undocumented, yet nevertheless very clear notion of boundary interest.

Local waters, global markets

The case of Greenex A/S[45] is perhaps the most relevant (as well as the most controversial) experience in the mining field involving a foreign company, the authorities and their negotiations with – or better, lack of negotiations – with the nearby community. Although some legal aspects of the case are not relevant to the contemporary legal framework, as it predated home rule, the case nevertheless sheds light on aspects of offshore interest in the coast and the wider sea-ice environment from the perspective of the local users, and suggests how a strained relationship may unfold between the interests of multinationals, the state, and a local population when and if the said population has not been properly informed about relevant extraction activities – specifically, informed about seasonal use and access to adjacent community coastal and sea corridors for the transportation of extracted resources to southern markets.

In autumn 1973, Greenex A/S commenced extraction of zinc and lead on the southern shore of the Qaumarujuk Fjord, in the vicinity of the municipality of Uummannaq. Local hunters using the fjord sea-ice areas in everyday harvesting often place overnight long-lines on the ice and also hunt for seals on the wider ice and at the floe edge adjacent to the mine. When a Greenex-contracted cargo transporter arrived and started breaking the ice while plotting a course into the fjord for the purpose of loading minerals, it was quickly obstructed by an improvised blockade of dog-sleds and local hunters. The hunters pointed out that the transporter's actions were scaring away all their prey and destroying their nets, while their fellow hunters further north were in danger of being set adrift should the vessel continue. A negotiator from nearby Uummannaq was soon called out to the site of the improvised blockade on the sea ice to mediate between the parties. Despite a temporary agreement being reached between the company and the local hunters, an official resolution between Greenex A/S and the authorities in Copenhagen failed to be reached. Not until an invitation was issued by the nearby municipality could an accord be signed between Greenex A/S and the residents of Uummannaq. In this case, it was not the mediation efforts of the authorities in Copenhagen, which served to facilitate a resolution to the dispute, but rather the repeated efforts of the municipality of Uummannaq to bring the company to the negotiation table.

It is also relevant to focus on the problems related to public involvement under the current self-governmental regime in Greenland. Just south of Uummannaq, in Qeqertarsuaq on Disko Island, the offshore environment constitutes both a niche for wildlife and crucial eco-systems as a feeding ground for annually returning bowhead whales, and a subsistence platform providing a range of ecosystem services for the local communities in the bay area. In legal terms, sea ice[46] defies categorisation due to its inherently overlapping qualities (where land meets sea); but more than this, local usage of sea ice also features as a sort of platform for social and ecological spheres of interaction and interest. Individual hunters and fishers express very clear notions of interest and ownership in specific sites, and these are often referred to not only by their place-names, but also via triangulations between sites on land and sea areas, and finally by individual or family catch-sites on the ice. Harvey Feit's observation that people's histories 'are part of both hunting and landscape making'[47] conveniently translates to Qeqertarsuarmiut narratives about the coast, and how these form a vital part both of fishing and of seascape-making. The people of Qeqertarsuaq have been poorly consulted about the exploration activities of Cairn Energy plc because that company's activities are headquartered at its main port of call, the town of Aasiaat at the southern mouth of the bay area. When prompted about their attitude to multinational oil exploration activities, however, local hunters and their families are quick to point out that, although most of the activities and possible future noise in local waters will be further offshore, everyone agrees that the 'food chamber' should not be disturbed. There are two important aspects to this question which require further elaboration when the role of community stakeholders is considered in relation to future offshore activities on the Greenlandic west coast. On the one hand, the concern expressed over increased noise pollution has not only been heard already in relation to the disappearance of marine mammals such as walrus, but it continues to be heard in the context of local observations of increased ship traffic and of how the associated noise activities, especially during the last decade, have often been cited in connection with the loss of ecological diversity. On the other hand, although offshore activities in Disko Bay have not (or at least not yet) occurred in close proximity to community hunting territories, coastal residents in the adjacent bay area have nevertheless expressed their concerns over the environmental impact by hinting at wider socio-ecological interdependencies as they affect the sustainability of the local eco-systems upon which they continue to rely for subsistence. This latter observation should, moreover, be considered in the light of recent research findings on the reception of the oil industry in Upernavik district. This research documented many hunters expressing the desire to continue their traditional hunting activities, rather than take up possible job opportunities in a future offshore oil venture on the west coast.[48]

Conclusion

The chapter has argued that the recognition of community understandings, and by that definition their human–ecological extensions or spheres of interest as these relate to the management of land–sea space continuums in coastal environments, may offer a way in which to reconnect historically fractured jurisdictional domains, while at the same time addressing questions of social exclusion, sustainable development and the governance of Arctic coastal areas. In endangering local systems of marine tenure and occupancy, proposed oil exploration and related industrial offshore activities pose a severe threat to Inuit livelihoods. In the Arctic, local systems of tenure and the constituent land, water and sea-ice ecosystem, are often at odds with encroaching developments, which, it can be argued, erode these and concomitantly 'could render the system unworkable.'[49]

In speaking to colonial and post-colonial 'cognised environments', Nuttall notes that sub-surface resources have long formed part of the 'cognised environment' of the imagined-community discourse in Greenland; because mining has occurred previously, in colonial times, aspects of the contemporary discourse are indeed informed by previous experiences and outcomes.[50] Perhaps this should come as no surprise, as many contemporary developments in Greenland tend to resemble historical case material, in that it continues to be the Greenlandic elites (the politicians and business leaders) and the international contractors (primarily the extractive industries) that are privileged to engage in the collective enterprise of imagining, deciding upon, and gradually actualising Greenland's future.[51] Though often muted, the local voice in this discourse must remain central in any assessment of the Arctic region's observance of the ILO Convention 169 and UNDRIP.

Historical material and fieldwork data on how questions of ownership are approached and expressed *in situ* suggest that when it comes to attitudes and lasting reservations among the local population about what will locally inevitably be perceived as external or extra-community demarcations of land or sea areas or tenured territories the local Inuit population will without a doubt attempt to interpret their rights by grounding them in collective interpretations of usage and ownership.

Integrated strategies for long-term land, sea and resource management in Greenland's offshore areas will be best achieved through due recognition of indigenous customary ownership in the coastal zone including the offshore islands, reefs, mulls and similar environments that continue to feature as backdrop both to indigenous coastal subsistence and to the sea-ice eco-systems. In reopening the case for historical and contemporary aspects of territorial ownership and user rights in Greenland as a topic of public concern, this chapter has emphasised the need for a considered and timely, appreciation of community interests (or claims) in the ownership of the coastal, sea and wider sea-ice environments – anchored, as they remain, in customary notions of tenure.

Notes

1 Ballard and Banks 2003.
2 Hansen and Bankes 2013.
3 Article 14, §1, my emphasis.
4 Hansen and Bankes 2013, 299.
5 Hansen and Bankes 2013, 301.
6 Inuit Nunangat is the regional definition adopted by the Inuit. It comprises the totality of land and sea space whose places are named by Inuit. See also Mulrennan and Scott 2000, 696.
7 Nyvold 2013.
8 Dahl 1998, 61.
9 Dahl 1998, 62.
10 Anderson 1983.
11 Olsvig 2014.
12 Brøsted 1986, 317.
13 Petersen 1963, 274.
14 Brøsted 1986, 328.
15 Brøsted 1986, 331.
16 Brøsted 1986, 328.
17 Mulrennan and Scott 2000, 694.
18 Dahl 1998, 61.
19 Petersen 1963, 270.
20 Ingold 1987, 223.
21 Brøsted 1985, 43–44, see also Petersen 1963, 1965.
22 Petersen 1965, Dahl 2000.
23 Petersen 1963.
24 Ingold 2000, 185.
25 Ingold 2000, 189.
26 Ingold 1987, 223.

27 Herskovits 1952, 322.
28 Strang 2000, 99.
29 Mulrennan and Scott 2000, 696.
30 See for example, Porsild 1921, 316; Dahl 2000.
31 Petersen 1963.
32 See also Petersen 1963, 274–275.
33 Field notes, Qeqertarsuaq, 5 February 2008.
34 Brøsted 1986, 330
35 Ingold 1987, 224.
36 Ingold 1987, 239.
37 Mulrennan and Scott 2000, 682, Pálsson 1993, Gaffin 1996.
38 Dahl 1998.
39 Dahl 1998, 63.
40 Dahl 1998, 63.
41 Dahl 1998, Sejersen 2001.
42 Sejersen 2001.
43 Tejsner 2014.
44 The MLSA was formerly known as the Bureau of Minerals and Petroleum (BMP).
45 Dahl 1977.
46 Baker and Mooney 2012.
47 Feit 2004, 94.
48 Hansen and Tejsner 2016.
49 Mulrennan and Scott 2000, 694.
50 Nuttall 2012, 120.
51 Sejersen 2015.

References

Anderson, B. 1983. *Imagined Communities*. London: Verso.

Baker, B.B. and S. Mooney. 2012. 'The Legal Status of Arctic Sea Ice in the United States and Canada.' *Polar Geography* 35 (1): 1–19.

Ballard, C. and G. Banks. 2003. 'Resource Wars: The Anthropology of Mining.' *Annual Review of Anthropology* 32: 287–313.

Brøsted, J. 1985. 'Territorial Rights in Greenland: Legal Basis – Viewpoints and Considerations.' *Nordisk Tidsskrift* 54: 43–51.

Brøsted, J. 1986. 'Territorial Rights in Greenland: Some Preliminary Notes.' *Arctic Anthropology* 23 (1): 325–338.

Dahl, J. 1977. *Minedrift i et Fangersamfund*. Copenhagen: Forlaget Kragestedet.

Dahl, J. 1998. 'Resource Appropriation, Territories and Social Control.' In *Aboriginal Environmental Knowledge in the North*, edited by L.-J. Dorais, M. Nagy and L. Müller-Wille, 61–80. Quebec: University of Laval Press.

Dahl, J. 2000. *Saqqaq: An Inuit Hunting Community in the Modern World*. Toronto: University of Toronto Press.

Feit, H.A. 2004. 'James Bay Crees' Life Projects and Politics: Histories of Place, Animal Partners and Enduring Relationships.' In *In The Way of Development: Indigenous Peoples, Life Projects and Globalisation*, edited by M. Blaser, H.A. Feit and G. McRae, 92–110. London: Zed Books.

Gaffin, D. 1996. In Place: Spatial and Social Order in Faeroe Islands Community. Long Grove: Waveland Press.

Hansen, K.F. and N. Bankes. 2013. 'Human Rights and Indigenous Peoples in the Arctic.' In *Arctic Oil and Gas: Sustainability at Risk?*, edited by A. Mikkelsen and O. Langhelle, 291–317. New York: Routledge.

Hansen, A.M. and P. Tejsner. 2016. 'Challenges and Opportunities for Residents in the Upernavik District While Oil Companies are Making a First Entrance in Baffin Bay.' *Arctic Anthropology* 53 (1): 84–94.

Herskovits, M.J. 1952. *Economic Anthropology*. London: Knopf.

Ingold, T. 1987. 'The Principle of Individual Autonomy and the Collective Appropriation of Nature.' Chapter 9. In *The Appropriation of Nature: Essays on Human Ecology and Social Relations*, edited by T. Ingold, 222–242. Manchester: Manchester University Press.

Ingold, T. 2000. *The Perception of the Environment: Essays on Livelihood, Dwelling and Skill*. London: Routledge.

Mulrennan, M.E. and C.H. Scott. 2000. '*Mare Nullius*: Indigenous Rights in Saltwater Environments.' *Development and Change* 31: 681–708.

Nuttall, M. 2012. 'Imagining and Governing the Greenlandic Resource Frontier.' *The Polar Journal* 2 (1): 113–124.

Nyvold, M. 2013. 'Bliver Benjamin og Sakæus hørt.' *Sermitsiaq* 38: 4.

Olsvig, S. 2014. Interview. P-1 Orientering, Danmarks Radio 1. Accessed 27 November 2014 at www.radio24syv.dk.

Pálsson, G., ed. 1993. 'Household Words: Attention, Agency and the Ethnography of Fishing.' In *Beyond Boundaries: Understanding, Translation and Anthropological Discourse*, edited by G. Pálsson, 117–140. Oxford: Berg.

Petersen, R. 1963. 'Family Ownership and Right of Disposition in Sukkertoppen District, West Greenland.' *Folk* 5: 269–281.

Petersen, R. 1965. 'Some Regulating Factors in the Hunting Life of Greenlanders.' *Folk* 7: 107–124.

Porsild, M.P. 1921. 'Godhavn Distrikt.' *Meddelser om Grønland* 60: 272–341.

Sejersen, F. 2001. 'Hunting and Management of Beluga Whales (*Delphinapterus Leucas*) in Greenland: Changing Strategies to Cope with New National and Local Interests.' *Arctic* 54: 431–443.

Sejersen, F. 2015. *Rethinking Greenland and the Arctic in the Era of Climate Change*. London: Routledge.

Strang, V. 2000. 'Not So Black and White: The Effects of Aboriginal Law on Australian Legislation.' In *Land, Law and Environment*, edited by A. Abramson and D. Theodossopoulos, 93–116. London: Pluto Press.

Tejsner, P. 2014. 'Quota disputes and subsistence whaling in Qeqertarsuaq, West Greenland.' *Polar Record* 50: 430–439.

Part IV

Regulatory instruments and enforcement

13 Impact benefit agreements and economic and environmental risk management in the Arctic

Vladimir Pacheco Cueva

Introduction

The past 30 years have witnessed a number of trends in the regulation of the extractive industries. On the one hand, the deregulation of investment and taxation rules around the world[1] has made the movement of capital from different parts of the world significantly easier for international investors, as exemplified by the large number of cross-border mergers and acquisitions (M&As).[2] Companies in the extractive industries have, therefore, been able to consolidate their position within the world economy and enjoy the benefits that monopolies possess, such as being able to influence national economic policies, as well as having, through rent-seeking,[3] inordinate political power at their disposal.[4]

On the other hand, the extractive industry's predominance in the global economy has been accompanied by an increasing abundance in forms of regulation. For instance, apart from being subject to state laws and international treaties,[5] the largest players in the industry currently also adhere to 'world's best practice' standards, guidelines and voluntary schemes. These practices are created by international industry bodies and international organisations such as the International Petroleum Industry Environmental Conservation Association (IPIECA)[6] and the International Association of Oil and Gas Producers (IOGP).[7] Even though, generally, there are no enforcement mechanisms, failing to comply with such standards may lead to reputational loss or cancellation of industry certification. Some industry-based standards have become so influential that they form the basis of government guidelines, and government align their regulations to be able to adhere to the industry standard. One example is the NORSOK Norwegian oil and gas industry set of standards, which forms the basis for Greenland's drilling and related guidelines.[8] Some voluntary schemes involve more than one industry. The Equator Principles, for instance, are used by private financial institutions – such as Eksport Kredit Fonden, BNP Paribas and the Royal Bank of Canada – to tie social and environmental criteria to loans made to natural resource extraction projects.[9] Multilateral financial institutions – such as the International Finance Corporation (IFC) and the

World Bank (WB) – have developed standards and guidelines with which borrowers must comply before obtaining finance for projects operating in the global South. This practice could also be relevant in future developments in the Arctic, because private financial institutions follow the lead of multilateral financial institutions in this respect.[10] On the other side of the spectrum are NGOs that promote principles such as Free, Prior and Informed Consent (FPIC) – which require companies to consult local communities before starting up new extraction projects[11] – or work to improve transparency in extractive industry transactions, as exemplified by the objectives of the Extractive Industries Transparency Initiative, EITI.[12] Among these overlapping and competing standards there is a governance model whose objectives are to reduce social and environmental conflicts related to extractive industries while at the same time giving all parties involved the opportunity to maximise, manage and monitor the benefits of resource extraction of a given resource project. This model is variously called Community Benefit Agreement (CBA), Impact and Benefit Agreement (IBA) or Economic Benefit Agreement (EBA), and it assumes a negotiated arrangement for the distribution of benefits arising out of resource extraction between nominally equal parties, i.e. companies, states and communities.[13] This form of negotiation falls within the realm of what, in legal pluralism, is called 'negotiated justice': a regime that provides legitimation and regulation without direct prescription from the state; or, as Szablowski puts it: "regimes in which decision-making is to a material extent the result of negotiations rather than the product of adjudication, administrative decision-making, or purely private, individual decision-making."[14]

Even though the number of IBAs in resource-extraction projects is increasing, this chapter will show how this form of regulation, despite all its advantages, really needs strengthening, integrating and aligning with existing governance mechanisms before it is applied wholesale to the Arctic offshore oil and gas industry.

Apart from local employment, one of the most crucial aspects in IBA negotiations is subcontracting levels. The first part of the chapter will therefore provide a brief account of subcontracting trends within the oil and gas industry. The following section will describe what IBAs are and will examine their potential to improve local sustainable development and environmental management in the offshore oil and gas industry in Canada and Greenland. The final section of the chapter will discuss ways to improve the governance of existing IBAs.

Current subcontracting and outsourcing trends in the oil and gas industry

A *Wall Street Journal* article published in mid-2015 reported that Exxon Mobil and BP had suspended their 'Canadian Arctic Exploratory Drilling Programme in the Beaufort Sea,' and that Chevron had made a similar decision in December 2014 due to 'high costs and regulatory hurdles'.[15] In Greenland, the self-government made the decision to halt new oil drilling licences in 2013.[16] These accounts give the impression that the search for oil and gas in the Arctic is in overall decline but interest in exploration from both companies and governments continues. For instance, in Greenland, the Oil Industry Association (representing 8 oil companies) boasts of currently possessing 10 offshore exploration licenses for West Greenland and 5 offshore exploration licenses for East Greenland.[17] TGS-Nopec Geophysical Company ASA conducted seismic testing offshore Northeast Greenland in 2015 and the company submitted an application to the Mineral License and Safety Authority for similar testing to be carried out in July and October 2016. The company has a prospecting license valid until 2018 (Center for Marine and Coastal Studies, 2015). This is all in line with the government of Greenland's 2014–2018 Oil and Mineral Strategy 'to further the chances of making a commercially viable oil find.'[18] In Canada, a CBC news item dated March 2016, reported that BP and Imperial Oil have lobbied the federal government "so that their 9-year licences to explore for oil in the deep waters of the Beaufort Sea can be extended to 16 years."[19]

While the price of international oil remains low, companies are likely to maintain a quiet drilling profile in both the Beaufort Sea and the waters surrounding Greenland, but this is liable to change at any time.[20] History shows that the price of commodities such as oil and gas is very volatile. Oil prices began to climb steeply after the first oil crisis in 1973 until the mid-1980s, when – as a result of increased production and falling demand – prices began to decrease. That trend changed in 1998, when prices started to increase only to drop again in 2014 (after a brief recovery from a 2008 slump), to the current low price of US$47 per barrel.[21] The international price for natural gas remained relatively stable at around US$3 per million British thermal units (mmBtu) from 1980 to the year 2000, when it started rising, until it reached a high of US$10 per mmBtu in 2008. The price then slumped to US$5 per mmBtu within a year, then rose to US$9 per mmBtu in 2012, and has been on a slow downward trend ever since to its current level of US$4.53per mmBtu.[22] Therefore it is possible that if prices for both of these commodities rise again and other positive conditions exist in the future,[23] industry interest in exploiting the Canadian and Greenlandic reserves may re-emerge.[24]

Alongside the ups and downs of commodity prices is the upward trend in oil and gas companies moving towards outsourcing in order to remain competitive. The trend started in the early 1990s, when major vertically integrated companies around the world began the practice of sourcing from specialist firms, services and products that the 'verticals' did not consider part of their core competencies.[25] A major oil company can, for instance, contract a major catering company to provide meals for workers at oil rigs instead of organising this activity in-house. The advantage for the oil company is that it can focus on its areas of expertise and hire others to provide peripheral services. At the same time, worldwide deregulation of investment in services and the information technology revolution facilitated the establishment of companies in low-wage countries with highly educated workforces to supply some of these specialist services. The global market size of outsourced services has more than doubled from US$45.6 billion in the year 2000 to US$104.6 billion in 2014,[26] and the locations of these services are clustered in a few cities in India, China, the Philippines, Eastern Europe, Russia, Ireland and Latin America. A large proportion of the outsourcing for the oil and gas industry is carried out by large consulting companies such as Electronic Data Systems (currently trading as EDS), Tata Consulting Services and Chevron Holdings.[27]

At the beginning of the outsourcing trend mentioned earlier, information technology services formed the bulk of contracts, but now these include both upstream services such as oil and gas technical data and engineering and downstream services such as improving refinery performance and helping companies comply with health, safety and environmental standards (HSE).[28] The widening of options means that these companies are now starting to compete with older and more established suppliers to the oil and gas industry like the large EPCM consultancies, such as ABB, Chiyoda, Bechtel and SNC Lavalin, and the large accounting and auditing firms, such as EY, KPMG, PwC and Deloitte.[29]

Even though large oil and gas companies tend to contract out to large contractors, not all outsourcing goes to them. There is a vast array of smaller companies that perform similar functions on a smaller scale. These services include human resources, back-office support, maintenance, training, drilling, rig operations, surveying, labour hire, sea and air transport, catering, communications, health and emergency services, project management, materials and supply management, storage, waste management and environmental services, among others. These smaller companies also service many second- and third-tier oil and gas companies. Another distinguishing feature of the smaller companies is that they are more likely to be located closer to the point of resource extraction and are therefore found in rural and remote communities.

Opportunities and challenges with local subcontracting and outsourcing

In the Canadian Arctic, examples of these smaller companies abound, and include businesses owned by indigenous peoples and communities, such as the Arctic Oil and Gas Services (AOGS, a subsidiary of the Inuvialuit Development Corporation)[30] and Dehcho Regional Helicopters, an aviation company that has formed a partnership with Air Tindi, a larger company offering air transport services to oil and gas companies and other clients.[31] In Nunatsiavut, Nachyak Supply & Services Inc. provides and manages supplies (lubricants, greases, bottled gases and chemicals) to the petroleum industry.[32] In Greenland, there are many operators working with oil and gas companies such as Arctic Base Supplies (logistics) and KK Engross (food supplies and catering). Many of these companies have been working with oil and gas companies in the offshore exploration phase, and are expected to continue working with them through to the exploitation phase if that ever occurs. However, even during the exploration phase there is room to improve the current levels of local-contractor participation. For instance, Cairn Energy, a UK company active in Greenland, spent only 11 per cent of a total expenditure of US$1.2 billion on locally based suppliers,[33] and in Canada, Imperial Oil has spent a similar percentage out of an estimated US$1.7 billion in total exploration costs.[34] The companies usually blame low levels of local-contractor participation and local-content purchasing on lack of local supplies, expertise and know-how. However, in many cases, large oil and gas companies simply 'inherit' relationships with international suppliers even if local supplies, expertise and know-how can be found locally, or they might prefer to simplify the procurement process by dealing with one large supplier rather than many small ones.[35]

State regulation has a lot to do with this situation. Regulation that is weak or does not determine a certain level of local content[36] and participation in oil and gas projects provides ample room for companies to decide how much of their inputs will be sourced locally and internationally.[37] Many jurisdictions beyond the Arctic are addressing this problem in all sorts of ways. In Australia, for instance, a deal between EDS and the government of South Australia stipulates that EDS has to invest 10 per cent of its generated outsourcing revenue into the state's economic growth.[38] In Papua New Guinea, mining companies are obliged not only to comply with local content and employment rules, but also to monitor and publish the figures.[39] The latest Greenland Oil and Mineral Strategy (2014–2018) includes significantly enhanced local-content requirements,[40] and the government of the Northwest Territories (GNWT) in Canada has introduced a Business Incentive Policy (BIP), which provides tax credits for companies that demonstrate that a sufficient dollar value of their local labour, goods and services expenditure, as well as that of all subcontractors and suppliers proposed in a bid, is spent within the NWT.[41]

Even though increasing local content and participation in offshore oil and gas projects is possible via a combination of company corporate social responsibility commitments and state regulation, the resulting levels leave a lot to be desired, as the examples of Cairn Energy in Greenland and Imperial Oil in Canada show. Rogers and Cooley mention other factors that companies take into account when making decisions about choosing suppliers: value of currency – and its fluctuations – as well as high duties, tariffs and import taxes, benefits in terms of time, cash flow, flexibility, geographical or logistical barriers such as port infrastructure, ice management, cost of local sources, technology and labour.[42] At the height of the Greenland mineral exploration boom in 2012, logistics, lack of beds and high prices for local contractors were cited by company CEOs as challenges to getting more local content. Nick Rose, CEO of Avannaa Resources, for instance, complained about the prices of local subcontractors, adding that: "we have noticed that there aren't enough Greenlandic companies... We would otherwise like to hire them, but it should be on competitive terms."[43]

Another CEO, Nicholas Hall, from Angel Mining said: "There isn't much competition. Pricing in Greenland is generally higher than what we would pay in a competitive market."[44]

Many of the factors mentioned above by Rogers and Cooley are beyond the control of municipal councils or even national governments, so they too find themselves limited in what they can do to increase local content and thus improve the chances of economic development. Yet perhaps the most problematic of all of these aspects is that neither the authorities nor the oil and gas companies can claim that local-content policies and practices, even when successfully implemented, will guarantee a long-lasting developmental effect when applied on their own. The reason for this is that once the mineral resource becomes depleted, whatever the local capacity created to service the needs of the licensee cannot easily be transferred to many other industries. In other words, increasing economic activity for the sake of supplying an industry that is unsustainable cannot, without proper planning instruments and objectives, lead to sustainable local development. Many governments claim to have a long-term planning capacity, but in democratic societies – such as Canada and Greenland – many of the plans are related only to the duration of the election periods of the political parties in power. In many situations, the policy objectives may be well identified, but the accompanying set of instruments to carry out the policy may not match. And there is also the problem of lack of representation in policy-formation processes as a result of bureaucratically derived or 'top-down' policies lacking sufficient citizen or community input.[45] Cases where the licensee, the competent authorities and the affected communities have been able to achieve a shared vision of development *and* to successfully implement the policies that emanate from that shared vision are far and few, as the resource-curse literature shows in regard to national development.[46] So far, the most promising example of success in regard to local economic development comes in the form of the various IBAs signed in the Canadian Arctic for mining projects such as the Raglan mine in northern Quebec,[47] and IBAs in Greenland such as those signed by Cairn Energy's subsidiary, Capricorn Greenland Exploration, in 2010 and 2011.[48]

Are IBAs effective local sustainable development and environmental management tools?

Before answering this question, we need to look at IBAs more closely. In Chapter 14, Mortensen examines IBAs in Greenland in great detail, so this chapter will only provide a brief mention of their major characteristics and will concentrate on examining Canadian IBAs.

In various parts of the world, IBAs are legally binding agreements entered into between the communities most impacted by the resource project and the resource developer, with the intention of maximising, managing and monitoring the benefits of resource extraction for all parties involved. In many ways, IBAs integrate in a single package disparate benefit-sharing mechanisms that have developed in the extractive industries over the years. These IBAs may include conditions on local employment, compensation, community investments, procurement, beneficiation, multi-use infrastructure and community funds, trusts and foundations.[49] The prevalence of these agreements in the extractive industries shows that they have the potential to address some enduring social and economic problems faced by minorities, indigenous and rural and remote communities around the world.[50]

In Greenland, IBAs must be negotiated between the government of Greenland (Naalakkersuisut) and the licensee; they may include, at the discretion of Naalakkersuisut, the affected municipalities.[51] The final IBA document must explain how the project will contribute to the economic and social development of the impacted communities and of Greenland as a whole, and how these contributions will be measured and achieved. Some of the contributions taken into account in the current IBAs include: direct and indirect employment, involvement of local enterprises, knowledge transfer, education, research, work experience, and social and cultural well-being.[52] Apart from Capricorn Greenland Exploration, a number of mining companies are in the negotiation stages or have finalised agreements. For instance, London Mining Greenland A/S is currently in the process of negotiation,[53] and True North Gems signed its IBA in 2014.[54]

In Canada, IBAs are negotiated between the resource-project proponent and the landowners.[55] In principle, the agreements are ad hoc and not required by legislation, unless they involve land where ownership has been settled and granted to an indigenous land claimant.[56] In either case, it is becoming increasingly difficult for an extractive company to obtain a licence without an agreement with the affected community. In other words, even though the use of IBAs is not mandatory based on state legislation, they are an essential part of the social licensing process and projects cannot proceed if an agreement is not reached. The agreements include items such as employment, procurement, training, cultural well-being, the traditional economy, sustainable development and monitoring and evaluation of impacts. Apart from the Raglan mine, other projects that have agreements in place include the following: DeBeers Gahcho Kué Project, Canadian Zinc Prairie Creek Mine, Dominion Diamond Ekati Mine, Diavik Diamond Mine, DeBeers Snap Lake Project and the Mackenzie Gas Project.[57] In fact, this is only a small sample of the total. In a 2010 study, the World Bank found that Canada 'had over 150 projects with signed exploration agreements or IBAs in the country.'[58] From an indigenous standpoint, the agreements benefit local development by increasing the level of participation of the otherwise socially and economically disadvantaged indigenous population. For instance, 54 per cent of the total workforce at the Voisey's Bay nickel project, in Labrador, are local Inuit, and the IBA related to this project allows the community to save into a 'sustainability' trust to ensure future income after the project closes.[59] At the Diavik diamond mine in the Northwest Territories, O'Faircheallaigh reports that: "during the first six years after its construction started in 2000, [the mine] spent in excess of C$1 billion with Aboriginal businesses."[60]

The Inuvialuit Regional Corporation signed IBAs in 1995, 1996 and 2009 with Darnley Bay Resources Ltd to mine nickel, copper, platinum-group metals and diamonds in their lands.[61] In 2000, the Inuvik Community Corporation, based in the town of Inuvik, signed an agreement with Chevron Canada Resources to explore and develop natural gas in the Inuvik area. The agreement, worth over C$43.5 million, included royalties, surface-access fees, local gas-use provisions and prioritisation of contracts with Inuvialuit businesses.[62] In 2012, Imperial Oil – representing the Beaufort Sea Exploration Joint Venture, along with BP and Exxon Mobil – expressed, in the Preparatory Information Package (PIP)[63] for Exploration Licence (EL) 476 (Ajurak) and EL 477 (Pokak), their commitment to "support, *to the extent possible,* existing and new local businesses, employment, education and training and to provide a 'transparent and fair procurement and contract award process."[64] In the same section of the document, the company:

> considers local content to be an important component of its business and employment strategy for the programme because it gives Imperial the ability to offer meaningful opportunities for community members to participate and benefit from the programme.[65]

From the foregoing, it is clear that, even at the low levels of subcontractor expenditure found in the cases of Cairn Energy in Greenland and Imperial Oil in Canada, IBAs can be used as mechanisms to improve local development, but of a type that is not necessarily sustainable. Also, even though many of these agreements include environmental monitoring clauses, they are rarely stipulated at the same level of scrutiny that an Environmental Impact Assessment (EIA) requires of project proponents. This is a problem particularly in Canada, because the IBA process is not sufficiently integrated with the EIA process.[66] In actual fact, authors such as Fidler and Hitch have argued that the IBA negotiation process (which aims at maximising community benefits from a project) when carried out separately from an EIA process (which aims at avoiding or mitigating a project's adverse biophysical and social impacts) can undermine the effectiveness of the latter, because the IBA may not make environmental considerations a priority.[67] IBAs in Inuit areas are no different, since these agreements: "are primarily intended to ensure that Inuit benefit from mining and other developmental projects and are compensated for the expected negative impacts of those projects on communities, land and traditional way of life."[68]

Given the above description of the IBAs, the next section will discuss a number of areas that may reinforce the governance of IBAs, and therefore make them more suited to improving local sustainable development and improving environmental management.

Factors to improve IBA governance

Two governance areas need to be mentioned when discussing improvement of offshore-project IBAs. The first area has to do with improvements of the design of IBAs as a government tool to improve local sustainable development and to align the content of the IBAs with the government's larger planning processes; the other refers to exogenous or external parts of the process, such as environmental governance, maintenance of autonomous political identity, and avoiding inequality.

Endogenous factors in IBA making

Despite the increasing number of IBAs and the relative success in improving local economic participation (especially in regard to local employment and, to a certain degree, local subcontractors), the effectiveness of IBAs is largely dependent on the negotiating power of the community, municipal or national government. As a result, so far, there is 'no predetermined outcome resulting from this type of mining-communities negotiation,'[69] which means that even though IBAs have the potential to improve local development, this may not always be the case. This applies especially to environmental management, and holds despite all the legislative apparatus and IBA environmental mitigation clauses that are designed to protect the environment.[70] To this end, it is imperative that national governments provide the necessary advisory, technical and legal infrastructure to decrease the power and information asymmetries that exist between communities or local governments/ municipal councils and the companies. The Inuvialuit and other Inuit in Canada are now experienced at negotiating with oil and gas companies, but this was not always the case.[71] In Greenland, municipal councils, when they are involved, sign IBAs in conjunction with Naalakkersuisut. Ideally, this association *should* give municipal councils access to technical and legal expertise, but this is not currently the case.[72] Unfortunately, the level of knowledge and skills required to negotiate agreements is not something that small remote communities elsewhere in the Arctic readily possess, or that is easily accessible to them. Therefore, for agreements to become effective tools of local sustainable development, it is necessary to avoid a situation in which one party enters an agreement with no prior negotiating skills and knowing little about the judicial mechanisms already available to it to support its case in the negotiations, or to support its withdrawal from the process.[73]

Within this area, one aspect that needs to be clarified by governments is the need to make negotiations more inclusive and transparent.[74] In Canada, community leaders at the local levels carry out negotiations on behalf of their constituents and, in ideal circumstances, should give constituents the right to have the knowledge needed in respect to the contents and process of the negotiations as they occur, and to object if they so desire.[75] The spirit of the negotiations should be such that confidentiality clauses embedded in Canadian IBAs should not harm the interests of indigenous community members and of the broader public.[76] In Greenland, the licensee must submit a Social Sustainability Assessment (SSA) and on the basis of the SSA recommendations, an IBA must be negotiated.[77] The final document, once an agreement is reached, becomes part of the public domain.[78] On a procedural basis alone, Greenlandic IBAs may look more transparent and amenable to public input than their Canadian counterparts. However, many observers have argued that this is far from the case,[79] and the situation may be worsening. As recently as 2014, the government tabled a proposal to reduce public access to information relating to raw materials.[80]

It is also important that, whether through legislated means or policy instruments, the process of IBA negotiation is aligned, as O'Faircheallaigh argues, with formal 'broader processes for community planning and decision-making.'[81] This is of special relevance to Greenland only in those cases where agreements include a municipal council, as these local authorities already have planning processes in place.[82] For instance, some observers argue for the development of 'flexible settlements' near a mine, or the closest onshore location to offshore operations, in order to resolve housing shortages in Greenlandic towns.[83] If this proposal was ever considered by a municipality as part of its planning objectives, then the development of flexible settlements would, ideally, have to be part and parcel of any IBA negotiation with the licensee. This also applies to plans for increasing local subcontractor participation in offshore oil and gas projects, since simply engaging more subcontractors may make the local economy over-dependent on the fate of the licensee. Identifying larger national and global trends in subcontracting and outsourcing can help communities and municipal governments integrate these trends into their own development plans, improve their bargaining position vis-à-vis the licensee, and expand their choices. For instance, oil and gas companies' reliance on subcontracting FOC-registered ships and oil platforms forms part of a global subcontracting trend within the industry, which severely curtails the ability of governments to implement local content and employment rules.[84] Greenland and Canada also face forgone tax revenues, as they cannot apply their tax laws to vessels that are not registered under their jurisdiction – and make no use of those countries' resources – thus missing opportunities to fund sustainable development projects in their own territories.[85] In other words, it is important to know how particular types of subcontracting fit with longer and strategic planning efforts at the municipal and national levels. For instance, in comparing the subcontracting of local firms to build accommodation for offshore workers with subcontracting to carry out maintenance on FOC-registered vessels, it becomes clear that the former provides skills and training that can be used at a later stage by the local workforce for other housing projects in-country, whereas the skills and training acquired in the latter can only be transferred effectively if there is strong domestic demand in the local vessel fleet. In most cases, however, FOC registration allows vessel owners to employ third-country nationals[86] to carry out maintenance tasks, thus circumventing the need to pay them Canadian or Greenlandic wages.

A subset of long-term community and local-government planning is closure planning for offshore projects. Companies now know with much certainty how long it will take to extract a resource in a particular location, and they plan accordingly. Communities and municipal councils (especially those reliant on single-resource projects) should, in their own planning exercises, make this their most important long-term planning consideration.[87] Offshore-project closure planning needs to consider the factors required for a successful economic transition from being dependent on a single resource to becoming more economically diverse while improving the sustainability of current economic activities. This type of planning also needs to consider appropriate monitoring mechanisms that tell communities if and when social and economic goals are achieved. Long-term community planning and monitoring is significant because most Arctic formal economies are already highly dependent on a single or few commodities. For instance, fish and shellfish make up 85 percent of Greenland's exports.[88] It is therefore essential that project closure planning and broader economic planning are integrated and support existing drivers of the formal economy. As a final point, IBAs should be subject to existing global standards like the ones mentioned at the beginning of this chapter, especially as they apply to long-term planning, transparency, human rights issues, security, environmental management, local participation and sustainability.

All these extra planning tasks are difficult to implement, and require a certain level of institutional capacity. This is a problem for the Greenlandic public administration which, until only recently, has had to consider large, complex projects. In his analysis of the proposed ALCOA aluminium smelter, Hansen argues that the Greenlandic authorities showed a degree of improvisation and agility in dealing with the proposal and that 'in several cases, the necessary procedures have been invented on the run'. The downside of this is that the project proponent has been able to take advantage of this on-the-run approach and has, in many cases, had 'an easy play.'[89] Similarly, one of the most important recommendations in the 2014 report *To the Benefit of Greenland* is that the institutional capacity of the Greenlandic public administration needs to be improved so as to be able to deal effectively with large-scale resource-extraction projects.[90]

So far, the foregoing has touched on only two relevant endogenous aspects of agreement-making that need improvement, but there are many others that for reasons of space cannot be included in this chapter. In this regard, perhaps the best resource is the newly released IBA Toolkit, developed by the Gordon Foundation in Canada and available at the foundation's website.[91] This unique toolkit is designed to help communities and civil-society organisations strengthen their negotiation power and knowledge base vis-à-vis companies using existing regulatory mechanisms.

Exogenous factors in IBA making

Exogenous areas in agreement-making are governance mechanisms that are not explicitly related to IBAs, but nevertheless affect their effectiveness. The focus here is on environmental governance and issues to do with political autonomy and inequality.

In terms of environmental governance it is important that national governments support communities and/or municipal councils in starting to negotiate IBAs as early as possible in the project lifecycle, and certainly in conjunction with the EIA process, rather than after it, as is the case in both Canada and Greenland. Reorganising the order of events will allow the negotiating parties some time to determine each other's goodwill in sharing the potential benefits of the proposed project, as well as a 'cooling off' period before economic commitments are made.[92] The objective of this move is to establish some level of trust between the negotiating parties.

IBAs in offshore oil and gas projects should be subject to integrated resource planning in addition to long-term community and/or local policy-planning processes in order to make sure that the project is carried out within a previously nationally agreed approach to environmental risk-taking. Bouchard and Delisle argue that an integrated resource planning (IRP) approach could be used for resource projects in the oil and gas industry, just as it is currently applied to renewable energy projects in Canada. The IRP is an analysis that allows for 'smart growth decisions at lower risks and environmental costs' through the ranking of lower-cost alternative projects and internationalisation of externalities 'which may or may not be monetised.'[93]

In terms of political autonomy, IBAs and other forms of negotiated justice give rise to political and legal identities that confer specific economic and ownership rights on certain communities. This kind of economic regime or 'the kind and degree of political recognition that is conferred by a legal order on those who are subject to it' limits communities' capacity to access other forms of rights.[94] In other words, once a potentially affected population enters into an IBA agreement with a company, it becomes a 'holder of stakes' in the proposed project, at the expense of being a 'holder of rights' that are independent of the interests of the project. In this regard, some experts advise indigenous landowners in Canada to reflect carefully before moving to accept an agreement. For instance, Nancy Morgan, from Morgan and Associates, says:

> [Y]ou need to decide what your First Nation's priorities are so you can determine when you want to negotiate arrangements with governments or third parties and when you want to oppose a project or initiative because it will have too significant an impact on your First Nation.[95]

But the same author warns:

> However, by consenting to a project or entering into an agreement, *you may be limiting your ability to advance a legal claim at a later date opposing the project based on your aboriginal rights.* It is likely that governments and third parties would use such an agreement to show that you were consulted, your interests were accommodated and you were provided with the opportunity to share in the economic benefits.[96]

The decision to become a stakeholder in a project can also lead to other problems. In preparing for negotiating an agreement, indigenous communities realise that benefit-sharing is only possible through the legal recognition of traditional titles.[97] From traditional systems that are imprecise and fluid, they move to systems that are precise and rigid. Many times, this transition leads to divisions and conflict before the project starts, and this situation permeates all phases of the project's lifecycle. Later on in the project, the distribution of benefits becomes a highly contested affair among indigenous leaders, which may lead to internal disputes. In this regard, a World Bank study on IBAs found that indigenous organisations in charge of managing and distributing resource rents: "are characterised by political infighting and devote a disproportionate amount of their time and resources on litigation and legal expenses."[98]

Some of the infighting can be traced to community members not knowing the details of the agreements and relates to problems of representation, increasing inequality between members and, as mentioned above, transparency. In this regard Prno, Bradshaw and Lapierre say that in Canada:

> [T]he details of IBAs are not well known in communities due to the confidentiality of these agreements or due to limited information-sharing by Aboriginal organisations. This makes it difficult for community members to know if they are receiving what they are entitled to.[99]

Increasing inequality also creates problems for indigenous communities in Canada because IBAs, as Shanks points out: "are not effective instruments for wealth distribution… [as] some will benefit from participating in the wage economy, but others will be disproportionably affected by its negative effects."[100]

A related problem is the regional inequalities that are created as a result of the way IBAs distribute benefits. Both in Canada and Greenland, IBAs invariably give greater precedence to the interests of some communities or municipalities over the interest of non-affected communities or municipalities, and this may exacerbate problems such as joblessness and economic migration.[101]

As IBAs are negotiated by Naalakkersuisut – and sometimes, the municipalities – the transformation of communities from being rights holders to being stakeholders in resource projects is less of a problem in Greenland. Still, the problem of unequal local development persists in both jurisdictions. It is therefore important that the existing regulatory structures are strengthened to ensure that benefits from IBAs, such as employment, procurement, royalties and infrastructure development are not disproportionately going to one area and creating massive inequalities between the different areas. It is also important that organisations in charge of managing and distributing resource rents become subject to transparency and accountability mechanisms already in place; or, in their absence, that new ones be established to deal with this type of organisations. As a final point, it is essential that the governance structures allow communities to maintain autonomous political identities that are separate from market identities when resource-extraction decisions are being made. In Canada, for instance, companies seem to prefer treating indigenous communities as 'stakeholders' in order to obtain approval for their projects, despite the existence of reconciliation legislation that gives indigenous communities rights beyond economic interests.[102]

Conclusion

This chapter has shown that IBAs offer a model for market-driven, local-level sustainable development, especially among indigenous peoples. Looking at their respective local expenditures, it is evident that both Imperial Oil and Cairn use local subcontracting, but not in a manner that ensures optimal local benefits. Neither company's level of local expenditure is particularly high when compared to the total level of expenditure. This indicates that local contractors working with these companies are benefiting only from a small proportion of the exploration expenditure that occurs in the Beaufort Sea and the waters surrounding Greenland. There is also no indication that this type of subcontracting will support the development of sustainable economies for Inuvialuit and Greenland.

Another important point made in this chapter is that despite the increasing amount of regulation occurring at the international and national levels as exemplified by the enactment of various international treaties, industry standards and national laws designed to protect the Arctic environment and its people, it seems that IBAs used for onshore projects in Canada are not sufficiently aligned with existing planning, reconciliation and environmental regulations. Given that some of the research indicates that IBAs offshore are being signed voluntarily, the following question must be posed: should onshore IBAs be used as models for offshore oil and gas projects?

In Greenland, IBAs suffer because there is limited institutional capacity and local communities' involvement is weak. IBAs in offshore projects should therefore not proceed until reasonable improvements are achieved in the negotiating, planning and implementing capacities of Greenlandic institutions – to ensure that local procurement, expenditure and taxes from resource-extraction activities are maximised. Similarly, improvements in citizen involvement and transparency must be made in order to ensure that offshore projects obtain a social licence to operate.

As a last point, if national governments with a stake in the Arctic are interested in improving the chances of success with local sustainable development and environmental management without having to establish, implement and enforce more layers of regulation, then more needs to be done to integrate and align the IBA model of local development with existing regulation. Oil and gas companies wanting to do likewise should start by not avoiding their legal tax obligations and by adhering to section 7.3 of the Circumpolar Inuit Declaration on Resource Development Principles in Inuit Nunaat: "the proponent of a resource development project bears the burden of demonstrating that the proposed development is sustainable."[103]

Notes

1 The first wave of deregulation in Greenland occurred when, through Danish Law #203 of 1969, companies could be exempted from paying taxes on earnings from mining activities (Hansen 2014: 141). The second wave of deregulation started in the early 1990s with further revisions of mining and taxation laws. According to Poole, Pretes and Sinding other changes included the 'conversion of Royal Greenland, the Home Rule Authority's trawling, production and sales enterprise, and other public enterprises into limited companies' (Poole, Pretes and Sinding 1992, 191 and 197). Nowadays, apart from NunaOil, all of the oil and gas companies operating in Greenland are foreign owned. See www.govmin.gl/images/stories/minerals/list_of_licences/list_of_licences.pdf.

In Canada, the process of deregulation started earlier. From 1985 onwards, targeted taxes to oil and gas were abolished, the federal government sold its shares in Petro-Canada to national and international investors, and the signing of the Canada–US Free Trade Agreement meant the Canadian federal government could no longer impose sales taxes on oil and gas exporters (Plourde 2010, 7). As a result, the stock of foreign direct investment (FDI) grew from US$10.4 billion in 1985 to US$33.7 billion in 2005 (UNCTAD 2007, 103).

2 From 1990 to 2006, cross-border M&As in oil and gas accounted for almost three-quarters of all such deals in extractive industries worldwide. In mining and quarrying, cross-border M&As reached a record value of $55 billion in 2006 (UNCTAD 2007, 100).

3 Poole, Pretes and Sinding (1992, 198) define rent-seeking as 'any activity that attempts to improve a person or group's well-being by escaping the forces of competition in the market place.'

4 This is clearest in the oil sector. Of the 100 largest transnational corporations ranked by sales, the top four are oil companies (UNCTAD 2007, 25). In the

minerals sector, 149 metal mining companies out of 4,000 worldwide account for 'some 60 percent of the total value at the mining stage of all non-energy minerals produced' (UNCTAD 2007, 108–109).

5 See Basse, Pelaudeix, Baker and Sidortsov, this volume. One example of an international convention safeguarding life at sea that applies to industry is the SOLAS Convention (IMO, 2015).

6 IPIECA has produced a number of guidelines for the oil and gas industry. These include, among others: The Oil and Gas Industry Guidance on Voluntary Sustainability Reporting; Good Practices for the Collection of Biodiversity Baseline Data; Response Strategy Development Using Net Environmental Benefit Analysis (NEBA); The Good Practice Guidelines for Incident Management and Emergency Response Personnel. For a full list see www.ipieca.org/library?tid_1%5B%5D=12&date_filter%5Bvalue%5D%5Byear%5D=&k.

7 Instead of creating its own guidelines, the IOGP urges its members to adhere to procedures set by the International Standards Organisation (ISO) for the various processes found within the industry. ISO 3183:2007, for instance, specifies the characteristics of steel pipelines for pipelines transportation systems, whereas ISO 3977–5:2001 applies to procurement procedures of gas turbines. The full list can be found at www.ogp.org.uk/pubs/4210.pdf.

8 Dagg et al. 2011, 36. See Greenland Exploration Drilling Guidelines at: https://www.govmin.gl/petroleum/approval-of-activities/exploration-drilling. The NORSOK standards for petroleum can be found at www.standard.no/en/sectors/energi-og-klima/petroleum/.

9 The full list of principles can be found on the Equator Principles Association website. According to the association, 81 financial institutions in 36 countries have officially adopted the principles. This effectively covers over 70 percent of international project finance debt in emerging markets. www.equator-principles.com/index.php/about-ep/about-ep.

10 It is pertinent to add that the latest version of the Equator Principles (EPIII), published in 2013, has adopted many of the IFC's Performance Standards. http://www.equator-principles.com/index.php/ep3.

11 Szablowski 2010.

12 As of 2015, neither Canada nor Greenland are part of the EITI. However, many companies operating therein and elsewhere in the Arctic are registered in countries that are part of the initiative. These include Norway, the United States and the UK. For a full list see https://eiti.org/countries.

13 A World Bank study has identified at least 15 different terms for this type of agreement around the world (ERM 2010, 16). In Greenland the term Impact Benefit Agreement (IBA) is used, whereas in Canada the terms include Participation Agreement, Impact Benefit Agreement and Benefit Agreement (Indigenous Bar Association, cited in Knotsch and Warda 2009, 10). For the purposes of this chapter they will be referred to as Impact Benefit Agreements (IBAs).

14 Szablowski 2010, 113.

15 Dawson 2015.

16 MacAlister 2013.

17 See www.goia.gl/en-us/reportsandpresentations.aspx.

18 Naalakkersuisut 2014a, 7.

19 See www.cbc.ca/news/canada/north/beaufort-sea-inuvialuit-oil-gas-licence-review-1.3506808. In order to facilitate oil and gas exploration in the Beaufort Sea Jeremko 2014 reports that companies are lobbying the federal government to abandon "the same season relief well capability." This safety requirement gives companies time to drill a second well when an accident happens to "siphon off a blowout before the end of a summer work season."

20 The decline in drilling activity does not mean that exploratory drilling has ceased. To the contrary. See www.cbc.ca/news/canada/north/imperial-oil-bp-delay-beaufort-sea-drilling-plans-indefinitely-1.3129505.
21 Pacheco 2015, 232, UNCTAD 2007, 88, and Milne, Adams and Crooks 2015. Current price level based on NASDAQ's Crude Oil WTI (NYMEX). See www.nasdaq.com/markets/crude-oil.aspx.
22 Prices based on the UKNBP Index. See www2.nationalgrid.com/UK/Industry-information/Future-of-Energy/FES/Winter-Outlook/ and www.bp.com/en/global/corporate/energy-economics/statistical-review-of-world-energy.html.
23 Some of these positive conditions include: capping liability costs associated with oil spills clean up (US), maintaining low royalty rates (all jurisdictions in the Arctic), not imposing a carbon tax (all jurisdictions in the Arctic), maintaining favourable exploration block leasing terms (Canada and Greenland), providing direct support for state owned companies (Russia) and constructing better infrastructure such as large deep water ports (all jurisdictions except Norway): Byers 2015; Naalakkersuisut 2014a, 10–11; Wilson Centre no date, 12–13.
24 Elsewhere in the Arctic, companies such as Shell in Alaska, Statoil and Rosneft in Norway and Cairn in Greenland continue their drilling campaigns in order to, in the short term, secure reserve ratios (Byers 2015) and, in the long term, have access to the vast resources in the region (Byers 2015; Schaps 2015), which according to a US Geological Survey may amount to '90 billion barrels of oil, 1,669 trillion cubic feet of natural gas, and 44 billion barrels of natural gas liquids'. Of this total, 'approximately 84 percent is expected to occur in offshore areas' (Bird et al. 2008, 1). See also Mooney 2015.
25 Hirschheim and Heinzl 2002.
26 Statista 2015.
27 Ravago 2007, 8–9.
28 In a vertically integrated extractive company, upstream services are those that are close to the point of extraction (ores, crude oil, natural gas, coal, etc.), while downstream services are those related to further processing of the original resource (refineries, smelters, foundries, etc.).
29 EPCM stands for Engineering, Procurement, Construction and Management and refers to firms that are engaged in all aspects of a project's lifecycle. These firms enter into a contractual relationship with the resource developer or licence holder to design, build and manage resource projects but do not own the resource itself.
30 Inuvialuit Development Corporation subsidiaries that work closely with oil and gas companies include: Inukshuk Geomatics Inc., Akita Equatak Drilling Ltd., Inuvialuit Oilfield Services and IEG Consultants. The full list of subsidiaries can be found at http://www.idc.inuvialuit.com/our-companies/
31 See http://dehchoregional.com/.
32 Nachvak Supply & Services Inc. entry under the Nunatsiavut business directory: http://www.nunatsiavut.com/business/inuit-business-directory/.
33 Cairn Energy 2011, 117, and Kay and Thorup 2014.
34 CBS News 2013.
35 Rogers and Cooley 2004, 2.
36 Local-content rules include regulation and/or policy measures that determine a certain percentage of intermediate goods used in the process of extraction to be sourced from local or domestic suppliers. The final objective of this type of regulation is to increase local employment levels, widen the economic base of regions and countries, and strengthen local suppliers vis-à-vis foreign suppliers (Hackenbruch and Davis, 2011, 2).

37 Oil and gas industry usage of oil platforms registered in FOCs may be impacting the ability of governments in Greenland and Canada to enforce local content and employment regulation.
38 Hirschheim and Heinzl 2002, 6.
39 Pacheco 2015, 231.
40 Naalakkersuisut 2014a, and Kay and Thorup 2014.
41 GNWT 2013.
42 Rogers and Cooley 2004, 2.
43 Nyvold 2012, 30.
44 Ibid., 30.
45 Wake 2013, iii.
46 Rosser 2006, 7.
47 Roy Grégoire 2013.
48 Naalakkersuisut, 2010 and Mortensen, this volume.
49 IFC 2010, 10, 109 and Pacheco 2012, 747. In some instances, IBAs may include the sharing of royalties between various levels of government and the affected communities and the sharing of taxes between various levels of government. In Newfoundland Labrador, the provincial government requires a Benefits Agreement be signed between it and the offshore oil and gas licensees. The negotiation includes royalties, as well as employment commitments and targets, and industrial benefits for the province (http://www.nr.gov.nl.ca/nr/royalties/oil_gas.html).
50 O'Faircheallaigh 2010, 69. IBAs are part of a larger family of benefit-sharing agreements called Community Development Agreements (CDAs). Like IBAs, CDAs allow private and state companies (in industries such as real estate, extractive industries, tourism, forestry, hydroelectric dams and national parks to name a few) and affected communities to negotiate the future perceived benefits of a development project (O'Faircheallaigh 2013, 222).
51 As stipulated in Section 78a of the Mineral Resource Act. See Chapter 14.
52 BMP 2012, 25.
53 Naalakkersuisut 2015.
54 Naalakkersuisut 2014b.
55 Since an IBA is a prerequisite to obtain a licence, the term 'resource proponent' is used instead of licensee.
56 All four Inuit regional corporations (Nunavut, Inuvialuit, Nunavik and Nunatsiavut) have settled land claims, which mean that they are the owners of the land. Out of the four, only Inuvialuit and Nunavut settlements include sub-surface rights to oil, gas and minerals on a section of their land. The Nunatsiavut government is entitled to receive 25 percent of provincial government revenues from sub-surface resources in Labrador Inuit lands. Regardless of the existence of sub-surface rights, IBAs are required for most large resource projects by all regional corporations except for Nunavik, where the government of Quebec is bound to facilitate and encourage the signing of agreements in mining projects (Knotsch and Warda 2009, 46–48).
57 GNWT 2015.
58 ERM 2010, 17.
59 O'Faircheallaigh 2010, 72.
60 Ibid., 72
61 These and other publicly available IBAs can be found in the Natural Resources Canada 'Table of Agreements'. A similar table is provided by the IBA Research Network and can be found here http://www.impactandbenefit.com/IBA_Database_List/. Unfortunately, neither of the tables provides the value and contents of the agreements, as this is considered confidential information. The exception

is a small, detailed table provided by Knotsch and Warda of the most notorious IBAs in Canada (2009: 50–3). None of the tables list all the IBAs in Canada, as there is no legal obligation to make the agreements public. One recent publicly available IBA is the Mary River Project Inuit Impact Benefit Agreement, signed between the Qikiqtani Inuit Association and the Baffinland Iron Mines Corporation in Baffin Island. This agreement and others signed in the Northwest Territory and Nunavut are available at http://www.miningnorth.com/commitments.

62 Gorrill 2000. For this project, Chevron Canada Resources commissioned IEG Consultants (a subsidiary of the Inavialuit Development Corporation) to complete the project description in order to 'to meet the requirements of Indian and Northern Affairs Canada (INAC) and fulfil the Operating Guidelines and Procedures of the Environmental Impact Screening Committee (EISC)' (AINA, no date).

63 As part of the licensing process, oil and gas companies in Canada have to present a PIP to the National Energy Board (NEB) after consulting with the affected community(ies) – in this case, the Inuvialuit Regional Corporation. See Section 2.2.2 of the NEB's *Filing Requirements for Offshore Drilling in the Canadian Arctic* (December 2011) at: https://www.neb-one.gc.ca/bts/ctrg/gnthr/rctcrvwflngrqrmnt/rctcrvwflngrqmnt-eng.pdf.

64 My emphasis. This phrase is usually added to agreements to avoid making concrete commitments.

65 Imperial Oil 2012, 5.1. In a 2013 project description document, Imperial commits to provide opportunities to Inuvialuit companies by notifying them of opportunities as soon as possible and by 'preparing work packages that encourage Inuvialuit companies to bid on the work or align with other companies in joint ventures to manage larger work packages' (Imperial Oil 2013, 6–35).

Despite repeated email enquiries to the Inuvialuit Regional Corporation's research liaison, it was not possible to establish whether the company's PIP commitments had been fulfilled and if an IBA had been signed in relation to Exploration Licence (EL) 476 (Ajurak) and EL 477 (Pokak). This does not mean that similar types of arrangements do not exist. The Western Arctic (Inuvialuit) Claims Settlement Act of 1984 says nothing about IBAs for offshore projects, so Inuvialuit and oil and gas companies may be reaching voluntary agreements instead. Fidler explains:

> When industries seek access to resources onshore they are required under the Inuvialuit Final Agreement to negotiate benefit agreements. Although industry is not legally required to do so offshore, some companies have voluntarily struck benefit agreements. For example, one industry participant explained that 'the Inuvialuit wish to have offshore plans tailored to them as long-term development; we [industry proponent] feel this is reasonable to respect and have entered into agreements with the IRC [Inuvialuit Regional Corporation]'. However, this particular company's opinion was not widely supported; other industry interviewees were opposed to reaching voluntary agreements with the Inuvialuit for offshore development, noting that regulatory framework does not require such actions. (2013, 72)

The reason why agreements are not required offshore is that the federal government retains jurisdiction over the offshore region of the Inuvialuit Settlement Region. See Fidler and Noble 2013, 180, and Rodon, this volume.

66 In Greenland, on the other hand, the EIA and, when applicable, the Social Sustainability Assessment (SSA) inform the IBA process, thus showing more integration between processes (see Chapter 14).

67 Fidler and Hitch 2007, 52.

68 There are, of course, environmental clauses in these agreements but they are usually designed to mitigate damage or compensate for expected damage. In Inuvialuit, for instance, IBAs require wildlife compensation, restoration and mitigation plans. Similarly, in Nunavik, agreements with mining companies include restoration of mining sites (Knotsch and Warda 2009, 7, 46–48).
69 Laforce, Campbell and Sarrasin 2012.
70 O'Faircheallaigh and Corbett 2005, 629.
71 The Inuvialuit have twenty years' experience in negotiating IBAs. Many onshore agreement provisions are in template form, and these have borrowed from provisions in publicly available IBAs, expert advice, IBA research and indigenous exchange.
72 Nuttall 2013.
73 O'Faircheallaigh 2010, 75; Knotsch and Warda 2009, 34.
74 The problem of lack of transparency in the oil and gas and other mineral industries does not affect Canada only; it is a widespread problem. NGOs like Public What You Pay and The Revenue Watch Institute have made this part of their campaigning. See for instance, Rosenblum and Maples 2009.
75 Fidler and Hitch 2007, 59. See also Section 7.5 of the Circumpolar Inuit Declaration on Resource Development Principles in Inuit Nunaat at http://inuit.org/?id=432.
76 First Nations governments, Shanks says, 'should be seen as part of the regulatory apparatus and part of the decision-making structure that regulates and approves development in the public interest' (Shanks 2006, 8). In this regard it is important to note that the federal government in Canada, in line with EITI, has recently introduced transparency legislation for the extractive industries (the Extractive Sector Transparency Measures Act) that treats First Nation governments like any other modern public administration. See http://www.martindale.com/environmental-law/article_Borden-Ladner-Gervais-LLP_2194526.htm.
77 See Mortensen, this volume, BMP 2009, 6, and https://www.govmin.gl/petroleum/approval-of-activities/exploration-drilling.
78 Naalakkersuisut 2014b.
79 Hansen 2013 and 2014; Hansen 2010; Rosing et al. 2014; Nuttall 2013; Boersma and Foley 2014, Buch Kristensen, Smed and Smed 2012.
80 Jacobsen 2014.
81 O'Faircheallaigh 2010, 70.
82 The authority to manage municipal land and conduct planning at that level was an area of responsibility transferred to the four newly formed municipalities in 2009 (Hansen 2014, 138). The law that lays down the requirements for planning is the Greenland Parliament Act no. 17 of 17 November 2010. For offshore areas, zoning exists, but the focus is on environmental impacts of exploration activities, with little community involvement. There is, however, no zoning at municipal level regarding mineral extraction conducted onshore (Rosing et al. 2014, 28).
83 Hendriksen, Hoffman and Jørgensen 2014.
84 Baker 2012 and Buchanan 2012.
85 The 2010 BP Deepwater Horizon oil-spill literature provides an answer as to why this trend is so compelling for oil and gas companies operating offshore. According to Baker, 'safety and security of the oil rig was not [jurisdictionally] the responsibility of the United States government, but that of the Marshall Island' where the platform was registered. Oil platforms and ship-owning companies prefer to register their vessels in FOCs for reasons explained above. These companies also save money by registering their legal domicile in low- or no-tax jurisdictions such as Switzerland, Jersey and the Cayman Islands. Transocean,

the owner of the platform contracted by BP, 'saved some 1.8 billion dollars in United States tax liability by moving its legal domicile from the Houston area to the Cayman Islands and later to Switzerland' (Baker, 2010, 691). Cairn oil platforms used in Greenland, the Stena Don and Leiv Eiriksson, are owned by Stena Don Cyprus Limited (domiciled in Cyprus) and Ocean Rig Offshore Management (domiciled in Jersey) respectively. In the Beaufort Sea, the respective owners of the oil platforms Kuluk, Molikpaq and SDC are Noble Corporation (domiciled in Switzerland), Sakhalin Energy (domiciled in the Russian Federation) and SDC Drilling Inc (domiciled in Liberia) (Callow, 2013). It is beyond the scope of this chapter to calculate how much tax the governments of Greenland and Canada each forego by allowing licensees the subcontracting of oil platforms to companies that have their legal domicile in jurisdictions that are beyond government control.

86 The term 'third country nationals' refers to seafarers whose nationality differs from the country where the vessel is registered. It is common for these seafarers to receive low wages, and sometimes be owed wages for long periods of time. The International Transport Federation, a trade union that represents seafarers worldwide, recovers millions of dollars in unpaid wages on behalf of seafarers working on FOC-registered vessels. See http://www.itfseafarers.org/defining-focs.cfm.

87 ERM 2010, 68 and Pacheco 2012 and World Bank 2010.

88 Hendriksen, Hoffman and Jørgensen 2014, 1.

89 Hansen 2013, 93. The whole of the Greenlandic public administration totals 600 civil servants. The competent authority in matters of offshore licencing, the Mineral Licence and Safety Authority (MLSA), had 27 employees in 2014. The MLSA replaced the Bureau of Minerals and Petroleum (BMP).

90 Rosing et al. 2014, 29.

91 http://gordonfoundation.ca/north/iba-community-toolkit.

92 Fidler and Hitch 2007, 59; Knotsch and Warda 2009, 11.

93 Bouchard and Delisle 1998, 218.

94 Szablowski 2010, 303.

95 Morgan 2002.

96 My emphasis. Morgan 2002. See also O'Faircheallaigh 2010, 83–84, and Knotsch and Warda 2009, 11.

It is important to mention that not all IBAs will lead to limiting political rights, as this depends on the way that IBAs are negotiated. Peterson St-Laurent and Le Billon note that despite:

> some Canadian (and Australian) IBAs requir[ing] Aboriginal signatories to refrain from participating in any regulatory or legal process that might result in imposition of conditions on a project... IBAs for two mines, respectively in Eastern Canada and the NWT, hav[e] provisions indicating that nothing shall restrict a Party's right to contest the project through official proceedings (e.g., opposing to an environmental licence or permit). (2015, 5 fn. 8)

See Rodon, this volume, in relation to Nunavut Inuit asserting their political autonomy through legal and political avenues.

97 See Tejsner, this volume.

98 ERM 2010, 68.

99 Prno, Bradshaw and Lapierre 2010.

100 Shanks 2006, 40.

101 ERM 2010, 68.

102 Fidler and Hitch 2007, 52; Morgan 2002; Knotsch and Warda 2009, 11, 14.

103 A Circumpolar Inuit Declaration on Resource Development Principles in Inuit Nunaat available at http://inuit.org/?id=432.

References

AINA (Arctic Institute of North America). No date. *Project Description for the Proposed Chevron Canada Resources Langley South 3D Seismic Programme.* Hydrocarbon Impacts/Incidences des Hydrocarbures, Publications Clés. Calgary: Arctic Institute of North America. No date. Accessed 9 October 2015. www.aina.ucalgary.ca/scripts/mwimain.dll/145/hiprof/hiprofaa/sisn+50234+ou+sisn+50235+ou+sisn+58648?COMMANDSEARCH.

Baker, B. 2012. 'Flags of Convenience and the Gulf Oil Spill: Problems And Proposed Solutions.' *Houston Journal of International Law* 34 (3): 687–716.

Bird, K., Charpentier, R., Gautier, D., Houseknecht, D., Klett, T., Pitman, J., Moore, T., Schenk, C., Tennyson, M. and Wandrey, C. 2008. *Circum-Arctic Resource Appraisal: Estimates of Undiscovered Oil and Gas North of the Arctic Circle.* Factsheet 2008–3049. Menlo Park, CA: US Geological Survey. Accessed 25 August 2015. http://pubs.usgs.gov/fs/2008/3049/.

BMP. 2009. Guidelines for Social Impact Assessments for mining projects in Greenland. Nuuk: Bureau of Minerals and Petroleum.

BMP. 2012. Report to Inatsisartut, the Parliament of Greenland concerning mineral resources activities in Greenland. Nuuk: Greenland Bureau of Minerals and Petroleum.

Boersma, T. and Foley, K. 2014. The Greenland Gold Rush: Promise and Pitfalls of Greenland's Energy and Mineral Resources. Washington, DC: Brookings Institution.

Bouchard, M. and Delisle, C. 1998. 'A comparison of the EIA of the Great Whale Hydroelectric and Raglan Mine projects: lessons learned on societal views towards natural resources.' In *Assessment and Impacts of Megaprojects,* edited by M. Colbo and P. Ryan. Proceedings of the 38th Meeting of the Canadian Society of Environmental Biologists, in collaboration with the Newfoundland and Labrador Environment Network, St John's, Newfoundland, 213–227. 1–3 October 1998. Toronto, Ontario: Canadian Society of Environmental Biologists.

Buchanan, P. 2012. *Risk Assessment: Selling Sovereignty and Declining Responsibility: Flags of Convenience in the South Pacific.* Auckland, New Zealand: 36th Parallel Assessments. Accessed 16 October 2015. http://36th-parallel.com/2012/08/28/risk-assessment-selling-sovereignty-and-declining-responsibility-flags-of-convenience-in-the-south-pacific/.

Byers, M. 2015. 'Is Arctic Oil a Losing Gamble?' *The Globe and Mail,* 27 June 2015. Accessed 9 October 2015. www.theglobeandmail.com/report-on-business/rob-commentary/is-arctic-oil-a-losing-gamble/article25150809/.

Cairn Energy. 2011. *Corporate Responsibility Report.* Edinburgh: Cairn Energy PLC.

Callow, L. 2013. *Oil and Gas Exploration & Development Activity Forecast: Canadian Beaufort Sea 2013–2028.* Vancouver, British Columbia: LTLC Consulting, for Aboriginal Affairs and Northern Development Canada (AANDC).

CBC News. 2015. 'Oil Companies Seek to Drill in Deep Beaufort Sea.' Accessed 26 August 2015. www.cbc.ca/news/canada/north/oil-companies-seek-to-drill-in-deep-beaufort-sea-1.1871343.

Center for Marine and Coastal Studies. 2015. 'North East Greenland 2016 Seismic Survey'. Accessed 12 December 2016. http://naalakkersuisut.gl/~/media/Nanoq/

Files/Hearings/2016/TGS%20NEG16%20Scope%20of%20Works/Documents/English.pdf.

Dagg, J., Holroyd, P., Lemphers, N., Lucas, R. and Thibault, B. 2011. *Comparing the Offshore Regulatory Regimes of the Canadian Arctic, the US, the UK, Greenland and Norway.* Drayton Valley, Alberta: Pembina Institute.

Dawson, C. 2015. 'Exxon Mobil, BP Suspend Canadian Arctic Exploratory Drilling Programme in Beaufort Sea.' *New York Times,* 26 June 2015. Accessed 25 August 2015. www.wsj.com/articles/exxon-mobil-bp-suspend-canadian-arctic-exploratory-drilling-program-in-beaufort-sea-1435348381.

ERM. 2010. *Mining Community Development Agreements: Final Report for the World Bank.* Washington DC: Environmental Resources Management. Accessed 29 August 2015. www.sdsg.org/wp-content/uploads/2011/06/CDA-Report-FINAL.pdf.

Fidler, C. 2013. 'Arctic Offshore Oil and Gas Development: Advancing the Efficacy of Environmental Management through Regional Strategic Environmental Assessment.' PhD diss., Department of Geography and Planning, University of Saskatchewan. Accessed 13 October 2015. https://ecommons.usask.ca/bitstream/handle/10388/ETD-2013-02-952/FIDLER-DISSERTATION.pdf?sequence=5.

Fidler, C. and Hitch, M. 2007. 'Impact and Benefit Agreements: A Contentious Issue for Environmental and Aboriginal Justice.' *Environments Journal* 35 (2): 49–69.

Fidler, C. and Noble, B. 2013. 'Stakeholder Perceptions of Current Planning, Assessment and Science Initiatives in Canada's Beaufort Sea.' *Arctic* 66 (2): 179–190.

GNWT (Government of the Northwest Territories). 2013. *Business Incentive Policy: NWT and Local Contents.* Yellowknife: Department of Industry, Tourism and Investment. Accessed 27 August 2015. www.iti.gov.nt.ca/en/publications.

GNWT (Government of the Northwest Territories). 2015. *Socio-Economic Agreements.* Yellowknife: Department of Industry, Tourism and Investment. Accessed 28 August 2015. www.iti.gov.nt.ca/en/services/socio-economic-agreements.

Gorrill, M. 2000. 'Seal of Approval: ICC Members Unanimously Ratify Deal with Chevron.' *Northern News Service Online,* 23 June 2000. Accessed 12 October 2015. www.nnsl.com/frames/newspapers/2000-06/jun23_00explore.html.

Hackenbruch, M. and Davies, J. 2011. Commercial Value from Sustainable Local Benefits in the Extractive Industries: Local Content. Copenhagen: BSR (Business for Social Responsibility).

Hansen, A. M. 2010. 'SEA Effectiveness and Power in Decision-making: a Case study of aluminium production in Greenland. Aalborg, Institut for Samfundsudvikling og Planlægning, Aalborg Universitet. Accessed 2 September 2015. http://vbn.aau.dk/files/46686491/samlet_afhandling_finito.pdf.

Hansen, K. 2013. 'The Aluminium Smelter Project in Greenland – New Aspects of an Industrialisation Process?' In *Urbanisation and the Role of Housing in the Present Development Process in the Arctic,* edited by K. Hansen, S. Bitsch and L. Zalkind, 85–101. Stockholm: Nordic Centre for Spatial Development.

Hansen, K. 2014. 'Greenlandic Perspectives on Offshore Oil and Gas Activities: An Illustration of Changes in Legitimacy Related to Democratic Decision Processes.' *Journal of Rural and Community Development* 9 (1): 134–154.

Hendriksen, K., Hoffmann, B. and Jørgensen, U. 2014. 'Mineral Exploitation and Development in Greenland: Engaging Local Workforce and Planning Flexible Settlements.' In *Arctic Yearbook*, edited by L. Heininen, H. Exner-Pirot and J. Plouffe. Akureyri: Northern Research Forum.

Hirschheim, R. and Heinzl, A. 2002. *Information Systems Outsourcing: Enduring Themes, Emergent Patterns and Future Directions*. Berlin: Springer-Verlag.

IFC (International Finance Corporation). 2010. Strategic Community Investment: A Good Practice Handbook for Companies Doing Business in Emerging Markets. Washington DC: International Finance Corporation.

IMO (International Maritime Organisation). 2015. *International Convention for the Safety of Life at Sea (SOLAS), 1974*. London: International Maritime Organisation. Accessed 1 November 2015. www.imo.org/en/About/Conventions/ListOfConventions/Pages/International-Convention-for-the-Safety-of-Life-at-Sea-%28SOLAS%29%2c-1974.aspx.

Imperial Oil. 2012. Beaufort Sea Exploration Joint Venture: Drilling Programme: Preliminary Information Package. Calgary, Alberta: Imperial Oil Resources Ventures Limited.

Imperial Oil. 2013. Beaufort Sea Exploration Joint Venture: Drilling Programme: Project Description. Calgary, Alberta: Imperial Oil Resources.

Jacobsen, M. 2014. 'Proposed Law Amendment May Threaten Good Greenlandic Governance.' Washington: The Arctic Institute. Accessed 27 February 2017. www.thearcticinstitute.org/proposed-law-amendment-good-governance-greenland/.

Jeremko, G. 2014. 'Canada Considering Relaxing Offshore Relief Well Requirement.' *NGIs Daily Gas Price Index*, 20 June 2014. Accessed 9 October 2015. www.naturalgasintel.com/articles/98772-canada-considering-relaxing-offshore-relief-well-requirement.

Kay, J. and Thorup, S. 2014. Oil and Gas in Greenland-Still on Ice?' *Notes from the Field: An English Law Perspective on the Oil & Gas Market*. London: Andrews Kurth, November 2014. Accessed 27 August 2015. www.andrewskurth.com/insights-1165.html.

Knotsch, C. and Warda, J. 2009. *Impact Benefit Agreements: A Tool for Healthy Inuit Communities?* Ottawa: National Aboriginal Health Organisation.

Kristensen, B., Smed, M. and Smed, L. 2012. 'Integrity Study on the public sector in Greenland.' Taastrup: Nordic Consulting Group, for Transparency International Greenland. Accessed November 15, 2015. www.ncg.dk/reports/69-integrity-study-on-the-public-sector-in-greenland.

Laforce, M., Campbell, B. and Sarrasin, S. 2012. *Pouvoir et régulation dans le secteur minier: leçons à partir de l'expérience canadienne*. Boisbriand, QC: Presses de l'Université du Québec.

Macalister, T. 2013. 'Greenland Halts New Oil Drilling Licences.' *The Guardian*, 27 March 2013. Accessed 25 August 2015. www.theguardian.com/world/2013/mar/27/greenland-halts-oil-drilling-licences.

Milne, R., Adams, C. and Crooks, E. 2015. 'Oil Companies Put Arctic Projects into Deep Freeze.' *Financial Times*, 5 February 2015.

Mooney, C. 2015. 'The Real Reason Arctic Drilling is Faltering Right Now.' *The Daily Herald*, 25 October 2015.

Morgan, N. 2002. *The State of the Law on the Obligation to Consult With First Nations*. Vancouver, BC: Aboriginal Mapping Network/EcoTrust Canada, Accessed 13 October 2015. www.nativemaps.org/?q=node/2050.

Naalakkersuisut. 2010. *Impact Benefit Agreement under Licence 2008/10 for 2010*. Nuuk: Naalakkersuisut. Accessed 28 August 2015. http://ccsi.columbia.edu/files/2015/03/Greenland-Qaasuitsup-Qeqqata-Sermersooq-Capricorn-Greenland-2010-IBA.pdf.

Naalakkersuisut. 2014a. *Greenland's Oil and Mineral Strategy 2014–2018*. Nuuk: Greenland Bureau of Minerals and Petroleum. Accessed 27 August 2015. www.govmin.gl/images/stories/about_bmp/publications/Greenland_oil_and_mineral_strategy_2014-2018_ENG.pdf.

Naalakkersuisut. 2014b. *Impact Benefit Agreement under Mineral Exploration Licence 2014/21*. Nuuk: Ministry of Industry, Labour and Trade. Accessed 28 August 2015. http://naalakkersuisut.gl/~/media/Nanoq/Files/Publications/Raastof/ENG/Signed%20IBA%20TNG%20ENG%2016%2006.pdf.

Naalakkersuisut. 2015. 'New Strong Force behind London Mining Greenland.' Accessed 27 August 2015. http://naalakkersuisut.gl/en/Naalakkersuisut/News/2015/01/080115-London-Mining.

Nuttall, M. 2013. 'Zero-Tolerance, Uranium and Greenland's Mining Future.' *The Polar Journal* 3 (2): 368–383. Accessed 13 November 2015 www.tandfonline.com/doi/abs/10.1080/2154896X.2013.868089.

Nyvold, M. 2012. 'Logistics and Lack of Beds, Biggest Challenges, Miners Say.' *Greenland Oil & Minerals,* Issue 3 (2012): 30–31. Accessed 29 August 2015. http://projekter.aau.dk/projekter/files/80438732/Appendix_5.pdf.

O'Faircheallaigh, C. 2010. 'Aboriginal–Mining Company Contractual Agreements in Australia and Canada: Implications for Political Autonomy and Community Development.' *Canadian Journal of Development Studies/Revue Canadienne d'études du développement* 30 (1–2): 69–86. doi:10.1080/02255189.2010.9669282.

O'Faircheallaigh, C. 2013. 'Community Development Agreements in the Mining Industry: an Emerging Global Phenomenon.' *Community* 5 February 2015. doi:10.1080/15575330.2012.705872.

O'Faircheallaigh, C. and Corbett, C. 2005. 'Indigenous Participation in Environmental Management of Mining Projects: The Role of Negotiated Agreements.' *Environmental Politics* 14 (5): 629–647. doi:10.1080/09644010500257912.

Pacheco, V. 2012. 'Foundations, Trusts and Funds in Near Mine Closure and Post-Closure Environments: A Case from Bolivia.' In *Mine Closure,* edited by A. Fourie and M. Tibbett, 747–758. Proceedings of the Seventh International Conference on Mine Closure in collaboration with the Australian Centre for Geomechanics, Brisbane, Queensland, 25–27 September 2012.

Pacheco, V. 2015. 'From Transnational Trends to Local Practices: Monitoring Social Impacts in a Papua New Guinea Mining Community.' In *Globalisation and Transnational Capitalism in Asia and Oceania,* edited by J. Sprague. Abingdon, Oxon, New York: Routledge.

Peterson, G. and Le Billon, P. 2015. 'Staking Claims and Shaking Hands: Impact and Benefit Agreements as a Technology of Government in the Mining Sector.' *Extractive Industries and Society* 2 (3): 590–602. doi:10.1016/j.exis.2015.06.001.

Plourde, A. 2010. *Oil and Gas in the Canadian Federation.* Working Paper No. 10–001 (June 2010): 1–25. Evanstone, Illinois: Buffet Center for International and Comparative Studies.

Poole, G., Pretes, M., and Sinding, K. 1992. 'Managing Greenland's Mineral Revenues: A Trust Fund Approach.' *Resources Policy* 18 (3): 191–204.

Prno, J., Bradshaw, B. and Lapierre, D. 2010. 'Impact and Benefit Agreements: Are they working?' Paper presented at The Canadian Institute of Mining, Metallurgy and Petroleum's 2010 Conference and Exhibition. Vancouver, British Columbia. Accessed 14 October 2015. www.impactandbenefit.com/UserFiles/Servers/

Server_625664/File/IBA%20PDF/CIM%202010%20Paper%20-%20Prno,%20 Bradshaw%20and%20Lapierre.pdf.

Ravago, M. 2007. *Outsourcing in the Global Oil and Gas Industries.* Fall Church, VA: Tholons. Accessed 23 August 2015. www.tholons.com/nl_pdf/071130_ OutsourcingintheOilGasIndustry.pdf.

Rogers, S. and Cooley, L. 2004. 'Deciding Where to Source: Local, National, Regional, or Global.' Paper presented at the 89th Annual International Supply Management Conference, Nashville, Tennessee. Accessed 27 August 2015. www.instituteforsupplymanagement.org/files/pubs/proceedings/bfcooleyrogers.pdf.

Rosenblum, P. and Maples, S. 2009. *Contracts Confidential: Ending Secret Deals in the Extractive Industries.* New York: Revenue Watch.

Rosing, M., Knudsen R., Heinrich, R. and Rasmussen, L. 2014. *For the benefit of Greenland.* Nuuk: Ilisimatusarfik (University of Greenland); Copenhagen: University of Copenhagen, for Committee for Greenlandic Mineral Resources to the Benefit of Society. Accessed 12 November 201. http://greenlandperspective.ku.dk/this_is_greenland_perspective/background/report-papers/To_the_benefit_of_Greenland.pdf.

Rosser, A. 2006. *The Political Economy of the Resource Curse: A Literature Survey.* IDS Working Paper 268: 1–34. Brighton: Institute of Development Studies, 2006.

Roy Grégoire, E. 2013. The Contribution of Impact and Benefit Agreements to the Regulation of Mining Projects: Lessons from the Raglan Agreement in Northern Quebec. Montreal: CIRDIS (Centre Interdisciplinaire de Recherche en Développement International et Société). Accessed 23 August 2015. www.ieim.uqam.ca/IMG/pdf/roy-gregoire.pdf.

Schaps, K. 2015. 'Royal Dutch Shell Pulls Plug on Arctic Exploration.' *Reuters Business News,* 28 September 2015. Accessed 10 October 2015. www.reuters.com/article/us-shell-alaska-idUSKCN0RS0EX20150928.

Shanks, G. 2006. Benefits of Resource Developments: A Study of First Nations–Industry Impact Benefits Agreements: Final Report. Ottawa: Public Policy Forum/Forum des Politiques Publiques.

Statista. 2015. 'Global Market Size of Outsourced Services from 2000 to 2014 (in billion US dollars).' New York: Statista (Statistics Portal). Accessed 26 August 2015. www.statista.com/statistics/189788/global-outsourcing-market-size/.

Szablowski, D. 2010. 'Operationalising Free, Prior, and Informed Consent in the Extractive Industry Sector? Examining the Challenges of a Negotiated Model of Justice.' *Canadian Journal of Development Studies/Revue Canadienne d'études du développement* 30 (1–2): 111–130. doi:10.1080/02255189.2010.9669284.

UNCTAD. 2007. World Investment Report: Transnational Corporations, Extractive Industries and Development. New York: UNCTAD.

Wake, B. 2013. Foreword to Policy Governance in Multi-level Systems: Economic Development and Policy Implementation in Canada, by Charles Conteh, ii–iii. Montreal: McGill-Queens University Press.

Wilson Centre. No date. Opportunities and Challenges for Arctic Oil and Gas the Wilson Center.

World Bank. 2010. *Towards Sustainable Decommissioning and Closure of Oil Fields and Mines: A Toolkit to Assist Government Agencies, Version 3.* Washington, DC: World Bank. Accessed 23 August 2015. http://siteresources.worldbank.org/EXTOGMC/Resources/336929-1258667423902/decommission_toolkit3_full.pdf.

14 Impact and benefit agreements in Greenland

Bent Ole Gram Mortensen

Introduction

Any exploitation of local resources normally has an effect on the local community, including if it takes place offshore. Pollution and other negative effects of offshore operations on hunting and fisheries are well documented in the Arctic, but there will also be additional socioeconomic effects, such as the immigration of non-local workers, as well as opportunities for the local workforce and local companies, skills transfers, and revenues from taxes and royalties.[1]

This chapter focuses on the protection of the Greenlandic area and Greenlandic society in connection with offshore hydrocarbon activities. No onshore drilling for oil and gas has yet taken place in Greenland, and onshore activities in general will not be discussed here.

It is important to take into account that local exploitation of hydrocarbons and other minerals does not always guarantee local gain. In fact, one can often see very limited gain for either the local community or the host country in general. On several occasions in other regions of the world, both local communities and host countries have been left with depleted resources, significant environmental damage, and no lasting gain when the operation closes down. This has been referred to as the 'resource curse.'[2]

A further factor is that the interests of the Greenlandic government – Naalakkersuisut – and the local communities may not always be identical on the question of the resource exploitation. In the overall perspective, Naalakkersuisut and the four Greenlandic municipalities do have the same interests in connection with the extraction of minerals: namely, to ensure the recruitment of the Greenlandic workforce and to ensure knowledge transfer (e.g. education programmes) to Greenlandic society in order to ensure long-term capacity-building. However, the municipalities may have interests that conflict with those of Naalakkersuisut when it comes to the protection of local interests in hunting, fisheries, and tourism, as well as in sociocultural values and traditions. Interests among citizens in the geographically huge municipalities[3] may also be in conflict.

Various regulatory options are available in different parts of the world for safeguarding the priority of local interests, for instance, regulatory conditions requiring companies to deliver social and economic benefits.[4] An alternative to general statutory rules is to insert conditions related to special benefits for the local community into a licence as a requirement, or to require the licensee to enter into a separate agreement negotiated between the state and/or the local authorities on the one hand and the licensee on the other hand. Such agreements have been quite common in various forms, including community development agreements (CDAs), community development initiatives, voluntary agreements, indigenous land-use agreements, model mining development agreements, partnering or partnership agreements, social trust funds, investment agreements, benefits-sharing agreements, and Impact and Benefit Agreements (IBAs). All these types of agreement are similar in function. The last of these – IBAs[5] – is the one that has been used in Greenland.

A number of plans (the Benefit and Impact Plan, the Monitoring Plan, and the Evaluation Plan) form part of the IBA model used in Greenland, and must be kept updated by the licensee. It is the Benefit and Impact Plan that constitutes the detailed IBA.

This chapter is based on the five IBAs concluded to date in Greenland, as well as on the so-called draft model IBA which was designed as inspiration. These five IBAs were signed within a period of seven years (2010–2016). Three of the five relate to onshore mining projects. Despite the fact that these two projects are neither offshore nor include exploitation of hydrocarbons, they are included in this chapter for the simple reason that the total number of IBAs drafted is so small and the onshore mining projects are the most recent of them. These non-hydrocarbon IBAs may contribute to analysis of the use of IBAs in relation to future exploitation of hydrocarbons offshore. The analysis of these onshore IBAs constitutes an exception to the general focus on offshore projects.

First, an attempt will be made to define the legal nature of an IBA, as it has been used in Greenland. Second, regulation of the use of the IBA will be discussed. Third, parts of the draft model IBA, as well as the five IBAs, will be analysed and their content will be discussed, focusing on the provisions regarding labour. The chapter concludes that the IBAs used in Greenland to date contain obligations that are hard to enforce, and that the definition of 'Greenlandic workers' represents a particular problem.

Mineral resources and the autonomy of Greenland

Greenland is an autonomous region within the Kingdom of Denmark, but sharing the constitution and citizenship of Denmark and the Faroe Islands. According to the Self-Government Act[6] Sections 1 and 3 (2) and the Schedule's list II, No. 26, the Greenlandic authorities have taken over responsibility for mineral resources, giving them the right to regulate and exploit the subsoil resources. The mineral resource area was transferred to the Greenlandic self-government authorities on 1 January 2010. As a consequence of this, the self-government authorities can exercise legislative and executive power in the field of mineral resources. Executive power now lies with the Greenland government, Naalakkersuisut, and legislative power with the Greenland parliament, Inatsisartut, under Section 1 of the Act.

Since the transfer of the mineral resource area, the Mineral Resources Act has been the primary act[7] regulating the exploitation of mineral resources in the subsoil.[8] As used in this chapter the term 'mineral' includes hydrocarbons and the term 'mining' includes exploration and exploitation, not only of hydrocarbons but also of hard minerals.[9] Mineral resources in the subsoil of Greenland belong exclusively to the self-government authorities, according to the Act's Section 2 (1). Exploitation of minerals is based on a concession system of licences. The granting of licences for the extraction of hydrocarbons is regulated by part 6 (Sections 22–28) of the Act, together with a number of general provisions covering all minerals.

Granting mineral resource licences

The ownership of mineral resources in the Greenlandic subsoil thus belongs to the government – in this case, the self-government authorities. This is explicitly stated in Section 2 of the Mineral Resources Act. This contrasts with the situation in other places, where mineral rights do follow land ownership.

Offshore, according to the United Nations Convention on the Law of the Sea (UNCLOS) and the older Convention on the Continental Shelf (CSC), states have sovereign rights. As part of the Kingdom of Denmark, Greenland is covered by these conventions.[10] The geographical scope of the Mineral Resources Act, according to Section 9, covers the territorial land, the territorial sea, the exclusive economic zone, and the continental shelf. The Act's Section 98 (3) amends the Act on the Continental Shelf.[11]

A number of licences for offshore hydrocarbons have been issued.[12] However, no commercial valuable resources have been found to date, even though expectations have been high.[13] At present, exploration activities are limited due to the low oil price in the world market.

Where does this leave the local Greenlandic municipalities? The municipalities have no competences offshore. Exploitation of oil and gas includes positive as well as negative impacts,[14] and one might fear that the local community will be left with the lion's share of the negative impact and only a little of the positive impact. The purpose of the IBA is to increase the positive impact for the local community.

Community agreements

An IBA can generally be described as an agreement between licensee and local community, outlining commitment and responsibilities in order to secure benefits to be passed on to the local community and to reduce negative impacts from major projects, primarily mineral exploitation.[15] No international definition exists.

Based on the international use of the term IBA, certain characteristics can be identified. First, an IBA addresses the impact (social, cultural, environmental and economic) of mining operations on *local communities*. Second, an IBA is normally seen as a *formal contract* under private law, outlining the commitment and responsibilities of the mining company (the licensee) and the local community (and others). Third, an IBA is a tool to secure benefits (positive impacts) to be passed on to the local community (maximising development opportunities) and to reduce negative impacts resulting from mining projects. In fact, IBAs can be seen as part of the concept of corporate social responsibility.[16] The ability to conclude agreements could also be seen as expression of economic efficiency, i.e. Pareto efficient allocation of externalities.[17]

No limitation has been placed on the elements that may be incorporated in an IBA. Often, a number of elements are specified[18]:

- disruption of *animal migration, game trails, trap lines and fishing areas* and interruption of *traditional economies* in general
- possible *health impacts*
- additional necessary *infrastructure* such as roads and buildings
- use of *local workforce and local companies.*

Legislation regarding IBA

The regulation regarding IBAs is mainly found in the Mineral Resources Act. A number of other laws and guidelines, however, are also relevant to the IBAs.

The Mineral Resources Act

No formal definition of an IBA exists in Greenlandic legislation. The Mineral Resources Acts Section 78a states[19]:

> In a licence under Section 16, the Greenlandic Government must specify terms on the extent to which a licensee must enter into and comply with an agreement on social sustainability and other socioeconomic issues.
>
> (2) The agreement referred to in subsection (1) may relate to agreements on the licensee's compliance with obligations pursuant to Section 18 (1)–(4) and on the education or training of Greenlandic manpower.

As can be seen in this extract, the term IBA is not mentioned. The Act uses the phrase 'an agreement regarding socio-related sustainability and other socio-economic relations.'[20] The obligation for the licensee to enter into an IBA is meant to be decided on a discretionary basis by Naalakkersuisut, as the authority awarding the licence. Who should be the parties to the IBA is not determined by the Act. In the preparatory work to Section 78a, it is stated that the parties to the agreement shall be the licensee, Naalakkersuisut, and one or more municipalities.

The Large-Scale Projects Act

The Large-Scale Projects Act[21] applies to the establishment of projects for, *inter alia*, the exploitation of minerals when the capital expenditure involved exceeds DKr5 billion (€670 million).[22] The Act aims to promote foreign investment in Greenland by allowing companies to hire workers from outside the Kingdom of Denmark covered by collective agreements negotiated with non-Greenlandic trade unions. This means lower salary and less favourable conditions. The regulation was issued to prevent companies and investors deselecting Greenland for economic reasons, i.e. due to Greenland's high salary levels. Government approval is required for the conditions in the Large-Scale Project Act to apply.

The Act presupposes the conclusion of an IBA. According to Section 7 (5) of the Act, to the extent possible, the use of Greenlandic companies and labour is to be encouraged by inviting tenders and by awarding tripartite agreements (IBAs) between Naalakkersuisut, other public authorities and the project company. According to Section 9 (3) of the Act, the IBA is to be concluded as a condition for use of the right to hire foreign workers (migrant workers) in collective agreements negotiated with non-local trade unions.

Section 9 (6) of the Act defines a special obligation to use Greenlandic companies for contracts, supplies and services. Naalakkersuisut may allow companies from other countries to be used if the licensee, contractor, supplier or service provider can demonstrate that Greenlandic companies are not technically or commercially competitive.

Section 9 (4) of the Large-Scale Projects Act sets a number of demands for the content of an IBA. First, it must be based on 'Common conditions for works and services in the construction industry in Greenland,'[23] a codex issued by Naalakkersuisut. Further, it must include appropriate provisions for training or education of the local workforce and the development of local companies' skills and knowledge. The IBA must also contain a jurisdiction provision, choosing the Court of Greenland for settlement of disputes. These demands are mandatory for approval of a large-scale project.

The Large-Scale Project Work Permit Act

The use of non-Greenlandic workers requires such workers to be given residence permits. Although different rules may apply regarding offshore drilling operations for staff working on foreign-flagged vessels, still personnel on shorebases must have work permits.

To avoid the delays involved in applying case-by-case, the Danish parliament in 2014 passed the Large-Scale Projects Work Permit Act.[24] Based on this Act, an employer can submit a single digital application on behalf of a group of workers from outside the Kingdom of Denmark, thereby limiting the time used to process the applications. If such a worker has entered into an agreement on – or has been offered employment to perform tasks covered by – the Large-Scale Projects Act, residence and work permits can be granted for one year at a time, but shall not exceed five years.

Further, the minimum requirements guaranteed to a non-local worker will not be equivalent to the wage and employment conditions customary in Greenland at the present time, and will therefore not fulfil the requirements of Section 9 (2) of the Danish Immigration Act,[25] which specifies that residence and work permits are conditional upon wages and other work conditions being equivalent to current wage and employment conditions in Greenland. According to the Large-Scale Projects Work Permit Act, these minimum requirements will not prevent the issuing of work permits in connection with large-scale projects in Greenland.

The licence standard terms

The interests of the local community in hydrocarbon extraction can be addressed in the terms of the licence. Further, the demand for an IBA could be specified in the terms of the licence, whether or not such a demand explicitly existed in the Mineral Resources Act. In fact, Cairn Energy entered into an IBA before the above-mentioned Section 78a of the Mineral Resources Act came into force.

No standard terms for the exploration of hydrocarbons seem to have been developed. In the standard terms for exploration licences and for prospecting licences (excluding hydrocarbons) as issued on 25 June 2013, IBAs are not mentioned.[26] However, in Section 22.05 of the model licence designed for the 2017 licensing round for offshore areas in Baffin Bay, it is stated that the 'licensee shall negotiate and conclude an impact benefit agreement… with the Government of Greenland, see Section 78a of the Mineral Resources Act.'[27] The municipalities are not mentioned as a party to the agreement, but can be seen as included in the reference to Section 78a of the Mineral Resources Act.[28]

The relation between IBA and SSA

The draft model IBA is closely connected with Section 76 of the Mineral Resources Act, in accordance with which, if a mining activity under the Act is assumed to have a significant impact on social conditions, Naalakkersuisut can only grant a licence if a Social Sustainability Assessment (SSA) is submitted. An SSA is similar to a Social Impact Assessment (SIA).[29] According to Section 9 (3) of the Large-Scale Projects Act, the SSA report is to form the basis for the IBA.

According to Section 76 of the Mineral Resources Act, Naalakkersuisut can decide whether the SSA is to be made, and can stipulate certain criteria that should be considered as well as approve the SSA in its entirety. An SSA must be completed by the licence applicant with the involvement of the Mineral Licence and Safety Authority.[30] The aims of the SSA do not, however, follow from the words of the Act, or the preparatory work explaining the intentions behind the Act. In the area of mining, guidelines are issued to explain the aims of this instrument.[31] These aims include the recruiting of the Greenlandic workforce and the engagement of Greenlandic enterprises.

The non-exhaustive components in the guidelines, Section 5.1, include: the purpose of the agreement and its guiding principles, principles for planning significant project modifications, employment practices, quantitative employment targets for Greenlandic workforces, hiring commitments from contractors, employment incentives, employment requirements, human resource development, business development, social well-being, cultural well-being, involvement of local community, and monitoring of the implementation of the IBA.

Entering into an IBA

The Mineral Resources Act contains no provisions regarding the procedure for negotiating an IBA. However, the decision-making process is described in the guidelines.[32] According to these guidelines, the negotiation of the IBA should span at least three months of concentrated negotiations. The IBA is normally signed after the approval of the revised SSA.

The IBA is seen as closely associated with the grant of the exploitation licence, with the agreement's conclusion and signature immediately preceding (or immediately following) the grant of the licence.[33]

Before the conclusion of an IBA, hearings must take place including the local public authorities, Greenlandic employer and worker organisations, and local organisations that are statutorily intended to safeguard essential interests regarding social sustainability or environmental protection. Parties to the hearing parties are to be provided with information which can form the basis for giving an opinion on the matters in the IBA of significant importance to Greenlandic enterprises and workers or the project's impact on societal or environmental conditions, cf. the Large-Scale Projects Act, Section 9 (5).

Existing IBAs

Cairn Energy's Greenlandic subsidiary, Capricorn Greenland Exploration, signed two IBAs in 2010 and 2011 regarding offshore drilling activities (exploration). These two IBAs are identical. Both were signed before Section 78a of the Mineral Resources Act came into force.[34]

True North Gems Greenland (TNG) signed an IBA in 2014 as part of the conditions for its licence to start up a minor onshore mine for the extraction of rubies and sapphires.[35]

Hudson Greenland A/S, a subsidiary of Canadian Hudson Resources Inc., signed in September 2015 an IBA regarding the extraction of anorthosite (calcium feldspar) in the Naajat (White Mountain) mine.

Ironbark Zinc A/S, a subsidiary of Australian Ironbark Zinc Limited, signed in September 2016 an IBA regarding the extraction of zinc and lead in Citronen Fjord.

Below, the draft model IBA, as well as a number of characteristic elements of the five IBAs concluded so far, will be discussed.

The draft model IBA agreement

A draft model IBA posted on the home page of the former Greenlandic Bureau of Minerals and Petroleum has at the time of writing been removed from the home page, presumably for revision. No new draft model IBA has been published.[36]

According to the draft model IBA agreement, an IBA is a tripartite agreement with the municipality, the licensee and Naalakkersuisut as parties.

The draft model IBA contains a number of different clauses concerning social and cultural issues related to mining projects. It contains provisions on the use of Greenlandic workforces (Section 10), training and recruitment (Section 11), the involvement of Greenlandic enterprises (Section 12), 'social well-being' (Section 13) and 'cultural well-being' (Section 14). Further liability is dealt with in Section 19 of the draft model IBA.

No special provisions regarding the insufficient performance or breach of contract are included in the draft model IBA. The only dispute mechanism mentioned is the Greenlandic or Danish courts with jurisdiction in Nuuk, Greenland (Section 22). This choice of jurisdiction is a little unclear, as there are no Danish courts in Greenland with jurisdiction in Nuuk. The Greenlandic local courts, the Court of Greenland and the High Court of Greenland are under the Danish judiciary, but the administration of justice in Greenland is regulated by the Greenlandic Administration of Justice Act. The equivalent Danish Administration of Justice Act is not applicable in Greenland. Any case related to IBAs has, if not otherwise provided for in an Act, to be initiated at the competent local court, and the request referred to the Court of Greenland in the first instance.[37]

Tripartite Agreements

All five signed IBAs are tripartite agreements involving the licensee, Naalakkersuisut, and one or more municipalities as parties.

The two Cairn Energy IBAs involve three municipalities as partners and the Ironbark Zinc IBA, four municipalities (i.e. all municipalities in Greenland), while the TNG IBA and the Hudson IBA include only one municipality among the parties. One reason for this difference may be that Cairn's prepared projects are related to offshore extraction and the Ironbark Zinc project relates to an area outside the municipal division.[38] Conversely, both the TNG project and the Hudson project are onshore mining projects within the municipal division. Various different kinds of shorebase in the three municipalities were included in the two Cairn Energy IBAs,[39] and the wells drilled were beyond the coastline of these municipalities. Only the Kujalleq municipality (in the southern tip of Greenland) was not included in the IBA.

Monitoring

The draft model IBA has a Section 8 regarding monitoring and evaluation of performance by the licensee in accordance with the terms of the IBA. According to that Section, the licensee shall monitor the performance of the extraction process and other activities under the terms established by the IBA, and it is mandatory for the licensee to make an annual monitoring report and send it to the other IBA parties. Further, the parties are required to hold biannual evaluation meetings. The monitoring and reporting of provisions were repeated in Cairn Energy's IBAs of 2010 and 2011, Section 9, and in TNG's and Hudson's IBAs in Section 6.

Local workforces

In the Cairn Energy IBAs of 2010 and 2011, Cairn made a commitment to hire Greenlanders. However, these commitments were in the form of vague estimates of the use of Greenlandic workers. In a performance report, it was stated that the local employment level for the 2010 drilling programme was 7.7 percent.[40]

In the TNG IBA, the wording is different. Here it is stated in Annex 4 that '... at all times the licensee will *do its utmost to ensure* that employment of Greenlandic Workers by the Licensee and its contractors, suppliers and service providers will be at least '70 percent during building and construction and 70 percent during the first year of performance increasing to 80 percent in year three' (emphasis added).

In the Hudson IBA, Appendix 4, a minimum percentage of employment of Greenland workers is likewise applied (repeating the phrase 'do its utmost to ensure'):

- minimum 50 percent of the total workforce in connection with carrying out construction activities
- minimum 50 percent in year one and two of the operation phase
- minimum 80 percent in year three of the operation phase and until closure.

The Ironbark Zinc IBA repeats the phrase 'do its utmost to ensure' and operates with less percentage of Greenlandic workers in the start and a higher in the end:

- minimum 20 percent of the total workforce in connection with carrying out construction activities
- minimum 20 percent in year 1–4 of the operation phase
- minimum 50 percent in year 5–6 of the operation phase
- minimum 90 percent in year 7 of the operation phase and until closure.

This formulation of the conditions sounds much more favourable to Greenland than that used in the Cairn Energy IBAs. It can be argued that the three onshore IBAs do not contain guarantees of a minimum level of the use of the local workforce, given the wording 'do its utmost to ensure.' But with specific percentages mentioned, a stronger 'burden of proof' rests on the shoulders of the licensee. This difference between the offshore and onshore IBAs may be due to expectations that a large ratio of local labour is easier to achieve at onshore mines than on offshore drilling activities.[41]

The mineral legislation in Greenland does not deal with the term 'Greenlandic'.[42] It is left to the IBAs. In the Cairn IBAs, no definition of the content of the terms 'Greenlandic workers' is included. One can therefore speculate as to whether everyone with Greenlandic residence has the status of Greenlandic worker. In the TNG IBA, the Hudson IBA and the Ironbark Zinc IBA this question has been dealt with. According to Appendix 10, the Greenlandic resident (worker) is defined as a person who:

1 was born in Greenland and had permanent residence in Greenland for the first 5 years of his or her life, or
2 has had permanent residence in Greenland in the last two years or seven of the last 10 years, or
3 is married to, or is in a civil partnership of at least one year with, a person who satisfies (1) or (2) or is employed… in Greenland…
4 otherwise has a particular connection to Greenland…

These provisions limit which persons 'count' when it comes to benefiting the Greenlandic workforce. They are partly in contradiction with the general principle of inclusiveness in Danish citizenship, which applies also to Greenland's autonomy.[43] Inclusiveness means that every Danish citizen (whether Dane, Faroese or Greenlander) has full citizenship rights in that part of the Kingdom where the person resides (for instance, regarding voting in parliamentary elections). It seems that the more narrow definition of 'Greenlandic' is meant to protect against the attempt to bypass the intentions behind the IBA by importing a workforce from other parts of the Kingdom.

If the licensee is unable, despite doing their 'utmost', to hire local workers, they are not obliged to do so. The problem may reside in the Greenlandic labour market and the available workforce. In fact, the availability of labour in Greenland and the capabilities and entrepreneurial culture at local potential supplier and/ sub-contractor level are also important.[44]

So far, the experience concerning mining company's use of local labour is limited. However, a 'Monitoring and Evaluation Report' was made in 2015 regarding the TNG IBA.[45] The report has monitored the use of Greenlandic labour in the initial phase. The proportion of local labour was high, but it is doubtful whether the results can be transferred to offshore activities.

Enforcement of the IBA

Both the draft model IBA and the five IBAs actually concluded contain a clause regarding liability for damages, insurance and indemnification as well as a further clause regarding jurisdiction. The Hudson IBA and the Ironbark Zinc IBA also contains an arbitration clause. The IBAs thereby regulate non-performance independent of the licence.[46] The ultimate reaction to breach of contract is often termination of the contract. The risk of having an IBA terminated does not in itself give the licensee an incentive not to breach contract. It is questionable whether the risk of having to pay compensation for damage and loss caused by activities performed or by non-performance of obligations under the IBA is a sufficient incentive not to breach contract.

The main interest of the licensee is the licence granted. The standard terms for exploration[47] state in Section 16 that the licence may be revoked if the licensee breaches the terms of the provisions laid down pursuant to the Mineral Resources Act or pursuant to the terms included in the licence. The standard terms do not mention the IBA. The same applies to the model licence for the licensing round for offshore areas in Baffin Bay to take place in 2017. Article 22 requires the licensee to carry out its obligations under the IBA and act in accordance with the IBA 'in the performance of activities under the licence.'[48] The consequences of a breach of the IBA are not spelt out. Even though the IBA is a condition for being granted the licence, it appears unclear whether insufficient implementation of the IBA can be regarded as a breach of the licence. It is likely that the courts or an arbitration tribunal would hesitate to allow the licence to be revoked based solely on breach of the provisions in an agreement which can be enforced in its own right, especially since such a consequence is stated in neither the Mineral Resource Act, the licence agreement nor the IBA.

According to Section 18 (2) of the TNG IBA, Section 19 (2) of the Hudson IBA and Section 21(2) of the Ironbark Zinc IBA, the licensor may order the licensee to suspend all activities or revoke the exploitation licence in the event of non-performance. It seems surprising that such a provision is made in a tripartite agreement. In fact, as a consequence of the drafting of the IBA, the relation between licensee and municipality becomes a condition in the licence; such a condition in the IBA is, in fact, a consequence of the use of the parties' competences under private law, whereas the licence is granted under public law. Such provisions are not contained in the draft model IBA or the two Cairn Energy IBAs.

Conclusion

Although a new instrument in Greenland, the IBAs and similar agreements are internationally used instruments which aim to secure benefits for the local community from mining activities by maximising development opportunities. As described above, the IBAs address the effect of mining operations on local communities socially, culturally, environmentally and economically.

The Mineral Resource Act stipulates that the use of IBAs may or may not be required by Naalakkersuisut as a condition for grant of a licence, and this to a certain extent makes the IBA a private negotiating arrangement rather than a requirement of public law. However, with the licensor as a party to the IBA, the IBA easily becomes a sort of condition connected to the content of the licence.

The relationship between IBA and license agreement seems quite unclear. In particular, the possibility of suspending activities or revoking a licence in the event of non-fulfilment of the IBA seems rather problematic. The licensor must exercise proportionality between means and ends.

The definition of a Greenlandic workforce has also caused particular problems. More detailed rules are called for in IBAs and have in recent IBAs been implemented to assure that workers from the rest of the Kingdom do not take advantage of the opportunity at the expense of local workers. Efforts to secure opportunities for workers in the municipalities have not been tried. Greenland is seen in the IBAs as a common labour market.

The IBA is a potentially valuable instrument for the promotion of Greenlandic and local interests in connection with the extraction of hydrocarbons. What matters is whether Greenland can provide a workforce that can exploit opportunities for jobs and training. Greenland's capacities are limited by its small population size, and, as a result, the timing of new projects becomes very important. In this context, it is pleasing that the three most recent IBAs concerns projects that seem to offer great potential for domestic manpower. However, these are onshore projects. The opportunities connected with the drilling of offshore exploration wells in 2010 and 2011 benefited the Greenland workforce only to a limited extent.

Notes

1 Mortensen 2012 and Committee for Greenlandic Mineral Resource to the Benefit of Society 2014.

2 The resource curse refers to the paradox that countries with many non-renewable natural resources tend not to use that capital to boost their economy. See for instance Ross 1999.

3 Two of the municipalities (Qaasuitsup and Sermersooq) cover a very large area. They are at the present time the world's two largest municipalities, with areas of 660,000 and 531,900 km^2 respectively.
4 They are used in Chile, Papua New Guinea, South Africa, Egypt, Eritrea, Guinea, Mozambique, Nigeria, Sierra Leone and Yemen; cf. World Bank 2010, 16.
5 World Bank 2010, 16 A list of terms can be found used for IBAs can be found in Centre for Social Responsibility in Mining (2011).
6 Danish Act No. 473 of 12 June 2009 on Greenland Self-Government, which entered into force 21 June 2009.
7 Inatsisartut Act No. 7 of 7 December 2009 on Mineral Resources and Mineral Resource Activities with later amendments.
8 See Section 5 of the Mineral Resources Act.
9 See Section 5 of the Mineral Resource Act.
10 In some international conventions signed by Denmark, Greenland is excluded. However, this is not the case regarding the CSC and UNCLOS. On the CSC and UNCLOS in relation to Greenland, see Sandroos 2015, 76 ff. and Mortensen 2013, 339 ff.
11 Consolidated Act no. 1101, 18 November 2005.
12 See Naalakkersuisut 2016.
13 It is assumed (but not yet confirmed) that there are significant oil and natural gas resources offshore of both north-east and north-west Greenland. The United States Geological Survey (USGS) estimates that there are reserves of about 7.3 billion barrels of oil and 52 billion cubic feet of natural gas offshore between north-west Greenland and north-east Canada. See USGS 2008. The USGS estimates that there is oil and natural gas equivalent to 31.4 billion barrels of oil offshore of north-east Greenland. See USGS 2007.
14 See Committee for Greenlandic Mineral Resources to the Benefit of Society 2014 for a discussion of the potential impact of mining in Greenland. The report is based on a number of background papers produced by academics, all of which are available on the internet.
15 IBA has been widely used in Canada as a tool to secure Aboriginal communities a share of the income from mining projects, see e.g. Sosa and Keenan 2001.
16 Mouyal 2016.
17 Coase 1960.
18 Sandroos 2015, 275 and www.miningfacts.org/Communities/What-are-Impact-and-Benefit-Agreements-(IBAs).
19 Article 78a was not originally part of the Mineral Resource Act. It was included by Act No. 26 of December 18 2012 and entered into force 1 January 2013.
20 When the term IBA is used in this chapter, it refers to an agreement in accordance with Section 78a of the Mineral Resource Act.
21 The Greenland Act No. 25 of 18 December 2012 on Works and Construction in Large Scale Projects.
22 Further, the Act only applies to projects if the need for labour in connection with the construction phase exceeds the suitable, available and accessible workforce, or if the technical and financial demands on the companies performing the construction work exceed the capacity of the Greenlandic companies. Considering the Greenlandic labour market, this will normally be the case for such large-scale projects.
23 In Danish: 'Fælles betingelser for arbejder og leverancer i bygge- og anlægsvirksomhed i Grønland' ('Common conditions for the provision of works and supplies within building and engineering in Greenland'), also known as AP 95.
24 Act no. 715 of 26 June 2014 (Lov for Grønland om udlændinges adgang til opholds-og arbejdstilladelse i anlægsfasen af et storskalaprojekt).

25 Consolidated Act No. 1021 of 19 September 2014.
26 These standard terms are reprinted in Sandroos, 2015, 450 ff. and 470 ff.
27 See Sandroos 2015, 403.
28 See above in the section *The Mineral Resources Act* regarding the municipalities as a party to the IBA being mentioned in the preparatory work.
29 On SIA in Greenland in connection with mining project, see Hansen and Mortensen 2013, 365 ff. The term SSA will be used in the following.
30 The MLSA was formerly known as the Bureau of Minerals and Petroleum (BMP).
31 See Bureau of Minerals and Petroleum 2009.
32 Bureau of Minerals and Petroleum 2009.
33 As an example, it took three months from the grant of an exploitation licence covering the Aappaluttoq ruby-sapphire deposit dated 3 March 2014 to True North Gems Greenland A/S (TNG) to the signature of an IBA between TNG, Sermersooq municipality, and the government of Greenland on 16 June 2014. The drafting process is described in Hansen and Mortensen 2013, 380 ff.
34 See for a comment to the two Cairn IBA's in Mouyal 2016, 57–62.
35 See for a comment to the TNG IBA's in Mouyal 2016, 62–65.
36 The draft model IBA can still be found on the internet by googling *iba_draft_model_website.doc* – last accessed 7 October 2016.
37 Hansen and Mortensen 2013, 383.
38 Citronen Fjord is located within Greenland's National Park Nuna allanngutsaaliugaq.
39 According to the Cairn IBA of 2011, the shorebases consisted of a country office in Nuuk, a helicopter base in Ilulissat, a supply base and project office in Aasiaat, and an office for personnel transfer, oil spill, contingency and equipment in Kangerlussuad.
40 Capricorn 2012.
41 Offshore jobs often require minimum requirements such as good English skills, passing a medical examination and passing offshore safety and survival training courses.
42 Mortensen, Su and Ulfbeck 2016, 74.
43 On inclusive and exclusive self-government, see Suksi, 2014.
44 Borch, 2014.
45 True North Gems Greenland 2015.
46 Sanctions in case of non-performance will not be dealt with further in this chapter.
47 Sandroos, 2015, 467.
48 Sandroos, 2015, 403.

References

Borch, O.J. 2014. 'Greenland Natural Resources: How to Improve Regional Value Creation and Ripple Effects.' Background Paper for Committee for Greenlandic Mineral Resources to the Benefit of Society. Available at http://greenlandperspective.ku.dk/this_is_greenland_perspective/background/report-papers/Greenlandic_natural_resources___how_to_improve_regional_value_creation_and_ripple_effects.pdf. Accessed 7 October 2016.

Bureau of Minerals and Petroleum. 2009. *Guidelines for Social Impact Assessments for mining projects in Greenland.* Available at https://www.govmin.gl/images/stories/petroleum/SIA_guidelines.pdf. Accessed 7 October 2016.

Capricorn. 2012. IBA Performance Report, April 2012. Available at http://dk.vintage.nanoq.gl/Emner/Landsstyre/Departementer/R%C3%A5stofdirektoratet/~/media/Naalakkersuisut/Raastof/VurderingafSamfundsm%C3%A6ssigBaeredygtighed/Impact%20Benefit%20Agreement%202011%20Report%20on%20Progress%20April%202012%20rev%201a%20_2_.ashx. Accessed 7 October 2016.

Centre for Social Responsibility in Mining. 2011. 'World Bank Extractive Industries Source Book: Good Practice Notes on Community Development Agreements.' Available at http://www.csrm.uq.edu.au/Portals/0/docs/CSRM-CDA-report.pdf. Accessed 7 October 2016.

Coase, R.H. 1960. 'The Problem of Social Cost'. In *The Journal of Law & Economics*, Vol. III, 1–44.

Committee for Greenlandic Mineral Resource to the Benefit of Society. 2014. *To the Benefit of Greenland.* Nuuk and Copenhagen. Available at http://greenland-perspective.ku.dk/this_is_greenland_perspective/background/report-papers/To_the_benefit_of_Greenland.pdf. Accessed 7 October 2016.

Hansen, T.T. and Mortensen, B.O.G. 2013. 'Social Impact Assessment, including related impact assessments in relation to mineral extraction in Greenland.' In *Yearbook of Polar Law*, Vol. 5, 359–386. Leiden: Brill.

Mortensen, B.O.G. 2012. 'Mining and pollution.' In *Yearbook of Polar Law*, Vol. 4, 673–88. Leiden: Brill.

Mortensen, B.O.G. 2013. 'Greenland' in *Upstream Law and Regulation: A Global Handbook*, eds. Pereira, E. and Talus, K., 337–354. London: Globe Business Planning.

Mortensen, B.O.G.; Su, J. and Ulfbeck, V. 2016. 'Workers' rights and chain liability' in *Responsibilities and Liabilities for Commercial Activity in the Arctic*, eds. Ulfbeck, V., Møllmann, A. and Mortensen, B.O.G., 72–82, London & New York: Routledge.

Mouyal, L.W. 2016. 'Corporate social responsibility in the light of contract law' in *Responsibilities and Liabilities for Commercial Activity in the Arctic*, eds. Ulfbeck, V., Møllmann, A. and Mortensen, B.O.G., 50–71, London & New York: Routledge.

Naalakkersuisut 2016. 'Current Licences.' Available at https://www.govmin.gl/minerals/current-licences. Accessed 7 October 2016.

Ross, M.L. 1999. 'The Political Economy of the Resource Curse.' In *World Politics* Vol. 51 (2), 297–322.

Sandroos, B. 2015. *The Greenland Mineral Resource Act.* Copenhagen: Djøf Publishing.

Sosa, I. and Keenan, K. 2001. 'Impact Benefit Agreements between Aboriginal Communities and Mining Companies: Their Use in Canada.' Toronto, ON: Canadian Environmental Law Association; Victoria, BC: Environmental Mining Council of British Columbia. Available at http://www.cela.ca/sites/cela.ca/files/uploads/IBAeng.pdf. Accessed 7 October 2016.

Suksi, M. 2014. 'Territorial autonomy: The Åland Islands in comparison with other sub-state entities.' In *Territorial Autonomies in Europe: Solutions and Challenges*, ed. Kántor, Z., 37–58. Budapest: NPKI and Harmattan.

The United States Geological Survey (USGS). 2007. 'Assessment of Undiscovered Oil and Gas Resources of the East Greenland Rift Basins Province.' https://pubs.usgs.gov/fs/2007/3077/pdf/FS07-3077_508.pdf. Accessed 7 October 2016.

The United States Geological Survey (USGS). 2008. 'Assessment of Undiscovered Oil and Gas Resources of the West Greenland–East Canada Province.' Available at https://pubs.usgs.gov/fs/2008/3014/. Accessed 7 October 2016.

True North Gems Greenland. 2015. 'Monitoring and Evaluation Report 2015 for the Impact Benefit Agreement in relation to the Aappaluttoq Ruby- Pink Sapphire Project Greenland.'

World Bank/ERM. 2010. 'Mining Community Development Agreements: Practical Experiences and Field Studies.' Available at http://siteresources.worldbank.org/INTEXTINDWOM/Resources/CDA_Report_FINAL.pdf. Accessed 7 October 2016.

15 The interplay between environmental research and environmental regulation of offshore oil activities in Greenland

Anders Mosbech, David Boertmann, Susse Wegeberg and Kim Gustavson

Introduction

Any regulation of the environmental impact of oil activities in the Arctic must take into account both the ecological characteristics and the current challenges facing the Arctic ecosystems. Many Arctic species, including copepods and marine mammals, are characterised by high levels of body fat, slow maturation and long lifespan and a simple food chain. The relatively high levels of body fat serve partly as an energy reserve to withstand long periods of starvation or hibernation, partly as body thermo-insulation. These factors, together with seasonal reproduction and feeding and consequent seasonality in the metabolic activity of Arctic organisms, may interact with any environmental stressor that takes the form of chemical pollution. Additional factors that must be taken into account are that biological and chemical degradation of chemicals generally takes place more slowly at low temperatures, while the ecological processes of the Arctic are less well understood than those of temperate zones. At the same time, the Arctic ecosystems are already affected by long-range pollution and are more affected by climate change than temperate ecosystems. As a result, there is often uncertainty associated with assessing the potential impact of oil activities. Special caution is therefore called for with emissions and discharges, as well as a focus on the environmental monitoring of such activities. This chapter is about how Greenland has dealt with this challenge in the interplay between research, monitoring and regulation.

Our focus here is on the impact and regulation of regular oil-exploration activities in the marine environment. Dealing with major accidents and oil-spill responses would require a chapter in its own right.[1] To set the stage in the Greenland context, we first give short introductions to the challenges facing the management of the marine ecosystem (part one) and to the regulatory framework for oil activities in Greenland (part two). Then we describe how research and monitoring are an integrated part of the planning, the mitigation of negative impact and the regulatory process of oil-exploration activities (part three). We focus on three topics: the development of strategic environmental impact assessments (SEIAs, also called SEAs); drilling discharges during the most recent drilling campaigns in West Greenland; and the noise from seismic surveys in Baffin Bay 2012. We demonstrate how the authorities in some cases have to deal with considerable uncertainty due to lack of basic knowledge, and how they manage to do so in an adaptive manner. Finally, in part four, we discuss how research and monitoring are fundamental for implementing ecosystem-based management when adapting to Arctic change.

The marine ecosystem: human use and management challenges

Greenland has a low population density and very extensive and relatively untouched marine areas, with room for unique populations of animals of both local and international importance, such as narwhals and polar bears. The protection and management of the fauna are important issues for the local population and are frequent hot topics in the public debate. Greenland has large marine areas and as yet there is limited environmental impact from oil activities. Nevertheless, oil activities are increasing, and the ecosystems are not unaffected by human impact from other activities. Today, the effects are noticeable in the following three main areas: (1) fishery and hunting, (2) long-range pollution from the industrial world and (3) climate change.

In connection with the ongoing development of the oil industry in this area, it is important to keep in mind that the environmental impact of oil activities should be dealt with in the context of the need to protect a nature that is already exposed to impact in the above-mentioned three areas, and the need for the oil industry to coexist in a sustainable way with fishery and hunting.

Fishery is Greenland's main export industry, and the modern and effective fishery for northern shrimp and Greenland halibut accounts for approximately 80 percent of exports. Fishing quotas are regulated in accordance with scientific advice from organisations such as NAFO (the Northwest Atlantic Fisheries Organisation), the international non-governmental organisation ICES (the International Council for the Exploration of the Sea) and the Greenland Institute of Natural Resources (Pinngortitaleriffik). It is also worth mentioning that the important shrimp fishery off the coast of West Greenland has recently been certified as sustainable by MSC (the Marine Stewardship Council). In addition to the size of the catch, it is particularly the impact on the seafloor fauna from bottom trawling that may have a negative impact on the sustainability of the shrimp fishery. Although trawler fishery dominates the economy, subsistence fishery and hunting from small boats is also very important for the socio-economy and well-being in the Greenland communities. Hunting for birds and mammals is important culturally, for the meat supply and for employment, especially in Qaasuitsup municipality. Hunting for marine mammals is regulated in accordance with scientific advice from international forums such as NAMMCO (the North Atlantic Marine Mammal Commission), JCNB (the Joint Commission on

Narwhal and Beluga) and IWC (the International Whaling Commission). Most marine mammals are exploited sustainably, but the ongoing unsustainable exploitation of certain species presents a challenge.[2] Some populations, such as the harbour seal, walrus and thick-billed murre, were historically under pressure from excessive hunting for some decades as increasingly effective hunting equipment, in particular faster motor boats with a larger range, made hunting more efficient, while regulations and population monitoring failed to keep pace. However, there are now examples of very successful nature management, where effective regulations have restored former populations. This is the case for the common eider in West Greenland, where limitations to spring hunting introduced in 2001 are presumed to be the main cause of the increase in the breeding population from approximately 15,000 pairs to approximately 70,000 pairs in the period 2001–2009.[3]

Long-range pollution from the industrial world already constitutes a major environmental problem in Greenland.[4] This applies to heavy metals such as mercury and also to slowly degradable environmental persistent organic pollutants such as PCB (polychlorinated biphenyl) and dioxin, which spread via air and ocean currents and become part of the marine food chain.[5] The highest accumulation of these contaminants occurs in the animals at the top of the food chain, such as seals and polar bears, partly because the contaminants are fat-soluble and therefore become incorporated in the fatty Arctic marine food chains, and partly because animals in the Arctic grow relatively slowly and reach a greater age than animals at more southern latitudes.[6] Some of the contaminant breaks down slowly in the liver, and some is excreted only very slowly from the animals.

Although the concentrations of contaminants such as mercury and PCB have been higher in seals in areas such as the Baltic Sea, where they live closer to the sources of pollution,[7] the concentrations of contaminants in several marine mammals in Greenland are at levels where they may have an impact both on the health of the animals and on the people who consume them. The polar bear's immune system and ability to produce viable offspring are particularly affected.[8] Seals and polar bears are food sources in Greenland, and Greenlanders living on traditional food sources are therefore among the world's peoples with the highest body-load of substances such as mercury and PCB.[9] The health authorities recommend limiting the intake of seal and whale. It is particularly important to limit the consumption of fatty tissue, liver and kidneys, which are the organs and tissues with the highest concentrations of most contaminants.[10]

Climate change is considered to be by far the greatest threat to Arctic biodiversity as we know it today.[11] Increasingly robust models show that global climate change with rising temperatures and greater climate variability will have a very strong impact in Arctic regions. The changed climate conditions affect the snow and ice cover, ocean currents and the phenology (seasonal rhythm) and distribution of flora and fauna. The warmer conditions will benefit some animals, while other species, especially those that are sea-ice dependent, will meet difficulties. The greater variability in the weather from year to year that is another consequence of global warming also makes it difficult for organisms to adapt to the new conditions. Researchers are particularly concerned that important food chains may be disrupted because changes are occurring so rapidly that animals have difficulty adapting to the changes in food availability,[12] resulting in a mismatch between the occurrence and availability of food (trophic mismatch).[13]

Any assessment of the environmental impact of oil activities must therefore take into account not only that the ecosystems are already exposed to long-range pollution and affected by climate change, but, additionally, that the Arctic is characterised by slow animal growth (with resulting potentially higher contaminant accumulation over a lifespan) and slow biological breakdown of contaminants, oil, offshore chemicals, etc. As a result, there is a need for special caution with emissions and discharge from mineral-resource activities, as well as with the environmental monitoring of such activities. To fully support an ecosystem-based management, monitoring should ideally include studies that shed light on which changes are caused by mineral-resource activities, by climate change or by other human activities, by a combination of these factors (cumulative effects), or by natural variations.

The environmental regulatory framework for oil activities

All mineral-resource activities, including their environmental aspects, are governed by the Mineral Resources Act, adopted by the parliament of Greenland. Licences for exploration and exploitation are granted by the government of Greenland after consideration by the Mineral Resource Authority. The Mineral Resources Act sets out the principles that govern performance-based environmental regulations. These include requirements for the industry to carry out all activities in a responsible way as regards safety, health, environment, resource exploitation and social sustainability. Special emphasis is placed on application of the principles of Best Available Technique (BAT) and Best Environmental Practice (BEP).

The Inatsisartut (Greenland parliament) Mineral Resources Act Committee's 2009 report to the Naalakkersuisut (the government of Greenland) on the Mineral Resources Act states as follows:

> **The purpose of the Mineral Resources Act – a difficult balancing act**
> Seen in a greater perspective, the Mineral Resources Act serves several purposes: it aims to provide a framework for mineral-resource activities in Greenland that makes investment in exploration projects attractive to mining and oil companies. It aims to ensure that Greenland society benefits financially from mineral-resource activities in the country, including increased employment. Finally, it should prevent mineral-resource activities from causing irreversible damage to the environment, including the very vulnerable Arctic nature in particular. To some extent, these considerations are contradictory: increased requirements for societal

> benefits and environmental protection make investment in exploration projects less attractive to mining and oil companies. The process therefore involves a difficult balancing act. The Bill sets out the general framework for this balancing act. Within this framework, it will be up to the government of Greenland to determine the detailed provisions by means of executive orders, standard conditions and model permits, etc.[14]

Chapter 15 in the act is dedicated to environmental impact assessment. All projects and activities that may impact the environment require that the applicant carry out an environmental impact assessment (EIA). The EIA report is subject to public consultation before the government of Greenland, with the assistance of the Mineral Resource Authority, makes a decision regarding approval. In the EIA, the applicant must explain all relevant environmental conditions and document that the above-mentioned BAT and BEP principles are being applied. The EIA must be based on actual baseline studies of the environmental conditions in the area, and the Mineral Resource Authority may request that the company undertakes additional studies if it considers there is insufficient information about the potential environmental impact and the technologies to be used.

A number of guidelines and threshold values prepared and implemented by the Mineral Resource Authority make up the framework of environmental regulations that governs the mineral-resource industry's activities in Greenland. The guidelines summarise the requirements, considerations and limitations that apply to companies preparing project-specific EIAs for large-scale activities. Based on the EIA report and the formal application, the authorities draft specific requirements and conditions for the project in question, including a framework for environmental control and monitoring.

Guidelines in relation to offshore hydrocarbon exploration activities have been introduced for:

- oil exploration and exploitation (*Guidelines for preparing an environmental impact assessment [EIA] report for activities related to hydrocarbon exploration and exploitation offshore Greenland*)
- Offshore Seismic Surveys in Greenland (*Guidelines to Best Environmental Practices, Environmental Impact Assessments and Environmental Mitigation Assessments 2015*)
- stratigraphic drilling (*BMP Guidelines for preparing an environmental impact assessment [EIA] report related to stratigraphic drilling offshore Greenland*)

To this should be added general rules-sets governing oil-industry activities:

- exploration drilling (*Exploration Drilling Guidelines, May 2011*)
- other exploration activities (*MLSA Guidelines for application, execution and reporting of offshore hydrocarbon exploration activities [excluding drilling] in Greenland, February 2016*)

All guidelines are available at the Mineral Resource Authority website (www.govmin.gl).

The guidelines are generally based on international standards. Applied, for instance, are the Norwegian standards for adequate safety in the petroleum industry (NORSOK), British standards for seismic surveying (JNCC guidelines),[15] the Arctic Council's guidelines for offshore oil activities in the Arctic (PAME 2009)[16] and the environmental provisions of the OSPAR convention (the Oslo and Paris Convention for the Protection of the Marine Environment of the North–East Atlantic), by the Greenland Self-government unilaterally extended to include West Greenland. The OSPAR convention has been very effective in reducing pollution from the oil industry in the North Sea.

Environmental research and the regulation of offshore oil activities

In this section, we will present examples of the interplay between research and regulation from some of the issues that have been most sharply in focus in recent years in Greenland. First, we will deal with the environmental planning involved in government decisions about opening new areas for licensing; then, the two most environmentally important exploration activities, exploration drilling and seismic exploration, will be presented.

Planning of offshore oil-industry activity

Spatial planning and the careful choice of location for oil-industry activities are essential to minimise the harmful impact on the environment. To manage and meet the environmental challenges and potential consequences associated with offshore oil activities, the Greenland self-government has commissioned a number of regional strategic environmental impact assessments (SEIAs, also called SEAs), including a large number of scientific background studies.[17] An SEIA summarises the available knowledge and environmental status of a region without oil activities (a zero solution) and describes how the region may be affected if oil activities are permitted. The SEIA is submitted for public hearing before the self-government makes a decision about the opening and demarcation of licence areas in the region. In this process, some areas have been excluded from licence rounds due to environmental considerations. In the last decade, most offshore marine areas around Greenland have been covered by the SEIA programme, and the available knowledge of the area has been summarised. Key environmental risks and gaps in knowledge have also been described in the background reports. It was, for example, based on the SEIA submitted in the licensing process for North-East Greenland that the current efficiency of technology available for oil-spill response in ice was not considered adequate for establishing an effective oil-spill response plan for exploratory drilling. It was clear to all that this issue has to be solved before exploratory drilling can begin.

All SEIAs and the background research have been carried out at a scientific level, and all data organised in a data centre, where the knowledge associated with the individual regions is stored for use in connection both with the development of EIAs for oil activities and with further administrative regulation and planning. The body of knowledge about nature and the environment generated by EIA research programmes is also available for the planning and regulation of other sectors. As an example, this has constituted an important part of the data used for the analysis carried out to identify marine areas vulnerable to shipping[18] and in the development of the oil-spill sensitivity atlas,[19] and a considerable amount of information is available at the government's geographical information system portal, NUNAGIS.

Exploration drilling

Offshore drillings for hydrocarbons take place during both the exploration and the production phases. Historically, the seabed in the North Sea was heavily polluted by oil drillings around 30–40 years ago, especially because of discharges of drilling mud containing oil and chemicals. A targeted campaign by the North Sea countries, coordinated through the OSPAR convention, resulted in a considerable reduction of environmentally harmful discharges from exploration drillings. Due to a higher number of drillings per year, the discharge of drilling mud continues to impact the environment in the North Sea, although the most hazardous components have been substituted with substances with better environmental properties.[20]

Drilling mud is used for lubrication and cooling of the drill bit, as a means to transport drill cuttings, to stabilise the well bore and to balance the pressure in the drill line. Large quantities are involved. In connection with drillings in Greenland in 2011, for example, the amount used per well thus varied from 350 tonnes (2 wells) to approximately 1,500 tonnes (3 wells), depending on the depth of the hole and the geological formations involved. The drilling mud consists of a carrier fluid, weighting material (typically barite) and various different chemicals, mainly selected according to the geology of the layers drilled. The carrier fluid may be water (water-based drilling mud) or oil (oil-based drilling mud). The barite itself causes no harm to the environment, apart from the physical impact of sedimentation, but several of the potential chemicals may have environmentally harmful properties. Barite also contains impurities in the form of heavy metals. Cold-water corals and sponge gardens are particularly vulnerable to the impact of sedimentation in the form of drill cuttings and mud. This is why the seabed fauna must be studied before discharge can be approved, in order to protect particularly vulnerable species and communities (Figure 15.1).

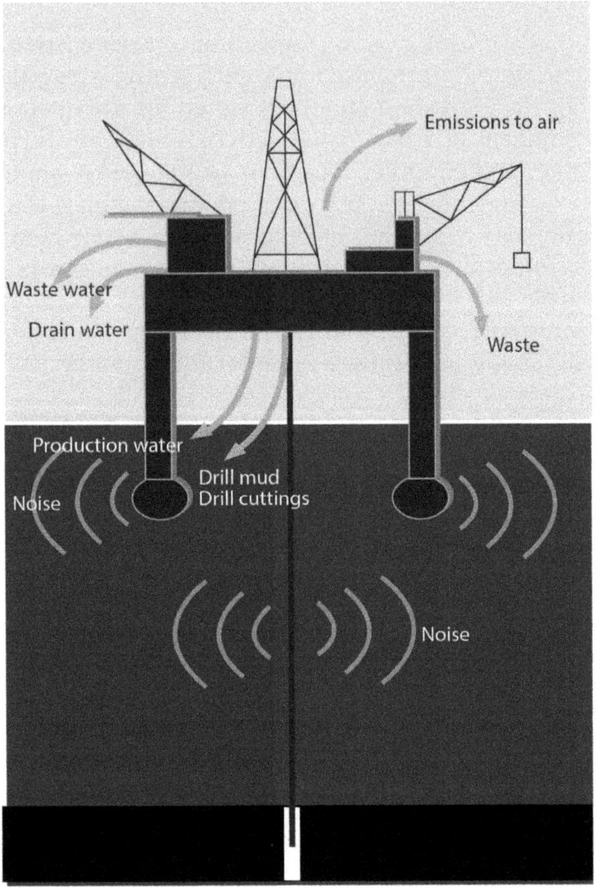

Figure 15.1 Discharge and impact from a drilling platform. The self-government decided before the 2010 drilling campaign that the OSPAR convention's discharge guidelines apply all over Greenland. It later developed a strategy for further minimizing impacts from discharges of drilling waste, as discussed in the text. (© DCE).

The choice of drilling mud is of key importance to the drilling process. According to choice, drilling mud may have a severe impact on the environment when disposed of at the end of the drilling period. Water-based drilling mud generally has the least impact on the environment, and in the North Sea, is normally discharged directly into the ocean. Oil-based drilling mud has proven much more hazardous to the environment, which is why Denmark and Norway require that oil-based drilling mud be collected and transported to shore for further processing (cleaning, disposal and/or recycling). The advantage of using oil-based drilling mud is that it allows

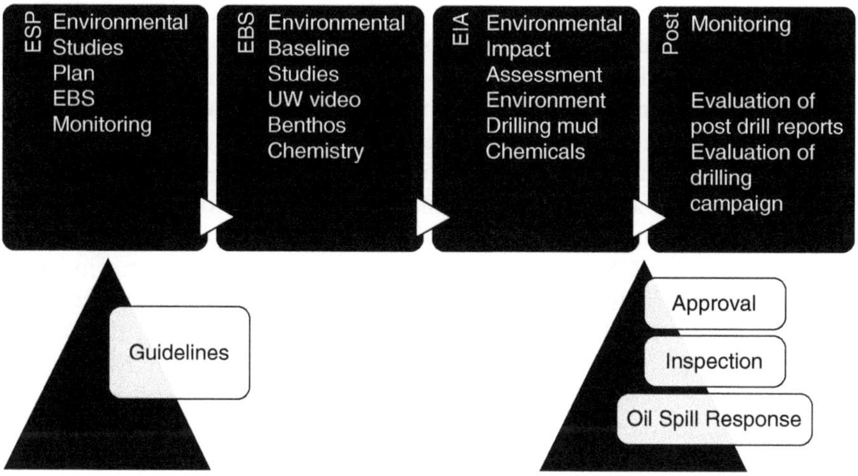

Figure 15.2 Environmental studies and approval processes in connection with exploration drillings in Greenland (© DCE).

for higher drilling speeds and reduces the amount of drilling mud required compared with water-based drilling mud (Figure 15.2).

In the wake of the exploration drillings in West Greenland in 2010 and 2011, the overall view was that the environmental conditions after the drillings were as expected and that there was no significant or unexpected impact on the marine environment. However, as a result of the drilling campaign's monitoring programme for the seabed, certain deviations from environmental requirements and predicted concentrations on the seabed were of concern.[21] There was focus on the discharge of drilling-mud chemicals and on concentrations of heavy metals in the form of impurities in the barite. The authorities demanded further environmental studies in 2013 of the 2011 drilling locations, with a view to obtaining further information about the presence of drilling chemicals in the sediment. The Greenland authorities have since then raised the requirements regarding the concentrations – and their documentation – of mercury as an impurity in barite and have initiated a study of release and bioavailability of mercury in drilling mud and sediment. Hence, the mercury content of barite planned for use in drilling mud must be documented and approved by the authorities before use, and must be the documentably lowest on the market. This means considerably lower than 1 ppm. The earlier <1 ppm threshold limit for mercury concentration in barite was introduced in the 2011 drilling activities that followed US Environmental Protection Agency (EPA) guidelines (2004),[22] as no threshold limits on mercury concentrations in barite are stated by OSPAR.[23] Neither does the Norwegian regulation indicate a threshold limit, but it is indicated in the Norwegian petroleum activities regulation that the operator shall use chemicals with the lowest possible content of contaminants.[24]

The purpose of the environmental monitoring of drillings is to map any unexpected impact on the marine environment and to document failures to comply with environmental requirements. In this case, the environmental monitoring programme turned out to be effective, but the results also highlighted the need for the systematic control of chemicals to be used as well as discharges and concentrations in the environment.

Past environmental regulation of oil activities in Greenland has largely been inspired by the Norwegian legislation, especially for the Barents Sea. The Greenland authorities have also chosen to apply the provisions and regulations of the OSPAR convention on discharges to the marine environment, although the exploration drillings have so far taken place in the ocean off West Greenland, which is outside the area covered by the OSPAR convention. Under that convention, drilling chemicals are environmentally assessed according to their toxic properties, their biodegradability and their ability to bioaccumulate.

DCE – the Danish Centre for Environment and Energy – has thus recommended following the OSPAR recommendations on reducing the discharge of chemicals in the category of 'red' (chemicals of environmental concern and for which approval of use and discharge can be given only under certain circumstances).[25] To meet this objective, chemicals categorised as red must be substituted by more environmentally friendly alternatives, or oil-based drilling mud can be introduced, whose discharge is prohibited. This strategy follows the trend in Norway and Denmark. DCE[26] has therefore recommended that, prior to the selection and approval of drilling-mud system and chemicals in connection with oil-exploration drilling applications for Greenland, an analysis of the environmental pros and cons of several relevant drilling-mud systems is presented, and that the analysis should also include treatment technologies for drilling waste as part of the EIA so as to ensure that the drilling-mud system selected in an overall environmental context will impact the Greenlandic marine environment the least. If the results of the analysis point towards selecting an oil-based drilling-mud system, DCE recommends (1) that no drilling mud or cuttings are discharged to sea and that the risk of spills is minimised through HSE requirements; and (2) that requirements for self-control and inspections be raised.

Chemicals are normally assessed on the basis of data from standard laboratory tests carried out under temperate conditions and using organisms that are not always relevant in an Arctic context. The assessments may accordingly be subject to a higher degree of uncertainty, and a new strategy[27] proposes to focus on reducing this uncertainty by developing and performing tests specifically designed for Arctic conditions. More knowledge is required about the breakdown and ecotoxicology of chemicals and oil components under Arctic conditions so as to predict the potential effect of discharges in the Arctic environment: a work which is expected to take place in international cooperation with further development of OSPAR recommendations for the Arctic area.

Disturbance of fauna from traffic and seismic surveys

Disturbance of the fauna by traffic is often of brief duration and with no major impact, but in certain areas and at certain times, the fauna may be particularly sensitive to disturbance. Walrus haul-out sites and bird cliffs with breeding seabirds are typical examples. Disturbances in these areas at critical times may have impact on the populations. Disturbances may also scare animals away from hunting areas, but these would normally occur in a small area and be of short duration. In Greenland and elsewhere, studies have been carried out to determine the distance at which different animal species react to disturbing activities. Based on these results, the Mineral Resource Authority has defined 'traffic rules' that govern these activities so as to limit disturbance in areas and during periods of particular importance to the fauna. If these rules are adhered to, disturbance can be greatly minimised.

Animals can, under certain circumstances, habituate to disturbances. This typically occurs if the disturbance 'behaves' predictably and does not constitute a threat, for example, if a ship sails past on a regular basis along fixed lanes, does not get too close to the animals and is not associated with hunting. If oil activities in an area intensify, careful planning of traffic and other activities may promote habituation among animals in the affected areas and thereby reduce impacts in the animal populations.

Seismic activities are the most critical source of noise in connection with offshore oil exploration. Seismic surveys are carried out to obtain an image of the subsurface seabed that can be used to identify possible pockets of oil and gas. During the exploration phase, such surveys are carried out over vast offshore areas. Pressure waves from a powerful sound source are transmitted into the seabed, and the reflections are captured by a multitude of microphones.

At sea, underwater airguns are used as a sound source and are towed behind a ship. The microphones recording the sound reflections are located in a cable several kilometres long, which is also towed behind the source ship. The airguns emit a very strong, albeit brief, signal at intervals of approximately ten seconds. Underwater, the signal can be registered hundreds of kilometres away, and at times more than a thousand kilometres away, as sound attenuates much more slowly in water than in air. Especially in the Arctic, certain layers of water may act as sound transmitters, because the sound is reflected between adjacent layers in the often highly stratified water column. The sound impact from seismic activities is therefore an environmental problem that must be dealt with both in the planning process and through regulation. Behavioural changes in whales and fish are the main consequence.

If the whales are kept away from their best foraging areas for an extensive period of time, it is likely to have a major impact, but if they change to alternative foraging areas of the same quality, the effects on the population may be minimal – although the hunting potential may be affected. If the migration pattern of the whales is affected, this may also have serious consequences for certain populations, which may face a greater risk of being trapped by ice (Sassat).[28] Seen in an international perspective, the regulations on seismic activity in Greenland waters for the protection of marine mammals are quite comprehensive. A number of areas are closed to seismic surveys during sensitive periods, and companies are required to collaborate in preparing a joint noise model for the activities applied for if their noise propagation affects the same areas. This gives the authorities a better basis for assessing whether the total impact will be acceptable. There is nevertheless much uncertainty about the effect of seismic activities on species most sensitive to noise, such as the narwhal. For this reason, the Greenland government launched a research project in connection with a large seismic campaign in Baffin Bay in 2012. In this area, the narwhal hunt is of considerable socioeconomic and cultural importance for local hunters. Studies included noise propagation from the seismic vessels,[29] aerial surveys of distribution and numbers of narwhals and interviews with narwhal hunters.[30] Results from these studies indicate that the narwhals did not leave Melville Bay or change the time of their autumn migration due to the 2012 seismic activities. The conclusion was not entirely clear, however. It is possible that the seismic noise of 2012 caused the narwhals to prefer the central part of Melville Bay, where they were more clumped than was observed in 2007. However, the results from the aerial survey of 2014 suggest that the clumping of narwhals in the inner part of the Melville Bay is a long-term trend unrelated to seismic exploration. Other human activities in the bay involve increased boat traffic (including dinghies used for transport to the hunting grounds, as documented by the hunter studies). Non-human changes in Melville Bay involve the retreat of glaciers and increased advection of warm water. It is at present impossible to distinguish the effects of seismic exploration from other human activities and ongoing natural changes. Continued monitoring of the relatively small population of narwhals in the bay will presumably lead to a better understanding of the observed behavioural changes in the narwhal population.

The next step towards greater understanding of the impact of seismic noise on narwhals – both individually and at population level – is to conduct targeted studies of the behavioural and physiological effects on individual narwhals during controlled exposure to noise from airgun arrays. The long-term impact of seismic noise on distribution, migration patterns and population size should be documented by annual aerial surveys in areas where seismic surveys have been carried out and where the level of hunting pressure is known (e.g. Melville Bay).[31]

This example illustrates how difficult it is to single out a clear cause–effect relationship between the various factors involved and to determine a safe level of impact in a complex ecosystem. Further studies will be necessary to evaluate the long-term effect of disturbances on the population, and an ecosystem-based approach with a strong monitoring programme will be needed to keep track of what is going on and to identify the relevant management options.

Conclusion

We have here highlighted the value of SEIAs for setting the stage and for pinpointing key knowledge gaps, uncertainties and environmental risks as a tool in the governance process before opening for licensing. The SEIAs are also important, however, at later stages, underlining the research and monitoring that is required in following an innovative and adaptive approach. We used discharges from exploratory drilling and noise from seismic surveys as examples of offshore activities to illustrate the importance of research and monitoring for dealing with uncertainty in the environmental management of the activities.

In general, the monitoring should include both a baseline survey before the start of exploration and exploitation activities and impact monitoring after they have been begun.[32] To provide the knowledge necessary for an ecosystem-based management as recommended by the Arctic Council, this monitoring should include both a local and a regional level. The regional monitoring should include indicators of ecosystem health (both biodiversity and system processes) and should provide information not only about the environmental impact of a particular activity, but also about the multi-sector overall (cumulative) effects on the ecosystem of climate change, long-distance pollution, industry, and fishery and hunting. An example of this complexity was illustrated in our case of the narwhals in Baffin Bay: it is difficult to understand and manage the impact of seismic noise on narwhals without taking into account that this animal is a key species for hunters in the area.

More specifically, the local assessment and monitoring of drilling should follow an approach in which biological and chemical samples and analyses are performed in an integrated framework. Such an integrated approach is defined by international institutions and conventions such as OSPAR and HELCOM.[33] Monitoring includes key environmental matrices, water sediment, biota and an appropriate combination of biological effects and chemical measurements, as well as the design of sampling programmes to allow the chemical concentrations, the biological effects data and other supporting parameters to be combined for assessment.

We conclude that, given the many unknowns in this frontier area, a close linkage between research, monitoring and the regulation of offshore activities in Greenland is necessary to secure an innovative and adaptive management. Greenland has established environmental governance based on regional strategic assessments (SEIAs or SEA), company responsibility through the approval of EIAs and the use of mandatory guidelines based on international standards (such as OSPAR). These regulatory instruments are research-based, and as we have shown, it is pivotal that they are supported by area-specific research focused on minimising the uncertainty for key environmental issues in the Greenland area, such as the impact of noise on narwhals. Relevant research-based knowledge is also vital in the democratic debate and governance processes, which include not only local communities, but industry and government.

Notes

1 AMAP 2010, See Skjoldal et al. 2010.
2 Boertmann 2008, AMAP 2013.
3 Merkel 2010.
4 AMAP 1998.
5 AMAP 2004, 2011a,c.
6 AMAP 1998, 2004, and 2011a, b and c.
7 Nyman et al. 2002; Roos et al. 2012.
8 Dietz et al. 2013; Letcher et al. 2010; Sonne 2010.
9 AMAP 2009.
10 AMAP 2009.
11 AMAP 2011a, AMAP 2013, CAFF 2013.
12 Høye et al. 2013.
13 Post and Forchhammer 2008.
14 Our translation, Mineral Resource Committee (2009).
15 JNCC is the abbreviation for the Joint Nature Conservation Committee in the UK.
16 PAME 2009.
17 All reports can be found at: www.govmin.gl/petroleum/environment/environmental-reports.
18 Christensen et al. 2012, 2015; AMAP 2013.
19 E.g. Clausen et al. 2012. For full list see www.govmin.gl/petroleum/environment/environmental-reports.
20 SFT 2008, Research Council of Norway 2012.
21 DCE 2013, dated 7 February 2013; Bureau of Minerals and Petroleum. 2011.
22 US EPA guidelines (2004).
23 DCE 2011, dated 31 October 2011.
24 Aktivitetforskriften § 66, http://www.ptil.no/aktivitetsforskriften/category379.html#_Toc408811857.
25 OSPAR 2006.
26 Gustavson et al. 2013.
27 Gustavson et al. 2013.
28 Heide-Jørgensen et al. 2013a.
29 Wisniewska et al. 2014.
30 Heide-Jørgensen et al. 2013b; Heide-Jørgensen et al. 2014.
31 DCE and GINR 2015.
32 Arctic Council 2013.
33 The Baltic Marine Environment Protection Commission, also known as the Helsinki Commission.

References

AMAP (The Arctic Council working group on Arctic Monitoring and Assessment Programme). 1998. *AMAP Assessment Report: Arctic Pollution Issues.* Oslo: Arctic Monitoring and Assessment Programme.

AMAP. 2004. *AMAP Assessment 2002: Persistent Organic Pollutants in the Arctic*. Oslo: Arctic Monitoring and Assessment Programme. www.amap.no/.

AMAP. 2009. *AMAP Assessment 2009: Human Health in the Arctic*. Oslo: Arctic Monitoring and Assessment Programme. www.amap.no/.

AMAP. 2010. *Assessment 2007: Oil and Gas Activities in the Arctic – Effects and Potential Effects*. Vols. 1 and 2. Oslo: Arctic Monitoring and Assessment Programme. www.amap.no/oil-and-gas-assessment-oga.

AMAP. 2011a. *AMAP Assessment 2011: Mercury in the Arctic*. Oslo: Arctic Monitoring and Assessment Programme.

AMAP. 2011b. *Snow, Water, Ice and Permafrost in the Arctic (SWIPA): Executive Summary*. Assessment Summary. Oslo: AMAP Secretariat.

AMAP. 2011c. *Arctic Pollution 2011*. Oslo: Arctic Monitoring and Assessment Programme.

AMAP. 2013. *Identification of Arctic Marine Areas of Heightened Ecological and Cultural Significance: Arctic Marine Shipping Assessment (AMSA) IIc: AMAP/CAFF/SDWG*. Oslo: Arctic Monitoring and Assessment Programme.

Arctic Council. 2013. *Ecosystem-Based Management*. Report submitted to Senior Arctic Officials by the Expert Group on Ecosystem-Based Management. Tromsø: May 2013.

Boertmann, D. 2008. *Greenland's Red List 2007* [in Danish]. Aarhus: University of Aarhus Danish Centre for Environment and Energy (DCE); Nuuk: Greenland Self-Government.

Bureau of Minerals and Petroleum. 2011. *Extract from Approval of up to 7 (Seven) Exploration Drillings in Accordance with Section 15 in the Permits 2002/15, 2005/06, 2008/11 and 2011/16* [in Danish]. Nuuk: Greenland Self-Government, Bureau of Minerals and Petroleum, May 2011.

CAFF. 2013. *Arctic Biodiversity Assessment*. Conservation of Arctic Flora and Fauna. Arctic Council.

Christensen, T., K. Falk, T. Boye, F. Ugarte, D. Boertmann and A. Mosbech. 2012. *Identification of Vulnerable Marine Areas in the Greenland/Danish Part of the Arctic* [in Danish]. Aarhus: University of Aarhus Danish Centre for Environment and Energy. www.dmu.dk/pub/sr43.pdf.

Christensen T., et al. 2015. Analyse af mulig økosystembaseret tilgang til forvaltning af skibstrafik i Disko Bugt og Store Hellefiskebanke. Aarhus Universitet, DCE – Nationalt Center for Miljø og Energi, 103 s. – Teknisk rapport fra DCE – Nationalt Center for Miljø og Energi nr. 61 http://dce2.au.dk/pub/TR61.pdf.

Clausen, D., K.L. Johansen, A. Mosbech, D. Boertmann and S. Wegeberg. 2012. *Environmental Oil Spill Sensitivity Atlas for the West Greenland (68°–72° N) Coastal Zone*, 2nd revised edition. Scientific Report 44. Aarhus: University of Aarhus Danish Centre for Environment and Energy. www.dmu.dk/Pub/SR44.pdf.

DCE (Danish Centre for Environment and Energy). 2011. 'Koncentrationer af naturligt forekommende kviksølv i baryt anvendt i boremudder i forbindelse med olieefterforskningsboringer ved Grønland 2011.' Memo 31 October 2011. Aarhus: University of Aarhus Danish Centre for Environment and Energy.

DCE (Danish Centre for Environment and Energy). 2013. 'Post-drill monitoring evaluation, environmental assessment and recommendation of the Capricorn Drilling Campaign 2011.' Memo 7 February 2013. Aarhus: University of Aarhus Danish Centre for Environment and Energy.

DCE (Danish Centre for Environment and Energy) and GINR (Greenland Institute of Natural Resources, Nuuk). 2015. 'Summary of environmental studies designed to assess the effects of seismic exploration in the Baffin Bay 2012.' Memo 22 September 2015. Aarhus: University of Aarhus Danish Centre for Environment and Energy.

Dietz, R., et al. 2013. 'What are the Toxicological Effects of Mercury in Arctic Biota?' *Science of the Total Environment* 443: 775–790.

Gustavson et al. 2013. 'Forslag til strategi for miljøvurdering og bortskaffelse af boremudder og borekemikalier i forbindelse med olie-og gasaktiviteter i grønlandske farvande.' Memo 14 May 2013. 4th edition. Aarhus: University of Aarhus Danish Centre for Environment and Energy.

Heide-Jørgensen, M.P., R.G. Hansen and M.H.S. Sinding. 2014. *Abundance and Distribution of Narwhals in Melville Bay in 2014.* Nuuk: Greenland Institute of Natural Resources.

Heide-Jørgensen, M.P., R.G. Hansen, K.K. Westdal, R.R. Reeves and A. Mosbech. 2013a. 'Narwhals and Seismic Exploration: Is Seismic Noise Increasing the Risk of Ice Entrapments?' *Biological Conservation* 158: 50–54.

Heide-Jørgensen, M.P., R.G. Hansen, S. Fossette, N.H. Nielsen, M.V. Jensen and P. Hegelund. 2013b. *Monitoring Abundance and Hunting of Narwhals in Melville Bay During Seismic Surveys in 2012.* Nuuk: Greenland Institute of Natural Resources.

Høye, T.T., E. Post, N. Schmidt, K.T. Nielsen and M.C. Forchhammer. 2013. 'Shorter Flowering Seasons and Declining Abundance of Flower Visitors in a Warmer Arctic.' *Nature Climate Change* 3: 759–763.

Letcher, R.J., et al. 2010. 'Exposure and Effects Assessment of Persistent Organic Pollutants in Arctic Wildlife and Fish.' *Science of the Total Environment* 408: 2995–3043.

Merkel, F.R. 2010. 'Evidence of Recent Population Recovery in Common Eiders Breeding in Western Greenland.' *Journal of Wildlife Management* 74 (8): 1869–1874.

Mineral Resource Committee. 2009. *The Analysing Report of 21 November 2009 from the Committee on the Naalakkersuisut's Bill on the Greenlandic Mineral Resources Act Presented for Inatsisartut under its Second Reading of the Bill.* J. No. EM2009/1020. Nuuk: Mineral Resource Committee.

Nyman, M., J. Koistinen, M.L. Fanta, T. Vartiainen and E. Helle. 2002. 'Current Levels of DDT, PCB and Trace Elements in the Baltic Ringed Seals (*Phoca hispida baltica*) and Grey Seals (*Halichoerus grypus*).' *Environmental Pollution* 119: 399–412.

OSPAR (Oslo and Paris Convention for the Protection of the Marine Environment of the North–East Atlantic). 2006. *Recommendation 2006/3 on Environmental Goals for the Discharge by the Offshore Industry of Chemicals that Are, or Which Contain Substances Identified as Candidates for Substitution.* London: OSPAR Secretariat.

PAME (The Arctic Council working group on the Protection of the Arctic Marine Environment). 2009. *Arctic Offshore and Gas Guidelines.* Tromsø: Arctic Council. p. 92.

Post, E. and M.C. Forchhammer. 2008. 'Climate Change Reduces Reproductive Success of an Arctic Herbivore through Trophic Mismatch.' *Philosophical Transactions of the Royal Society B* 363 (1501): 2369–2375.

Research Council of Norway. 2012. *Long-Term Effects of Discharges to Sea from Petroleum-Related Activities: The Results of Ten Years' Research* www.npd.no/en/

Publications/Reports/Long-term-effects-of-discharges-to-sea-from-petroleum-activities/.
Roos A., B.-M.V.M. Bäcklin, B.O. Helander, F.F. Rigét and U.C. Eriksson. 2012. 'Improved Reproductive Success in Otters (*Lutra lutra*), Grey Seals (*Halichoerus grypus*) and Sea Eagles (*Haliaeetus albicilla*) from Sweden in Relation to Concentrations of Organochlorine Contaminants.' *Environmental Pollution* 170: 268–275.
SFT (Norwegian Pollution Control Authority). 2008. *Costs and Benefits for the Environment and Society by Requiring Injection/Reinjection of Produced Water, Zero Discharge of Cuttings and Drilling Fluid, including Radioactivity in Zero Discharge Goal* [in Norwegian]. Oslo: Norwegian Radiation Protection Authority (NRPA), Norwegian Petroleum Directorate (NPD) and Norwegian Pollution Control Authority (SFT).
Skjoldal, H.R., et al. 2010. *Oil and Gas Activities in the Arctic: Effects and Potential Effects.* Scientific Findings and Recommendations Chapter 7, AMAP Assessment 2010. Oslo: Arctic Monitoring and Assessment Programme.
Sonne, C. 2010. 'Health Effects from Long-Range Transported Contaminants in Arctic Top Predators: An Integrated Review Based on Studies of Polar Bears and Relevant Model Species.' *Environment International* 36: 461–491.
US Environmental Protection Agency. 2004. *Electronic Code of Federal Regulations Title 40: Protection of Environment, Part 435: Oil and Gas Extraction Point Source Category.* Washington, DC: US Environmental Protection Agency.
Wisniewska, D.M., et al. 2014. *Propagation of Airgun Pulses in Baffin Bay 2012.* Aarhus: University of Aarhus Danish Centre for Environment and Energy: http://dce2.au.dk/pub/SR109.pdf.

16 Towards an integrated and participatory governance of the Arctic marine areas

Cécile Pelaudeix

Offshore oil and gas exploration and exploitation activities in the Arctic in the 2000s took place on a much greater scale than the drilling activities that started in the early 1970s in Canada and off the coast of Greenland. Despite an increasing production of renewable energy (the majority of which will be competitive by 2040 without subsidies[1]), oil demand will grow in sectors where substitutes are scarce or not easily available, such as freight, aviation fuels and petrochemicals. In all regions of the world, energy demand has grown in recent years, and the percentage of oil-generated energy used in the transport sector (land, water and air) is close to 100%, whereas shipping is not subject to emission reduction targets in the Paris Agreement.[2] As a result of energy globalisation, and notwithstanding low oil prices in early 2017, oil and gas exploration and exploitation continue in the Arctic offshore, in particular in Russia and in Norway. In 2016, 33 companies showed an interest in new blocks in the Barents Sea, some blocks located further east and further north than ever before; and later the same year, the Norwegian Ministry of Petroleum and Energy opened, with the 24th licensing round, new blocks for exploration in the Barents Sea.

This continued exploration and exploitation unfolds in the context of climate change, which impacts the respective activities in several ways. Induced change in the atmosphere from growing amounts of greenhouse gases has resulted in higher temperatures and melting ice. While the shift in ice regimes has increased opportunities for development and extended the geographical area for offshore hydrocarbon activities on the one hand, on the other hand, hazardous ice conditions remain a threat to the stationary and mobile infrastructure used by the offshore industry.[3] In addition, the unfolding of oil and gas activities in the Arctic constitutes what is called the Arctic paradox, for these activities contribute to climate change while the Arctic region is already impacted by rising temperatures twice as much as the rest of the world.

As highlighted in this volume, the governance of offshore hydrocarbon extraction must be based on acknowledgement of the especially high risks of environmental damage connected to such activities. The impacts of oil spill and related pollution will affect a vulnerable natural environment whose ecosystems have low resilience, a changing climate and the living resources of the marine areas. The governance of offshore oil and gas activities needs to accommodate the various uses of the ocean: fishing is the most important economic sector in Greenland, and also accounts for an important part of the Norwegian and Russian coastal economies; and indigenous coastal communities have traditionally depended on the resources of the Arctic marine areas. The question thus arises not only of public (and indigenous) participation in decision-making, but also of distribution of benefits.

This conclusion first synthesises the state of the art of existing governance systems at international, regional, national and sub-national levels, then highlights the various challenges arising for the governance systems due to the continuing oil and gas activities, and finally proposes three pathways for reflection.

State of the art of governance systems

The preceding chapters have analysed the governance of offshore oil and gas activities in the Arctic with an approach relying on the concept of multi-level governance, with the aim of analysing how interactions between those levels structure the policy process and impact the efficiency of environmental management and an effective public participation, including the participation of indigenous peoples. Indeed, beyond the technical challenge, the offshore exploration and extraction of hydrocarbons in the Arctic also brings into play legal and political challenges in the form of the recognition of sub-state entities, the rights of indigenous peoples and the demands of peripheral regions to benefit from economic development. At all levels, the governance systems are complex and heterogeneous throughout the Arctic.

International level

The current governance of oil and gas activities in the Arctic involves a state-based governance system characterised by fragmentation and legal pluralism arising from the overlap of various legal regimes. It is also characterised by partial compliance with international law. The principle of customary international law codified in the wording of UNCLOS, the Biodiversity Convention, the OSPAR Convention, the Ramsar Convention, the Espoo Convention and the Agreement between the Arctic Countries on Cooperation on Marine Oil Pollution Preparedness and Response in the Arctic are important conventions with consequences for the signatories with regard to their responsibilities for marine areas with relevance for offshore oil and gas activities. However, none of the conventions have all the Arctic states as parties, and they cannot be the only basis for the protection of the Arctic from the risk connected to offshore hydrocarbon activities. In addition, these conventions do not necessarily take into consideration the specific environmental and geographical features of the Arctic region. This is the case with regard to the International Convention on Oil Pollution Preparedness Response and Co-operation 1990 (OPRC), which is signed by all Arctic states, but lacks an Arctic focus. The regional agreement on oil spill response prepared under the auspices of the Arctic Council and discussed below intends to fill this gap.

Various authors in this volume have provided evidence of a tendency to shy away from commitments under international law. To offer an attractive investment environment, states can manoeuvre within an array of aspects of regulation, including environmental concerns (pollution at sea, safety and liability rules), indigenous peoples' rights and international standards regarding public participation. The rights related to public participation are stated in the Rio Declaration[4] and codified in the Aarhus Convention (the UNECE Convention). The Aarhus Convention, which only covers Europe but is open to all states interested in taking part, has not been ratified by Russia and has been ratified by Denmark only with a reservation for Greenland. Canada and the US have opted to refrain from taking part in this European agreement. The procedural rights laid down in the convention comprise respect for the local communities and cultures of indigenous peoples. Access to such rights is also a way of building capacity, as the exchange of information and knowledge supports awareness of environmental status, and opportunities for public participation and access to justice make it possible for the public to bring cases regarding the enforcement of environmental legislation before the courts.

Regarding the rights of indigenous peoples to land and property – rights that are linked to their rights to culture – it is argued in this volume that even if the central principle of free, prior and informed consent included in UNDRIP is not accepted as hard law, the uncertainty regarding the status of the principle, and the speed at which the law can evolve, gives cause for developers – and the states governing them – to pursue this principle and reduce the potential for legal liability (Johnstone).

Regional level

At the regional level, the development of inter-state cooperation includes cooperation on marine oil pollution, preparedness and response and environmental security. Cooperation between the Arctic states remains, however, focused more on response than on prevention, although prevention will always be more effective than clean-up. Cooperation is also currently based on very fragmented and complex regulation. The 2013 Agreement on Cooperation on Marine Oil Pollution Preparedness and Response, a binding agreement signed by all the Arctic states under the auspices of the Arctic Council, offers a framework for coordinated response, but sets only limited constraints on the parties. The responsibilities of the Arctic states are described in Section 2 of this agreement with the wording '*as appropriate*' and '*if appropriate*' so as to ensure flexibility; in Appendix IV, the 'Operational Guidelines' for the agreement, which describes assistance, response operation and so on, is not binding.

Even with these deficiencies, the Arctic Council plays an important role in shaping the discourse and promoting values and standards of best practices, in particular through considerable support for scientific research on the Arctic environment. However, regarding discourse shaping and values, Humrich stresses that the concept of sustainable development can no longer serve as a suitable policy-guiding frame for identifying what is problematic about Arctic offshore hydrocarbon activities, because shifts in the discursive and functional dimensions of this concept have opened up for economic development rather than constraining it. The Arctic Council thus promotes codes of conduct (the need to have an environmental impact assessment procedure) and recommends practices for the regulation of offshore oil and gas exploration and extraction. The 2009 Arctic Council Offshore Oil and Gas Guidelines (AOOGG) in particular laid a foundation for information sharing between national offshore hydrocarbon regulators in each of the Arctic Council member states. The AOOGG is a comprehensive document that specifically addresses the concerns of the offshore Arctic (Koivurova). It also laid the foundation for two further practical outcomes: a 2014 *Systems Safety Management and Safety Culture Report, Avoiding Major Disasters in Arctic Offshore Oil and Gas Operations*; and a web-based information sharing portal, *Arctic Offshore Oil and Gas Management, Regulation and Enforcement*, launched in 2014 (Baker).

National level

The national systems of governance of the US, Russia, Canada, Norway and Greenland as a sub-state differ significantly when it comes to environmental protection and public participation. The governance system of the US encompasses complex federal, state and substate legal interests in Alaska and a multiplicity of actors (including over 20 federal agencies and various groups of Alaskan Natives). The Outer Continental Shelf Lands Act seeks to balance development and environmental standards in consistence with the 'maintenance of competition and other national needs'. An emerging trend indicates that growing communication involving industry, federal/state government and tribes creates opportunities for dialogue (Canuel): the objective is to advance a more coordinated and inclusive management approach 'to improve efficiency and operational certainty' and 'direct and meaningful partnership with stakeholders'.[5] In Russia, the governance system, which like the US system is based on a prescriptive regime, is complex but remains *de facto* very centralised, and the process through which companies gain access to offshore oil and gas deposits lacks transparency and inclusiveness. As a result, critical stakeholder groups such as indigenous communities are often left out of the decision-making, and the Russian regulatory framework lacks a balance between financial incentive and appropriate environmental and socioeconomic checks (Sidortsov).

The comparison made between the governance systems of offshore oil and gas activities in Canada, Norway and Greenland, all based on a goal-setting approach, shows that regulation not only reflects technical rationality but that energy strategies are related to regulatory governance and lead to a differentiated trade-off between economic incentive, public participation and environmental protection (Pelaudeix). The Norwegian governance system contains strong environmental requirements, and it also benefits from a culture of inclusiveness of actors in decision-making, such as a tripartite collaboration between companies, unions and government regulators (Baker). Still, all national governance systems for offshore energy activities are facing challenges of integrated management and public participation, in particular with regard to indigenous peoples' rights to land and participation in decision-making.

Sub-national level and indigenous peoples' rights

Various authors in this volume have documented a lack of involvement of indigenous peoples in decision-making and/or a limited recognition of land rights in Canada, in Greenland and in Norway. Indigenous customary ownership in the coastal zone of Greenland has still not been recognised under Greenlandic law (Tejsner), and the coastal Sámi in Norway only enjoy weak protection of their historical rights (Ravna and Svendsen). In Canada, where all the Inuit-inhabited regions have land-claims agreements that have been signed by the Federal Government and Territories, these agreements offer the Inuit little control over offshore development in their territorial land and sea area (Rodon). The full endorsement of UNDRIP – as proposed by Prime Minister Trudeau in 2016 – could lead to a notable change in the Canadian position vis-à-vis the principle of free, prior and informed consent as a politically accepted principle. Neither the Canadian courts nor the Federal Government have ever recognised this principle as hard law.

Relations between state, local communities and industry

The spectrum of instruments available as described in this volume is wide. It includes a combination of procedural guarantees as laid down in the Aarhus Convention, marine spatial planning, environmental impact assessments (EIAs), strategic environmental assessments (SEAs) and economic and market-based instruments such as Impact Benefit Agreements (IBAs), combined with traditional top-down regulation. Private corporate actors have a dual position in the complex regulatory environment as both rule-takers and rule-makers. As rule-takers, they are exposed to the complex and non-systematised legal rules (legal uncertainty); as rule-makers, they contribute to the creation of law, primarily through contracting – incorporating the industry-based standards such as 'world's best practice' standards, guidelines and voluntary schemes, and especially through the use of IBAs (Cueva).

The value of ecosystem services that are essential to the ecosystem balance and to the living conditions of indigenous peoples is currently not taken into account on a fully calculated basis in the licensing of offshore hydrocarbon activities. The same lack of recognition characterises the supplementary IBAs and other tools used by the state and sub-state authorities in their regulation of such activities. IBAs contain provisions such as indirect employment, the involvement of local enterprises, knowledge transfer, education, research, work experience and social and cultural well-being. Yet, they rarely *de facto* include local sustainability and environmental risk-management criteria for offshore projects as part of their objectives. Corporations enjoy significant flexibility in the way they implement impact-benefit agreements and make use of outsourcing. Even though increasing local content and participation in offshore oil and gas projects is possible – via a combination of corporate social responsibility commitments and state regulation – the resulting levels leave a lot to be desired (Cueva, Mortensen).

Challenges arising for the governance systems due to the continuing oil and gas activities

As offshore oil and gas activities continue in the Arctic marine areas, and as new areas for exploration are opened, some challenges arise for the current governance systems: cutting through all levels of governance, these challenges pertain to technical, ecological/environmental, political, legal and normative aspects.

Drilling, extracting oil and gas and shipping in the Arctic marine areas require technical expertise which is still lacking today, as the weather and geographic conditions are not only severe in the region, but are also undergoing changes due to the effects of climate change on sea-ice regimes, ocean currents, weather patterns and other factors. In the context of a changing Arctic, harsh conditions are even worsened by an increase in unpredictability. Local weather forecasting in remote coastal areas, sea-ice and iceberg monitoring, oil-spill detection in ice-infested waters and oil fate in sea ice are some of the dimensions of knowledge which need to be deepened in order to make activities in the marine areas of the Arctic safer.

The ecological and environmental aspect constitutes another major challenge. There is a lack of knowledge about the actual baseline for environmental conditions in the area, on which EIAs must be based. Another lack of knowledge detrimental to sustainable activities in the region relates to the lack of standards adapted to the Arctic, like standards for the use of chemicals in drilling activities that are usually assessed on the basis of data from standard laboratory tests and using organisms that are not always relevant in an Arctic context (Mosbech et al.). Biodiversity loss in the Arctic, whether caused by climate change or new, high-risk activities, has its consequences, as it is likely to impair the natural resilience of the ecosystems on whose services not only other species, but also local communities, depend. The loss of ecosystem services would have strong negative effects both on welfare and on human capital, and the loss of natural capital could exceed the gains generated by economic activities. Such an outcome would undermine the ability to sustain future growth, especially for the local communities, and the consequent imbalances in the natural system would threaten to impair the regenerative balance or productive capacity of environmental systems.[6]

The political challenges connected to continuing and extending offshore oil and gas activities, as examined in this volume, relate mainly to protection of the environment, participation and distribution of benefits. The governance of offshore hydrocarbon extraction needs to be based on acknowledgement of the especially high risks of environmental damage connected to such activities; but as shown by several authors, Arctic states vary a great deal in terms of their commitment to environmental protection. It is thus not surprising that the Arctic Waters, which form the region 1 in the OSPAR convention, show the lowest degree of marine protected areas (MPAs), with only 1.94% of this area being protected by the OSPAR Network of MPAs.[7] Regarding participation, an increasing demand for democratic legitimisation and recognition of the rights of indigenous peoples emerges in the civil spheres of society. Even so, participation throughout the Arctic is limited – even when Strategic Environmental Impact Assessments are performed – and neither the Aarhus Convention nor the rights of indigenous peoples over resources are fully implemented or recognised. Furthermore, a balanced equation is needed between lower taxation systems to attract investments in the frontier fields of the Arctic, and the distribution of benefits through various mechanisms such as the sovereign funds in Norway and in Greenland, and though IBAs which need to incorporate in practice local content, in the context of especially high risks of environmental damage.

Finally, another challenge lies in the lack of an analytical perspective on policy practice and on the concepts that can carry with them a normative substance in order to steer sound policy decisions. Some framings have been highlighted in this volume, touching on an alleged race for resources, or on the constraints of environmental and climate change factors in questioning the issue of exploitation of oil and gas in the Arctic (Koivurova). More analytical work is needed to understand the differentiated role of the various actors in shaping the issue of offshore oil and gas in the Arctic region. In that perspective, it is also important to pay attention to the conceptual framework used for supporting reflection on the issue, and for guiding the practice of actors. It has been shown that the concept of sustainable development has lost its capacity to compel economic development (Humrich). It is also necessary to look at some principles which are also commonly used, like the best available technique (BAT) or best environmental practice (BEP) in order to question their relevance in the Arctic context, which is still a little-known region in many respects, but which is also a region in a state of change.

Pathways of reflection for the future

Given the technical, ecological, political and conceptual challenges mentioned above, three pathways of reflection can be proposed for developing the governance structure of oil and gas activities in the marine areas of the Arctic, based on good examples or best practices mentioned in the chapters but also based on complementary perspectives. These pathways of reflection include the strengthening of law and its implementation, the development of integrated management and a reflection on the problematisation of the issue of oil and gas extraction in the Arctic.

Strengthening of law and implementation

It is unlikely that a dualistic vision – one which forces us to choose between hard law and soft law – will open new avenues for solutions. Still the evolution of international law and of customary international law deserves attention, and national regulations can be strengthened. The need for a stronger climate change regime has been highlighted (Koivurova). Baker in particular sees in the current relative lull in oil and gas activity an opportunity to consider how climate change can reshape offshore regulation by tying permits more closely to potential climate impacts of the activity in question. In this respect, and as noted above, it is relevant to note that the Paris Agreement, important as it is, does not take shipping into consideration in the emission reduction targets.

Two principles need to be part of the national regulatory systems: the precautionary principle and its corollary that environmental damage must, as a priority, be ratified at source, as well as the principle that environmental conditions are diverse in the various geographical areas of the Arctic region. One of the recommendations presented here is to promote the vertical and horizontal harmonisation of ecosystem-based marine strategy and spatial planning, as well as the offshore safety standard established by the EU (Basse). It is argued that there is a need for the EU's eco-system marine and maritime governance in the Arctic, and that harmonisation with international and regional standards and the extraterritorial effects of the EU's environmental and social norms makes it possible to ensure a higher level of environmental protection (Basse).

The issues of precaution, monitoring, supervisory activities and – if necessary – enforcement of environmental standards at the national level (for instance the disposal of drilling waste onshore when this is possible) remain central as offshore extraction activities unfold in remote areas lacking infrastructure in an environment that is at once harsh and very vulnerable. Guidelines for EIAs exist and can be implemented. Finally, to ensure that IBAs have the potential to improve local development, it is imperative that national governments provide the necessary advisory, technical but also legal infrastructure to reduce the power and information asymmetries that exist between communities or local governments/municipal councils and companies (Cueva). In Greenland, IBAs should contain clearer obligations which are easier to enforce (Mortensen).

A certain level of harmonisation between national regulations may be welcome, for instance, to enable states with different norms to cooperate efficiently on the prevention of oil spills and their response to them.[8] This cooperation on regulatory systems and more generally on governance processes should be of particular interest for states which share maritime borders, such as Canada and Greenland/Denmark, in view of their signature of the Agreement for Cooperation Relating to the Marine Environment in 1983 and their 3,000-km shared maritime border. The 2010 agreement between Russia and Norway in the Barents Sea provides general provisions like 'continuous consultation and exchange of information', but says little about what a cross-border joint unitisation agreement must specify about the level of contact required between regulators in the two countries (Baker).

Integrated management

Regulation is not the be-all and end-all of this process. Communication and cooperation between actors also appear to be very important, especially in an area such as offshore oil and gas extraction, where a high level of knowledge is required to operate safely and where knowledge sharing can only be achieved through the active involvement of all relevant actors. The chapters in this volume show that increased interactions between the various levels of governance – involving actors with diverse interests, authorities and cultures – could help in the identification of ways to increase efficiency in the governance of more secure offshore hydrocarbon activities, environmental management and public participation. In Norway, the practice of integrated management plan dates back to 2006 and was introduced first in the Barents Sea.[9] In the US, the interest for the Arctic has recently created enhanced opportunities for dialogue involving industry, federal/state government and tribes (Canuel). As for public participation, the Strategic Environmental Assessments offer an opportunity for engagement and influence at the strategic tier, but in effect they spark 'less interest in engagement due to the high level, and often abstract nature of decisions', a challenge exacerbated in the offshore context 'traditionally deemed out-of-sight, out-of-mind'.[10]

As far as indigenous peoples are concerned, although they are more extensively protected by international law than non-indigenous communities (Johnstone), their interaction with public administration and authority can be complicated with regard to both participation in decision-making and the right to appeal against decisions. In Greenland, the regulation related to oil resources does not contain any specific provision or protection of indigenous rights: the Government of Greenland believes that the interests of the Inuit are represented, but municipalities may have interests that conflict with those of the Government when it comes to the protection of local interests in hunting, fishing and tourism, as well as in sociocultural values and traditions. And the regulation in Greenland does not require the municipalities to be parties in the negotiation of IBAs, either (Mortensen).

In Nunavut, an example that complements Rodon's chapter on Canada relates to a difference in standing right in courts between local actors, even if they are all indigenous peoples: in a recent case between indigenous peoples in Clyde River and a consortium of companies regarding seismic surveys,[11] the lawyers for the consortium, as well as the Crown, argued against the applicant's right to file the legal challenge. The applicants were the Hamlet of Clyde River, the Nammautaq Hunters & Trappers Organization and the mayor of Clyde River. The lawyers of the consortium and the Crown suggested that the application should instead have been filed on their behalf by a regional or territorial *Inuit* association, which enjoys specific rights under the Nunavut Land Claims Agreement. It is thus expected that with conflicting interests between local populations on the one hand and corporations (in which indigenous peoples may also have shares in some Canadian regions) and regional/national governments on the other hand, the development of offshore resources will lead to an increase in the number of cases ending up in court.

How can we ensure that integrated management based on a dialogue between regulators, industry and stakeholders actually leads to effective and meaningful participation and efficient management and enforcement? Offshore activities in the Arctic take place in remote marine areas where environmental monitoring is difficult to enforce. As an example, the need for a systematic control of chemicals to be used as well as discharges and concentrations in the environment has been emphasised (Mosbech et al.). As the enforcement of environmental protection and public participation appear crucial, one option to ensure effective integrated management and efficient enforcement has a procedural character and lies in the use of specific contracts that are binding on the regulator (the public authority, which has monitoring rights and duties) and the licensee, who will also establish subcontracts with other companies. Rather than focusing on short-term competitiveness and effectiveness like the transactional contracts do, such contracts known as relational contracts emphasise long-term relations and rely on obligations such as commitment and loyalty.[12] Relational contracts may not only optimise the operator-regulator interface and ensure the effective performance of monitoring, but also more generally offer a stable framework for inclusive dialogue between actors, so as to develop a culture of trust, particularly in terms of risk acceptance.

As described in this volume, however, the use of negotiation needs to be connected to capacity-building in local communities, in particular institutional capacity, and the role of the state is still important in that perspective. National governments should support communities and/or municipal councils in starting to negotiate IBAs as early as possible in the project lifecycle, and certainly in conjunction with the EIA process, rather than after it (Cueva). Furthermore, close linkage between research and the monitoring and regulation of offshore activities in Greenland is necessary to secure an innovative and adaptive management, a democratic debate and governance processes involving the local communities, the municipalities, the industry and the Government of Greenland (Mosbech et al.).

Further research

Observation capacities in the Arctic and regional models for adequate monitoring, forecasts or impact assessments of oil and gas activities need more scientific research. In particular, as sea ice is a clear challenge to offshore infrastructures, more knowledge about local surface wind and ocean current observations is needed for ice motion modelling.[13] Further knowledge is required about the baseline for environmental conditions in the Arctic and about the breakdown and ecotoxicology of chemicals and oil components used during the drilling process (Mosbech et al.). Oil spills may affect a region for decades or longer,[14] but over time microbial activity does degrade pollutants.[15] However, little is known about the effect of microbial biodegradation in the cold climate of the Arctic. Offshore oil and gas activities also produce undesirable effects like the emission of atmospheric pollutants generated by the operation of machinery on offshore oil rigs as well as the burn-off of gases, and by activities associated with shipping, the impact of which needs to be assessed in the Arctic context. More studies are also necessary to evaluate the long-term effect of disturbances of seismic activities on species most sensitive to noise like narwhals (Mosbech et al.), and to identify the relevant management options.

Beyond technical and ecological requirements to foster a safer operational environment for oil and gas extraction, there is a need for a better understanding of the problems involved in the policy process, and for innovative legal solutions. Little is known about the way policy makers, social actors and the corporate sector question the issue of offshore oil and gas exploitation in the Arctic, and how the problems involved impact the governance process. To what extent are regulatory frameworks and governance processes related to energy and national policies (Sidortsov, Pelaudeix)? Whereas Arctic states are energy self-sufficient or net exporters, how energy security, in a global context, can impact national energy strategies in the Arctic region and what are the effects of an externalization of the energy security issue from a regional to a global one?[16] Under which conditions can relational contracts more effectively engage the actors involved in the governance process in order to lead to increased management efficiency? As debates question the nature of a licence – is it a contract (private law), or is it public law – to what extent does the design of a licence pertaining to contract law allow more powerful leverage in terms of the enforcement of terms and the protection of the environment? What is the potential of relational contracts in the offshore industry to overcome the issue of increased risks through subcontracts and ensure the effective fulfilment of monitoring duties? Developing knowledge in this area could open new perspectives when the governance of offshore oil and gas activities involves an increasing number of actors. Finally, what are the options to ensure that the concepts that drive policy making retain a normative substance and have the potential to steer sound policy decisions?

Offshore oil and gas activities in the Arctic region unfold in a complex geographic, climatic, global energy, economic and societal context in which the interests of the various actors associated with the governance process may diverge significantly. Besides being a very challenging area, unknown in many respects and with little infrastructure, the Arctic Ocean is also in a state of change owing to climate change and is subject to increasingly unpredictable weather events and sea ice behaviour. Any governance system for Arctic offshore oil and gas activities that is to be politically and environmentally sustainable will have to be based on coordination across various levels of decision-making and regulation. There is a need for vertical and horizontal coordination between the UN's international regulatory bodies, the regions (e.g. OSPAR regions), the EU, the Arctic states, Greenland, the local communities, the industry and the indigenous peoples. It is also necessary to develop integrated management conceived not only as a process that takes into consideration the interconnection between cross-sectorial issues related to the development of offshore activities and local sustainable development, but also as a process that includes various actors, including the public (individuals and their associations). Regulatory activities and enforcement activities are traditionally the reserve of states, but there is room for improvement in the Arctic. It seems that we have no alternative but to move away from solely state-centred decision-making regarding offshore oil and gas extraction activities with its predominantly top-down and sectorial approach, towards a governance system based on an integrated management and participatory approach.

Notes

1 IEA 2016.
2 IPCC 2007a, b and IPCC 2014.
3 Barber et al. 2014.
4 At the 1992 Earth Summit in Rio, governments adopted the Rio Declaration including Principle 10, which stressed that environmental issues are best handled with the participation of all concerned citizens. In 1995 the members of UNECE adopted the Sofia Guidelines on the importance of public information, public participation and access to justice. The UNECE Convention on Access to Information, Public Participation in Decision-Making and Access to Justice in Environmental Matters (the Aarhus Convention) was the next step in this development.
5 Interagency Working Group 2013, 2.
6 OECD 2011, 9 and 29, where climate change, global nitrogen cycles and biodiversity loss are mentioned as examples of imbalance.
7 OSPAR Commission 2014, 16.
8 Baker 2012.
9 Fidler and Noble 2012.

10 Ibid.
11 Hamlet of Clyde River, Nammautaq Hunters & Trappers Organization – Clyde River, and Jerry Natanine versus TGS-NOPEC Geophysical Company ASA (TGS), Petroleum Geo-Services Inc. The applicants tried to reverse a 2014 National Energy Board (NEB) decision to allow a consortium of three seismic companies to survey in Baffin Bay and Davis Strait. Cf. also Rodon's chapter in this volume.
12 Olsen et al. 2005.
13 Barber et al. 2014.
14 Peterson et al. 2003.
15 Kimes et al. 2014.
16 Pelaudeix 2015b.

References

Baker, B. 2012. 'Offshore Oil and Gas Regulation in the Arctic: Room for Harmonisation?' In *Yearbook of Polar Law*, 4: 475–504. Leiden: Brill Nijhoff.

Barber, D.G. et al. 2014. 'Climate-Change and Ice Hazards in the Beaufort Sea.' *Elementa: Science of the Anthropocene* 2: 000025. doi:10.12952/journal.elementa.000025. Available at: www.elementascience.org/articles/25.

Fidler, C. and B. Noble. 2012. 'Advancing Strategic Environmental Aassessment in the Offshore Oil and Gas Sector: Lessons from Norway, Canada and the United Kingdom.' *Environmental Impact Assessment Review*, 34: 12–21.

IEA 2016. International Energy Agency fact sheet 2016.

Interagency Working Group on Coordination of Domestic Energy Development and Permitting in Alaska, 2013. *Managing for the future in a rapidly changing Arctic: A Report to the President.*

IPCC, 2007a. 'Energy supply.' Chapter 4. Available at: www.ipcc.ch/pdf/assessment-report/ar4/wg3/ar4-wg3-chapter4.pdf.

IPCC, 2007b. 'Transport and its infrastructure.' Chapter 5. Available at: www.ipcc.ch/pdf/assessment-report/ar4/wg3/ar4-wg3-chapter5.pdf.

IPCC, 2014. 'Transport,' Chapter 8. Available at: www.ipcc.ch/pdf/assessment-report/ar5/wg3/ipcc_wg3_ar5_chapter8.pdf.

Kimes, N.E., A.V. Callaghan, J.M. Suflita and P.J. Morris, P.J. 2014. 'Microbial Transformation of the Deepwater Horizon Oil Spill – Past, Present, and Future Perspectives.' *Frontiers in Microbiology* 5: 603.

OECD. 2011. *Towards Green Growth.* OECD Green Growth Studies. Paris: Organisation for Economic Cooperation and Development. Available at: doi: 10.1787/9789264111318-en.

Olsen B.E. et al., 2005. 'Governance of Complex Procurements in the Oil and Gas Industry.' *Journal of Purchasing & Supply Management* 11: 1–13.

OSPAR Commission. 2014. 2014 Status Report on the OSPAR Network of Marine Protected Areas:16.

Peterson, C.H., S.D. Rice, J.W. Short, et al. 2003. 'Long-Term Ecosystem Response to the Exxon Valdez Oil Spill.' *Science* 302(5653): 2982–2086.

Pelaudeix, C. 2015. 'Governance of offshore hydrocarbon resources development in the Arctic: conceptualising energy security.' Paper given at the international conference Security and governance in the Global Arctic: Nordic and International Perspectives, Aarhus 12–13 November 2015.

Index

For Product Safety Concerns and Information please contact our EU representative GPSR@taylorandfrancis.com
Taylor & Francis Verlag GmbH, Kaufingerstraße 24, 80331 München, Germany

www.ingramcontent.com/pod-product-compliance
Ingram Content Group UK Ltd.
Pitfield, Milton Keynes, MK11 3LW, UK
UKHW020018200926
475702UK00014B/1944
* 9 7 8 1 0 3 2 0 9 6 7 5 9 *